HYBRID CONSTITUTIONALISM

This is the first book that focuses on the entrenched, fundamental divergence between the Hong Kong Court of Final Appeal and Macau's Tribunal de Última Instância over their constitutional jurisprudence, with the former repeatedly invalidating unconstitutional legislation with finality and the latter having never challenged the constitutionality of legislation at all. This divergence is all the more remarkable when considered in the light of the fact that the two regions, commonly subject to oversight by China's authoritarian party-state, possess constitutional frameworks that are nearly identical; feature similar hybrid regimes; and share a lot in history, ethnicity, culture, and language. Informed by political science and economics, this book breaks new ground by locating the cause of this anomaly, studied within the universe of authoritarian constitutionalism, not in the common law–civil law differences between these two former European dependencies, but in the disparate levels of political transaction costs therein.

Eric C. Ip (D.Phil., University of Oxford) is an Associate Professor of Law at The University of Hong Kong. His award-winning research on comparative public law has been published in peer-reviewed periodicals such as *The American Journal of Comparative Law, Oxford Journal of Legal Studies* and *International & Comparative Law Quarterly*. He is the author of *Law and Justice in Hong Kong* (2016).

Prior to joining The University of Hong Kong, he taught at University College London (UCL) and The Chinese University of Hong Kong.

COMPARATIVE CONSTITUTIONAL LAW AND POLICY

Series Editors

Tom Ginsburg *University of Chicago*
Zachary Elkins *University of Texas at Austin*
Ran Hirschl *University of Toronto*

Comparative constitutional law is an intellectually vibrant field that encompasses an increasingly broad array of approaches and methodologies. This series collects analytically innovative and empirically grounded work from scholars of comparative constitutionalism across academic disciplines. Books in the series include theoretically informed studies of single constitutional jurisdictions, comparative studies of constitutional law and institutions, and edited collections of original essays that respond to challenging theoretical and empirical questions in the field.

Books in the Series

The Invisible Constitution in Comparative Perspective
Edited by Rosalind Dixon and Adrienne Stone

Constituent Assemblies
Edited by Jon Elster, Roberto Gargarella, Vatsal Naresh, and Bjorn Erik Rasch

Judicial Review in Norway
Anine Kierulf

The DNA of Constitutional Justice in Latin America: Politics, Governance, and Judicial Design
Daniel M. Brinks and Abby Blass

The Adventures of the Constituent Power: Beyond Revolutions?
Andrew Arato

Constitutions, Religion and Politics in Asia: Indonesia, Malaysia and Sri Lanka
Dian A. H. Shah

Canada in the World: Comparative Perspectives on the Canadian Constitution
Edited by Richard Albert and David R. Cameron

Courts and Democracies in Asia
Po Jen Yap

Proportionality: New Frontiers, New Challenges
Edited by Vicki C. Jackson and Mark Tushnet

Constituents before Assembly: Participation, Deliberation, and Representation in the Crafting of New Constitutions
Todd A. Eisenstadt, A. Carl LeVan, and Tofigh Maboudi

Assessing Constitutional Performance
Edited by Tom Ginsburg and Aziz Huq

Buddhism, Politics and the Limits of Law: The Pyrrhic Constitutionalism of Sri Lanka
Benjamin Schonthal

Engaging with Social Rights: Procedure, Participation and Democracy in South Africa's Second Wave
Brian Ray

Constitutional Courts As Mediators: Armed Conflict, Civil–Military Relations, and the Rule of Law in Latin America
Julio Ríos-Figueroa

Perils of Judicial Self-Government in Transitional Societies
David Kosař

Making We the People: Democratic Constitutional Founding in Postwar Japan and South Korea
Chaihark Hahm and Sung Ho Kim

Radical Deprivation on Trial: The Impact of Judicial Activism on Socioeconomic Rights in the Global South
César Rodríguez-Garavito and Diana Rodríguez-Franco

Unstable Constitutionalism: Law and Politics in South Asia
Edited by Mark Tushnet and Madhav Khosla

Magna Carta and Its Modern Legacy
Edited by Robert Hazell and James Melton

Constitutions and Religious Freedom
Frank B. Cross

International Courts and the Performance of International Agreements: A General Theory with Evidence from the European Union
Clifford J. Carrubba and Matthew J. Gabel

Reputation and Judicial Tactics: A Theory of National and International Courts
Shai Dothan

Social Difference and Constitutionalism in Pan-Asia
Edited by Susan H. Williams

Constitutionalism in Asia in the Early Twenty-First Century
Edited by Albert H. Y. Chen

Constitutions in Authoritarian Regimes
Edited by Tom Ginsburg and Alberto Simpser

Presidential Legislation in India: The Law and Practice of Ordinances
Shubhankar Dam

Social and Political Foundations of Constitutions
Edited by Denis J. Galligan and Mila Versteeg

Consequential Courts: Judicial Roles in Global Perspective
Edited by Diana Kapiszewski, Gordon Silverstein, and Robert A. Kagan

Comparative Constitutional Design
Edited by Tom Ginsburg

Hybrid Constitutionalism

THE POLITICS OF CONSTITUTIONAL REVIEW IN THE CHINESE SPECIAL ADMINISTRATIVE REGIONS

ERIC C. IP
The University of Hong Kong

CAMBRIDGE
UNIVERSITY PRESS

CAMBRIDGE
UNIVERSITY PRESS

University Printing House, Cambridge CB2 8BS, United Kingdom

One Liberty Plaza, 20th Floor, New York, NY 10006, USA

477 Williamstown Road, Port Melbourne, VIC 3207, Australia

314–321, 3rd Floor, Plot 3, Splendor Forum, Jasola District Centre, New Delhi – 110025, India

79 Anson Road, #06–04/06, Singapore 079906

Cambridge University Press is part of the University of Cambridge.

It furthers the University's mission by disseminating knowledge in the pursuit of education, learning, and research at the highest international levels of excellence.

www.cambridge.org
Information on this title: www.cambridge.org/9781107194922
DOI: 10.1017/9781108163804

First published 2019

Printed and bound in Great Britain by Clays Ltd, Elcograf S.p.A.

A catalogue record for this publication is available from the British Library.

Library of Congress Cataloging-in-Publication Data
NAMES: Ip, Eric Chi Yeung, author.
TITLE: Hybrid constitutionalism: the politics of constitutional review in the Chinese special administrative regions / Eric Ip.
DESCRIPTION: New York: Cambridge University Press, 2019. | Series: Comparative constitutional law and policy | Includes bibliographical references and index.
IDENTIFIERS: LCCN 2018044282 | ISBN 9781107194922 (hardback)
SUBJECTS: LCSH: Law – China – Macau (Special Administrative Region). | Law – China – Hong Kong. | Constitutional law – China. | Legal polycentricity – China. | BISAC: LAW / Constitutional.
CLASSIFICATION: LCC KNQ9408.16 2019 | DDC 342.510095125–dc23
LC record available at https://lccn.loc.gov/2018044282

ISBN 978-1-107-19492-2 Hardback

Contents

Figures

Tables

Acknowledgments

This book was made possible with the support of many teachers, colleagues, friends, and institutions. I am deeply indebted to Denis Galligan, my doctoral supervisor at Oxford, and thankful to David Erdos, Yuka Kobayashi, Marina Kurkchiyan, Bettina Lange, and Cristina Parau for their advice throughout my years as a research student. I am grateful to Albert Chen, Anne Cheung, Richard Cullen, Christopher Gane, Sara Jordan, and Benny Tai for their encouragement and support. My gratitude goes to Cora Chan, Peter Chau, Jianlin Chen, Frank Choi, Kelvin Kwok, David S. Law, Michael Law, Siu Yau Lee, Franz Mang, Stephen Thomson, Mila Versteeg, Xiaojun Yan, Po Jen Yap, and Samson Yuen, whose comments have shaped the ideas in this book. Jerry Bain's mind-boggling questions greatly enhanced the robustness of my arguments. Lorraine Wu's excellent assistance is critical to the richness of the data presented on the pages that follow. All remaining errors are purely my own.

I have been researching the issues in this book for more than a decade. I must acknowledge the support of several institutions that, at various times, have provided me with comfortable and resourceful settings in which to develop my ideas. These include the Centre for Socio-Legal Studies and the Faculty of Law, University of Oxford; Wolfson College Oxford; Oriel College Oxford; the Oxford Bodleian Libraries; the United Nations University Institute on Comparative Regional Integration Studies; the School of Public Policy at University College London; the Faculty of Law, and New Asia College at The Chinese University of Hong Kong; and the Department of Politics and Public Administration, the Faculty of Law, and St. John's College at The University of Hong Kong.

Thanks to my editor, Joe Ng, and the anonymous reviewers at Cambridge University Press for enthusiastically supporting this book. It contains heavily modified content derived from earlier articles of mine that appeared in several periodicals: Eric C. Ip, *Comparative Subnational Foreign Relations Law in the Chinese Special Administrative Regions*, 65(4) INT'L & COMP. L. Q. 953 (2016); Eric C. Ip, *The Evolution of Constitutional Adjudication in the Chinese Special Administrative Regions: Theory and Evidence*, 61(4) AM. J. COMP. L. 799 (2013); and Eric C. Ip, *The Politics of Constitutional Common Law in Hong Kong under Chinese Sovereignty*, 25(3) WASH. INT'L L. J. 565 (2016). I also wish to thank my wife, Giselle Yuen, for her caring support. The unconditional love of my parents, Carol and Pang Fei Ip, has been crucial to the success of my research. I dedicate this book to my daughter, Alexandra.

Abbreviations

ACM	Associação Comercial de Macau
AKP	*Adalet ve Kalkınma Partisi* (Justice and Development Party)
AO	Administrative Officer
CCTV	China Central Television
CFA	Hong Kong Court of Final Appeal
DAB	Democratic Alliance for the Betterment and Progress of Hong Kong
FTU	Hong Kong Federation of Trade Unions *or* Macau Federation of Trade Unions
GDP	Gross Domestic Product
GUNA	General Union of Neighbors Association of Macau
ICCPR	International Covenant on Civil and Political Rights
POAS	Political Officials Accountability System
SAR	Special Administrative Region
SARS	Severe Acute Respiratory Syndrome
MLC	Member of the Legislative Council
TUI	Tribunal de Última Instância of Macau
UN	United Nations
UNESCO	United Nations Educational, Scientific and Cultural Organization

1

The Rise of Hybrid Constitutionalism

INTRODUCTION

Constitutional review, or the competence of courts to review legislation and administrative acts for consistency with constitutional norms, has spread to every inhabited continent since its birth in the United States in the early nineteenth century.[1] Politically consequential constitutional courts[2] have arisen in nascent democracies from South Korea to Brazil, and courts in entrenched parliamentary democracies in the Commonwealth have assumed greater power to protect individual rights and nullify government policies.[3] As a result, the democratic world has experienced a profound "judicialization of politics."[4] Courts all over the world are regularly petitioned to protect individual freedoms from governmental encroachment, regulate campaign finance, resolve electoral disputes, remove elected officials, and mediate conflicts between government bodies.[5] The political importance of courts has come to transcend the resolution of particular issues. For all practical purposes, courts now make and unmake

[1] Rosalind Dixon & Tom Ginsburg, *The Forms and Limits of Constitutions as Political Insurance*, 15(4) INT'L J. CONST. L. 988, 988 (2017) ("Constitutional review has spread all over the world in recent decades, to the point where some three-quarters of all constitutional systems have it in some form.").

[2] Two well-known models of constitutional review exist: the American "decentralized" review model by ordinary courts, and the Continental European model of "centralized" review by a specialized constitutional court. *See* Albert H.Y. Chen & Miguel Poiares Maduro, *The Judiciary and Constitutional Review*, *in* ROUTLEDGE HANDBOOK OF CONSTITUTIONAL LAW 97 (Mark Tushnet et al. eds., 2015). This book uses the term "constitutional court" broadly to encompass both specialized constitutional courts and apex courts in decentralized review systems.

[3] Diana Kapiszeswiki et al., *Introduction*, *in* CONSEQUENTIAL COURTS: JUDICIAL ROLES IN GLOBAL GOVERNANCE 1, 1 (Diana Kapiszeswiki et al. eds., 2013).

[4] Mark Tushnet & Madhav Khosla, *Unstable Constitutionalism*, *in* UNSTABLE CONSTITUTIONALISM: LAW AND POLITICS IN SOUTH ASIA 3, 9 (Mark Tushnet & Madhav Khosla eds., 2015).

[5] Tom Ginsburg & Aziz Z. Huq, *Assessing Constitutional Performance*, *in* ASSESSING CONSTITUTIONAL PERFORMANCE 3, 19 (Tom Ginsburg & Aziz Z. Huq eds., 2016).

public policy[6] by way of standard, authoritative interpretations of constitutional texts, clothed in the imprimatur of the law,[7] that have gradually altered the former meaning of constitutional norms and adapted statutory and administrative acts to ever-changing circumstances, mostly absent meaningful popular participation.[8]

It is now a truism in constitutional scholarship that independent constitutional review is a precondition of a nation's entitlement to global respect;[9] a credible signal to foreign and international actors of a regime's commitment to property rights;[10] and an essential characteristic of democratic constitutionalism,[11] good governance, and the rule of law, under which political power is subject to genuine legal accountability and judicial checks.[12] Constitutional review by judicial bodies has become a dominant, nearly universal trait of liberal democracies.[13] It is no surprise that the spread of constitutional review in the last three decades of the twentieth century coincided with the so-called third wave of democratization,[14] which hit much of Africa, Asia, Latin America, and the Eastern bloc.[15] Since the Portuguese Carnation Revolution of 1974 and until 2004, the number of formally liberal democratic regimes has doubled worldwide.[16]

6 Robert M. Howard & Amy Steigerwalt, Judging Law and Policy: Courts and Policymaking in the American Political System 177 (2012).

7 Haig Patapan, *Leadership, Law, and Legitimacy: Reflections on the Changing Nature of Judicial Politics in Asia*, *in* The Judicialization of Politics in Asia 219, 223 (Björn Dressel ed., 2012).

8 Julio Ríos-Figueroa, Constitutional Courts as Mediators: Armed Conflict, Civil-Military Relations, and the Rule of Law in Latin America 200 (2016).

9 Tom Ginsburg & Robert Kagan, *Introduction: Institutionalist Approaches to Courts as Political Actors*, *in* Institutions and Public Law: Comparative Approaches 1, 5 (Tom Ginsburg & Robert Kagan eds., 2005).

10 *See* Nuno Garoupa and Maria Maldonado, *The Judiciary in Political Transitions: The Critical Role of U.S. Constitutionalism in Latin America*, 19 Cardozo J. Int'l & Comp. L. 593 (2011).

11 *See generally* David Robertson, The Judge as Political Theorist: Contemporary Constitutional Review (2010).

12 *See* Aylin Aydin, *Judicial Independence across Democratic Regimes: Understanding the Varying Impact of Political Competition*, 47(1) Law & Soc'y Rev. 105 (2013); Carlo Guarnieri, *Judicial Independence in Authoritarian Regimes: Lessons from Continental Europe*, *in* Judicial Independence in China: Lessons for Global Rule of Law Promotion 234, 235 (Randall Peerenboom ed., 2010).

13 Georg Vanberg, *Constitutional Courts in Comparative Perspective: A Theoretical Assessment*, 18 Annu. Rev. Polit. Sci. 167, 167 (2015).

14 Ran Hirschl, *The Strategic Foundations of Constitutions*, *in* Social and Political Foundations of Constitutions 157, 157 (Denis J. Galligan & Mila Versteeg eds., 2013).

15 Kelly M. McMann, Economic Autonomy and Democracy: Hybrid Regimes in Russia and Kyrgyzstan 174 (2006).

16 The resilience of the third wave of democratization is unprecedentedly in international history. *See* Andreas Schedler, *The Logic of Electoral Authoritarianism*, *in* Electoral Authoritarianism: The Dynamics of Unfree Competition 1, 2 (Andreas Schedler ed., 2006).

Not all are liberal democratic in substance: elite accession to a constitutional instrument does not guarantee its observance in actual governmental practice.[17] It is hardly disputed that the prevalence of liberal democratic ideology after the downfall of Communism has incentivized many of the ruling politicians who seized power in the aftermath of single-party dictatorships and military juntas across Africa, Eurasia, and Latin America during the close of the Cold War, to take up democratic mantles and showcase multiparty elections notwithstanding their lack of commitment to the liberal democratic ideal.[18] In brief, new regimes prefer speaking the language of liberal democracy,[19] and coupling plebiscitarianism with authoritarianism "in an astounding rate,"[20] to committing themselves to contested, free, fair elections, enabled by civil and political rights.[21] By the early twenty-first century, no less than half of all countries, from Azerbaijan to Zimbabwe, from Russia to Singapore, from Belarus to Cameroon, from Egypt to Uzbekistan, can be said to have regimes that adhered at least superficially to these political patterns.[22]

A sizeable part of the "third wave" of democratization was thus a "dramatic trend" toward a new kind of authoritarianism, variously branded "hybrid regime,"[23] "semi-democracy,"[24] "semi-authoritarianism,"[25] "electoral authoritarianism,"[26] "competitive authoritarianism,"[27] "democratically

[17] Yasuo Hasebe & Cesare Pinelli, *Constitutions*, *in* ROUTLEDGE HANDBOOK OF CONSTITUTIONAL LAW 9, 15 (Mark Tushnet et al. eds., 2015).

[18] Steven Levitsky & Lucan A. Way, Competitive Authoritarianism: Hybrid Regimes after The Cold War 3 (2010); Matthew Y.H. Wong, Comparative Hong Kong Politics: A Guidebook for Students and Researchers 106 (2017).

[19] Elections are necessary but not sufficient for the endurance of democracy: SAMUEL ISSACHAROFF, FRAGILE DEMOCRACIES: CONTESTED POWER IN THE ERA OF CONSTITUTIONAL COURTS 6 (2015).

[20] Jason Brownlee, *Portents of Pluralism: How Hybrid Regimes Affect Democratic Transitions*, 53 (3) AM. J. POL. SCI. 515, 515 (2009).

[21] Carlos Gervasoni, *The Dimensions of Democratic and Hybrid Subnational Regimes: Evidence from an Expert Survey in Argentina*, *in* ILLIBERAL PRACTICES: TERRITORIAL VARIANCE WITHIN LARGE FEDERAL DEMOCRACIES 120, 129 (Jacqueline Behrend & Laurence Whitehead eds., 2016).

[22] MCMANN, *supra* note 15, at 174.

[23] Larry J. Diamond, *Thinking about Hybrid Regimes*, 13(2) J. DEMOCRACY 21, 27 (2002). For the sake of clarity, the term "hybrid regime" will be used throughout this book.

[24] John P. Burns, *Editorial Introduction: Special Issue on the Second Decade of the Hong Kong Special Administrative Region of China: Themes and Overview*, 39(2) ASIA PAC. J. PUB. ADMIN. 79, 79 (2017).

[25] *See* MARINA OTTAWAY, DEMOCRACY CHALLENGED: THE RISE OF SEMI-AUTHORITARIANISM (2003).

[26] Schedler, *supra* note 16, at 1.

[27] LEVITSKY & WAY, *supra* note 18, at 4.

disguised dictatorship,"[28] "the gray zone,"[29] and so on. Ironically, this authoritarianism spread much more rapidly than actual liberal democracy during the third wave, and has become the most common form of authoritarianism, above absolute monarchies, single-party regimes, and military dictatorships.[30] The hybrid has even spilled over to the local level, such that subnational authoritarian enclaves can be found in federated countries, liberal democratic or not, such as Argentina, Brazil, Mexico, India, and Russia.[31] The considerable diversity of terms used to describe hybrids at both national and subnational levels[32] implies that neither a satisfactory definition nor a standard way to classify them exists.[33] Nevertheless, it is safe to say that hybrid regimes generally lack either of two, but not both, components of liberal democracies or else they would have been fully fledged closed authoritarian regimes,[34] and could be called, with more generality, "illiberal democracies"[35] or "liberal autocracies."[36] As noted above, there are competing ways in political science to conceptualize hybrid regimes.[37] This book will not engage in that debate. It suffices to summarize the

[28] Paul Brooker, Non-Democratic Regimes 2 (2014).

[29] Thomas Carothers, *The End of the Transition Paradigm*, 13(1) J. Democracy 5, 9 (2002).

[30] Beatriz Magaloni, *The Game of Electoral Fraud and the Ousting of Authoritarian Rule*, 54(3) Am. J. Pol. Sci. 751, 751 (2010). Each year, The Economist Magazine releases a well-known list of "flawed democracies" and "hybrid regimes" in its annual Democracy Index. *See* The Economist Intelligence Unit, Democracy Index 2017: Free Speech under Attack 2 (2017).

[31] André Borges, *Subnational Hybrid Regimes and Democratization in Brazil: Why Party Nationalization Matters*, *in* Illiberal Practices: Territorial Variance within Large Federal Democracies 162, 162 (Jacqueline Behrend & Laurence Whitehead eds., 2016); *See generally* Jacqueline Behrend & Laurence Whitehead, *Setting the Comparative Agenda: Territorially Uneven Democratization Processes in Large Federations*, *in* Illiberal Practices: Territorial Variance within Large Federal Democracies 1 (Jacqueline Behrend & Laurence Whitehead eds., 2016); Edward L. Gibson, Boundary Control: Subnational Authoritarianism in Federal Democracies (2012).

[32] Agustina Giraudy, Democrats and Autocrats: Pathways of Subnational Undemocratic Regime Continuity within Democratic Countries 37 (2015).

[33] Ottaway, *supra* note 25, at 7. *See* Honorata Mazepusa et al., A *Comparative Study of Legitimation Strategies in Hybrid Regimes*, 37(4) Pol'y Stud. 350 (2016); Steffen Kailitz, *Classifying Political Regimes Revisited: Legitimation and Durability*, 20(1) Democratization 39 (2013).

[34] Gervasoni, *supra* note 21, at 125.

[35] Fareed Zakaria, *The Rise of Illiberal Democracy*, 76(6) Foreign Aff. 22, 29 (1997).

[36] Tom Ginsburg, *East Asian Constitutionalism in Comparative Perspective*, *in* Constitutionalism in Asia in the Early Twenty-First Century 32, 37 (Albert H.Y. Chen ed., 2014).

[37] *See* Samuel Handlin, *Observing Incumbent Abuses: Improving Measures of Electoral and Competitive Authoritarianism with New Data*, 24(1) Democratization 41 (2017);

state of research in two methods of classification – namely a continuum with liberal democracy on one extreme and fully fledged authoritarianism on the other, with electoral democracy, hybrid ambiguous regimes, hybrid competitive authoritarian regimes, and hybrid hegemonic electoral authoritarian regimes in between.[38] Regardless of their differences, hybrid regimes tend to be officially civilian and provide electoral channels for the Opposition legally to contend for official positions, albeit disadvantagedly,[39] in that electoral institutions are "heavily skewed" in favor of incumbent rulers.[40] Opposition political parties, civil society organizations, an independent press, and political debate are intermittently tolerated, provided that they do not directly threaten regime security.[41]

It is coming to be recognized that hybrid regimes are "a persistent and unique regime form" that cannot be presumed to be trending in a democratic direction.[42] Belarus and Russia have become more authoritarian, Malaysia and Singapore remain fairly stable,[43] and formerly liberal democratic Venezuela and Turkey have slipped into hybrid authoritarianism.[44] It is no longer in serious dispute that the hybrid regime is a type in its own right, and not transitional between closed authoritarianism and liberal democracy.[45] It follows that hybrids are not necessarily by-products of failed attempts to establish either closed autocracies or liberal democracies.[46] They may be intentionally designed by elites to extract the *bona fides* and international goodwill of liberal democratic institutions,[47] while reducing the risk of losing political control at home.[48] Elections can be used by rulers as a cost-effective mechanism to reveal crucial information about popular preferences and

Leah Gilbert & Payam Mohseni, *Beyond Authoritarianism: The Conceptualization of Hybrid Regimes*, 46 St. Comp. Int'l Dev. 270 (2011).

38 Wong, *supra* note 18, at 95; Diamond, *supra* note 23, at 26.

39 Graeme B. Robertson, The Politics of Protest in Hybrid Regimes: Managing Dissent in Post-Communist Russia 6 (2011).

40 Levitsky & Way, *supra* note 18, at 5.

41 Schedler, *supra* note 16, at 3.

42 Gabrielle Bardall, *Coding Competitive Authoritarianism*, 10 Z. Vgl. Polit. Wiss. (Suppl.) 19, 20 (2016).

43 Levitsky & Way, *supra* note 18, at 4.

44 Mark V. Tushnet, *Authoritarian Constitutionalism*, 100 Cornell L. Rev. 391, 394, 435 (2015).

45 McMann, *supra* note 16, at 174.

46 Ottaway, *supra* note 25, at 7.

47 The logic of hybrid regimes establishing electoral mechanisms is much more sophisticated than mere window dressing. *See* Sherzod Abdukadirov, *The Problem of Political Calculation in Autocracies*, 21(4) Const. Pol. Econ. 360 (2010).

48 Robertson, *supra* note 39, at 12.

regime support, enabling incumbents to coopt the opposition and segments of the electorate, and to modify policies that are not central to the regime.[49]

Liberal democratic constitutional texts are drafted by authoritarian elites to elicit "an enthusiasm for and loyalty to the constitutional order and [they] have more to do with rhetorical appeal than with practical efficacy, more to do with symbols than with reality, more to do with their ability to raise a cheer than with their ability to serve interests."[50] In short, hybrid regimes are more adaptive and flexible than closed autocracies, but at the same time are far more authoritarian than liberal democracies. The proliferation of a liberal democratic *form* of government must therefore not mislead us to believe that undemocratic higher control has been consigned to the dustbin of history.[51] Authoritarianism has been the norm for most of human history, and is likelier than not to remain so.[52]

The two liberal democratic institutional forms adopted most prominently, almost universally, by hybrid regimes are multiparty elections[53] and independent judiciaries armed with constitutional review powers.[54] The adoption of constitutional review and its exercise by independent courts are, of course, two separate developments. Founding documents do not distribute review competence once for all: their provisions, viewed as desirable by framers at the moment of constitutional making, do not necessarily explain the perdurable influence of such a court in day-to-day politics.[55] The court may claim primacy over constitutional meaning, but whether its assertions will be tolerated by political actors is another question.[56] At the end of the day, independent and consequential constitutional review cannot be presumed, simply

49 Clara Boulianne Lagacé & Jennifer Gandhi, *Authoritarian Institutions, in* ROUTLEDGE HANDBOOK OF COMPARATIVE POLITICAL INSTITUTIONS 278, 288 (Jennifer Gandhi & Rubén Ruiz-Rufino eds., 2015).

50 *See* Geoffrey Brennan & Alan Hamlin, *Constitutions as Expressive Documents, in* THE OXFORD HANDBOOK OF POLITICAL ECONOMY 329, 342 (Barry R. Weingast & Donald A. Wittman eds., 2006).

51 BROOKER, *supra* note 28, at 1.

52 Stephen Haber, *Authoritarian Government, in* THE OXFORD HANDBOOK OF POLITICAL ECONOMY 693, 693 (Barry R. Weingast & Donald A. Wittman eds., 2006).

53 *See* JASON BROWNLEE, AUTHORITARIANISM IN AN AGE OF DEMOCRATIZATION (2007).

54 Stephen Gardbaum, *Are Strong Constitutional Courts Always a Good Thing for New Democracies?*, 53 COLUM. J. TRANSNAT'L L. 285, 287 (2015); Tamir Moustafa, *Law and Courts in Authoritarian Regimes*, 10 ANNU. REV. LAW SOC. SCI. 281, 294 (2014).

55 Vanberg, *supra* note 13, at 169.

56 *See* KEITH E. WHITTINGON, POLITICAL FOUNDATIONS OF JUDICIAL SUPREMACY: THE PRESIDENCY, THE SUPREME COURT, AND CONSTITUTIONAL LEADERSHIP IN U.S. HISTORY (2007).

because it is bound, eventually, to inconvenience those wielding political power.[57]

Indeed, it is hard to imagine that a dictator, regardless of ideological orientation, would invite or allow even nominally independent judges potentially to obstruct the making of major public policies, or tolerate checks and balances that give priority to adherence to procedural rights over achievement of desired substantive outcomes.[58] The presence of democratic forms thus appears to be a necessary, though certainly not a sufficient, condition for consequential constitutional review to be entrenched.[59] A settled consensus in the comparative constitutional law literature holds that "[i]t seems very unlikely that one will encounter the judicialization of politics outside democratic polities."[60] Often it is casually assumed that judicial independence is impossible in non-democracies, including hybrid regimes, in which legal institutions are unable to restrain political power, and judges are faithful tools of the ruling regime.[61] This assumption is understandable. After all, "abrasive" constitutional review could provoke dictators to abort entire constitutions by brute force.[62] There is no shortage of examples of hybrid regimes prepared to inflict extralegal sanctions on courts and judges according to political needs.[63] In September 1993, Russian President Boris Yeltsin preemptively suspended the entire Constitutional Court after the Court became embroiled in a power struggle between the presidency and the Duma.[64] In April 2011, under the auspices of Prime Minister Viktor Orbán, an open advocate of "illiberal democracy," the Hungarian parliament passed a new Constitution that curbed the jurisdiction of and access to the country's previously powerful

57 Keith E. Whittington, *Legislative Sanctions and the Strategic Environment of Judicial Review*, 1(3) INT'L J. CONST. L. 446, 446 (2003).

58 David S. Law & Mila Versteeg, *Constitutional Variation among Strains of Authoritarianism*, *in* CONSTITUTIONS IN AUTHORITARIAN REGIMES 165, 166 (Tom Ginsburg & Albert Simpser, eds., 2014).

59 C. Neal Tate, *Why the Expansion of Judicial Power?*, *in* THE GLOBAL EXPANSION OF JUDICIAL POWER 27, 29 (C. Neal Tate & Torbjörn Vallinder eds., 1995).

60 *Id.* at 28.

61 Randall Peerenboom, *Introduction*, *in* JUDICIAL INDEPENDENCE IN CHINA: LESSONS FOR GLOBAL RULE OF LAW PROMOTION 1, 3 (Randall Peerenboom ed., 2010).

62 PO JEN YAP, COURTS AND DEMOCRACIES IN ASIA 207 (2017).

63 Terence C. Halliday, *Why the Legal Complex Is Integral to Theories of Consequential Courts*, *in* CONSEQUENTIAL COURTS: JUDICIAL ROLES IN GLOBAL GOVERNANCE 337, 349 (Diana Kapiszeswiki et al. eds., 2013).

64 JANE HENDERSON, THE CONSTITUTION OF THE RUSSIAN FEDERATION: A CONTEXTUAL ANALYSIS 205 (2011).

Constitutional Court.[65] In January 2013, Sri Lanka's parliament, dominated by the ruling Freedom Party, defied a Supreme Court ruling in removing the Chief Justice from her office after the Court had imposed stringent procedural hurdles on a development budget proposed by the President's brother.[66] More recently, in February 2018, Maldivian President Abdulla Yameen declared a state of emergency in response to the Supreme Court's decision to release political prisoners, including convicted but exiled former President Mohamed Nasheed, and to reinstate twelve ousted Opposition parliamentarians; consequently, two justices, including the Chief Justice, were arrested, and the controversial judgment was rescinded by the Court's remaining members.[67]

Recent detailed case studies of constitutional review under authoritarian regimes – a nascent field of study[68] – have also discovered that courts in at least some hybrid regimes have from time to time aggrandized power with impunity.[69] The reconstituted Constitutional Court of the Russian Federation has, since 1995, "done far better than its counterpart constitutional courts in most post-Soviet countries,"[70] and has endured "as an arbiter of

65 Miklos Bankuti et al., *Hungary's Illiberal Turn: Disabling the Constitution*, *in* THE HUNGARIAN PATIENT: SOCIAL OPPOSITION TO AN ILLIBERAL DEMOCRACY 37, 38–39 (Peter Krasztev et al. eds., 2015).

66 Gardbaum, *supra* note 54, at 287–88.

67 Editorial Board, *China's Man in the Maldives How Xi's Belt and Road Project Is Promoting A Political Crisis*, THE WALL STREET JOURNAL, Feb. 19, 2018.

68 *See* Moustafa, *supra* note 54, at 282.

69 Examples include, but are not limited to, Argentina: Gretchen Helmke, *The Logic of Strategic Defection: Court-Executive Relations in Argentina under Dictatorship and Democracy*, 96(2) AM. POL. SCI. REV. 291 (2002); Benin: Theodore Holo, *Handling of Petitions by the Constitutional Court of Benin*, *in* CONSTITUTIONAL ADJUDICATION IN AFRICA 315 (Charles M. Fombad ed., 2017); Egypt: TAMIR MOUSTAFA, THE STRUGGLE FOR CONSTITUTIONAL POWER: LAW, POLITICS, AND ECONOMIC DEVELOPMENT IN EGYPT (2007); Nigeria: Ameze Guobadia, *Constitutional Adjudication in Nigeria: Formal Structures and Substantive Impact*, *in* CONSTITUTIONAL ADJUDICATION IN AFRICA 136 (Charles M. Fombad ed., 2017); Pakistan: PAULA NEWBERG, JUDGING THE STATE: COURTS AND CONSTITUTIONAL POLITICS IN PAKISTAN (2002); Singapore: Lynette J. Chua & Stacia L. Haynie, *Judicial Review of Executive Power in the Singaporean Context, 1965–2012*, 4(1) J. L. & CTS. 43 (2016); Soviet Union and Russia: ALEXEI TROCHEV, JUDGING RUSSIA: CONSTITUTIONAL COURT IN RUSSIAN POLITICS 1990–2006 (2008); Turkey: Yaniv Roznai & Serkan Yolcu, *An Unconstitutional Constitutional Amendment – The Turkish Perspective: A Comment on the Turkish Constitutional Court's Headscarf Decision*, 10(1) INT'L J. CONST. L. 175 (2012); Zimbabwe: DANIEL COMPAGNON, A PREDICTABLE TRAGEDY: ROBERT MUGABE AND THE COLLAPSE OF ZIMBABWE 150–152 (2011). *See* Brad Epperly, *Political Competition and de facto Judicial Independence in Non-Democracies*, 56(2) EUR. J. POL. RESEARCH 279 (2017).

70 Peter H. Solomon, Jr., *Judicial Power in Authoritarian States: The Russian Experience*, *in* RULE BY LAW: THE POLITICS OF COURTS IN AUTHORITARIAN REGIMES 261, 279 (Tom Ginsburg & Tamir Moustafa eds., 2008).

political disputes and increasingly as a guarantor of stable constitutional rules" for more than two decades till the present day.[71] In spite of formidable political limits, it has effectively abolished the death penalty in all of Russia,[72] and from time to time upheld the civil rights of individuals in cases involving state officials.[73] In 2014 alone, in the teeth of backlash from Prime Minister and later President Erdoğan, the Constitutional Court of Turkey struck down legal provisions that would have conferred on the Minister of Justice sweeping powers over judicial and prosecutorial appointments; invalidated government bans on social media as breaching the freedom of expression; nullified legal impediments on high-ranking civil servants returning to their positions within two years of being unjustly removed; and ruled unconstitutional a law that empowered the state to shut down websites within four hours without a court order.[74]

Overall, the constitutional courts of nondemocratic regimes show ever greater tendencies to converge on common patterns of behavior and reasoning with their counterparts, and biases in favor of secularism and modernism.[75] Constitutional courts have been found to produce stabilizing effects that hold even authoritarian elites themselves together, and also vital "focal points" that coordinate state-society conflict.[76] It is therefore imprudent uncritically to presume that constitutional review matters only in democracies.[77] The above developments have led some scholars to discern the emergence of alternative constitutionalisms, ranging from "sham constitutionalism"[78] and "authoritarian constitutionalism"[79] through "abusive constitutionalism,"[80] to "mixed constitutionalism"[81] and "hybrid constitutionalism,"[82] within the universe of authoritarian regimes. "Constitutional-oligarchic regimes ... [that]

[71] Carla L. Thorson, Politics, Judicial Review and the Russian Constitutional Court 156 (2012).
[72] Tamara O. Kuznetsova et al., Russian Constitutional Law 45 (2014).
[73] Thomas F. Remington, Politics in Russia 235 (2015).
[74] Rethink Institute, 2015 Turkey Country Report 12–13 (2014).
[75] Ran Hirschl, Constitutional Theocracy 162 (2010).
[76] Samuel Issacharoff, Fragile Democracies: Contested Power in the Era of Constitutional Courts 10 (2015).
[77] Moustafa, *supra* note 69, at 2.
[78] David S. Law & Mila Versteeg, *Sham Constitutions*, 101 Cal. L. Rev. 863, 878 (2013).
[79] Tushnet, *supra* note 44, at 450.
[80] David Landau, *Abusive Constitutionalism*, 47 U.C. Davis L. Rev. 189 (2013).
[81] Graham Walker, *The Idea of Nonliberal Constitutionalism*, *in* Ethnicity and Group Rights 164 (Ian Shapiro & Will Kymlicka eds., 1997), cited in Li-ann Thio, A Treatise on Singapore Constitutional Law 61–62 (2012).
[82] Albert H.Y. Chen, *The Achievement of Constitutionalism in Asia: Moving beyond "Constitutions without Constitutionalism," in* Constitutionalism in Asia in the Early Twenty-First Century 1, 14 (Albert H.Y. Chen ed., 2014).

combine high levels of constitutionalism with low levels of electoralism" can indeed be found in jurisdictions such as Singapore, Malaysia, and Hong Kong.[83] In any event, with over half of all countries recognized as closed authoritarian or hybrid regimes, little can excuse our neglect of the constitutional and judicial dynamics in these political settings.[84]

CONSTITUTIONAL REVIEW IN THE CHINESE SPECIAL ADMINISTRATIVE REGIONS

Under what conditions will the final appellate courts[85] of two subnational hybrid regimes diverge fundamentally in their understandings of and approaches to constitutional review, despite endowment with identical jurisdiction by kindred constitutions, overseen by a common sovereign in roughly the same time frame? This book ventures to address this question with the Hong Kong and Macau Special Administrative Regions (SARs) of the People's Republic of China as case studies. Both Regions are located on the northern edge of the South China Sea, bordering Guangdong Province, and only 60 kilometers apart from each other.[86] The two Chinese SARs are in many ways "most similar" to each other, politically, economically, and socially (see Tables 1.1 and 1.2). They were the only European dependencies left on East Asian soil at the resumption of Chinese sovereignty in 1997 and 1999, respectively. Hong Kong was founded by the British in the midst of the First Anglo-Chinese War (1839–42) on one of the islands lying off the coast of the Cantonese County of Bao'an. In 1842, Qing China, by the Treaty of Nanking, ceded to the British Crown in perpetuity.[87] The geographical

83 *See* Mikael Wigell, *Mapping "Hybrid Regimes": Regime Types and Concepts in Comparative Politics*, 15(2) DEMOCRATIZATION 230 (2008).

84 Tamir Moustafa & Tom Ginsburg, *Introduction: The Function of Courts in Authoritarian Politics*, *in* RULE BY LAW: THE POLITICS OF COURTS IN AUTHORITARIAN REGIMES 1, 1 (Tom Ginsburg & Tamir Moustafa eds., 2008).

85 Gretchen Helmke & Julio Ríos-Figueroa, *Introduction: Courts in Latin America*, *in* COURTS IN LATIN AMERICA 1, 7 (Gretchen Helmke & Julio Ríos-Figueroa eds., 2011) (political economy analyses of judicial behavior are "interested first and foremost in how judges interact with other political actors and how these interactions shape policy outcomes. Whereas lower-level courts can sometimes play this role, courts imbued with constitutional review jurisdiction – whether they are supreme courts, constitutional chambers, or separate constitutional courts – hold the proverbial last word over whether to enforce the political rules of the game, at least within the judicial hierarchy.").

86 Bill K.P. Chou, *Interest Group Politics in Macau after Handover*, 14(43) J. CONTEMP. CHINA 191, 192 (2005).

87 *See* G.B. ENDACOTT, A HISTORY OF HONG KONG (1964).

TABLE 1.1 *Hong Kong and Macau: a legal-political comparison*

Jurisdiction	Constitutional document (Year in force)	Universal suffrage election for chief executive?	Establishment majority in legislature? (% in 2017)	Constitutional review (centralized or decentralized?)
Hong Kong	Basic Law (1997)	No	Yes (57%)	Decentralized
Macau	Lei Básica (1999)	No	Yes (88%)	Decentralized

TABLE 1.2 *Hong Kong and Macau: a socioeconomic comparison*

Jurisdiction	Total land area	Population (2016 est.)	Largest ethnic group(%) (2011 est.)	Most spoken language (%) (2011 est.)	GDP (PPP) (2016 est.)	GDP (PPP) per capita (2016 est.)
Hong Kong	1,073 km^2	7,167,403	Han Chinese (93.1%)	Cantonese (89.5%)	US$427.4 billion	US$58,100
Macau	28.2 km^2	646,800	Han Chinese (92.4%)	Cantonese (83.3%)	US$63.22 billion	US$96,100

Source: Central Intelligence Agency, THE WORLD FACTBOOK, www.cia.gov/library/publications/the-world-factbook/

boundaries of the Crown Colony were expanded twice in the nineteenth century under the First Convention of Peking 1860 and the Second Convention of Peking 1898, ultimately covering the entire landmass and surrounding islands to the south of modern-day Shenzhen. Although Macau in modern history predated Hong Kong by several centuries,[88] beginning with Ming China's 1557 acquiescence in Portuguese occupation after four decades of unofficial settlement,[89] it was not until 1887 that Peking formally recognized the Portuguese right of "perpetual occupation" by way of the Treaty of Friendship and Commerce between Portugal and China.[90] Macau consists

88 Carmen Amado Mendes, *Macau in China's Relations with the Lusophone World*, 57 REV. BRAS. POLÍT. INT. 225, 225 (2014).

89 Jaw-ling Joanne Chang, *Settlement of the Macao Issue: Distinctive Features of Beijing's Negotiating Behavior*, 20 CASE W. RES. J. INT'L L. 253, 255–56 (1988).

90 Paulo Cardinal, *Macau: Transformation of an Historic Autonomy*, *in* PRACTISING SELF-GOVERNMENT: A Comparative Study OF AUTONOMOUS REGIONS 383, 385 (Yash Ghai & Sophia Woodman eds., 2013).

of a small peninsula and two tiny islands. Its area was, however, widened considerably through land reclamation, which took off in the 1970s as its economy began to develop rapidly. Between 1972 and 1994, the geographical size of Macau expanded by one-third.[91] Both SARs lack raw materials but possess modern, developed economies and high standards of living. By the late 2000s Hong Kong had climbed from its modest origins as an obscure fishing village in the Far East to become a leading international financial center in many ways on a par with New York and London.[92] Immediately after the Handover, Macau already possessed a world-class telecommunications system, an advanced off-shore financial system, and a rising high-tech industry.[93] It is home to the world's largest casinos, and its gaming revenue now exceeds those of Las Vegas and Atlantic City combined.[94] In 2013, Macau became the world's fourth-richest economy by gross domestic product (GDP) per capita.[95]

The international bargains that forged, even before the Cold War ended, the unprecedented merger of the world's most populous Leninist state with two capitalist, cosmopolitan polities deviated significantly from the typical process of decolonization in the twentieth century.[96] In December 1984, the Sino-British Joint Declaration, a treaty registered with the United Nations, set in motion the transition of Hong Kong to an exceptionally autonomous SAR under Chinese sovereignty,[97] vested with executive, legislative, and independent judicial powers,[98] and headed by a locally selected Chief Executive.[99] The contracting parties undertook to preserve the pre-existing

91 Herbert S. Yee, Macau in Transition: From Colony to Autonomous Region 13 (2001).

92 *See* City of London and Z/Yen Group, The Global Financial Centers Index 2009, www.cityoflondon.gov.uk/GFCI; Michael Elliott, *NyLonKong: A Tale of Three Cities*, Time Magazine, Jan. 28, 2008.

93 Fok Kaicheong, *The Existence of Macau: A Chinese Perspective, in* Macau on the Threshold of the Third Millennium 13, 13 (Macau Ricci Institute ed.,2001).

94 *See* Sonny Lo, *Hong Kong*, in Politics in China: An Introduction 364 (William A. Joseph, ed., 2010).

95 Ieong Meng U, *Macao and Hong Kong, Convergence or Divergence? The 2014 Retirement Package Bill Protest and Macao's Governance Crisis*, 57 (3) Asian Surv. 504, 505 (2017).

96 *See* Ming K. Chan, *Democracy Derailed: Realpolitik in the Making of the Hong Kong Basic Law, 1985–90, in* The Hong Kong Basic Law: Blueprint for "Stability and Prosperity" under Chinese Sovereignty? 6 (Ming K. Chan & David J. Clark eds., 1991); Lilly W.Y. Heong, *One Country, Two Ideologies: The Rule of Law in the Hong Kong Special Administrative Region*, 16 Temp. Int'l & Comp. L. J. 447 (2002).

97 Joint Declaration of the Government of the United Kingdom of Great Britain and Northern Ireland and the Government of the People's Republic of China on the Question of Hong Kong, 26 Sept. 1984 [hereinafter "Sino–British Joint Declaration"], arts. 3(1) & 3(2).

98 Sino–British Joint Declaration, art. 3(3).

99 Sino–British Joint Declaration, art. 3(4).

legal,[100] social, economic systems, lifestyle, rights and liberties of the British dependency[101] by way of one document known as the Hong Kong Basic Law.[102] The Lei Básica de Macau of 1993,[103] authorized by the Sino–Portuguese Joint Declaration of 1987,[104] set up for post-1999 Macau institutions "remarkably similar"[105] to Hong Kong's,[106] reproducing much of the Basic Law verbatim.[107] However, nothing more than Beijing's goodwill guaranteed the observance of those grandiose promises after the withdrawal of British and Portuguese rule from Hong Kong and Macau respectively. As mainland Chinese Basic Law drafter Wu Jianfan noted, "[The Sino–British Joint Declaration] says nothing about who decides whether the laws enacted are in accordance with the Basic Law and legal procedures or how to handle laws which do not accord with the Basic Law and legal procedures."[108]

Significantly, the two constitutional documents guaranteed that "[t]he socialist system and policies [of mainland China] shall not be practised … [and] the previous capitalist system and way of life shall remain unchanged for 50 years,"[109] and declared moreover that "[n]o department of the Central People's Government and no province, autonomous region, or municipality

100 Sino–British Joint Declaration, art. 3(3); Kevin Kwok-yin Cheng, *Prosecutorial Procedural Justice and Public Legitimacy in Hong Kong*, 57(1) Brit. J. Criminol. 94, 100 (2017) ("The previous legal institutions, including the law (both legislation and case law), the judiciary and prosecution, remain largely unchanged.")

101 Sino–British Joint Declaration, art. 3(5).

102 Sino–British Joint Declaration, art. 3(12).

103 Lei Básica da Região Administrativa Especial de Macau da República Popular da China (Basic Law of the Macao Special Administrative Region of the People's Republic of China) (adopted by the First Session of the Eighth National People's Congress on Mar. 31, 1993, effective Dec. 20, 1999) [hereinafter "Lei Básica"].

104 Joint Declaration of the Government of the People's Republic of China and the Government of the Republic of Portugal on the Question of Macao, Apr. 13, 1987.

105 Judith R. Krebs, *One Country, Three Systems? Judicial Review in Macau after* Ng Ka Ling, 10 (1)Pac. Rim L. & Pol'y J. 126 (2000).

106 Basic Law of the Hong Kong Special Administrative Region of the People's Republic of China (adopted at the Third Session of the Seventh National People's Congress on Apr. 4, 1990, effective on Jul. 1, 1997) [hereinafter "Basic Law"].

107 Simon N.M. Young, *Fundamental Rights and the Basic Laws of the Hong Kong and Macau Special Administrative Regions*, *in* One Country, Two Systems, Three Legal Orders – Perspectives of Evolution: Essays on Macau's Autonomy after the Resumption of Sovereignty by China 683 (Jorge Oliveira & Paulo Cardinal, eds., 2009).

108 Jianfan Wu, *Several Issues Concerning the Relationship between the Central Government of the People's Republic of China and the Hong Kong Special Administrative Region*, 2 J. Chinese L. 65, 75 (1988).

109 Basic Law, art. 5; Lei Básica, art. 5.

directly under the Central Government may interfere in the affairs which the [SARs] administer, on [their] own."[110] Nevertheless, the Hong Kong SAR is described by political scientists as "oligarchic,"[111] "liberal authoritarian,"[112] "semi-democratic,"[113] "nondemocratic,"[114] a "hybrid regime,"[115] a "partial democracy,"[116] and an "electoral authoritarian regime."[117] The Macau SAR is likewise described as "undemocratic,"[118] "semi-democratic,"[119] "somewhere between a democratic and an authoritarian state,"[120] "a transitional democracy,"[121] "a subnational authoritarian regime,"[122] and "fundamentally a liberal authoritarian regime featuring some electoral authoritarian elements."[123]

The hybrid regimes of Hong Kong and Macau[124] were not accidents of history, but, as this book argues, deliberately established as such by the framers of the Basic Law and the Lei Básica under the auspices of China. Both are run by corporatist regimes,[125] under ruling circles known as "Establishment

110 Basic Law, art. 21; Lei Básica, art. 21.

111 Richard C. Bush, Hong Kong in the Shadow of China: Living with the Leviathan 48 (2016).

112 Matthew Y.H. Wong, *Party Models in a Hybrid Regime: Hong Kong 2007–2012*, 15(1) China Rev. 67, 69 (2015).

113 Graham Greenleaf, Asian Data Privacy Laws: Trade & Human Rights Perspectives 20 (2014).

114 Daniel A. Bell, The China Model: Political Meritocracy and the Limits of Democracy 117 (2016).

115 *See* Julius Yam, *The Role of Courts in Hybrid Regimes and a Reconceptualization of Separation of Powers: The Case of Filibuster in Hong Kong*, 17(1) Australian J. Asian L. art. 3 (2016).

116 Eliza W.Y. Lee et al., Public Policymaking in Hong Kong: Civic Engagement and State-society Relations in a Semi-Democracy 1 (2013).

117 *See* Brian C.H. Fong, *In-between Liberal Authoritarianism and Electoral Authoritarianism: Hong Kong's Democratization under Chinese Sovereignty, 1997–2016*, 24(4) *Democratization* 724 (2017).

118 Bill K.P. Chou, *Interest Group Politics in Macau after Handover*, 14(43) *J. Contemp. China* 191, 196 (2005).

119 Bill K.P. Chou, *Legitimacy-Building and Public Sector Reform in Macao: Administrative Measures to Address Political Problems*, 10(3) China: An Int'l J. 133, 148 (2012).

120 Yufan Hao et al., Political Economy of Macao since 1999: The Dilemma of Success 216 (2017).

121 Herbert S. Yee, *The 2001 Legislative Assembly Elections and Political Development in Macau*, 14(43) J. Contemp. China 225, 227 (2005).

122 Ieong, *supra* note 95, at 506.

123 Ying-ho Kwong, *Ruling Coalition Restructuring under Macao's Hybrid Regime*, 17(3) China Rev. 111, 112 (2017).

124 Brian C.H. Fong, *State-Society Conflicts under Hong Kong's Hybrid Regime*, 53(5) Asian Surv. 854, 854 (2013).

125 Edmund W. Cheng, *Street Politics in a Hybrid Regime: The Diffusion of Political Activism in Post-colonial Hong Kong*, 226 China Q. 383, 384–47 (2016).

Coalitions" without any comprehensive, competitive elections, headed by indirectly elected Chief Executives exempt from rigorous checks and balances by partially elected legislatures dominated by loyalists.[126] As of 2017, both Chief Executives are selected by minuscule Election Committees and appointed by the State Council in Beijing. Hong Kong's Election Committee comprises only 1,200 members, and Macau's is even smaller, comprising just 400.

Beijing can count on an overwhelming majority of Election Committee members, most of whom are not popularly elected, to ensure that only an acceptable candidate is chosen as Chief Executive, in spite of the lack of popular support.[127] In Hong Kong, thirty-five out of seventy members of the Legislative Council, or 50 percent, belong to the corporatist "Functional Constituencies," selected by means other than universal suffrage. These tend to be members of the Establishment Coalition, the informal alliance of pro-government parties and politicians. In Macau, up to nineteen out of thirty-three (58 percent) members of the Sixth Legislative Assembly (2013–17) were chosen by Functional Constituencies (twelve) and by direct appointment by the Chief Executive (seven). In other words, the Establishment Coalitions of both Chinese SARs have been able to command overall majorities in their respective parliaments without having to win a majority of the vote in direct elections.[128] Hong Kong's Establishment Coalition has, of late, been accused of resorting to authoritarian manipulation tactics more and more, such as disqualifying allegedly separatist candidates from Legislative Council elections, selectively prosecuting activists, rigging pseudo-independent civil society groups to protest against Pan-Democratic protests, and harassing media outlets sympathetic to Opposition causes.[129] In similar vein, its Macau counterpart has secured the passage of a national security act in 2009 that outlaws treason, secession, sedition, and subversion against the Chinese state; and in 2014 arrested activists who had been demanding more democratic procedures through organizing an unofficial referendum.[130]

126 Stan Hok-Wui Wong, *Resource Disparity and Multi Level Elections in Competitive Authoritarian Regimes: Regression Discontinuity Evidence from Hong Kong*, 33 ELECTORAL STUD. 200, 201–02 (2014).

127 SIMON YOUNG & RICHARD CULLEN, ELECTING HONG KONG'S CHIEF EXECUTIVE 79, 91 (2010).

128 As of March 2018, thirty-five seats in the Legislative Council are constituted through universal suffrage in Geographical Constituencies elections, while another thirty-five seats are constituted through Functional Constituencies elections. *See* PO JEN YAP, COURTS AND DEMOCRACIES IN ASIA 46 (2017).

129 *See* Fong, *supra* note 117.

130 *See* Andrew J. Nathan, *China's Challenge*, *in* AUTHORITARIANISM GOES GLOBAL 23, 32 (Larry Diamond et al., 2016).

Consistent with the trend of hybrid regimes described above, and unique among subnational polities, both the Basic Law and the Lei Básica establish final appellate courts – the Hong Kong Court of Final Appeal (CFA) and the Tribunal de Última Instância of Macau (TUI) – independent of China's apex court, the Supreme People's Court in Beijing. The judges enjoy *de jure* security of tenure and legal immunity in the performance of their functions,[131] and are entitled to "exercise judicial power independently, free from any interference."[132] However, if the two documents establish any system of constitutional review, it is, at best, one of "weak-form review."[133] The Standing Committee of the National People's Congress, China's paramount interpretive authority was obligated to authorize the SAR courts "to interpret on their own, in adjudicating cases, the provisions of [the Basic Law or Lei Básica] which are within the limits of the autonomy of the Region[s]."[134] But on matters implicating national sovereignty or the relationship between the Chinese central government and the SARs, both jurisdictions are required to refer interpretive questions to the Standing Committee, from whose authority there is no appeal.[135] Either Court could easily have forsworn the power of constitutional review by holding that it is vested in the Standing Committee exclusively; that any legislation not vetoed by the latter shall be presumed consistent with the Basic Law or Lei Básica and enforced by the courts.[136]

Counterintuitively, constitutional review in the SARs over the last two decades has followed two diametrically opposite paths. The CFA's "activism"[137] is now accepted as an unquestioned and "highly significant"[138] part of the constitutional landscape.[139] Within its first two decades of existence, the CFA has held that persons "unlawfully" detained by the police "are

131 Basic Law, arts. 85 & 89; Lei Básica, arts. 87 & 89.

132 Basic Law, art. 85; Lei Básica, art. 83.

133 Mark Tushnet & Rosalind Dixon, *Weak-Form Review and Its Constitutional Relatives: An Asian Perspective, in* COMPARATIVE CONSTITUTIONAL LAW IN ASIA 102, 105 (Rosalind Dixon & Tom Ginsburg, eds., 2014).

134 Basic Law, art. 158; Lei Básica, art. 143.

135 *Id.*

136 Albert H.Y. Chen, *The Relationship between the Central Government and the SAR, in The Basic Law and Hong Kong's Future* 107, 124 (Peter Wesley Smith & Albert H.Y. Chen eds., 1988).

137 Laifan Lin & Mingkang Gu, *Can Courts in Hong Kong Examine the Constitutionality of the Legislative Conduct of the PRC?, in* HONG KONG IN TRANSITION: ONE Country, TWO SYSTEMS 175, 188 (Robert Ash et al. eds., 2003).

138 RICHARD GORDON & JOHNNY MOK, JUDICIAL REVIEW IN HONG KONG vii (2d ed. 2014).

139 Swati Jhaveri & Anne Scully-Hill, *Executive and Legislative Reactions to Judicial Declarations of Constitutional Invalidity in Hong Kong: Engagement, Acceptance or Avoidance?*, 13(2) INT'L J. CONST. L. 507, 507–08 (2015) ("Following [the Basic Law's] promulgation, the courts have exercised far more extensive powers than those that existed

entitled to use reasonable force to free themselves";[140] and that the executive has "a positive duty ... to take reasonable and appropriate measures to enable lawful assemblies to take place peacefully."[141] It has declared as unconstitutional a criminal law provision that subjected homosexual men to unjustified differential treatment on the basis of their sexual orientation;[142] recognized the right of postoperative transsexuals to marry in their new gender;[143] affirmed the right of non-permanent residents to travel and return from overseas;[144] invalidated statutory limits on its own competence to hear parliamentary election petitions;[145] quashed a seven-year residence requirement before new immigrants may apply for social security payments;[146] and demanded that the Legislative Council enact corrective covert surveillance legislation within a specified time limit.[147] It has even designed new procedures of constitutional review, reviving defunct British Imperial laws as additional grounds for judging the validity of legislation passed before July 1, 1997;[148] striking down a non-infringing provision to better achieve statutory ends;[149] and applying remedial interpretation to "read down" constitutionally defective statutes.[150] These developments have led one notable comparative constitutional law expert to describe Hong Kong's evolution as to a "juristocracy,"[151] in which courts are weighty political decision-makers.

The TUI, in stark contrast, has yet to invalidate one legislative provision for inconsistency with Macau's Lei Básica, including its comprehensive charter of rights contained in Chapter III, and has been described by scholars as

prior to 1997, to judicially review the constitutionality of legislation. Judicial review is consequently a more prominent aspect of the law and policy-making environment than was the case prior to 1997.") *See* Johannes M.M. Chan, *Basic Law and Constitutional Review*, 37 Hong Kong L. J. 407 (2007); Po Jen Yap, *10 Years of the Basic Law: The Rise, Retreat and Resurgence of Judicial Power in Hong Kong*, 36(2)Commonwealth L. World Rev. 166 (2007).

140 Yeung May Wan v. HKSAR (2005) 8 H.K.C.F.A.R. 137, 160 (H.K.C.F.A.).

141 Leung Kwok Hung v. HKSAR (2005) 8 H.K.C.F.A.R. 229, 249 (H.K.C.F.A.).

142 Sec'y for Justice v. Yau Yuk Lung (2007) 10 H.K.C.F.A.R. 335 (H.K.C.F.A.).

143 W v. The Registrar of Marriages (2013) 16 H.K.C.F.A.R. 112 (H.K.C.F.A.).

144 Gurung Kesh Bahadur v. Dir. of Immigration (2002) 5 H.K.C.F.A.R. 480 (H.K.C.F.A.).

145 Mok Charles v. Tam Wai Ho (2010) 13 H.K.C.F.A.R. 762 (H.K.C.F.A.).

146 Kong Yunming v. Dir. of Soc. Welfare (2013) 16 H.K.C.F.A.R. 950 (H.K.C.F.A.).

147 Koo Sze Yiu v. Chief Exec. of the HKSAR (2006) 9 H.K.C.F.A.R. 441 (H.K.C.F.A.).

148 Solicitor v. Law Soc. of Hong Kong (2003) 6 H.K.C.F.A.R. 570 (H.K.C.F.A.).

149 Koon Wing Yee v. Insider Dealing Tribunal (2008) 11 H.K.C.F.A.R. 170 (H.K.C.F.A.)..

150 HKSAR v. Hung Chan Wa (2006) 9 H.K.C.F.A.R. 614 (H.K.C.F.A.)..

151 Ran Hirschl, Towards Juristocracy: The Origins and Consequences of the New Constitutionalism 223 (2004).

"inactive,"[152] "timid,"[153] and "uncreative,"[154] if not actually suffering from "a problem of invisibility."[155] Notably, it is still controversial, more than a decade after the end of Portuguese rule, whether the Macau courts are at all entitled to rule on the constitutionality of legislation. Early on, the Tribunal forestalled the writ of *amparo* for protecting fundamental constitutional rights,[156] rejecting incompatibility of statutes with the Lei Básica as grounds per se for litigating in the courts;[157] ruled that the courts may not declare any legal norm unconstitutional with general and binding effect;[158] denied non-permanent residents a right to family reunion;[159] affirmed discretion in the Chief Executive to decree laws independently of the overriding or authorizing effect of primary legislation;[160] rejected the right of an official, convicted of corruption in a politically controversial case, to apply for a review of his sentence,[161] arguably in violation of the International Covenant on Civil and Political Rights, which was incorporated by reference in the Lei Básica;[162] and allowed the Legislative Assembly to legislate with "free discretion" unless it breaches labile thresholds such as "flagrant inequality"[163] and "total unreasonableness"[164] that are far less demanding than the CFA doctrine of structured proportionality. Judicial activism and its opposite, judicial restraint or deference, are loaded terms. But understood narrowly, judicial activism may refer to a court's successful track record of asserting its powers to invalidate statutes.[165] It is safe to conclude that, in comparison with each other, the

152 YUANYUAN ZHANG, ROLE ANALYSIS IN THE LEGALIZATION OF MACANESE GOVERNANCE 130 (One Country, Two Systems Research Centre of the Macao Polytechnic Institute 2009).

153 Jorge Godinho & Paulo Cardinal, *Macau's Court of Final Appeal*, *in* HONG KONG'S COURT OF FINAL APPEAL: THE DEVELOPMENT OF THE LAW IN CHINA'S HONG KONG 608, 618 (Simon N.M. Young & Yash Ghai eds., 2014).

154 CHAOYANG JIANG, A STUDY ON THE BASIC LAW OF MACAU AND THE RULE OF LAW OF THE MACAU SPECIAL ADMINISTRATIVE REGION 136 (2016).

155 Paulo Cardinal & Yihe Zhang, *Subnational Constitutionalism in the SARS of the People's Republic of China: An Exceptional Tailored Suit Model?*, 4(2) PERSP. ON FEDERALISM 101, 128–29 (2012).

156 Case 1/2000 (T.U.I.M.).

157 Case 8/2000 (T.U.I.M.); Case 4/2000 (T.U.I.M.); Case 9/2006 (T.U.I.M.).

158 Case 8/2007 (T.U.I.M.).

159 Case 21/2007 (T.U.I.M.).

160 Case 28/2006 (T.U.I.M.).

161 Case 60/2015 (T.U.I.M.).

162 Cardinal & Zhang, *supra* note 155, at 129.

163 Case 5/2010 (T.U.I.M.).

164 Case 69/2016 (T.U.I.M.).

165 *See* Nuno Garoupa, *Comparing Judicial Activism – Can We Say that the US Supreme Court Is More Activist Than the German Constitutional Court?*, 72(4) REVISTA PORTUGUESA DE FILOSOFIA 1089 (2016); Cora Chan; A *Preliminary Framework for Measuring Deference in Rights Reasoning*, 14(4) INT'L J. CONST. L. 851 (2016).

CFA is activist and the TUI deferential – or, to put it more neutrally, the CFA is politically consequential and the TUI is politically inconsequential.

How can such a radical variance in the dependent variable be explained? The two Chinese SARs share so much of constitutional law, history, ethnicity, culture, and demographics; how could such a difference in apex court activism have arisen between them? The CFA–TUI divergence contradicts received wisdom, that like constitutional designs bring like incentives to bear on policy-making – itself a rule-dependent activity – and yield like levels of political dynamics.[166] It is all the more paradoxical from the standpoint of comparative constitutional law, given that the provisions on judicial power in the Basic Law and the Lei Básica are near identical and have remained constant since 1997 and 1999, respectively, suggesting that something other than constitutional provisions is spelling the difference.[167] It should be clarified, at the outset, that the CFA's and the TUI's trajectories in constitutional review are not polarized merely because of differences between English common law and Portuguese civil law. Macau's former *suzerain* saw decades of rights-based judicial review in the Constitutional Court of Portugal; British Hong Kong, by contrast, never had a tradition of constitutional review of primary legislation, due to lack of an entrenched bill of rights and a powerful doctrine of parliamentary sovereignty in the United Kingdom.

The Chinese SARs furnish a natural experiment, after the "most similar cases" logic, upon the dynamics of constitutional review under hybrid regimes in very similar political contexts. A careful small-*n* analysis of "most similar cases" may therefore give rise to causal inferences applicable beyond these cases.[168] In a seminal study, Tom Ginsburg investigated the political conditions conducive to the empowerment of constitutional courts, using Taiwan, South Korea and Mongolia – three nascent Asian democracies – as case studies[169] grounded in "most similar

166 James M. Buchanan, *Same Players, Different Game: How Better Rules Make Better Politics*, 19 CONST. POL. ECON. 171, 172 (2008); JASON BROWNLEE, AUTHORITARIANISM IN AN AGE OF DEMOCRATIZATION 207 (2007). *See* Tom Ginsburg, *Public Choice and Constitutional Design*, *in* RESEARCH HANDBOOK ON PUBLIC CHOICE AND PUBLIC LAW 261 (Daniel A. Farber & Anne Joseph O'Connell eds., 2010); Roger D. Congleton & Birgitta Swedenborg, *Introduction: Rational Choice Politics and Institutions*, *in* DEMOCRATIC CONSTITUTIONAL DESIGN AND PUBLIC POLICY: ANALYSIS AND EVIDENCE 1 (Roger D. Congleton & Birgitta Swedenborg eds., 2006); Torsten Persson & Guido Tabellini, *Constitutions and Economic Policy*, 18(1) JOURNAL OF ECONOMIC PERSPECTIVES 75 (2004).

167 RÍOS-FIGUEROA, *supra* note 8, at 37.

168 RAN HIRSCHL, COMPARATIVE MATTERS: THE RENAISSANCE OF COMPARATIVE CONSTITUTIONAL LAW 193, 244 (2014).

169 *See* TOM GINSBURG, JUDICIAL REVIEW IN NEW DEMOCRACIES: CONSTITUTIONAL COURTS IN ASIAN CASES (2003).

cases" logic.[170] All three shared important similarities of geography, culture, and history, yet featured different trajectories of judicial review. What differed across the cases was the level of electoral uncertainty. Ginsburg inferred that the more uncertain electoral futures are, the more likely it is that the incumbent regime will opt for judicial empowerment as an insurance strategy against the succession of opponents; concluding that "neither culture nor history is as important as [political] structure in determining outcomes [in relation to judicial empowerment]."[171] The similarities between Hong Kong and Macau, neither of which is expecting wholesale democratization in the near future, are manifestly much closer than those between Taiwan, Korea, and Mongolia. In yielding so stark a variation on the dependent variable, the CFA-TUI divergence yet controls for many background variables, such as historical, cultural, and colonial legacies, and dispenses with the need to take account of divergent national contexts, as is typical of cross-country studies.[172] The contrast of the CFA with the TUI furnishes an invaluable opportunity to undertake a balanced and in-depth examination of the political conditions for the presence or absence of judicial activist behavior, the latter of which is neglected in the literature on judicial politics.[173]

ARGUMENT

This book argues that high transaction cost politics in Hong Kong and low transaction cost politics in Macau are keys to understanding the divergence or antithesis in the exercise of constitutional review by the CFA and the TUI. The strategic model of judicial decision-making is chosen as the vantage point for the theory offered by this book because of the peculiar features of the cases studied and the type of research question asked. Consider the applicability of the attitudinal model and the legal model, the two other dominant models of judicial behavior in the law and courts literature.[174] The attitudinal model assumes judges to be unconstrained, single-minded, policy-seeking actors who act on their own individual political preferences[175] As this model takes the partisan affiliation of judges as a reliable predictor of judicial attitudes,

[170] Hirschl, *supra* note 168, at 249.

[171] Ginsburg, *supra* note 169, at 261.

[172] *See* Markus Freitag & Adrian Vatter, *Patterns of Democracy: A Subnational Analysis of the German Lander*, 44(4) Acta Politica 410, 411 (2009).

[173] Trochev, *supra* note 69, at 22.

[174] David W. Neubauer & Stephen S. Meinhold, Judicial Process; Law, Courts, and Politics in the United States 494 (5th ed. 2010).

[175] Jeffrey A. Segal & Harold J. Spaeth, The Supreme Court and the Attitudinal Model Revisited 434 (2002).

ideology, and behavior,[176] its applicability outside the United States in general[177] and the Chinese SARs in particular is problematic given that no partisan realignment of executives or legislatures has ever taken place in Hong Kong or Macau since the resumption of Chinese sovereignty.[178] The judges of the CFA or the TUI never belonged to political parties, and they were nominated by independent judicial commissions and appointed by their Chief Executives as a matter of formal procedure.[179] And the divergence of constitutional review trajectories in the teeth of the convergence of the Basic Law and the Lei Básica offends the doctrinal thinking characteristic of the legal model, which assumes that legal rules and principles determine the policy choices of courts.[180] To put it another way, the similarities between the Basic Law and the Lei Básica are supposed to predict that the two courts' constitutional jurisprudence should overlap, if law is the primary factor shaping judicial behavior. As the approaches to constitutional review of the CFA and the TUI bore little resemblance to each other, it is likely that factors other than law underlie their disjunction.

The strategic model is premised on the twin assumptions that courts anticipate the reactions of other political actors when making policy choices to attain certain goals, and that these choices are structured by the institutional environment in which they are made.[181] The power of constitutional courts is robust only insofar as other actors take no steps to overturn its rulings.[182] They may "declare" legislative acts invalid, but the efficacy of such orders depends on political compliance, or at least acquiescence.[183] Judicial rulings must accommodate political reality if they are to stand the test of time,[184] as even apex courts have few resources to defend against those wielding the means of

176 C. L. Ostberg & Matthew E. Wetstein, Attitudinal Decision Making in the Supreme Court of Canada 46 (2007).

177 Laarni Escresa & Nuno Garoupa, *Testing the Logic of Strategic Defection: The Case of the Philippine Supreme Court – An Empirical Analysis (1986–2010)*, 21(2) Asian J. Pol. Sci. 189, 190 (2013).

178 *See* Sofia Amaral-Garcia et al., *Judicial Independence and Party Politics in the Kelsenian Constitutional Courts: The Case of Portugal*, 6(2) J. Empirical Legal Stud. 381 (2009).

179 Basic Law, art. 88; Lei Básica, art. 87.

180 *See* Richard L. Pacelle, Jr. et al., Decision Making by the Modern Supreme Court (2011).

181 *See* Tonja Jacobi, *The Impact of Positive Political Theory on Old Questions of Constitutional Law and the Separation of Powers*, 100 Nw. U. L. Rev. 259 (2006).

182 *See* Lee Epstein & Jack Knight, The Choices Justices Make (1998).

183 *See* Mary L. Volcansek, *Constitutional Courts as Veto Players: Divorce and Decrees in Italy*, 39 Eur. J. Pol. Research 347 (2001).

184 *See* John A. Ferejohn & Barry R. Weingast, *A Positive Theory of Statutory Interpretation*, 12 Int'l Rev. L. & Econ. 263 (1992).

coercion.[185] Courts must anticipate the reactions of others and not outrage their sentiments and preferences if they expect to be obeyed.[186]

In the literature on strategic judicial behavior, it is well established that systemic and consequential constitutional review can only exist under divided governments that are either reluctant or unable to restrain courts.[187] Scholars have theorized on the American context that a decentralized party system and frequently divided control of the Presidency and Congress contributed to enabling the Supreme Court to deliver activist rulings with impunity.[188] The implication is that partisan infighting between the executive and the legislature opens up political space for constitutional courts to claim more power. These perspectives are perhaps best summed up in the words of Matthew Stephenson: "independent judicial review serves as a valuable insurance function for competitors in a stable democracy."[189] If this is correct, then high-energy constitutional review[190] should be unable to arise or develop stably in polities lacking in whole or in part institutionalized electoral and inter-branch competition. Authoritarian or semi-authoritarian regimes consolidate executive and legislative powers in the same hands, by definition, and so exempt themselves from the pressures and constraints of precisely this

185 *See* Rebecca Bill Chavez et al., *A Theory of the Politically Independent Judiciary: A Comparative Study of the United States and Argentina*, *in* COURTS IN LATIN AMERICA 219 (Gretchen Helmke & Julio Ríos-Figueroa eds., 2011).

186 James L. Gibson, *Judicial Institutions*, *in* THE OXFORD HANDBOOK OF POLITICAL INSTITUTIONS 514, 522 (R.A.W. Rhodes et al. eds., 2006) (noting that strategic behavior is not necessarily normatively appropriate. Not a few people expect judges to act sincerely, and only act upon reasons firmly based on legality and justice).

187 *See* JODI FINKEL, JUDICIAL REFORM AS POLITICAL INSURANCE: ARGENTINA, PERU, AND MEXICO IN THE 1990S (2008); J. Mark Ramseyer & Eric B. Rasmusen, *Judicial Independence in a Civil Law Regime: The Evidence from Japan*. 13(2) J. L. ECON. & ORG. 259 (1997); J. Mark Ramseyer, *The Puzzling (In)Dependence of Courts: A Comparative Approach*, 23 J. LEGAL STUD. 721 (1994); William Landes & Richard Posner, *The Independent Judiciary in an Interest-Group Perspective*, 18 J. L. & ECON. 875 (1975).

188 *See* Mario Bergara et al., *Modeling Supreme Court Strategic Decision-making: the Congressional Constraint*, 28 LEGIS. STUD. Q. 247 (2003); John Ferejohn, *Independent Judges, Dependent Judiciary: Explaining Judicial Independence*, 72 S. CAL. L. REV. 353 (1999); William N. Eskridge, *Overriding Supreme Court Statutory Interpretation Decisions*, 101 YALE L. J. 331 (1991).

189 Matthew C. Stephenson, *When the Devil Turns . . . The Political Foundations of Independent Judicial Review*, 32 J. LEGAL STUD. 59, 85 (2003).

190 As noted above, "judicial activism" is a loaded term with muddled connotations. The term "high-energy constitutional review" will be used instead as shorthand for the ability of the court to issue constitutional judgments that result in politically significant consequences, such as the expansion of judicial power and/or compliance from the political regime. *See* GINSBURG, *supra* note 169, at 251; Kapiszeswiki et al., *supra* note 3, at 19. The opposite of "high-energy constitutional review" is, needless to say, "low-energy constitutional review."

competition.[191] On the other hand, as mentioned above, recent empirical studies have shown that autonomous judicial power does emerge from time to time in authoritarian regimes; that eventual purges of constitutional courts have frequently come at the end of long periods of judicial activism. These findings cast doubt on the assumption that democracy is prerequisite to judicial review,[192] corroborating Ran Hirschl's observation that "the reliance on courts and judicial means to address core political controversies that often define and divide whole polities – knows no democratic/authoritarian borders."[193] All too often, the strategic model assumes that undivided governments conserve sufficient power to rein in defiant courts, never facing insurmountable informational, bargaining, decision-making, agent-monitoring, or enforcement costs. This implicit presumption of zero political transaction costs disabled the conventional strategic model to predict the evolution of judicial politics in authoritarian countries.

The strategic model nonetheless could be corrected by explicitly incorporating positive transaction costs into the calculus of regime reaction to judicial activism as well as of courts' anticipation of that. Transaction cost analysis has been applied to the gamut of political situations;[194] nothing precludes its applicability to judicial behavior in general and constitutional review in particular. Political transaction costs can be broadly conceived as the cost of running a polity: making decisions; giving orders; and monitoring and enforcing compliance.[195] Our specific problem of transaction costs consists in that, like all human organizations, hybrid regimes cannot possibly collect information on everyone, and in the course of policy-making and enforcement must sometimes encounter not only external resistance, but also prohibitively costly ideological dissension or factional fragmentation, though the latter's intensity will seldom match that in liberal democracies.

Consider the relevance of political transaction costs to judiciary–regime relations.[196] The potential incongruity between the regime's preferences and

191 *See* Steven Levitsky & Lucan A. Way, *The Rise of Competitive Authoritarianism*, 13 J. DEMOCRACY 51 (2002).

192 *See* Gretchen Helmke & Frances Rosenbluth, *Regimes and the Rule of Law: Judicial Independence in Comparative Perspective*,12 ANNU. REV. LAW POL. SCI. 345 (2009).

193 RAN HIRSCHL, CONSTITUTIONAL THEOCRACY 248 (2010).

194 DAVID EPSTEIN & SHARYN O'HALLORAN, DELEGATING POWERS: A TRANSACTION COST POLITICS APPROACH TO POLICY MAKING UNDER SEPARATE POWERS 43 (1999). *See* Douglass C. North, *A Transaction Cost Theory of Politics*, 2 J. THEORETICAL POL. 355 (1990).

195 EIRIK G. FURUBOTN & RUDOLF RICHTER, INSTITUTIONS AND ECONOMIC THEORY: THE CONTRIBUTION OF THE NEW INSTITUTIONAL ECONOMICS 43–47 (2000).

196 RÍOS-FIGUEROA, *supra* note 8, at 160.

the jurisprudence of courts will sooner or later induce the former to rein in the latter. The regime may deploy, in addition to formal constitutional amendments, dynamic means such as impeachment, curtailment of jurisdiction, a supermajority threshold to find unconstitutional, budget slashing, court packing, and so on.[197] However, a regime must be capable of agreeing and implementing a response to judicial overreach in the first place. A regime burdened by political fragmentation incurs high transaction costs and so is prone to indecision as to whether and how to react to controversial rulings. The higher the transaction costs, the likelier apex courts will exercise high-energy constitutional review, devising aggressive doctrines of judicial review, and vice versa.

The implications of these insights on the CFA–TUI divergence are now obvious. Beneath the appearance of unified government in both SARs lie real differences in the size of political transaction costs stemming from regime fragmentation. Although it is something of an oversimplification, the effectiveness of the Macau SAR Government is certainly greater than that of its Hong Kong counterpart.[198] The picture will be more complete if we take the degree of discord within the ruling Establishment Coalition as a proxy of political transaction costs.[199] Between 1997 and 2013, the overall success rate of successive Hong Kong SAR Governments in passing legislative proposals in the Legislative Council, in spite of an Establishment majority, stood at a low 56.29 percent for any authoritarian regime.[200] By contrast, subject to extremely rare instances of Government withdrawal, no bill proposed by a Macau Chief Executive has ever been defeated in the Legislative Assembly since 1999.[201] In Hong Kong, high transaction costs also spring from the roughly 60 percent electoral support consistently garnered by Pan-Democratic Opposition candidates, who hold more than one-third of Legislative Council seats whence they can veto any proposal to amend the Basic Law. The Pro-Democracy Opposition in Macau has never attained more than 15 percent of Legislative Assembly seats, nor won more than 40 percent of the popular vote, as with their

197 *See* Todd Schneider, *David v Goliath? The Hong Kong Courts and China's National People's Congress Standing Committee*, 20 Berkeley J. Int'l L. 575, 597 (2002).

198 Ming K. Chan & Shiu-Hing Lo, Hong Kong SAR and the Macao SAR x (2006).

199 Ira Katznelson, *Historical Approaches to the Study of Congress: Toward a Congressional Vantage on American Political Development*, *in* The Oxford Handbook of The American Congress 115, 119 (Eric Schickler & Frances E. Lee eds., 2011).

200 Brian C.H. Fong, *Executive-Legislative Disconnection in the HKSAR: Uneasy Partnership between Chief Executives and Pro-Government Parties, 1997–2016*, *in* Hong Kong 20 Years after the Handover: Emerging Social and Institutional Fractures after 1997 45, 54–55 (Brian C.H. Fong & Tai-lok Lui eds., 2018).

201 Kwong, *supra* note 123, at 131.

Hong Kong counterparts. Clearly, fluctuations in political transaction costs translate into fluctuations in the energy of constitutional review: Hong Kong's high transaction cost politics has disabled the regime from credibly threatening the CFA, while reinforcing demands for constitutional review of unpopular statutes, whereas Macau's low transaction cost politics, as witnessed by the decisiveness and relative popularity of the Government, explain its ability and will to forestall any move of the TUI toward self-aggrandizement.

OTHER CONTRIBUTIONS

Besides adding to our knowledge of judicial politics and the politics of hybrid regimes, this book also contributes to the literature of two other important areas of research: comparative constitutional law and Asian law. Comparing constitutional review arrangements in both SARs enhances our understanding of constitutional law in general and subnational constitutional law in particular. Comparative constitutional law, one of the oldest fields in the social sciences, originating in Aristotle's POLITICS,[202] has re-emerged as a "new frontier of legal scholarship,"[203] and a "newly energized field" in the twenty-first century.[204] Contemporary comparative constitutional scholarship, nonetheless, has remained uneven in its development, for a select few jurisdictions, such as Australia, Canada, France, Germany, Israel, South Africa, the United Kingdom, and the United States, feature prominently in most studies, whereas other nations, if not whole regions, are ignored, severely compromising the comparativeness of the field.[205] The "national fixation"[206] of comparative constitutional law needs to be superseded in view of the scholarly realization that the distribution of rights across regions, provinces, states, and municipalities is often very uneven even in the same country.[207] Comparative constitutional law scholars would benefit immensely from subnational analysis, a powerful tool already deployed by political scientists who study Latin America and other regions, including the United States, to yield "rich new laboratories for theory

202 Fernando Mendez & Jonathan Wheatley, *Introduction*, *in* PATTERNS OF CONSTITUTIONAL DESIGN: THE ROLE OF CITIZENS AND ELITES IN CONSTITUTION-MAKING 1, 1 (Jonathan Wheatley & Fernando Mendez eds., 2007).

203 HIRSCHL, *supra* note 168, at 278

204 Rosalind Dixon & Tom Ginsburg, *Introduction*, *in* COMPARATIVE CONSTITUTIONAL LAW IN ASIA 1, 1 (Rosalind Dixon & Tom Ginsburg eds., 2014).

205 Tushnet & Khosla, *supra* note 4, at 3.

206 *See* Edward L. Gibson, BOUNDARY CONTROL: SUBNATIONAL AUTHORITARIANISM IN FEDERAL DEMOCRACIES 11 (2012).

207 Gervasoni, *supra* note 21, at 120.

building."[208] This book may be regarded as a departure from conventional comparative constitutional law studies that concentrate on national judicial institutions exclusively.[209] Subnational constitutional dynamics are especially susceptible to comparative analysis,[210] because the same application and interpretation issues are likely to arise in any substate within the same sovereign state, and so can be evaluated at a more general level.[211] The finding of heterogeneous judicial behavior in constitutionally homogeneous polities like the SARs stands in sharp contrast to the experiences of commensurable jurisdictions. The Supreme Courts of the several British Overseas Territories,[212] State Supreme Courts in the United States,[213] Supreme Courts of the States of Australia,[214] Constitutional Courts of the member Republics of the Russian Federation,[215] or Constitutional Courts of the Länder of the Federal Republic of Germany[216] may differ sharply on specific issues, but the trajectories of their own judicial review jurisprudence are not nearly as irreconcilable as that of the CFA is with that of the TUI. For example, none of the constitutional courts of the various German Länder could be classified as "weak."[217]

Secondly, this book expands our comparative knowledge of law in Asia in general and China in particular. Asia is interesting to social scientists not least because of its rapid economic development since the Second World War: first the rebuilding of Japan in the 1960s; then the miraculous growth of the Four Asian Tigers – Hong Kong, Singapore, South Korea, and Taiwan – in the 1980s; and, more recently, the rise to prominence of China and India.[218] Many Asian countries have brought forth vibrant

208 Rebecca Bill Chavez, The Rule of Law in Nascent Democracies: Judicial Politics in Argentina 164–65 (2004).

209 Matthew C. Ingram, Crafting Courts in New Democracies: The Politics of Subnational Judicial Reform in Brazil and Mexico xvii (2016).

210 *See* Tom Ginsburg & Eric Posner, *Subconstitutionalism*, 62 Stan. L. Rev. 1583 (2010).

211 Robert F. Williams, The Law of American State Constitutions 11 (2009).

212 *See* Ian Hendry and Susan Dickson, British Overseas Territory Law (2011)

213 *See* Laura Langer, Judicial Review in State Supreme Courts: A Comparative Study (2002).

214 *See* Russell Smyth & Vinod Mishra, *The Transmission of Legal Precedent across the Australian State Supreme Courts*, 45(1) L. & Soc'y Rev. 139 (2011).

215 See Alexei Trochev, *Less Democracy, More Courts: A Puzzle of Judicial Review in Russia*, 38 L. & Soc'y Rev. 513 (2004).

216 *See* Giacomo Delledonne, *Subnational Constitutionalism: A Matter of Review*, 4(2) Persp. on Federalism 294 (2012).

217 Freitag & Vatter, *supra* note 172, at 417.

218 Jiunn-Rong Yeh & Wen-Chen Chang, *Introduction: Asian Courts in Context: Tradition, Transition and Globalization*, *in* Asian Courts in Context 1, 1 (Jiunn-Rong Yeh & Wen-Chen Chang eds., 2015).

constitutional review practices[219] and highly visible courts. Courts in India, Indonesia, Malaysia, Pakistan, the Philippines, South Korea, Taiwan, and Thailand are regularly involved in politically charged cases.[220] The comparative study of Asian law is worthwhile in its own right, but also more generally, because it can add new material to comparative law and provide guidance for the solution of current and future legal problems.[221] The Hong Kong case is idiosyncratic, in light of the fact that while high energy constitutional review is the norm in Western Europe, North America and Australia but "a rarity" outside these regions.[222] This book is the first English-language publication to compare the constitutional jurisprudence of the Chinese SARs only, both doctrinally and interdisciplinarily. The TUI in particular has received far less attention from Anglophone scholarship than apex courts in Hong Kong, or in mainland China, or in Taiwan, despite Macau being the only East Asian jurisdiction that was ever colonized by a continental imperial power in living memory.

Thirdly, the politics of constitutional review in the two SARs will be of interest, moreover, to those studying Chinese law, in view of the fact that Hong Kong and Macau have long been used by Beijing as laboratories to test novel ideas and policies before applying them to mainland China, especially the five Special Economic Zones of Shenzhen, Haining, Zhuhai, Shantou, and Xiamen.[223] In the past two decades China has made important investments in the institutional performance and quality of its courts.[224] Since the 1980s, China has growingly turned to common law jurisdictions, including Hong Kong, for models of legal reform.[225] The conservation of Hong Kong and

219 Dixon & Ginsburg, *supra* note 204, at 1.

220 Björn Dressel, *The Judicialization of Politics in Asia: Towards a Framework of Analysis, in* The Judicialization of Politics in Asia 1, 1 (Björn Dressel ed., 2012).

221 Zentaro Kitagawa, *Development of Comparative Law in East Asia, in* The Oxford Handbook of Comparative Law 237, 259 (Mathias Reiman & Reinhard Zimmermann eds., 2006).

222 Maria Popova, Politicized Justice in Emerging Democracies: A Study of Courts in Russia and Ukraine 35 (2012).

223 Ignazio Castelucci, *Rule of Law with Chinese Characteristics*, 13 Ann. Surv. Int'l & Comp. L. 35, 80–82 (2007).

224 *See* Eric C. Ip & Kelvin H. F. Kwok, *Judicial Control of Local Protectionism in China: Antitrust Enforcement against Administrative Monopoly on the Supreme People's Court*, 13 (3) J. Competition L. & Econ. 549 (2017); Eric C. Ip, *Judicial Review in China: A Positive Political Economy Analysis*, 8(2) Rev. L. & Econ. 331 (2012); Eric C. Ip, *The Supreme People's Court and the Political Economy of Judicial Empowerment in Contemporary China*, 24(2)Colum. J. Asian L. 367 (2011); Eric C. Ip, *The Supreme Court and the Making of Public Policy in Contemporary China*, 7 Mich. J. Pub. Aff. 1 (2010).

225 Kwai Hang Ng, The Common Law in Two Voices: Language, Law, and the Postcolonial Predicament in Hong Kong 231 (2009).

Macau as largely cosmopolitan and open self-administered jurisdictions reflects the People's Republic's ability to address the opportunities and challenges emerging from globalization and marketization.[226] Nowadays, Hong Kong and mainland China as a whole are each other's largest source of foreign direct investment. In 2013 alone, foreign direct investment from Hong Kong into the mainland amounted to US$78.302 billion, accounting for 67 percent of the latter's national total.[227] In November 2014, and in December 2016, the Shanghai–Hong Kong Stock Connect, and the Shenzhen–Hong Kong Stock Connect, respectively, were set up.[228] As of February 2018, Hong Kong was China's largest source of overseas direct investment.[229] Macau currently monopolizes lawful casino gaming in all of China; the SAR's gross gaming revenue had amounted to about seven times more than that of Las Vegas.[230] In 2015, Macau's gaming revenue (US$62 billion) accounted for nearly 80 percent of casino revenue in all of Asia-Pacific (US$79 billion).[231] The SARs thus deserve closer monitoring not only by legal scholars and political scientists, but also Sinologists, as their political experiences are "key chapters in the Chinese quest for national unification and modernization";[232] by international relations scholars, as their economic growth implicates Beijing's relations with the World Trade Organization and Western industrial democracies;[233] and lastly by economists as, with so few natural resources, Hong Kong and Macau have amassed so much wealth, transforming themselves into model market economies in a very short time.[234] And yet, the current literature has rarely compared politics in the

226 CHAN & LO, *supra* note 198, at xiii.

227 Ministry of Commerce of the People's Republic of China, *Statistics of FDI in China in January-December 2013*, http://english.mofcom.gov.cn/article/statistic/foreigninvestment/201402/20140200498911.shtml

228 Peter T.Y. Cheung, *In Beijing's Tightening Grip*, *in* HONG KONG 20 YEARS AFTER THE HANDOVER: EMERGING SOCIAL AND INSTITUTIONAL FRACTURES AFTER 1997 225, 258 (Brian C.H. Fong & Tai-lok Lui eds., 2018).

229 Hong Kong Trade and Development Council Research, *Economic and Trade Information on Hong Kong*, http://hong-kong-economy-research.hktdc.com/business-news/article/Market-Environment/Economic-and-Trade-Information-on-Hong-Kong/etihk/en/1/1X000000/1X09OVUL.htm

230 Mingjie Shenga & Chaolin Gub, *Economic Growth and Development in Macau (1999–2016): The Role of the Booming Gaming Industry*, 75 CITIES 72, 72 (2018).

231 Linda Hancock & Zhidong Hao, *Gambling Regulatory Regimes and the Framing of "Responsible Gambling" by Transnational Casino Corporations: Asia-Pacific Regimes in Comparative Perspective*, 38(3) ASIA PAC. J. PUB. ADMIN. 139, 144 (2016).

232 CHAN & LO, *supra* note 198, at xiii.

233 *Id.*

234 *Id.* at v.

Hong Kong and Macau SARs, within their contexts as subnational hybrid regimes, all of which awaits further and deeper exploration.[235]

ORGANIZATION OF CHAPTERS

This book is organized as follows. Chapter 2 constructs a transaction cost theory of hybrid constitutionalism,[236] the theoretical explanation of the entire book, out of the distinct literatures on strategic judicial behavior and on the role of transaction costs in politics. A constitutional court reviewing the policy choices of the regime must anticipate the latter's response so as to gauge the enforceability of its rulings and/or avoid retaliation. The regime's responses, in turn, depend heavily on their political transaction costs. Genuine separation of powers seldom thrives in authoritarian regimes, but ruling elites are hardly adamantine monoliths either. Contradictory policy agendas and political visions vie among them,[237] as also contradictory evaluations of the utility of judicial power.[238] A regime incurring high transaction costs is plagued by "legislative inertia"[239] as to whether and how to react to controversial judicial decisions. Chronic internal incohesion, combined with potent resistance by media, civil society organizations, and mass movements, can handicap even an authoritarian government that might otherwise punish assertive judicial claims.[240] Examples drawn from hybrid regimes worldwide are used to substantiate the arguments of this theoretical framework.

Chapter 3 outlines the oft-overlooked authoritarian character of the Hong Kong Basic Law and of the Lei Básica de Macau, both of which deliberately establish in their respective regimes Chief Executives selected by corporatist electoral colleges, assisted by appointed Executive Councils, whose advice they may ignore; and weak, only partly elected, Legislative Councils whose bills they may refuse to sign.[241] The constitutional documents

235 Kwong, *supra* note 123, at 133.

236 Constitutionalism is mostly understood to be a normative concept by philosophers. This book approaches it as a descriptive shorthand, one that denotes the emergence and endurance of judicially imposed constitutional constraints on political power in hybrid regimes. *See* Mark V. Tushnet, *Authoritarian Constitutionalism*, 100 CORNELL L. REV. 391, 394 (2015).

237 Mark A. Graber, *Constitutional Politics in the Active Voice*, *in* CONSEQUENTIAL COURTS: JUDICIAL ROLES IN GLOBAL PERSPECTIVE 363, 369 (Diana Kapiszewski et al. eds., 2013).

238 John A. Ferejohn, *Judicial Power: Getting It and Keeping It*, *in* CONSEQUENTIAL COURTS: JUDICIAL ROLES IN GLOBAL PERSPECTIVE 349, 353 (Diana Kapiszewski et al. eds., 2013).

239 PO JEN YAP, CONSTITUTIONAL DIALOGUE IN COMMON LAW ASIA 85 (2015).

240 Alexei Trochev, *Fragmentation? Defection? Legitimacy? Explaining Judicial Roles in Post-Communist "Colored Revolutions,"* *in* CONSEQUENTIAL COURTS: JUDICIAL ROLES IN GLOBAL PERSPECTIVE 367, 369 (Diana Kapiszewski et al. eds., 2013).

241 STEVE TSANG, A MODERN HISTORY OF HONG KONG 18 (2007).

of the Chinese SARs thus guarantee "unified government" – the control of the executive and legislative branches by the same political group within a broadly hybrid framework. This chapter also analyses the web of constraints that the Basic Law and the Lei Básica use to entangle the constitutional authority of the CFA and the TUI. It demonstrates that nothing in the two instruments prevents them from descending into "nominal" instruments that function "partly as propaganda and partly as camouflage," much like the Chinese Constitution itself.[242] The interdisciplinary approach of this book does not preclude legal scholars concerned with doctrine from finding much of use and interest in Chapter 4. This chapter systematically and comprehensively contrasts the antithetical judicial doctrines of the CFA's high-energy constitutional review and the TUI's low-energy constitutional review in these five dimensions: constitutional review jurisdiction, interpretive methodology, abstract review, standards of review, and judicial petition.

Chapter 5 will apply the transaction cost theory of hybrid constitutionalism to correlate long-term political fluctuations with the two courts' antithetical approaches to constitutional review. It reveals that, despite the persistent denial of democratic self-rule, factional infighting amid Hong Kong's Establishment Coalition and formidable popular resistance to government initiatives have disabled the regime from credibly threatening the Court, while creating demand for constitutional challenges.[243] By contrast, the Macau Establishment Coalition enjoys high levels of harmony, minimal popular unrest, and very weak pressure to democratize. Macau's SAR regime, able to govern by decree, might credibly preempt, and thus has succeeded for all practical purposes in discouraging the Tribunal from engaging in unwanted aggression. This chapter demonstrates that the disparate levels of political transaction costs really appeared only after China's resumption of sovereignty over these Regions. It then evaluates the strongest explanatory alternative, the "legal origins hypothesis,"[244] which in the present context is grounded in the belief that differences between the common law and civil law traditions are significant enough to yield vastly different judicial outcomes in constitutional review.[245] It should surprise no one that the CFA's constitutional review yields more political energy than that of the TUI. This chapter

242 Peter Wesley-Smith, Constitutional and Administrative Law in Hong Kong 71 (2d ed. 1994).

243 *See* Eric C. Ip, *The Evolution of Constitutional Adjudication in the Chinese Special Administrative Regions: Theory and Evidence*, 61(4) Am. J. Comp. L. 799 (2013).

244 *See* Nuno Garoupa et al., Legal Origins and the Efficiency Dilemma (2016).

245 *See* Kwai Hang Ng and Xin He, Embedded Courts: Judicial Decision-Making in China 84–85 (2017).

then rejects the legal origins hypothesis in favor of the transaction cost theory of hybrid constitutionalism, which better explains the difference between the high-energy constitutional review of the CFA and low-energy constitutional review of the TUI, regardless of the resemblance of their jurisdictions and constitutions, and the persistent authoritarianism of the SARs. Chapter 6 summarizes the book's main findings and conclusions. It reviews the question of why the apex courts of Hong Kong and Macau have chosen such divergent approaches to constitutional review despite comparable constitutional outfits and political structures that have remained largely constant. It recounts how the polarization of Hong Kong and Macau along the spectrum of transaction costs is key to explaining why an antithesis emerged from the constitutional jurisprudence of the two jurisdictions, their institutional similarities notwithstanding.

2

A Transaction Cost Theory of Hybrid Constitutionalism

INTRODUCTION

Courts are by nature weak institutions, even in liberal democracies.[1] The emergence of constitutional review of any political consequence under hybrid regimes,[2] but particularly when it is global in scale, is puzzling and warrants closer attention by the academy. Second-guessing the constitutionality of legislation and administrative acts by judges with relative independence seems incompatible with the very nature of authoritarianism, which denotes the concentration of power in a dictator or elite circle.[3] The reality is that no regime whose liberal democratic constitutional text is to be implemented in meaningful ways that confer the legitimacy of the hybrid on itself can withhold *all* discretion from its constitutional court.[4] This entails the possibility of constitutional judgments straying from regime preferences. Even so, regimes have at their disposal a variety of steps to curb unwanted judicial aggression, such as constitutional amendments and the impeachment of defiant judges.[5] The question that concerns us in this chapter is this: Under what conditions would self-interested hybrid regimes whose dominant political coalition will, barring unforeseen developments, be in control of both the

[1] Georg Vanberg, *Constitutional Courts in Comparative Perspective: A Theoretical Assessment*, 18 ANNU. REV. POLIT. SCI. 167, 168 (2015).

[2] John Ferejohn et al., *Comparative Judicial Politics*, *in* THE OXFORD HANDBOOK OF COMPARATIVE POLITICS 727, 729 (Carles Boix & Susan C. Stokes eds., 2007) (judicial independence can be taken to mean a court's decisional autonomy from other political actors).

[3] Peter H. Solomon, Jr., *Courts and Judges in Authoritarian Regimes*, 60 WORLD POL. 122, 123 (2007).

[4] Martin Shapiro, *The Mighty Problem Continues*, *in* CONSEQUENTIAL COURTS: JUDICIAL ROLES IN GLOBAL PERSPECTIVE 380, 383–86 (Diana Kapiszewski et al. eds., 2013). This chapter uses the term "constitutional court" broadly, to encompass both specialized constitutional courts and apex courts in a decentralized review system.

[5] MARIA POPOVA, POLITICIZED JUSTICE IN EMERGING DEMOCRACIES: A STUDY OF COURTS IN RUSSIA AND UKRAINE 39 (2012).

political executive and the legislature well into the distant future, voluntarily permit constitutional courts to impose constraints on them?[6] To state this question more bluntly, "Why would people with money and guns ever submit to people armed only with gavels?"[7]

To answer this question, this chapter constructs a theoretical explanation out of the distinct literatures on strategic judicial behavior and transaction cost politics. It is organized as follows. The second section outlines the standard strategic model of judicial review, which holds that a final court reviewing the policy choices of the regime must anticipate the latter's response so as to gauge the enforceability of its rulings and avoid retaliation, and that the regime's ability to respond negatively to judicial invalidations depends on the existence of interparty and/or interbranch competition in the polity, both of which tend to be very weak or absent in hybrid regimes. This means that the emergence of consequential or "high-energy" constitutional review in hybrid regimes as a matter of fact implies a refinement of the theoretical model. The third section proposes, under the rubric of "Transaction Cost Theory of Hybrid Constitutionalism," that such refinement consists of properly recognizing the important role of political transaction costs of credibly threatening a negative response to unwanted judicial rulings. The fourth section, utilizing the "most different" logic in case selection,[8] examines the consistency between the theory and the actual trajectories of constitutional review in Singapore and Turkey, both of which, in spite of their differences in history, geography, and culture, are widely recognized as hybrid regimes.[9] The fifth section sums up and draws the main conclusions.

STRATEGIC CONSTITUTIONAL REVIEW

Classical legal scholarship holds apex constitutional courts to have the last word in the constitutional interpretive process, absent broader political

[6] Ferejohn et al., *supra* note 2, at 747.

[7] Matthew C. Stephenson, "*When the Devil Turns ...* ": *The Political Foundations of Independent Judicial Review*, 32 J. LEGAL STUD. 59, 60 (2003).

[8] RAN HIRSCHL, COMPARATIVE MATTERS: THE RENAISSANCE OF COMPARATIVE CONSTITUTIONAL LAW 193, 253 (2014) ("[u]nder the 'most different cases' approach to selecting comparable cases, researchers choose cases that are different for all variables that are not central to the study but similar for those that are. Doing so emphasizes the significance of the independent variables that are similar in both cases to the similar readings on the dependent variable.")

[9] ROD HAGUE ET AL., COMPARATIVE GOVERNMENT AND POLITICS: AN INTRODUCTION 60 (10th ed. 2016).

dynamics.[10] Constitutional law is assumed to be the ultimate legal constraint on political decision-making, and the only determinant of judicial behavior.[11] These assumptions can be self-defeating. If the law and the facts are supposed to yield only one legal outcome, but two observers or more disagree over whether a judgment has correctly applied the law, this involves the court rendering judgment in a political dispute over essentially contestable meanings.[12] Any judgment may be – and has been – either justified or attacked using preexisting legal norms.[13] It is an unfalsifiable proposition that aggressive assertions of judicial primacy over constitutional interpretation are nothing more than legal doctrine,[14] which contributes little to our understanding of constitutional review in actual practice.[15] In contrast, the strategic model explicitly recognizes that constitutional review is essentially political,[16] and that any constitutional court functions in an environment that is shaped by a plethora of constraints, both legal and extralegal.[17] The mere fact that the constitution formally enables judicial review does not guarantee that it will be exercised effectually,[18] exempt from extrinsic political pressures.[19] The "strategic" idea implies "interdependence";[20] meaning that a constitutional court's power is robust only insofar as other actors take no steps to overturn its rulings.[21] A court may "nullify" a legislative act, but the effect of such an order depends on legislative compliance or at least acquiescence.[22] Constitutional judgments that continually impede the

10 Mathew D. McCubbins & Daniel B. Rodriguez, *The Judiciary and the Role of Law, in* THE OXFORD HANDBOOK OF POLITICAL ECONOMY 273, 273 (Barry R. Weingas & Donald A. Wittman eds., 2006).

11 *Id.*

12 ROBERT M. HOWARD & AMY STEIGERWALT, JUDGING LAW AND POLICY: COURTS AND POLICYMAKING IN THE AMERICAN POLITICAL SYSTEM 175 (2012).

13 JEFFREY A. SEGAL & HAROLD J. SPAETH, THE SUPREME COURT AND THE ATTITUDINAL MODEL REVISITED 432 (2002).

14 *Id.* at 433.

15 KEITH E. WHITTINGON, POLITICAL FOUNDATIONS OF JUDICIAL SUPREMACY: THE PRESIDENCY, THE SUPREME COURT, AND CONSTITUTIONAL LEADERSHIP IN U.S. HISTORY 10 (2007).

16 Ran Hirschl, *The Strategic Foundations of Constitutions, in* SOCIAL AND POLITICAL FOUNDATIONS OF CONSTITUTIONS 157, 165 (Denis J. Galligan and Mila Versteeg eds., 2013).

17 MICHAEL A. BAILEY & FORREST MALTZMAN, THE CONSTRAINED COURT: LAW, POLITICS, AND THE DECISIONS JUSTICES MAKE 155 (2011).

18 MARK TUSHNET, ADVANCED INTRODUCTION TO COMPARATIVE CONSTITUTIONAL LAW 41 (2014).

19 TOM S. CLARK, THE LIMITS OF JUDICIAL INDEPENDENCE 5 (2011).

20 LEE EPSTEIN & JACK KNIGHT, THE CHOICES JUSTICES MAKE 12 (1998).

21 McCubbins & Rodriguez, *supra* note 10, at 273.

22 *See* Mary L. Volcansek, *Constitutional Courts as Veto Players: Divorce and Decrees in Italy*, 39 EUR. J. POL. RESEARCH 347 (2001).

interests of political officials in the executive and legislative branches pose a threat to sustainable judicial independence,[23] for they may trigger a political backlash that could subvert the independence and legitimacy of the court.[24] In brief, constitutional judgments cannot be understood as mechanical applications of preexisting principles to sets of facts; rather, they are products of political choices by both judicial and nonjudicial actors seeking to maximize utilities, both legal and extralegal, in interdependent interactions.[25]

Constitutional judgments must accommodate political reality if they are to stand the test of time,[26] as courts have few resources to defend against coercion and those who publicly wield it.[27] The strategic model assumes that constitutional court judges have policy preferences, and comprehend that their opportunities to achieve them depend on the preferences of other political actors as well as their common institutional environment;[28] and especially that they are aware of their weakness vis-à-vis political officialdom when the controversies before them affect core elite interests.[29] Constitutional judges cannot ignore the repercussions, beyond the case at bar, of a judgment that develops and revises the fundamental norms by which public – and even private – life is ordered.[30] The ease of reversing politically inconvenient constitutional judgments varies from polity to polity.[31] The strategic model holds that politically motivated threats against the constitutional court are much more difficult to mobilize, let alone sustain, in competitive polities than

23 Vanberg, *supra* note 1, at 179.

24 Juan Carlos Rodriguez-Raga, *Strategic Deference in the Colombian Constitutional Court 1992–2006*, *in* COURTS IN LATIN AMERICA 81, 84 (Gretchen Helmke & Julio Ríos-Figueroa eds., 2011).

25 GEORG VANBERG, THE POLITICS OF CONSTITUTIONAL REVIEW IN GERMANY 12 (2005) ("it is plausible that just as legislators may anticipate constitutional review, judges are likely to be aware of the fact that implementation requires cooperation by other institutions. Anticipations of reactions to their decisions may therefore shape their jurisprudence."); EPSTEIN & KNIGHT, *supra* note 20, at 11 (it is for the researcher to specify the content of justices' goals, the major of which is usually to have the law reflect their preferred policy outcomes).

26 *See* John A. Ferejohn & Barry R. Weingast, *A Positive Theory of Statutory Interpretation*, 12 INT'L REV. L. & ECON. 263 (1992).

27 *See* Rebecca Bill Chavez et al., *A Theory of the Politically Independent Judiciary: A Comparative Study of the United States and Argentina*, *in* COURTS IN LATIN AMERICA 219 (Gretchen Helmke & Julio Ríos-Figueroa eds., 2011).

28 JULIO RÍOS-FIGUEROA, CONSTITUTIONAL COURTS AS MEDIATORS: ARMED CONFLICT, CIVIL-MILITARY RELATIONS, AND THE RULE OF LAW IN LATIN AMERICA 10 (2016).

29 Tamir Moustafa, *Law and Courts in Authoritarian Regimes*, 10 ANNU. REV. LAW SOC. SCI. 281, 289 (2014).

30 KENNETH A. SHEPSLE, ANALYZING POLITICS: RATIONALITY, BEHAVIOR, AND INSTITUTIONS 479 (2d ed. 2010).

31 Ferejohn et al., *supra* note 2, at 744.

in noncompetitive ones.[32] A court in a competitive polity can easily become the arbiter between competitors rather than the pawn of monopolistic elites that it would be in a noncompetitive one.[33]

To explain the political foundations of consequential constitutional review, strategic theorists have developed two accounts that are not necessarily mutually exclusive. The first emphasizes the importance of electoral competition as an enabling condition for constitutionalism and judicial independence.[34] This strand of explanation implies that electoral uncertainty is what causes the empowerment of constitutional courts, as a form of political insurance prospectively protecting incumbent parties from the consequences of electoral losses.[35] Defeated partisans will be reluctant to vacate insofar as they face high expected costs, such as politicized justice or scorched-earth repeal of policies with nonnegligible popular backing.[36] A ruling party that foresees that it will lose power has a newfound incentive to elevate a potent constitutional court appointed with judges more sympathetic to its interests than the successor regime will be.[37] Such a court can shield the outgoing regime from persecution,[38] and impede moves by successors to raze every one of its policies, promoting both justice and continuity.[39] In the long run, independent judges facilitate tacit bargains between political competitors to mutualize moderation.[40] Intense electoral competition increases the number of political parties and decreases the likelihood of consensus,[41] making it hard for elite interests to conspire to overthrow a constitutional court.[42] So long as elections continue to be competitive, all political parties can expect to benefit in the long run from their constitutional court, which incentivizes them to refrain from

32 Keith E. Whittington, *Legislative Sanctions and the Strategic Environment of Judicial Review*, 1 (3) Int'l J. Const. L. 446, 474 (2003).

33 Rebecca Bill Chavez, The Rule of Law in Nascent Democracies: Judicial Politics in Argentina 15 (2004).

34 Stephenson, *supra* note 7, at 61.

35 Tom Ginsburg, Judicial Review in New Democracies: Constitutional Courts in Asian Cases 256 (2003).

36 Tom Ginsburg & Mila Versteeg, *Why Do Countries Adopt Constitutional Review?*, 30(3) J. Law. Econ. & Organ. 587, 588 (2014).

37 Hirschl, *supra* note 16, at 168.

38 Popova, *supra* note 5, at 29.

39 Ran Hirschl, Constitutional Theocracy 65 (2010).

40 Ginsburg, *supra* note 35, at 262.

41 Matthew C. Ingram, Crafting Courts in New Democracies: The Politics of Subnational Judicial Reform in Brazil and Mexico 79 (2016).

42 Terence C. Halliday, *Why the Legal Complex Is Integral to Theories of Consequential Courts*, *in* Consequential Courts: Judicial Roles in Global Governance 337, 353 (Diana Kapiszeswiki et al. eds., 2013).

ruining it for shortsighted gain.[43] It has recently been discovered, in a comparative Asian context, that, insofar as political power routinely rotates between competing parties, constitutional courts can facilitate "micro-systemic electoral changes" or offer "dialogic" electoral redress to vulnerable groups, if not also initiate "macro-institutional changes" to broader political environments.[44]

The second strategic school of judicial behavior stresses the explanatory power of interbranch competition for ultimate control of the regime.[45] The core argument is that prolonged one-party control of the executive and legislative branches, also known as "unified government," is not conducive to constitutional review.[46] Conversely, "divided government," in which the executive and legislature are controlled by political rivals, is apt to converge on independent judicial power.[47] This is likely to be a stable equilibrium, for if the executive, for example, proceeds to move legislation in order to diminish the court's jurisdiction in retaliation for an embarrassing ruling, the rival party in control of the legislature is likely to defend the court by vetoing the bill.[48] Constitutional judges thus maintain an independent course with impunity.[49] With this logic, scholars infer that the decentralized party system and divided control of the presidency and Congress in the United States underpin the boldness of the Supreme Court's activist and frequently divisive rulings.[50]

If either standard account is true, then consequential constitutional review will be impossible in polities characterized by one coalition holding both executive and legislative powers over an indefinite period.[51] This includes hybrid regimes, which subject the executive and legislative branches to

43 TUSHNET, *supra* note 18, at 44.

44 PO JEN YAP, COURTS AND DEMOCRACIES IN ASIA 4 (2017).

45 CHAVEZ, *supra* note 33, at 15.

46 *Id.* at 16.

47 Chavez et al., *supra* note 27, at 223.

48 McCubbins & Rodriguez, *supra* note 10, at 282.

49 Chavez et al., *supra* note 27, at 219.

50 Mark A. Graber, *Judicial Supremacy and the Structure of Partisan Conflict*, 50 IND. L. REV. 141, 143 (2016) ("elite polarization, divided government, and electoral instability unmoor the course of judicial decision making from the structure of partisan competition. Ideological parties and elite polarization fuel efforts to secure partisan control of the courts. Electoral instability and divided government prevent either party from claiming a durable mandate to make their constitutional vision the law of the land. In this political universe, neither party can contain a stable judicial majority, but each party controls the veto points necessary to prevent the other coalition from challenging any favorable decisions that happen to be made by the Supreme Court.")

51 *See* J. Mark Ramseyer & Eric B. Rasmusen, *Judicial Independence in a Civil Law Regime: The Evidence from Japan*. 13(2) J. L. ECON. & ORG. 259 (1997); J. Mark Ramseyer, *The Puzzling (In)Dependence of Courts: A Comparative Approach*, 23(2) J. LEGAL STUD.

unitary control and are exempt from the electoral pressures that lead to the circulation of elites.[52] Reality is messy but more interesting than theory that is tidy. Strategic models too often presume that unitary governments concentrate enough power to discipline defiant courts because the costs of information, bargaining, decision-making, agent monitoring or enforcement that they face are never insurmountable; that is, the strategic models presume that noncompetitive polities operate in a world without "friction." The real world of politics, of course, is not a "frictionless" one, and the strategic schools' unexamined presumptions disable them from predicting the emergence of judicial politics in hybrid regimes, among other nondemocracies, which is now an undeniable reality. As the next section argues, the strategic models' explanatory power could be significantly improved if they were to incorporate the pivotal role played by transaction costs.

TRANSACTION COST THEORY OF HYBRID CONSTITUTIONALISM

Transaction costs may be defined as the "comparative costs of planning, adapting, and monitoring task completion under alternative governance structures."[53] They arise whenever interacting individuals want to come to terms,[54] and typically include agency costs, bargaining costs, contract costs, decisional costs, search costs, and uncertainty costs.[55] They are analogous to friction in the physical sciences.[56] Concretely put, in order to conclude an archetypal market transaction, one cannot avoid certain costs: to identify parties willing to deal, to inform them about the terms of offer, to negotiate mutually acceptable terms, to exact the contract, and to do the inspections necessary to see that the terms are implemented.[57] The level of transaction costs in economic exchanges is determined by factors such as bounded

721 (1994); William Landes & Richard Posner, *The Independent Judiciary in an Interest-Group Perspective*, 18(3) J. L. & ECON. 875 (1975).

52 *See* Steven Levitsky & Lucan A. Way, *The Rise of Competitive Authoritarianism*, 13(2) J. DEMOCRACY 51 (2002).

53 OLIVER E. WILLIAMSON, THE MECHANISMS OF GOVERNANCE 58 (1996).

54 Jean-Philippe Platteau, *The Causes of Institutional Inefficiency: A Development Perspective, in* NEW INSTITUTIONAL ECONOMICS: A GUIDEBOOK 443, 443 (Éric Brousseau & Jean-Michel Glachant eds., 2008).

55 Philip Jones & John Hudson, *The Role of Political Parties: An Analysis Based on Transaction Costs*, 94(1/2) PUB. CHOICE 175, 177 (1998).

56 MICHAEL DIETRICH, TRANSACTION COST ECONOMICS AND BEYOND: TOWARD A NEW ECONOMICS OF THE FIRM 18 (1994); Paul Milgrom & John Roberts, *Bargaining Costs, Influence Costs, and the Organization of Economic Activity, in* PERSPECTIVES ON POSITIVE POLITICAL ECONOMY 57, 72 (James E. Alt & Kenneth A. Shepsle eds., 1990).

57 RONALD H. COASE, THE FIRM, THE MARKET, AND THE LAW 6, 18 (1988).

rationality, opportunities, and asset specificity.[58] In hypothetical markets with zero transaction costs, actors would converge on efficient allocations of resources,[59] regardless of the initial distribution of property,[60] because the resources would flow smoothly to those who valued them most.[61] In such a nonexistent world, institutions such as the firm would have no substance or purpose.[62] Our real world is one in which transaction costs are large,[63] and unambiguously viewed in a negative light for burdening individuals who would partake in voluntary market exchange, which is normally welfare enhancing.[64]

Transaction costs arise in politics, too, whenever individuals try to take collective action or overcome resistance to it.[65] Transactions between politicians and between them and their constituents are core elements of the political process in every country.[66] The political arena is far more prone to inefficiencies, however, because to measure what is being exchanged, and so to enforce agreements, is exceptionally difficult. The persistence of inefficient paths in politics is thus more characteristic of economic history than anything else.[67] These findings motivated political economists to call for the application of transaction cost analysis to political processes,[68] in which transaction costs are normally nonmonetary.[69] Some of them are even irreducible, because the "natural" costs of political action imposed by society's technological, scientific, and organizational capacities were always

58 WILLIAMSON, *supra* note 53, at 162.

59 Antonio Nicita & Ugo Pagano, *Law and Economics in Retrospect*, *in* NEW INSTITUTIONAL ECONOMICS: A GUIDEBOOK 409, 411 (Éric Brousseau & Jean-Michel Glachant eds., 2008); Michael A. Fitts, *The Foibles of Formalism: Applying a Political 'Transaction Cost Analysis' to Separation of Powers*, 47(4) CASE W. RES. L. REV. 1643, 1646 (1997).

60 JIM LEITZEL, CONCEPTS IN LAW AND ECONOMICS: A GUIDE FOR THE CURIOUS 71 (2015).

61 RANDALL G. HOLCOMBE, ADVANCED INTRODUCTION TO PUBLIC CHOICE 121 (2016).

62 Ronald H. Coase, *The Relevance of Transaction Costs in the Economic Analysis of Law*, *in* THE ORIGINS OF LAW AND ECONOMICS: ESSAYS BY THE FOUNDING FATHERS 119, 208 (Francesco Parisi & Charles K. Rowley eds., 2005).

63 *Id.* at 216.

64 Niclas Berggreni & Nils Karlson, *Constitutionalism, Division of Power and Transaction Costs*, 117 PUB. CHOICE 99, 99 (2003).

65 SCOTT GEHLBACH, FORMAL MODELS OF DOMESTIC POLITICS 60 (2013).

66 Gonzalo Caballero & David Soto Oñate, *Why Transaction Costs Are so Relevant in Political Governance? A New Institutional Survey*, 36(2) BRAZILIAN J. POL. ECON. 330, 344 (2016).

67 Douglass C. North, *A Transaction Cost Theory of Politics*, 2 J. THEORETICAL POL. 355, 366 (1990).

68 Jerry Mashaw, *Public Law and Public Choice: Critique and Rapprochement*, *in* RESEARCH HANDBOOK ON PUBLIC CHOICE AND PUBLIC LAW 19, 19 (Daniel A. Farber & Anne Joseph O'Connell eds., 2010).

69 B. Dan Wood & John Bohte, *Political Transaction Costs and the Politics of Administrative Design*, 66(1) J. POL. 176, 183 (2004).

just there.[70] "Artificial" and controllable transaction costs encompass the ex ante costs of negotiating and concluding political agreements, and the ex post costs of monitoring and enforcing them. Such agreements may be formalized as statutes or decrees.[71] In practical terms, the concept of political transaction costs captures the vast difficulties of running the polity; of making decisions; of giving orders; and of monitoring, measuring, and enforcing compliance. It follows that a political organization incurring lower political transaction costs will have better chances of acting decisively, while one with higher costs will be less decisive.

The great importance of transaction costs in politics is appreciated by imagining a polity in which such costs do not exist. Political institutions (constitutions, governments, legislatures, and political parties) could all be dissolved, because people could bargain and negotiate without cost until an efficient solution benefiting all and injuring no one were found.[72] Even in an autocracy, any suboptimal political decision could be remedied by voluntary bargaining between the dictator and his subjects, until the resulting policy outcome is universally efficient.[73] The prevalence of electoral and legislative institutions in both democratic and nondemocratic polities across the world strongly implies the existence of political transaction costs as a universal phenomenon.[74] Before proceeding, one must remind oneself that substantial differences exist between economic and political exchanges. Politics lacks exact equivalents to prices.[75] Political transactions tend to be less voluntary and more coercive than economic ones.[76] Economic competition can take property rights for granted, whereas political conflict concerns the very content of rights and authority.[77]

This implies considerable differences between economic and political transaction costs. Firstly, political agreements, unlike commercial contracts, are rarely concluded between two clearly demarcated contractors, and it is hard to observe and measure something as complex and subjective as political

70 Erik G. Furubotn & R. Richter, Institutions and Economic Theory: The Contribution of the New Institutional Economics 47 (1998).

71 Donald Wittman, Economic Foundations of Law and Organization 39 (2006).

72 Douglass C. North, Transaction Costs, Institutions, and Economic Performance 9 (1992).

73 Francesco Parisi, *Political Coase Theorem*, 115 Pub. Choice 1, 14 (2003).

74 Robert D. Cooter, The Strategic Constitution 54 (2000).

75 David Epstein & Sharyn O'Halloran, Delegating Powers: A Transaction Cost Politics Approach to Policy Making under Separate Powers 44 (1999).

76 *See* Mehrdad Vahabi, *Appropriation, Violent Enforcement, and Transaction Costs: A Critical Survey*, 147(1) Pub. Choice 227 (2011).

77 Caballero & Soto Oñate, *supra* note 66, at 338.

performance.[78] Secondly, unlike the negative effect of economic transaction costs, political transaction costs are not necessarily to be regarded as undesirable in every situation.[79] It may not be in the best interest of political actors to minimize political transaction costs.[80] Constitutionalism and the separation of powers, which are normatively advantageous arrangements, entail higher transaction costs.[81] It may or may not be salutary if political actors manipulate transaction costs to achieve their preferences. One may hide politically sensitive information from citizens,[82] but one may also create procedural hurdles to hinder administrative agencies from pursuing actions that deflect from the preferences of their democratically elected legislative principals. Thirdly, political deals are seldom enforceable by third-party routines of intervention.[83] Constitutional courts, it bears repeating, are endogenous to politics – not outside and above it. Fourthly, contrary to the norm in market exchanges, ideological perceptions can alter the level of political transaction costs,[84] usually increasing them by warping actors' mental models, disabling them to evaluate accurately the benefits and costs of alternative policies.[85]

The power of strategic models to explain constitutional review in hybrid regimes could be greatly enhanced by factoring the role of positive transaction costs into the calculus of reactions to constitutional review, as well as into courts' anticipation of those. In fact, transaction cost analyses have been applied to a wide variety of political situations;[86] nothing precludes its applicability to judicial behavior in general or judicial review in particular. Consider the relevance of political transaction costs to regime–court relations. In transaction cost economics, "asset specificity" refers to the notion that deep investment in specific assets, such as relationships, knowledge, privileges, and so on, increases the difficulty of actors agreeing to changes that endanger their assets.[87] Analogously, in transaction cost politics, political actors invest in specific assets: acquiring knowledge, building relations, forming coalitions, or

78 Avinash K. Dixit, The Making of Economic Policy: A Transaction-Cost Politics Perspective 48 (1996).
79 Berggreni & Karlson, *supra* note 64, at 104.
80 Charlotte Twight, *Political Transaction-Cost Manipulation: An Integrating Theory*, 6 J. Theoretical Pol. 189, 213 (1994).
81 Berggreni & Karlson, *supra* note 62, at 99.
82 Dixit, *supra* note 78, at 59.
83 Caballero & Soto Oñate, *supra* note 64, at 338.
84 Frederick J. Phillips-Patrick, *Political Risk and Organizational Form*, 34(2) J. L. & Econ. 675, 677 (1991).
85 North, *supra* note 72, at 9.
86 Jan-Erik Lane, Constitutions and Political Theory 149–50 (2d ed. 2011).
87 Paul Pierson, Politics in Time: History, Institutions, and Social Analysis 148 (2011).

enhancing reputations.[88] If such investments cannot be easily reallocated to other uses, political actors will strive to maintain existing arrangements and resist change.[89]

The founding of a constitutional court at the constitution-making stage can easily be theorized as an "investment"[90] intended to yield valuable returns, including but not limited to political stability and foreign investment, subject to the overriding demand to maintain regime security and power.[91] A regime that, acting as constituent authority, invests constitutional competence in the court is making an asset-specific investment. It must design and incorporate provisions for independent constitutional review in the constitution and ordinary statutes; find and appoint qualified constitutional judges over a substantial period; provide for the court an organizational structure and physical premises, trained administrative staff, and a budget; promote the reputation of the court to domestic and international stakeholders; respect the judgments issued by the court, and so on. Such assets have little or no use in other contexts. Common problems in investment in markets, such as irreversibility and uncertainty about future returns, confront regimes, too, in their investments in constitutional courts.[92] Firstly, the costs of them are "sunk" and cannot be recovered if the courts prove to be incompetent or defiant.[93] Secondly, most choices at the constitutional level are made under uncertainty about the future benefits of review. Even low-energy review by judges loyal to a regime imposes undesirable costs: it finds its policy preferences subject to transparent legal assessment; it must confront the legal mobilization of interest groups in open court; and it forgoes the opportunity to pursue other, valuable courses of action, to name but a few. In short, the range of formally permissible acts available to the regime is reduced.

Given the various benefits of having a liberal democratic façade of which constitutional review is part, hybrid regimes – in contrast to the authoritarian or totalitarian governments that remain hostile to liberal democratic forms of political organization – can still justify investing in constitutional courts despite everything. Examples include the Egyptian Supreme Constitutional Court set up in 1979 by Anwar Sadat to signal ideological commitment to

88 Caballero & Soto Oñate, *supra* note 64, at 344.

89 Daryl J. Levinson, *Parchment and Politics: The Positive Puzzle of Constitutional Commitment*, 124(3) HARV. L. REV. 657, 686, 713 (2011).

90 Eric C. Ip, *A Positive Theory of Constitutional Judicial Review: Evidence from Singapore and Taiwan*, 2(4) ASIAN J. L. & ECON. art. 5 (2011).

91 RÍOS-FIGUEROA, *supra* note 28, at 19.

92 FRANCESCO PARISI & VINCY FON, THE ECONOMICS OF LAWMAKING 31 (2009).

93 John Ferejohn, *Law, Legislation, and Positive Political Theory*, *in* MODERN POLITICAL ECONOMY 191, 207 (Jeffrey S. Banks & Eric A. Hanushek eds., 1995).

neoliberalism and the "rule of law" (as opposed to former President Gamal Nasser's socialism),[94] and the Soviet Union's Constitutional Supervision Committee (the precursor to the Russian Constitutional Court), part of Mikhail Gorbachev's Perestroika program to "renew socialism" and engender a "socialist rule-of-law state" in lieu of orthodox Leninism,[95] which had never before tolerated empowered and autonomous judicial review.[96] Viewed from this angle, it is unsurprising that constitutional courts emerged in military-ruled South Korea but not in the Communist-ruled North; in Hosni Mubarak's Egypt but not in Muammar Gaddafi's Libya; and in Nationalist China but not in Maoist China.

Because of this, asset specificity leads to the "judicial holdup problem."[97] In our present scenario, the problem could easily devolve into self-aggrandizement by a court exploiting its structural independence to assume powers not intended by the framers. Weak regimes are particularly prone to judicial defections.[98] The mismatch between the court's preferences and the regime's will sooner or later incite the latter to check the former, either preemptively or in retaliation, at the constitutional or subconstitutional level. Specific action against the court will essentially be a political agreement reached inside the regime itself. This will be our unit of analysis.[99] Preemptive ex ante steps to shape the incentive structure of the court at its creation include drafting a constitution that vests the court with but limited review jurisdiction in the first place, and then, post-ratification, enables tight control of the appointment process so that the court might be "packed" with deferential judges. Other preemptive steps are statutory amendments or binding parliamentary resolutions that "hardwire" procedural hurdles into the process of law, as by requiring unanimity or a supermajority to deliver constitutional judgments; and expanding the size of the court to make it logistically harder to reach a consensus; and limiting citizens' access to the court for redress.

94 Tamir Moustafa, The Struggle for Constitutional Power: Law, Politics, and Economic Development in Egypt 39 (2007).

95 Jane Henderson, The Constitution of the Russian Federation: A Contextual Analysis 149 (2011).

96 Peter H. Solomon, Jr., *Judicial Power in Authoritarian States: The Russian Experience*, *in* Rule by Law: The Politics of Courts in Authoritarian Regimes 261, 262 (Tom Ginsburg & Tamir Moustafa eds., 2008).

97 Joel P. Trachtman, The Economic Structure of International Law 169 (2008).

98 Alexei Trochev, *Fragmentation? Defection? Legitimacy? Explaining Judicial Roles in Post-Communist "Colored Revolutions,"* *in* Consequential Courts: Judicial Roles in Global Governance 67, 69 (Diana Kapiszeswiki et al. eds., 2013).

99 Epstein & O'Halloran, *supra* note 73, at 45.

Given the abovementioned judicial holdup problem, even a hypothetical, epistemically perfect court that makes no technical errors may still make decisions adverse to regime goals.[100] This can embroil a regime in retaliatory ex post measures that scandalously assault the court or coerce it to withdraw its decisions. This can take the form of an amendment to the constitution overturning the decision, curtailing the court's jurisdiction, or weakening provisions guaranteeing the security of tenure and salary of judges; or of amending organic law or binding parliamentary resolution to soften or delay the impact of the decision; of cutting the judicial budget; or of impeaching defiant judges.[101] Extraconstitutional steps, such as personally intimidating or even assassinating judges, or abolishing courts permanently, tend to cost hybrid regimes more than they do closed autocracies and totalitarian polities, as they crack the liberal democratic façade.[102] A summary of these measures in the form of a 2 2 typology can be found in Figure 2.1.

According to the strategic model, a credible threat by the regime to take any of these steps will have the "chilling effect"[103] of shoving the court toward compliance with regime preferences; thus, constitutional judgments must accommodate political reality if they are to stand the test of time.[104] Having few resources to withstand a determined backlash, the court will be well advised to anticipate the regime's reactions to avert court-curbing and vindicate constitutional values and rights in the long run.[105] In order for its interpretations to stick, a constitutional court must craft its judgment not only to maximize judicial power but also to return substantial benefits to diverse parties outside and inside the regime, in ways that raise the transaction costs of retaliating.[106]

In a world of positive political transaction costs, therefore, the credibility of such threats to take ex post steps depends on the regime's prior ability to take and implement negative decisions in response to court "malfeasance." All ex

100 Eric A. Posner, *Controlling Agencies with Cost-Benefit Analysis: A Positive Political Theory Perspective*, 68 U. CHI. L. REV. 1137, 1140 (2001).

101 Roderick A. Macdonald & Hoi Kong, *Judicial Independence as a Constitutional Virtue*, *in* THE OXFORD HANDBOOK OF COMPARATIVE CONSTITUTIONAL LAW 831, 848 (Michael Rosenfeld and Andras Sajo eds., 2012); Tom Ginsburg, *The Politics of Courts in Democratization*, *in* GLOBAL PERSPECTIVES ON THE RULE OF LAW 175, 176 (James J. Heckman et al. eds., 2010).

102 KELLY M. MCMANN, ECONOMIC AUTONOMY AND DEMOCRACY: HYBRID REGIMES IN RUSSIA AND KYRGYZSTAN 179 (2006).

103 Hirschl, *supra* note 16, at 176.

104 Ferejohn & Weingast, *supra* note 26, at 263.

105 Ferejohn et al., *supra* note 2, at 744.

106 WHITTINGON, *supra* note 15, at 27.

	Ex ante	Ex post
Constitutional	New constitution to: define or redefine the court's constitutional jurisdiction	Constitutional amendment to: overturn the court's judgment; curtail the court's jurisdiction; repeal provisions guaranteeing judges' security of tenure and salary; or abolish the court
Subconstitutional	Statutory amendment or binding parliamentary resolution to: control over judicial appointments; manipulate judicial procedures; limit access to the court	Statutory amendment or binding parliamentary resolution to: undermine the judgment's effects; withhold judicial funds; impeach defiant judges

FIGURE 2.1 A typology of regime counteractions against constitutional courts

post steps exact from the regime high informational and decisional costs against a background of uncertainty that springs from the need to invest resources to search, detect, and attack malfeasance.[107] A threat is not credible if the costs of agreeing to it are too high, and the benefits to its sponsors of execution are low.[108] There is a real possibility that the political transaction costs to the regime of taking action are higher than the benefits of backlash. In hybrid regimes, which adopt liberal democratic forms with an ostensible separation of powers, the executive's power to command a reliable majority in the legislature is "critical," because appointments to constitutional courts and to electoral authorities tend to require legislative approval.[109] But this power is not as stable as is commonly assumed. Hybrid regimes are vulnerable to internal crises triggered by splits in the governing coalition, resulting in strong electoral challenges from erstwhile insiders.[110] Incumbents who take harsh

[107] Murray J. Horn, The Political Economy of Public Administration: Institutional Choice in the Public Sector 49 (1995).

[108] William D. Ferguson, Collective Action and Exchange: A Game-Theoretic Approach to Contemporary Political Economy 84–85 (2013).

[109] Steven Levitsky & Lucan A. Way, Competitive Authoritarianism: Hybrid Regimes after The Cold War 63 (2010).

[110] *Id.* at 65.

autocratic steps to retain power in the face of momentous mass oppositional mobilization put their public support at risk, and cause fractures in regime factions, if they do not also risk international sanctions.[111] Even practically unelected authoritarians must solicit the acquiescence of the ruled,[112] hold on to their collaborating groups, institutionalized or not, who assisted their accession to power,[113] and avoid antagonizing powerful constituents.[114] They typically lack complete control of enforcement of agreements among various factions that supply them with political support, and consequently, have to make concessions of rents to selected factions.[115]

The level of regime cohesion, the incumbent's capacity to secure the cooperation of the regime's members,[116] is a reliable indicator of the size of the political transaction costs facing that regime when it considers punishing courts. Unified governments that formally control both executive and legislative branches are not always monolithic; several factions, each incapable of prevailing, may cherish conflicting preferences on certain policies, about which compromises between them may be prohibitively costly. Conventional wisdom on authoritarian politics as nothing more than "the eccentricities, longevity, and brutality of a few dictators and their regimes" is misleading:[117] most authoritarian systems have multiple veto-gates that prevent incumbents from behaving irrationally and arbitrarily.[118] Generally speaking, political transaction costs increase as the number of factions inside the regime that must converge on an agreement increase, and decrease as the factions are fewer.[119] The scale of political transaction costs will be very high if there are multiple factions that are evenly matched.[120] Strong cohesion within a regime fortifies the incumbent's power to manage intra-elite conflict, mobilize support, win elections, and

111 *Id.* at 69.

112 Jennifer Gandhi, Political Institutions under Dictatorship xvii (2008).

113 Stephen Haber, *Authoritarian Government*, *in* The Oxford Handbook of Political Economy 693, 696 (Barry R. Weingast & Donald A. Wittman eds., 2006).

114 Douglass C. North, Institutions, Institutional Change and Economic Performance 52 (1991).

115 Milan W. Svolik, The Politics of Authoritarian Rule 2 (2012).

116 Levitsky & Way, *supra* note 109, at 60.

117 Svolik, *supra* note 113, at 43–44.

118 Francis Fukuyama, *Development and the Limits of Institutional Design*, *in* Political Institutions and Development: Failed Expectations and Renewed Hopes 21, 29 (Natalia Dinello & Vladimir Popov eds., 2007).

119 Cooter, *supra* note 74, at 53.

120 Mushtaq H. Khan, *Rent-seeking as Process*, *in* Rents, Rent-seeking and Economic Development: Theory and Evidence in Asia 70, 110 (Mushtaq H. Khan & K.S. Jomo eds., 2000).

carry controversial policies;[121] weak cohesion and factional infighting, in contrast, raise transaction costs by retarding bargaining and reducing the demand for agreements.[122] Political transaction costs may therefore be theorized as inversely proportional to regime decisiveness.[123] A regime can only take steps against its court so long as it coheres as a collective actor so as to amass inter-factional support for each cause; bearing in mind that regime cohesiveness may vary from one move against the court to another, and one policy domain to another. Because of imperfect information and other limitations, the regime may, in the aggregate, be indifferent or semi-indifferent on the issue under review, and hence will tolerate a wider range of judicial preferences so long as the rulings do not overstep well-defined preferences and interests shared by most or all of the factions constituting the regime.[124]

Two interrelated factors – ideology and opportunism – prominently determine regime cohesiveness, hence the size of its political transaction costs. A regime of ideological homogeneity versus heterogeneity differs in its decisiveness. The subjective mental models that political actors use to interpret the reality around them, to simplify complicated policy positions, and to make political transactions constitute a form of bounded rationality.[125] Actors with strong ideological convictions are willing to pay higher prices in pursuit of their preferences.[126] Ideological homogeneity among elite factions promotes regime cohesion,[127] while heterogeneity complicates political bargaining between factions.[128] Differential preferences inside the regime entail that coalition building is prerequisite to the exercise of even authoritarian power.[129] Ideological heterogeneity is likelier to arise in a hybrid regime. To impose, top-down, a sophisticated state ideology in a hybrid regime may be counterproductive in light of the necessity of keeping up a liberal façade. Hence, hybrid regimes are less likely than totalitarian or closed authoritarian polities, but still likelier than liberal democracies, to adopt a cohesive and

121 Levitsky & Way, *supra* note 109, at 59 67.
122 Cooter, *supra* note 74, at 213.
123 Lane, *supra* note 86, at 196.
124 Yap, *supra* note 44, at 3.
125 John B. Londregan, Legislative Institutions and Ideology in Chile 17 (2007).
126 North, *supra* note 114, at 90.
127 Stephen Dunn, The "Uncertain" Foundations of Post Keynesian Economics: Essays in Exploration 169 (2010).
128 Berggreni & Karlson, *supra* note 62, at 103.
129 Claude Ménard, *Facing Crises: Economy, Democracy, and Political Transaction Costs*, *in* Democracy and an Open-Economy World Order 109–110 (George C. Bitros & Nicholas C. Kyriazis eds., 2017).

homogenous political ideology for their elites and constituencies. The legislature of a hybrid regime, normally offering opposition parties an institutionalized platform to influence policy-making, also aggravates the diversity of ideologies and embarrasses deal-making.[130]

Political opportunism among insiders may also undermine regime coherence. A hybrid regime typically suffers "inherent fragmentation" in the paradoxical marriage of the formal institutions of liberal democracy, including reasonably fair elections, with an authoritarian modus operandi.[131] Insiders such as parliamentarians affiliated with a hybrid regime typically answer to competing principals: their electoral constituencies and the regime itself, both of whose preferences may clash.[132] Even limited electoral competition incentivizes loyalist parliamentarians to attack the regime's shortcomings as a way of gaining popularity, and opens the door to civil society activism.[133] When the regime is weak, insiders have more incentive to seek advancement from outside the regime, rather than inside.[134] In regimes that have diffused lines of authority, it is not uncommon for parliamentarians and their followers to switch sides on specific issues, in the face of mounting external pressures caused by widespread protests, unrest, and coup d'état threats from the military.[135] If parliamentarians affiliated with the regime expect a strong public reaction to spring from a decision to punish the constitutional court, at least some may refrain from concurring, which heightens political transaction costs.[136] Recently, scholars have been tweaking the strategic model, in both the democratic and authoritarian contexts, by factoring in public support for the constitutional court and its constraint on purges of judges.[137] Potent resistance by opposition parliamentarians,[138] mass media, civil society, popular movements, and the military can induce incoherence or moderation even

[130] Witold J. Henisz & Bennet A. Zelner, *Explicating Political Hazards and Safeguards: A Transaction Cost Politics*, 13(6) INDUSTRIAL & CORP. CHANGE 901, 908 (2004).

[131] Trochev, *supra* note 98, at 87.

[132] Beatriz Magaloni, *The Game of Electoral Fraud and the Ousting of Authoritarian Rule*, 54(3) AM. J. POL. SCI. 751, 753 (2010).

[133] ELIZA W.Y. LEE ET AL., PUBLIC POLICYMAKING IN HONG KONG: CIVIC ENGAGEMENT AND STATE-SOCIETY RELATIONS IN A SEMI-DEMOCRACY 2 (2013).

[134] LEVITSKY & WAY, *supra* note 109, at 62.

[135] STEPHAN HAGGARD & ROBERT R. KAUFMAN, THE POLITICAL ECONOMY OF DEMOCRATIC TRANSITIONS 357 (1995).

[136] Aylin Aydin, *Judicial Independence across Democratic Regimes: Understanding the Varying Impact of Political Competition*, 47(1) LAW & SOC'Y REV. 105, 113 (2013).

[137] *See* Barry Friedman, *The Will of the People and the Process of Constitutional Change*, 78 GEO. WASH. L. REV. 1232 (2010); Arthur Dyevre, *Unifying the Field of Comparative Judicial Politics: Towards a General Theory of Judicial Behaviour*, 2(2) EUR. POL. SC. REV. 297 (2010).

[138] GANDHI, *supra* note 110, at xviii.

inside a unified hybrid regime that might otherwise have sanctioned assertive judicial claims.[139] It should surprise no one that rulers are prone to suppressing "judicial support networks,"[140] in order to preempt both elite and judicial defections.[141]

The following thesis can be deduced from the above theoretical exposition: *ceteris paribus*, regardless of unified or divided government or the presence or absence of intense electoral competition, the higher the political transaction costs of reining in the constitutional court, the likelier the court will act consequentially, and vice versa. A regime with lower political transaction costs – namely, one that exhibits greater cohesion in terms of ideology and organization – will be abler credibly to threaten or actually reverse adverse rulings. In such a political climate, even courts armed with formidable review powers will be compelled to defer to the regime in anticipation of the grave consequences of defiance: namely, being overruled, if not persecuted. Low-energy constitutional review ensues. By contrast, insurmountable internal incohesion, sometimes triggered by opposition from media, civil society, and mass movements, will likely circumscribe the power and will of even a unified government to punish high-energy constitutional review. Such a state of affairs will, in turn, encourage courts to assert themselves all the more, challenging the regime with ever less timidity.

This thesis allows us to predict changes in constitutional court jurisprudence through observing fluctuations in the regime's capacity to run the polity. Constancy in the size of political transaction costs predicts a comparable constancy in the consequentiality of constitutional review; while fluctuations in political transaction costs predict similar fluctuations in constitutional court jurisprudence. It also predicts what kind of response will be deployed by a regime against judicial malfeasance: where costs are very low, the regime will be able to enact constitutional measures that conclusively defeat judicial adventures, but where costs are high, the regime will likelier resort to subconstitutional measures such as manipulating the decisional rules and composition of the court.

SAMPLE APPLICATIONS

This section tests the above transaction cost theory of hybrid constitutionalism against the development of constitutional review in two hybrid regimes: Singapore and Turkey. Unified government is the norm in both countries.

[139] Trochev, *supra* note 98, at 69.
[140] MOUSTAFA, supra note 94, at 236.
[141] Macdonald & Kong, *supra* note 101, at 848.

Singapore has been described as a "hegemonic party system" and an "electoral authoritarian regime."[142] In Turkey, elected officials who control both the executive and the legislature, and exhibit "authoritarian tendencies,"[143] coexist with military officers who retain "considerable" power.[144] The two polities exhibit variation across important conditions, such as the authoritarianism style and the modus operandi of judicial review. The predictiveness of the theory will be vindicated if it can account adequately for the pathways taken by the constitutional courts of these two dissimilar polities, and we can have stronger confidence in our conclusions.[145] The exposition is in the form of an analytic narrative, which best befits methodologically problem-driven, contextualized, single-country case studies tracing processes specific to time and space that have produced interesting political outcomes.[146]

SINGAPORE

Modern Singapore was founded by the British Empire in 1848, granted self-governing status in 1959, joined the newly sovereign Federation of Malaysia in 1963, and achieved independence in 1965.[147] By the 1980s, it had emerged as one of the world's leading financial centers.[148] Since 1959, the People's Action Party, founded by former Prime Minister Lee Kuan Yew (1923–2015), has continuously governed through a version of the Westminster system under which a simple plurality voting system has maintained its dominant status in Singapore's unicameral Parliament.[149] Between 1968 and 1981, the party held

142 Netina Tan, *Institutionalized Succession and Hegemonic Party Cohesion in Singapore, in* Party System Institutionalization in Asia: Democracies, Autocracies, and the Shadows of the Past 49, 52 (Allen Hicken & Erik Martinez Kuhonta eds., 2015).

143 Hootan Shambayati, *Courts in Semi-Democratic/Authoritarian Regimes: The Judicialization of Turkish (and Iranian) Politics, in* Rule by Law: The Politics of Courts in Authoritarian Regimes 283, 283 (Tom Ginsburg & Tamir Moustafa eds., 2008).

144 Levitsky & Way, *supra* note 109, at 32.

145 Matthew C. Ingram, Crafting Courts in New Democracies: The Politics of Subnational Judicial Reform in Brazil and Mexico 42–43 (2016).

146 *See* Robert H. Bates et al., *The Analytical Narrative Project*, 94 Am. Pol. Sci. Rev. 696 (2000).

147 Franklin E. Zimring et al., *Executions, Deterrence, and Homicide: A Tale of Two Cities*, 7(1) J. Empirical Legal Stud. 1, 3 (2010).

148 Jolene Lin, *The Judicialization of Governance: The Case of Singapore, in* Administrative Law and Governance in Asia: Comparative Perspectives 287–88 (Tom Ginsburg & Albert H.Y. Chen eds., 2009).

149 Kenneth Paul Tan, *The Singapore Parliament: Representation, Effectiveness, and Control, in* Parliaments in Asia: Institution Building and Political Development 27, 46 (Zheng Yongnian et al. eds., 2014).

every single seat in Parliament. Even in the 2001 General Election, the People's Action Party managed to win a vote share as high as 75 percent, the negative growth rate of the economy notwithstanding.[150] Over the past six decades, the party has built a "highly interventionist and entrepreneurial state" that also exhibits "[a]uthoritarian, technocratic, and paternalistic" patterns of governance.[151]

Political transaction costs have been constantly low in Singapore's hybrid regime. The People's Action Party has a fairly well-defined center-right ideology, in contrast to which none of the opposition parties provides any articulate ideological alternatives.[152] The party's exclusivist, meritocratic, and centralized methods of elite cooptation have fostered its internal cohesion.[153] These methods consist of recruiting English-speaking, overseas-educated top achievers directly from the military, the civil service, the medical and legal professions, universities, and business, in preference to grassroots activists as candidates in parliamentary elections.[154] The party, and by extension the Government, experiences little elite factionalism.[155] What is more, external pressures on the regime are relatively low. Legal restrictions on public assemblies and rigorous fund-raising rules have constrained the development of opposition parties.[156] It has become a truism that interparty competition is nonexistent in Singapore.[157] Most nongovernmental organizations are not only not in opposition; they are even connected with the party.[158] And the mass media has neither the will nor the ability to check Government operations externally.[159] Recent lawsuits against certain Internet bloggers is said to have successfully achieved what political scientists regard as "low intensity coercion," the overall effect of which has been to restrict political activism outside the party.[160]

150 Tan, *supra* note 142, at 49.
151 Kenneth Paul Tan, Governing Global-City Singapore: Legacies and Futures after Lee Kuan Yew 15, 25 (2017).
152 Bilveer Singh, Politics and Governance in Singapore: An Introduction 47 (2d ed. 2012).
153 Tan, *supra* note 142, at 69.
154 Tan, *supra* note 151, at 27–28.
155 Dan Slater, Ordering Power: Contentious Politics and Authoritarian Leviathans in Southeast Asia 241 (2010).
156 Tan, *supra* note 142, at 55.
157 Tan, *supra* note 151, at 25.
158 Singh, *supra* note 152, at 88.
159 *Id.* at 96.
160 Lee Morgenbesser, *The Autocratic Mandate: Elections, Legitimacy and Regime Stability in Singapore*, 30(2) Pac. Rev. 205, 210 (2017).

Given its persistent supermajority status in Parliament, the People's Action Party could amend the Constitution decisively with little resistance, as witness the abolition of trial by jury in 1969 and the suspension of final appeals to the Judicial Committee of the Privy Council in London in 1994.[161] At the subconstitutional level, too, Parliament has plenary discretion to alter ordinary legislation, even to enact statutes that would be considered unfair by many.[162] Nothing in the Constitution obligates Parliament to enact only limitations on fundamental liberties that are reasonable, let alone proportionate.[163] As predicted, the threat that Parliament could swiftly overturn unwanted constitutional judgments has proved to be credible in Singapore. In *Chng Suan Tze v. Minister for Home Affairs*,[164] the Singapore Court of Appeal, on the basis of technical irregularities, struck down orders issued by the Minister of Affairs to detain four persons without trial, pursuant to internal security legislation, for alleged participation in a Marxist insurgency against the state.[165] Significantly, the Court declared that "[a]ll power has legal limits and the rule of law demands that the courts should be able to examine the exercise of discretionary power."[166] Although the Court did not address the merits of the impugned orders, presumably out of respect for the Government, the latter simply rearrested the detainees minutes after their release, backed by detention orders made in compliance with all required procedures, and just a month later Parliament even passed several amendments to the Constitution and ordinary legislation to exclude substantive judicial review from Government decisions issued under the Internal Security Act.[167]

The transaction cost theory of hybrid constitutionalism predicts that in a regime of persistently low costs, the constitutional court is likelier than not to defer and to be inconsequential. Clearly, Singapore is such a low transaction cost polity: the Government of the People's Action Party is able to act as one under effective leadership and is confronted only by weak oppositional groups. It wields the ultimate veto in the very low decisional cost of amending

161 *See* David Martin Jones, *Asian Values and the Constitutional Order of Contemporary Singapore*, 8(4) CONST. POL. ECON. 283 (1997).

162 KEVIN Y.L. TAN, THE CONSTITUTION OF SINGAPORE: A CONTEXTUAL ANALYSIS 213 (2015).

163 Jack Tsen-Ta Lee, *According to the Spirit and Not to the Letter: Proportionality and the Singapore Constitution*, 8 VIENNA J. ON INT'L CONST. L. 276, 302 (2014).

164 Chng Suan Tze v. Minister for Home Affairs [1988] 2 S.L.R. 132 (C.A.S.).

165 PO JEN YAP, CONSTITUTIONAL DIALOGUE IN COMMON LAW ASIA 74 (2015).

166 Chng Suan Tze v. Minister for Home Affairs [1988] 2 S.L.R. 132, at [86] (C.A.S.).

167 YAP, *supra* note 165, at 75.

the Constitution.[168] Aggressive and consequential judicial review by an apex constitutional court should not arise in such a polity. And this is exactly what we have observed in the constitutional jurisprudence of the Court of Appeal, the final appellate court of Singapore, since 1994.[169] The constitutional jurisdiction of the Court of Appeal to review and invalidate unconstitutional legislation is uncontroversial in light of Articles 4[170] and 93[171] of the Constitution. What is more, a new Article 100 was inserted into the Constitution in September 1994 to enable the President of the Republic to refer questions about the Constitution to a special tribunal of no less than three judges. Ironically, the existence of a codified Constitution guaranteeing the paramountcy of fundamental rights and due process means that the Court of Appeal of Singapore actually has more right to strike down Acts of Parliament as being unconstitutional than does the Supreme Court of the United Kingdom, which is constrained by the doctrine of parliamentary sovereignty.[172] On the whole, the Court of Appeal is held in very high esteem, having a solid reputation for impartiality and incorruptibility.[173] In spite of all these formal powers, however, the Court has never once struck down an Act of Parliament for unconstitutionality;[174] indeed, constitutional litigation takes up only a tiny share of the Court's docket, in which commercial cases predominate.[175] Consider the minimalism of the Court in constitutional review as evidenced in its judgments. In *Jabar bin Kadermastan v. Public Prosecutor*[176] the Court ruled that, "[a]ny law which provides for the

168 *See* Po Jen Yap, *The "Dead" Constitution: Crime and Punishment in Singapore*, 40(3) Hong Kong L. J. 577 (2010).

169 Kevin Y.L. Tan, *As Efficient as the Best Businesses: Singapore's Judicial System*, *in* Asian Courts in Context 228, 236 (Jiunn-Rong Yeh & Wen-Chen Chang eds., 2015) (from 1994 onwards, the Court of Appeal practically became the final arbiter on all legal questions in Singapore, following the closure of the Judicial Committee of the Privy Council under the Judicial Committee (Repeal) Act 1994).

170 Constitution of the Republic of Singapore 1965, art.4: "This Constitution is the supreme law of the Republic of Singapore and any law enacted by the Legislature after the commencement of this Constitution which is inconsistent with this Constitution shall, to the extent of the inconsistency, be void."

171 Constitution of the Republic of Singapore 1965, art.93: "The judicial power of Singapore shall be vested in a Supreme Court and in such subordinate courts as may be provided by any written law for the time being in force."

172 Lin, *supra* note 148, at 295.

173 Tan, *supra* note 169, at 262.

174 Lynette J. Chua & Stacia L. Haynie, *Judicial Review of Executive Power in the Singaporean Context, 1965–2012*, 4(1) J. L. & Courts 43, 44 (2016).

175 *See* Li-ann Thio, *Lex Rex or Rex Lex? Competing Conceptions of the Rule of Law in Singapore*, 20 U.C.L.A. Pac. Basin L. J. 1 (2002).

176 Jabar bin Kadermastan v. Public Prosecutor [1995] 1 S.L.R. (R.) 326 (C.A.S.).

deprivation of a person s life or personal liberty, is valid and binding so long as it is validly passed by Parliament," and that it "is not concerned with whether it is also fair, just and reasonable as well."[177] In *Public Prosecutor v. Taw Cheng Kong*,[178] the Court made it clear that the threshold for rebutting a judicial presumption of constitutionality of official acts is extremely high: "to discharge the burden of rebutting the presumption, it will usually be necessary for the person challenging the law to adduce some material or factual evidence to show that it was enacted arbitrarily or had operated arbitrarily."[179] Predictably, the Court of Appeal overturned the High Court's judgment in *Taw Cheng Kong v. Public Prosecutor*,[180] the one case in which a Singaporean court has ever struck down legislation.[181]

The past decade may have witnessed a gradual sea-change in argumentative style, in that the justices of the Court of Appeal have shown a more sophisticated willingness to engage with the academic literature, foreign laws, and public international law.[182] But the prevailing judicial philosophy continues to be fundamentally communitarian,[183] and the Singaporean judiciary has "shown great restraint in striking down governmental action and legislation as unconstitutional,"[184] and remained staunch in its rejection of more intrusive doctrines of substantive review, such as structured proportionality review, as standards for gauging the constitutionality of legislation.[185] This approach almost conclusively presumes that the Government of the day acts in society's best interests and is owed deference on matters of legal reform.[186] The Court has reportedly awarded "astronomically high damages"[187] in controversial political defamation suits against parties who dared to criticize Government leaders. The doctrinal trajectory of the Court of Appeal in review cases squares

177 Jabar bin Kadermastan v. Public Prosecutor [1995] 1 S.L.R. (R.) 326, at [52] (C.A.S.).
178 Public Prosecutor v. Taw Cheng Kong [1998] 2 S.L.R. (R.) 489 (C.A.S.).
179 Public Prosecutor v. Taw Cheng Kong [1998] 2 S.L.R. (R.) 489, at [80] (C.A.S.).
180 Taw Cheng Kong v. Public Prosecutor [1998] 1 S.L.R. (R.) 78 (C.A.S.).
181 *See* Li-ann Thio, A Treatise on Singapore Constitutional Law 254 (2012).
182 Li-ann Thio, *"We are Feeling Our Way Forward, Step by Step": The Continuing Singapore Experiment in the Construction of Communitarian Constitutionalism in the Twenty-First Century's First Decade*, *in* Constitutionalism in Asia in the Early Twenty-First Century 270, 282 (Albert H.Y. Chen ed., 2014).
183 *Id.* at 283.
184 Jack Tsen-Ta Lee, *Constraint or Restraint? Singapore's Constitution at 50*, *in* Singapore: Negotiating State and Society, 1965–2015 15, 15 (Jason Lim & Terence Lee eds., 2016)
185 Daniel Tan, *An Analysis of Substantive Review in Singaporean Administrative Law*, 25 Singapore Academy of Law J. 296, 323 (2013).
186 Jaclyn L. Neo, *Balancing Act: The Balancing Metaphor as Deference and Dialogue in Constitutional Adjudication*, in Constitutional Interpretation in Singapore: Theory and Practice 159, 164 (2017).
187 Thio, *supra* note 182, at 291.

perfectly with the conclusions of the theory. The expected costs in terms of the credible threat of political backlash against high-energy constitutional review best explains the Court's habitual reluctance to render constitutional judgments that defy the preferences of a unified government.[188] On the basis of the theory, one can predict that, barring unforeseeable changes in low political transaction costs in Singapore, it is very unlikely that high-energy constitutional review will emerge any time soon. And little change in the decisiveness of the Party, the fragmentation of the opposition, or the resistance from civil society is anywhere detectable.[189]

TURKEY

The founding of the Republic of Turkey in 1923 repudiated centuries of the Ottoman Empire's Islamist traditions. The Kemalist[190] armed forces historically took a leading role in constructing and maintaining a secularist republic devoid of Muslim institutions and equipped with legal structures borrowed from Western Europe. The state policy of laïcité (Laiklik) was entrenched in the Constitutions of 1921, 1924, 1961, and 1982, to quell the forces of political Islam, sectarianism and Kurdish separatist nationalism.[191] Between 1923 and 1950, the Kemalist center-left Republican People's Party governed the country in the context of a low transaction cost, single party-state framework, in which the party was able to act decisively, and was unchallenged, most of the time.[192] Notwithstanding the inception of a multiparty system in 1950, a split within the party[193] meant that Turkey was never able to settle on a fully fledged liberal democratic political system. Indeed, popularly elected governments were ousted by the armed forces in 1960, 1971, 1980, and 1997[194] against a backdrop of overt military superintendence of politics,

188 Lee, *supra* note 163, at 281.

189 In the 2015 General Election, the People's Action Party retained 69.9 percent of the total votes: TAN, *supra* note 151, at 1.

190 Kemalism is the secularizing, modernizing, and Westernizing founding ideology of the Republic of Turkey, named after inaugural president and military strongman Mustafa Kemal Atatürk. *See* Suna Kili, *Kemalism in Contemporary Turkey*, 1(3) INT'L POL. SCI. REV. 381 (1980).

191 HIRSCHL, *supra* note 39, at 152.

192 Ceren Belge, *Friends of the Court: The Republican Alliance and Selective Activism of the Constitutional Court of Turkey*, 40(3) LAW & SOC'Y REV. 653, 659 (2006).

193 JOHN M. VANDERLIPPE, POLITICS OF TURKISH DEMOCRACY, THE: ISMET INONU AND THE FORMATION OF THE MULTI-PARTY SYSTEM, 1938–1950 189 (2012).

194 Güneş Murat Tezcür, *Judicial Activism in Perilous Times: The Turkish Case*, 43(2) LAW & SOC'Y REV. 305, 307 (2009).

escalating polarization on ideological and ethnic matters, separatist violence, and abuses of human rights.[195] The Turkish Constitutional Court (*Anayasa Mahkemesi*) was established in 1962, in the aftermath of the 1960 military coup that ousted the moderately Islamist Democratic Party regime, and executed Prime Minister Adnan Menderes, Minister of Foreign Affairs Fatin Rüştü Zorlu, and Minister of Finance Hasan Polatkan. Before returning power to civilian hands in 1961, the military convened a constituent National Assembly to ratify a modernist, liberal Constitution, which contained a bill of rights.[196] Consistent with the logic of political insurance or "hegemonic preservation" theory,[197] the Court's founding can be understood as a strategic move by Kemalist groups to raise a secularist countermajoritarian stronghold against any resurgence of Islamism.[198]

A "competitive authoritarian" and "hybrid" regime"[199] has been consolidating since the Islamist Justice and Development Party (*Adalet ve Kalkınma Partisi* (AKP)), riding a popular wave of anti-secularism,[200] captured a parliamentary majority.[201] The Turkish polity shows a "wide gap between codified law and rule enforcement," as well as "cycles of enhanced authoritarianism and contestation."[202] The political style of the AKP leader Recep Tayyip Erdoğan, Prime Minister from 2003 to 2014 and President since 2014, has become increasingly personalist.[203] The AKP regime is widely accused of deploying massive repression against opposition groups; seizing control of the media and regulatory agencies; and exhausting opponents with lawsuits.[204]

195 Ali Resul Usul, Democracy in Turkey: The Impact of EU Political Conditionality 172 (2010).

196 Ríos-Figueroa, *supra* note 28, at 187.

197 Ran Hirschl, Towards Juristocracy: The Origins and Consequences of the New Constitutionalism 42, 50 (2006).

198 Belge, *supra* note 192, at 656–57.

199 Yusuf Sarfati & Aviad Rubin, *Introduction: Israel and Turkey in Comparative Perspective, in* The Jarring Road to Democratic Inclusion: A Comparative Assessment of State–Society Engagements in Israel and Turkey 1, 5 (Aviad Rubin & Yusuf Sarfati eds., 2016); Hasan Ersel, *Political and Economic Developments in Turkey and the Transformation of Political Islam (1950–2010), in* Understanding the Political Economy of the Arab Uprisings 193, 194 (Ishac Diwan ed., 2014).

200 Hirschl, *supra* note 39, at 153.

201 *See* Nikolaos Stelgias, *Turkey's Hybrid Competitive Authoritarian Regime: A Genuine Product of Anatolia's Middle Class*, 4 Levantine Rev. 201 (2015).

202 Ceren Lord, *Situating Change under the AKP, in* Contemporary Turkey at a Glance II: Turkey Transformed? Power, History, Culture 7, 19 (Meltem Ersoy & Ersa Ozyurek eds., 2017).

203 *Id.* at 20.

204 Berk Esen & Sebnem Gumuscu, *Rising Competitive Authoritarianism in Turkey*, 37(9) Third World Q. 1581, 1581 (2016).

But it still lacks the two-thirds supermajority in Parliament necessary to amend the Constitution,[205] and massive gridlock afflicts the executive branch due to Kemalist dominance of the armed forces. Military leaders perceive the AKP as the successor of the Islamist movement and have taken actions ranging from coup attempts to the promotion of anti-AKP mass campaigns.[206] The General Staff, which oversees the armed forces and is supposed to report to the Prime Minister, has openly spoken against the AKP candidate for the 2007 presidential election.[207] The credible threat of another military coup has become a real constraint on anti-Kemalist policies.[208] Such a regime, clogged with severe ideological contradictions and rife with opportunism, shows unmistakable signs of skyrocketing political transaction costs.

The Turkish Constitutional Court has been described as one of the "most activist" courts in the world,[209] issuing "frequent rulings" against Parliament[210] and functioning as a preeminent "negative legislator."[211] A closer inspection, however, presents a more nuanced picture of its constitutional review trajectory. The Court originated in a decision of the Kemalist military to raise a bulwark of secularism:[212] a view shared by Kemalist elites and members of the Court, who understood its role to be defender of the Westernizing agenda against potential threats from the electorate.[213] During periods of Kemalist government, subject to minor exceptions when the Kemalists were themselves divided,[214] the

205 Lord, *supra* note 202, at 20.

206 İsmet Akça & Evren Balta-Paker, *Beyond Military Tutelage? Turkish Military Politics and the AKP Government*, *in* DEBATING SECURITY IN TURKEY: CHALLENGES AND CHANCES IN THE TWENTY-FIRST CENTURY 77, 77 (Ebru Canan-Sokullu ed., 2013).

207 *Id.* at 84.

208 Ümit Cizre, *The Justice and Development Party and the Military: Recreating the Past after Reforming It?*, *in* SECULAR AND ISLAMIC POLITICS IN TURKEY: THE MAKING OF THE JUSTICE AND DEVELOPMENT PARTY 132, 154 (Ümit Cizre ed., 2007).

209 Esin Örücü, *The Constitutional Court of Turkey: The Anayasa Mahkemesi as the Protector of the System*, *in* CONSTITUTIONAL COURTS: A COMPARATIVE STUDY 196, 214 (Andrew Harding and Peter Leyland eds., 2009).

210 Shambayati, *supra* note 143, at 296.

211 Örücü, *supra* note 209, at 200.

212 Shambayati, *supra* note 143, at 285.

213 *Id.* at 288.

214 M. HAKAN YAVUZ, ISLAMIC POLITICAL IDENTITY IN TURKEY 65 (2003) ("From 1973 to 1980, therefore, Turkey had unstable coalition governments that failed to address the growing structural problems of the country. In the 1970s, political divisions were mostly based on ideological divisions between the Left and Right. These ideological divisions, however, relied on the cultural clevages they helped to politicize. Societal polarization inevitably was reflected in electoral politics. The formerly statist CHP (Cumhuriyet Halk Partisi) after

Court has indeed been deferential to the preferences of the regime, and the military had rarely struck down Kemalist initiatives,[215] and had shown little sympathy for civil rights claims that subvert Kemalism's hegemonic status.[216] Rather, it has acted as a handmaiden for Kemalism to marginalize political Islam in the electoral arena, taking steps such as closing Kurdish and Islamist political parties repeatedly in the 1980s and 1990s.[217] In the same period, when non-Kemalist governments were in power, the Court struck down statutory amendments lifting the ban on wearing the headscarf in educational establishments with a laic scientific milieu;[218] and invalidated section 441 of the Penal Code criminalizing adultery by men as contrary to the Constitution's protection of equality in Article 10.[219]

Escalating clashes between the military-backed Constitutional Court and AKP were predictable. In May 2007, the Court, in line with the preferences of the Kemalist military, nullified the parliamentary vote designating AKP nominee Abdullah Gül as President. Prime Minister Erdoğan responded by calling new parliamentary elections, which the AKP won by a landslide, backing by popular demand Gül's succession as Turkey's first Islamist President.[220] In June 2008, the Court struck down a proposed amendment to the Constitution that would have lifted the ban on headscarves at public universities as being contrary to the secular founding principles of the Constitution.[221] The Court received considerable support from the Kemalist Republican People's Party, the Turkish education board, and numerous academics, who viewed the amendment with misgiving. A month later, the Court stopped short of closing the AKP for advocating anti-secular worldviews, imposing instead a cut on the party's funding.[222] In January 2010, the Court annulled an AKP law empowering civilians to prosecute members of the armed forces for crimes not military in nature.[223] Turkey's high transaction

1971 defected to the left and became an advocate for ethnic (Kurdish) and religious (Alevi) minorities.")

[215] Ríos-Figueroa, *supra* note 28, at 189–91.

[216] Belge, *supra* note 192, at 657.

[217] Dicle Kogacioglu, *Progress, Unity, and Democracy: Dissolving Political Parties in Turkey*, 38 (3) Law & Soc'y Rev. 433, 434 (2004); *see* Decision 1989/12 (T.C.A.Y.M.); Decision 1994/2 (T.C.A.Y.M.); Decision 1998/1 (T.C.A.Y.M.).

[218] *See* Decision 1989/1 (T.C.A.Y.M.).

[219] *See* Decision 1996/15 (T.C.A.Y.M.); Decision 1996/34 (T.C.A.Y.M.).

[220] Hirschl, *supra* note 39, at 156.

[221] *Id.* at 158.

[222] *Id.* at 156.

[223] *See* Decision 2009/52 (T.C.A.Y.M.).

cost polity is what allowed the Constitutional Court to defy AKP preferences so boldly. The military, the Republican People's Party in Parliament, and students and the laicist university establishment cleared for the Court sufficient maneuvering room to overturn some of the AKP's major policies.[224] The inability of successive Turkish governments, including the AKP's, to command an enabling parliamentary supermajority also circumscribed the potential to amend the Constitution to directly reverse constitutional judgments, unlike their counterpart in Singapore.

After 2010, the AKP undertook the process of reducing the political transaction costs of the Turkish polity, and moved simultaneously to diminish the influence of the Court on politics through constitutional review. In September of that year the AKP won, by a 58 percent landslide, a pivotal referendum to amend the Constitution to redefine the numbers, term limits, selection procedures and eligibility criteria of Constitutional Court judges and to reshuffle the personnel of the Court and of the Supreme Council of Judges and Prosecutors, albeit that this drew criticism for court packing.[225] The number of judges on the Court was increased from eleven to seventeen, presuming to dilute the influence of the activist group.[226] In line with the theory's predictions, as political transaction costs fell, judicial boldness declined in tandem. The new Court has taken a far more restrained approach to constitutional review, occasionally even rubberstamping controversial AKP policies,[227] such as the law mandating Sunni Islamic instruction in secondary school curricula.[228] From time to time, the Court does reclaim its Kemalist stance, as in its decisions quashing the regime's bans on Twitter and YouTube,[229] and acquitting journalists Can Dündar and Erdem Gül, both of whom drew severe criticism from AKP leader Recep Tayyip Erdoğan.[230] The tensions between the AKP regime and the military erupted violently on July 15, 2016, when a coup d'état, implemented by a faction of the armed

224 Belge, *supra* note 192, at 686.

225 Bertil Emrah Oder, *Populism and the Turkish Constitutional Court. the Game Broker, the Populist and the Popular,* I-CONNECT: BLOG OF THE INTERNATIONAL JOURNAL OF CONSTITUTIONAL LAW, May 2, 2017, www.iconnectblog.com/2017/04/populism-and-the-turkish-constitutional-court-the-game-broker-the-populist-and-the-popular/

226 DAVID L. PHILLIPS, AN UNCERTAIN ALLY: TURKEY UNDER ERDOGAN'S DICTATORSHIP 26 (2017).

227 *See* Decision 2012/65 (T.C.A.Y.M.); Decision 2012/128 (T.C.A.Y.M.).

228 Oder, *supra* note 225.

229 *See* Decision 2014/3986 (T.C.A.Y.M.); Decision 2014/4705 (T.C.A.Y.M.); Decision 2014/256 (T.C.A.Y.M.); Decision 2013/2187 (T.C.A.Y.M.); Decision 2013/2552 (T.C.A.Y.M.); Decision 2015/18567 (T.C.A.Y.M.); Decision 2013/7800 (T.C.A.Y.M.); Decision 2014/912 (T.C.A.Y.M.).

230 *See* Decision 2015/18567 (T.C.A.Y.M.).

forces styling itself the "Peace at Home Council," was attempted on President Erdoğan, and did gain temporary control of Ankara, Istanbul, and elsewhere.[231] Within a week, the AKP Government declared a state of emergency for three months, prolonged for three more months with parliamentary approval. The AKP seized the opportunity of the abortive coup to deal a fatal blow to ideologues and dissidents within the regime, the military, and the intellectual establishment such that Turley's political transaction costs were lowered virtually to rock bottom. The emergency government decreed the closing of scores of American-based cleric Fethullah Gulen-linked schools, hospitals, foundations, associations, confederations, newspapers and television and radio stations, for supporting that alleged mastermind of the coup; as well as the outright dismissal of tens of thousands of public employees, including judges and prosecutors, without any evidentiary basis. Detention without access to a court for up to thirty days was authorized, and the passports of persons under investigation or prosecution were automatically cancelled without court order.[232]

The successful purge of Kemalist sympathizers at all levels of government means that the AKP can flout Kemalist principles without fear of retaliation by the armed forces. The AKP lost no time in flexing its political muscles against the Court. Among the 113 judges who were arrested were two justices of the Constitutional Court.[233] What empowered the regime so much was the steep fall in transaction costs. Threats to undo unacceptable judicial action were now credible. In August 2016, in a unanimous decision, the Court removed the two justices on the ground that they were linked to terrorism. They were replaced by Erdoğan appointees. In October and November 2016, the Court, again unanimously, rejected applications by the Republican People's Party claiming the unconstitutionality of four of the emergency decrees promulgated after the failed coup.[234] In its judgments the Court largely abdicated its

[231] Marc de Werd, Mercan v. Turkey: *ECtHR rejects first case of Turkish judge after attempted coup d'état of 15 July 2016*, European Courts: Case Law from the European Court of Human Rights and the Court of Justice of the European Union, Nov. 18, 2016, http://europeancourts.blogspot.hk/2016/11/ecthr-rejects-first-case-of-turkish.html

[232] Selin Esen, *Judicial Control of Decree–Laws in Emergency Regimes – A Self-Destruction Attempt by Turkish Constitutional Court?*, Blog of the IACL, Dec. 19, 2016, https://iacl-aidc-blog.org/2016/12/19/judicial-control-of-the-decree-laws-in-emergency-regimes-a-self-destruction-attempt-by-the-turkish-constitutional-court/

[233] Reuters Staff, *Two Members of Turkey's Constitutional Court Arrested: NTV*, Reuters, Jul. 21, 2016, www.reuters.com/article/us-turkey-security-judges-arrest-idUSKCN1002HW

[234] Ali Acar, *The Hamartia of the Constitutional Court of Turkey: Part II*, I-Connect: Blog of the International Journal of Constitutional Law, Apr. 4, 2017, www.iconnectblog.com/2017/04/the-hamartia-of-the-constitutional-court-of-turkey-part-ii/; *see*

competence to scrutinize emergency decrees in the future, in favor of virtually limitless presidential discretion in times of emergency.[235] The AKP's bid to consolidate its power further was boosted by the 2017 constitutional referendum in which 51.4 percent of the electorate voted for a package of amendments that will substantially curb Parliament's power, and lift checks and balances by concentrating in .the hands of the President as head of state and government executive power previously divided between the Prime Minister and the Council of Ministers.[236] The transaction cost theory of hybrid constitutionalism predicts that, given the transition of Turkey from a high to a low transaction cost polity under Erdoğan, the Constitutional Court will predictably continue to retreat into the background and cease to play the high-energy role that it once played.

CONCLUSION

This chapter has exposed not only the risks entailed when hybrid regimes cede competences and resources to constitutional courts that may behave defiantly or incompetently, but also the importance, in managing the dilemma, of the range of constitutional and subconstitutional steps that regimes may take to rein in courts, so that the latter can sustain a framework of constitutionalism in the polity without undermining state security as the regime perceives it. Hybrid regimes are not monolithic entities and do not always act decisively and with ease. The formal unity of executive and legislative competences, and the absence of intense electoral contention, do not always allow these regimes to act more decisively every time than divided governments in refuting defiant courts. This finding ought fundamentally to affect the way in which we study constitutional review in nonliberal democratic polities. Weighing up the decisional and informational costs incurred by regimes in overturning constitutional judgments or curbing judicial power should yield more insights

Decision 2016/159 (T.C.A.Y.M.); Decision 2016/160 (T.C.A.Y.M.); Decision 2016/164 (T.C.A.Y.M.); Decision 2016/165 (T.C.A.Y.M.).

235 Maria Haimerl, *The Turkish Constitutional Court under the Amended Turkish Constitution*, VerfBlog, Jan. 27, 2017, http://verfassungsblog.de/the-turkish-constitutional-court-under-the-amended-turkish-constitution/

236 Selin Esen, *Analysis: The 2017 Constitutional Reforms in Turkey: Removal of Parliamentarism or Democracy?*, Blog of the IACL, AIDC, Mar. 14, 2017, https://iacl-aidc-blog.org/2017/03/14/analysis-the-2017-constitutional-reforms-in-turkey-removal-of-parliamentarism-or-democracy/; Kemal Kirişci, *Referendum Results Risk Further Polarization in Turkey*, Order From Chaos: Foreign Policy in a Troubled World – A How-to Guide for Managing the End of the Post-Cold War Era, Apr. 17, 2017, www.brookings.edu/blog/order-from-chaos/2017/04/17/referendum-results-risk-further-polarization-in-turkey/

than obsessing on the effects of formal separation of powers or the existence and number of veto points.

Hybrid regimes across the world are trammeled by the delicate balancing act of saving the substance of authoritarianism while exploiting the ostentations of liberal democracy – an act that never ceases and often necessitates toleration of factionalism within the regime and opposition without. Indeed, the size of the political transaction costs can be gauged only by studying more than formal institutional indicators such as whether the ruling party enjoys a legislative supermajority, to bring a phenomenon like the regime's ideological coherence into the picture, or the incentives for opportunism by insiders to the polity. The transaction cost theory of hybrid constitutionalism refines the predictions of the strategic model to arrive at the conclusion that, regardless of unified government or the absence of electoral competition, higher political transaction costs for regimes, in terms of factionalism and external pressures, yield lower defiance costs for constitutional courts, allowing them to pursue judicial review more aggressively, and vice versa. A regime encumbered by political fragmentation incurs high transaction costs, and is liable to be indecisive as to whether and how to react to controversial judicial acts. In short, the higher the regime's political transaction costs, the lower its ability credibly to threaten consequences for judicial opportunism, hence the lower the cost of judicial opportunism. By observing changes in the regimes' transaction cost calculus, one can reliably predict corresponding changes to constitutional jurisprudence.

This chapter has adduced evidence from constitutional review in Singapore and Turkey – two "most different" cases. In the following chapters, evidence from the Chinese Special Administrative Regions of Hong Kong and Macau will be studied, to corroborate the theory further. Singapore has been a low transaction cost polity since its founding, and the Court of Appeal has consistently upheld the constitutionality of Acts of Singapore's Parliament in its exercise of low-energy constitutional review. Given the strong likelihood of the continuance of the People's Action Party status quo into the foreseeable future, one should be cautious about suggesting that the Court will alter its approach to constitutional adjudication in the same time frame. By contrast, Turkey started out as a high transaction cost polity due to the fragmentation of the elites controlling the civilian and military parts of the political executive between Kemalist and Islamist factions, making it possible for the largely pro-Kemalist Constitutional Court to invalidate anti-Kemalist laws and government measures from time to time. The great success enjoyed by Erdoğan's government in incrementally reducing political transaction costs after 2010 has upset this equilibrium, as translated into low-energy constitutional review.

If this trend continues, the Court will someday no longer be a consequential institution in the Turkish polity. That the theory can explain the divergent constitutional review trajectories of Singapore and Turkey, despite their vast differences, supports the argument that fluctuations in political transaction costs, rather than factors such as legal tradition, are the key determinant of the consequentialness of constitutional review in hybrid regimes.

Last but not least, the theory recasts the debate over why high-energy constitutional review appears more prevalent in liberal democracies than in either hybrids or other nondemocracies. Constitutional review is likelier to flourish where the bargaining between parties and factions, even after taking into account the reactions of diverse interest groups and the electorate, imposes higher political transaction costs on any decision to sanction judicial assertiveness. Such a polity is often liberal democratic, but this is not universally so. No reason exists to presume hybrid regimes to be universally immune to the repercussions of political transaction costs and imperfect information.

3

Hybrid by Constitutional Design

INTRODUCTION

Constitutions[1] in the universe of authoritarianism are far from meaningless: at various times, in various places, they have empowered incumbents to coordinate their factions, regulate bureaucratic agents, promote investment, and reward their cronies.[2] In particular, hybrid regimes have not always relegated their constitutional documents to mere façades;[3] these regimes are known to be more respectful of formal laws and regulations than closed autocracies, and more willing to implement policies through constitutionally established institutions.[4] Constitutions in hybrid regimes can indeed significantly shape

[1] ZACHARY ELKINS ET AL., THE ENDURANCE OF NATIONAL CONSTITUTIONS 49 (2009) ("Constitutions consist of those documents that either: (1) are identified explicitly as the Constitution, Fundamental Law, or Basic Law of a country; OR (2) contain explicit provisions that establish the documents as highest law, either through entrenchment or limits on future law; OR (3) define the basic pattern of authority by establishing or suspending on executive or legislative branch of government.") Vikas Kumar, *Negotiating Constitutions for Political Unions*, 31 INT'L REV. L. & ECON. 58, 58 (2011) ("A constitution helps conflicting interests within a state to commit to a scheme for distribution of power, which is underwritten by the actual distribution of the means to power. A constitution can be treated as a convention, a self-enforcing arrangement under which everyone is better-off by conforming as long as all others do so. Once the underlying distribution of the means to power changes some players will be better-off by deviating from the behavior prescribed by the convention and others will be obliged to follow the lead.")

[2] Michael Albertus & Victor Menaldo, *The Political Economy of Autocratic Constitutions*, *in* CONSTITUTIONS IN AUTHORITARIAN REGIMES 53, 53 (Tom Ginsburg & Alberto Simpser eds., 2014); Tom Ginsburg & Alberto Simpser, *Introduction: Constitutions in Authoritarian Regimes*, *in* CONSTITUTIONS IN AUTHORITARIAN REGIMES 1, 2 (Tom Ginsburg & Alberto Simpser eds., 2014); Henry E. Hale, *The Informal Politics of Formal Constitutions: Rethinking the Effects of "Presidentialism" and "Parliamentarism" in the Cases of Kyrgyzstan, Moldova, and Ukraine*, *in* CONSTITUTIONS IN AUTHORITARIAN REGIMES 218, 220 (Tom Ginsburg & Alberto Simpser eds., 2014).

[3] Zachary Elkins et al., *The Content of Authoritarian Constitutions*, *in* CONSTITUTIONS IN AUTHORITARIAN REGIMES 141, 142 (Tom Ginsburg & Alberto Simpser eds., 2014).

[4] MARINA OTTAWAY, DEMOCRACY CHALLENGED: THE RISE OF SEMI-AUTHORITARIANISM 155 (2003).

political actors' expectations about how everyday politics will be organized, the occasionally casual violation of formalities notwithstanding.[5] The efforts for political actors to assess the net risks of reaching and implementing political bargains and of acting on that, informed by constitutional provisions, are, by nature, transaction costs.[6] It can thus be said that constitutions in hybrid regimes can substantially influence the volume of political transaction costs to the polity in the aggregate,[7] as in liberal democratic regimes.[8]

This chapter studies the Basic Law of the Hong Kong Special Administrative Region (SAR)[9] and the Lei Básica of the Macau SAR[10] from a strategic perspective, with special attention to how these two documents structure interdependency between core political actors such as the regime and the apex court. It is organized as follows. The second section reviews the constitutional development of British Hong Kong and Portuguese Macau, from their colonial beginnings all through the conclusion of the Sino–British Joint Declaration in 1984 and the Sino–Portuguese Joint Declaration in 1987, on to the enactment of the Basic Law and the Lei Básica in 1990 and 1993, respectively. The third section sheds light on the oft-overlooked authoritarian characters of the Basic Law and the Lei Básica, both of which establish an undoubtedly hybrid regime in each Region, in the sense that features minimal electoral competition and interbranch scrimmage; a Chief Executive selected by an elite corporatist[11] electoral college, ring-fenced by an appointed

[5] HENRY E. HALE, PATRONAL POLITICS: EURASIAN REGIME DYNAMICS IN COMPARATIVE PERSPECTIVE 77 (2015).

[6] CHARLOTTE A. TWIGHT, DEPENDENT ON D.C.: THE RISE OF FEDERAL CONTROL OVER THE LIVES OF ORDINARY AMERICANS 19–20 (2002).

[7] Gonzalo Caballero & David Soto Oñate, *Why Transaction Costs Are so Relevant in Political Governance? A New Institutional Survey*, 36(2) BRAZILIAN J. POL. ECON. 330, 336 (2016).

[8] David A. Lake, *Hobbesian Hierarchy: The Political Economy of Political Organization*, 12 ANNU. REV. POLIT. SCI. 263, 267 (2009); ROBERT D. COOTER, THE STRATEGIC CONSTITUTION 53 (2000); *see* Jonathan R. Macey, *Transaction Costs and the Normative Elements of the Public Choice Model: An Application to Constitutional Theory*, 74(2) VA. L. REV. 471 (1988).

[9] Basic Law of the Hong Kong Special Administrative Region of the People's Republic of China (adopted at the Third Session of the Seventh National People's Congress on Apr. 4, 1990, effective on Jul. 1, 1997) [hereinafter "Basic Law"].

[10] Lei Básica da Região Administrativa Especial de Macau da República Popular da China (Basic Law of the Macao Special Administrative Region of the People's Republic of China) (adopted by the First Session of the Eighth National People's Congress on Mar. 31, 1993, effective Dec. 20, 1999) [hereinafter "Lei Básica"].

[11] Antonio Costa Pinto, *Corporatism and "Organic Representation" in European Dictatorships*, *in* CORPORATISM AND FASCISM: THE CORPORATIST WAVE IN EUROPE 3, 5 (Antonio Costa Pinto ed., 2017) ("*Political corporatism* can be defined as a system of political representation based on an 'organic-statist' view of society in which its organic units (families, local powers, professional associations and interest organizations and institutions) replace the individual-

Executive Council whose advice he can ignore; and a half-elected, semi-corporatist legislature whose bills he may refuse to sign.[12] The constitutions of the SARs thus guarantee "unified government" – control of the executive and legislature by the same political grouping, known in each Region as the "Establishment Coalition." The same section also argues that these subnational regimes were not predestined to evolve into liberal democracies, but programmed from the outset to persist as hybrid regimes for as long as the Chinese Communist Party is in power on the mainland.[13] Constitutional design is a critical factor influencing how judges act even in autocracies, let alone hybrids.[14] This concern brings us to the fourth section, which examines the webs of constraint wherein the framers of the two constitutions intended to entangle the jurisdictions of the Hong Kong Court of Final Appeal (CFA) and the Tribunal de Última Instância de Macau (TUI). The last section concludes.

HISTORICAL CONTEXT

British Hong Kong

Amid the First Anglo–Chinese War (1839–1842), the British Empire established what was to become Hong Kong on one of the over 260 islands lying off the coast of China bordering the north end of the South China Sea, which nominally belonged to the Cantonese County of Bao'an.[15] The British troops arriving in 1841 found the then-nameless island sparsely populated by some 5,000 fishermen and villagers, who organized their social life by custom.[16] In 1842, by the Treaty of Nanking the Daoguang Emperor ceded to the British Crown in perpetuity what was already known by then as Hong Kong, literally meaning "Fragrant Harbour"; a name chosen by the British for the entire island after one of its twenty settlements. Queen Victoria made the island

centred electoral model of representation and parliamentary legitimacy, becoming the primary and/or complementary legislative or advisory body of the ruler's executive.")

12 Steve Tsang, A Modern History of Hong Kong 18 (2007).

13 The Basic Law might seem to be facilitating the eventual establishment of a subnational liberal democracy in Hong Kong; but on closer inspection, it reads more like a roadmap for Beijing on how to veto democratization proposals at will. Michael C. Davis, *The Basic Law and Democratization in Hong Kong*, 3 Loy. U. Chi. Int'l L. Rev. 165, 178 (2006).

14 Xin He, *Black Hole of Responsibility: The Adjudication Committee's Role in a Chinese Court*, 47(4) Law & Soc'y Rev. 681, 681 (2009).

15 Eric C. Ip, Law and Justice in Hong Kong 27 (2d ed. 2016).

16 *See* Dennis Duncanson, *Hong Kong as a Crown Colony*, *in* Hong Kong: A Chinese and International Concern 9 (Jürgen Domes & Yu-ming Shaw eds., 1988).

a Crown Colony in 1843, the capital of which, the City of Victoria, was then named in her honor. It was to be administered as a commercial, diplomatic, and military outpost rather than as a foothold for the territorial expansion of the British Empire.[17] At the conclusion of the Second Opium War (1856–60), Kowloon Peninsula and Stonecutters Island to the north of Hong Kong were, by the First Convention of Peking of October 1860, ceded to the British Crown in perpetuity by the Xianfeng Emperor. And in June 1898, London persuaded Peking to lease it the entire landmass and its surrounding islands to the south of the Sham Chun River – an area roughly twelve times the size of the original Colony – for a term of 99 years, an agreement known as the Second Convention of Peking. In 1899, the British Army took over the newly leased territories after putting down a local rebellion in six days.[18]

The Letters Patent was the canonical document that served as British Hong Kong's constitution. The Crown in Council, as advised by Her Majesty's Government in Whitehall, had plenary and exclusive power to amend the Letters Patent, leaving local inhabitants, including the white expatriate community, no constitutional choice in the formal sense.[19] The Letters Patent constituted the Governor of Hong Kong the titular commander-in-chief and chief executive,[20] and an Executive Council to advise him,[21] whose members were to hold office at the Crown's pleasure.[22] Together they were competent "by and with the advice and consent of the Legislative Council" to "make laws for the peace, order, and good government of the Colony."[23] The local community, even influential business interest groups, had little say in the selection of the Governor, which took place behind closed doors in Whitehall.[24] The Letters Patent never purported to exhaustively

[17] John M. Carroll, Concise History of Hong Kong 12 (2007).

[18] Patrick H. Hase, The Six-Day War of 1899: Hong Kong in the Age of Imperialism 14–16 (2008).

[19] Carroll, *supra* note 17, at 46.

[20] Hong Kong Letters Patent [hereinafter "Letters Patent"], art. II.

[21] The Executive Council was not a proper Cabinet, but a "sounding board" for policies that mostly originated in the bureaucracy and modified by suggestions from advisory committees drawn from local business and social elites. Ian Scott, Public Administration in Hong Kong: Regime Change and its Impact on the Public Sector 33 (2005).

[22] Letters Patent, art. V.

[23] Letters Patent, art. VII.

[24] That said, a new Governor coming to Hong Kong with virtually no staff of his own and no experience of the local economy, educational affairs, housing policy, transport situation, and public opinion, could not have acquitted himself before Whitehall without the advice of the Official Members of the Executive and Legislative Councils, let alone act as a ruthless autocrat. John P. Burns, *Administrative Reform in Hong Kong: An Institutional Analysis of Food Safety*, 17 Research in Pub. Pol'y Analysis & Management 21, 24 (2008).

codify the constitutional framework, following the British tradition of unwritten constitutionalism. Multiple other sources were to be brought to bear from time to time,[25] from first principles of common law like the rule of law and judicial independence;[26] to prerogative power and imperial legislation like the Royal Instructions and the Colonial Laws Validity Act 1865, respectively. Unwritten conventions governed most important political practices;[27] in particular, Whitehall's entrenched deference to the Crown Colony government's judgment of how best to administer the territory. No bill enacted by the Governor and Legislative Council unanimous was disallowed by London after 1913.[28] Imperial Orders in Council and Acts of Parliament affecting Hong Kong were often drafted in the City of Victoria and merely rubber-stamped in the City of Westminster.[29] In 1958, the territory was given independence from the United Kingdom in finance and taxation.[30] In tandem with British commercial interests there, Crown Colony officials morphed into "champions of Hong Kong for its own sake" before Whitehall.[31] Its constitution was undoubtedly non-democratic, yet colonial authoritarianism in Hong Kong qualitatively differed from totalitarianism, in that the state and its societal penetration were minimal.[32] The constitutional conventions of civil service neutrality and the entrenched social and governmental commitment to the principles of positive non-interventionism resulted in benign laws and policies benignly applied to uphold practical liberty and a free and competitive market.[33]

The Letters Patent and the legal context in which they arose afforded a latitude that allowed a distinctive, low transaction cost political order to

25 J.F. Matthews, *The Legal System of the Hong Kong Special Administrative Region*, 18 U. PA. J. INT'L L. 3, 11 (1997).

26 Christopher Munn, *The Rule of Law and Criminal Justice in the Nineteenth Century*, *in* JUDICIAL INDEPENDENCE AND THE RULE OF LAW IN HONG KONG 19, 20 (Steve Tsang ed., 2001).

27 YASH GHAI, HONG KONG'S NEW CONSTITUTIONAL ORDER: THE RESUMPTION OF CHINESE SOVEREIGNTY AND THE BASIC LAW 16 (2d ed. 1999).

28 Norman J. Miners, *Constitution and Administration*, *in* THE OTHER HONG KONG REPORT 1, 8 (Joseph Y.S. Cheng ed., 1990).

29 *See* Peter Wesley-Smith, *The Present Constitution of Hong Kong*, *in* THE BASIC LAW AND HONG KONG'S FUTURE 5 (Peter Wesley-Smith & Albert Chen eds., 1988).

30 Shu-hung Tang, *The Hong Kong Fiscal Policy: Continuity or Redirection?*, *in* POLITICAL ORDER AND POWER TRANSITION IN HONG KONG 189 (Pang-kwong Li ed., 1997).

31 Duncanson, *supra* note 16, at 11.

32 Wai Fung Lam & Kwan Nok Chan, *How Authoritarianism Intensifies Punctuated Equilibrium: The Dynamics of Policy Attention in Hong Kong*, 28(4) GOVERNANCE: AN INT'L J. POL'Y ADMIN. & INSTITUTIONS 549, 567 (2015).

33 Michael E. Degolyer, *The Civil Service*, *in* THE OTHER HONG KONG REPORT 73, 113 (Joseph Y.S. Cheng ed., 1990).

emerge early on. Between 1843 and 1976, a simulacrum of the Westminster model saw formally impartial, unelected, generalist civil servants known as "Administrative Officers,"[34] who staffed all ministerial offices, constitute the Legislative Council majority as "Official Members."[35] In other words, subject to the direction of the Governor, bureaucrats monopolized almost all political power in the Crown Colony "from policy making to policy execution, and from law making to law enforcement."[36] Unofficial Members of the Legislative Council were handpicked by the Governor, through an informal corporatist system,[37] from among leaders of major business houses such as HSBC or Jardines, the General Chamber of Commerce, and major Chinese-run companies. The coopted business and professional elites owed their political positions to the Governor rather than to bottom-up support from real constituents, whereas the non-partisan government never depended for its survival or the enactment of legislation on the Unofficial Members' support in the Legislative Council or on the myriad advisory committees. It follows that the contribution of such "constituents" to the drafting of legislation by the Government Secretariat was at most "informal."[38]

Societal resistance to government decisions was minimal in light of the fact that the vast majority of residents settled by choice in Hong Kong, and volunteered for its economic, political, and social traditions.[39] The Cultural Revolution in China did spill over into Maoist riots in 1967, but society had formed a consensus that the continuation of British overlordship was preferable to a takeover on any terms by the People's Republic, whence most had fled for fear of Communism.[40] By the 1970s, residents had come to embrace a hybrid culture all their own: economic liberty and the rule of law, coupled with Confucian moral and educational values.[41] The dominant popular view was that mass democracy added little value to, and might actually break the spell of a minimal government confined to the mere provision of order and

34 John Burns et al., *Changing Governance Structures and the Evolution of Public Services Bargains in Hong Kong*, 79(1) Int'l Rev. Admin. Sci. 135, 136 (2012).

35 Carroll, *supra* note 17, at 199.

36 Kathleen Cheek-Milby, *The Changing Political Role of the Hong Kong Civil Servant*, 62(2) Pac. Aff. 219, 221 (1989).

37 Ngok Ma, *The Making of a Corporatist State in Hong Kong: The Road to Sectoral Intervention*, 46(2) J. Contemp. Asia 247, 250 (2016).

38 Denis Bray, Hong Kong Metamorphosis 236 (2001).

39 Ghai, *supra* note 27, at 21.

40 Albert H.Y. Chen, *A Tale of Two Islands: Comparative Reflections on Constitutionalism in Hong Kong and Taiwan*, 37(2) Hong Kong L. J. 647, 658 (2007).

41 Kin Ming Kwong & Hong Yu, *Identity Politics*, *in* Hong Kong under Chinese Rule Economic Integration and Political Gridlock 125, 129 (Yongnian Zheng & Chiew Ping Yew eds., 2013).

infrastructure.[42] Throughout British rule, little enthusiasm about democracy ever emerged among residents, who at the end embraced democratization mostly as a firewall against interference with their freedoms from the Chinese mainland.[43]

The British Commonwealth policy in the aftermath of the Second World War was to empower the colonies to achieve at least representative self-government if not full independence. Decolonization and democratization occurred in every corner of the Empire just about, ranging from India to Singapore to the Falkland Islands, except Hong Kong. Without significant natural resources or residents of British descent, difficult to defend militarily, financially independent of Whitehall, and industrialized but recently,[44] few pragmatic motives justified omitting the same decolonization agenda.[45] By process of elimination, the single factor excepting the territory from the rest of the British Empire the most was the vicinity of Communist China,[46] and its categorical intolerance, backed up by a credible military threat, of an independent, democratic Hong Kong. In 1972, having replaced the Republic of China on Taiwan as China's international personhood in the United Nations, the People's Republic wasted no time in persuading that organization to remove Hong Kong and Macau from the list of non-self-governing territories awaiting self-determination under the Chapter XI of the United Nations Charter. Throughout the evolution, neither Beijing nor the United Nations consulted the people of either territory on anything.[47] The recent history of European colonialism, Japanese aggression, and Chinese civil war, still fresh in the mind, together with the ideological retreat of Maoism, had turned the People's Republic toward obsessive nationalism as a source of unity and self-esteem.[48] In September 1981, Ye Jianying, Chairman of the Standing Committee of the National People's Congress, proposed that Nationalist-ruled Taiwan be declared a "Special Administrative Region" of Communist China. Expectedly, Taipei's staunchly anti-Communist rulers, who had retained American political support, showed no interest in reunification on

42 Siu-kai Lau & Hsin-chi Kuan, The Ethos of the Hong Kong Chinese 150 (1988).
43 Andrew Scobell, *Hong Kong's Influence on China: The Tail That Wags the Dog?*, 28(6) Asian Surv. 599, 604 (1988).
44 Charles Hauss & Melissa Haussman, Comparative Politics: Domestic Responses to Global Challenges 311 (8th ed. 2013).
45 Ip, *supra* note 15, at 48.
46 Tang, *supra* note 30, at 317.
47 Yash Ghai, *Hong Kong's Autonomy: Dialects of Powers and Institutions*, *in* Practising Self-Government: A Comparative Study if Autonomous Regions 315, 320 (2013); James Crawford, The Creation of States in International Law 249 (2d ed. 2006).
48 Christopher R. Hughes, Chinese Nationalism in the Global Era 15 (2006).

terms proposed by Beijing.[49] In June 1982, Deng Xiaoping publicly claimed Chinese sovereignty over Hong Kong and Macau, declaring that these territories would be reintegrated into China within a few years under the rubric of "One Country, Two Systems," which was designed to prevent political dynamics within the mainland from affecting the capitalist systems in the two former occupied territories.[50] In December of that year, the National People's Congress adopted a new Constitution for China, Article 31 of which provided that, "The State shall establish Special Administrative Regions when necessary. The systems to be instituted in Special Administrative Regions shall be prescribed by law enacted by the National People's Congress in the light of the specific conditions."[51]

Emboldened by the UK's costly victory in the Falklands in 1982, China made it abundantly clear that London had little option but to acquiesce, and, moreover, exacted the status of Hong Kong to be a decision strictly between the two sovereign states, the international negotiation of which, impending directly upon their future, the citizenry of Hong Kong were to be shut out of. It was a grim irony that Beijing should arrogate to itself representation of the interests of Hong Kong residents, many of whom had fled there out of fear and loathing of Communism.[52] After much negotiation back and forth – without submitting it to a local referendum – Britain finally agreed to transfer Hong Kong to Chinese sovereignty on July 1, 1997 under the terms and conditions set forth in the Sino–British Joint Declaration of 1984, a United Nations (UN)-registered treaty that obligated China to enact a Basic Law constitutionalizing the twin principles of "One Country, Two Systems" and "Hong Kong People Rule Hong Kong," so as to build confidence in the future SAR's high degree of autonomy.[53]

Considered an unjust fait accompli by not a few,[54] the Joint Declaration nevertheless established a Hong Kong SAR under Chinese sovereignty,

49 Richard C. Bush, Hong Kong in the Shadow of China: Living with the Leviathan 225 (2016).

50 Kaicheong Fok, *The Existence of Macau: A Chinese Perspective*, *in* Macau on the Threshold of the Third Millennium 13, 21 (Macau Ricci Institute ed., 2001).

51 William Partlett & Eric C. Ip, *Is Socialist Law Really Dead?*, 48 N.Y.U. J. Int'l L. & Pol. 463, 485 (2016) ("The 1982 Constitution of the People's Republic of China – which is still in place today – has clear roots in the Russo-Leninist ideas of the Soviet model.")

52 Kwong & Yu, *supra* note 41, at 129.

53 Michael C. Davis, *Interpreting Constitutionalism and Democratization in Hong Kong*, *in* Interpreting Hong Kong's Basic Law: The Struggle for Coherence 77, 78 (Hualing Fu et al. eds., 2007).

54 Ian Scott, *"One Country, Two Systems": The End of a Legitimating Ideology?*, 39(2) Asia Pac. J. Pub. Admin. 83, 89 (2017).

comprising Hong Kong Island, Kowloon, and the New Territories,[55] which was to enjoy "a high degree of autonomy, except in foreign and defence affairs,"[56] and, "vested with executive, legislative and independent judicial power, including that of final adjudication,"[57] would be headed by a locally sourced but Beijing-appointed Chief Executive,[58] at the head of a government "composed of local inhabitants,"[59] the Principal Officials of which the Chief Executive would nominate for appointment by the State Council of the People's Republic.[60] The Region would conserve its own "social and economic systems,"[61] and the "laws currently in force,"[62] especially those protecting "[p]rivate property, ownership of enterprises, the legitimate right of inheritance, and foreign investment."[63] These terms would protect the pre-existing "life-style" of Hong Kong[64] and its rights and freedoms "of the person, of speech, of the press, of assembly, of association, of travel, of movement, of correspondence, of strike, of choice of occupation, of academic research and of religious belief [which] will be ensured by law in the Hong Kong Special Administrative Region."[65] The SAR would retain a free port,[66] status as an international financial center,[67] public security,[68] customs,[69] financial[70] and taxation systems[71] separate from those of mainland China. It would even have external relations competences to "maintain and develop economic and cultural relations and conclude relevant agreements with states, regions and relevant international organisations,"[72] "establish mutually beneficial economic relations with the United Kingdom and other countries,"[73] and "issue

[55] Joint Declaration of the Government of the United Kingdom of Great Britain and Northern Ireland and the Government of the People's Republic of China on the Question of Hong Kong, 26 Sept. 1984 [hereinafter "Sino–British Joint Declaration"], art. 1.
[56] Sino–British Joint Declaration, art. 3(1) & art. 3(2)
[57] Sino–British Joint Declaration, art. 3(3).
[58] Sino–British Joint Declaration, art. 3(4).
[59] Sino–British Joint Declaration, art. 3(4).
[60] Sino–British Joint Declaration, art. 3(4).
[61] Sino–British Joint Declaration, art. 3(5).
[62] Sino–British Joint Declaration, art. 3(3).
[63] Sino–British Joint Declaration, art. 3(5).
[64] Sino–British Joint Declaration, art. 3(5).
[65] Sino–British Joint Declaration, art. 3(5).
[66] Sino–British Joint Declaration, art. 3(6).
[67] Sino–British Joint Declaration, art. 3(7).
[68] Sino–British Joint Declaration, art. 3(11).
[69] Sino–British Joint Declaration, art. 3(6).
[70] Sino–British Joint Declaration, art. 3(7).
[71] Sino–British Joint Declaration, art. 3(8).
[72] Sino–British Joint Declaration, art. 3(10).
[73] Sino–British Joint Declaration, art. 3(9).

its own passports."[74] All of the above, known as "basic policies of the People's Republic of China regarding Hong Kong," would be codified into a "Basic Law of the Hong Kong Special Administrative Region of the People's Republic of China" and "remain unchanged for 50 years."[75] Through the Joint Declaration, China committed itself to recreating a Chinese version of the British Hong Kong constitution as it had stood in the 1980s.[76] It was a pragmatic choice, as the principles of China's legal system are fundamentally at odds with those of Hong Kong in almost every conceivable respect.[77]

Portuguese Macau

In 1513, at the height of the Age of Discovery, the Portuguese explorer Jorge Álvares made landfall on China's coast through the Strait of Malacca, anchoring his ship in Tuen Mun, which today is the westernmost of Hong Kong's eighteen Districts. The Portuguese subsequently established fortifications there until their expulsion by the Ming Empire then ruling China, largely for their enslavement of local Chinese.[78] This was followed by a series of armed conflicts, culminating in the Ming army's defeat of the Portuguese in 1521 at the Battle of Tuen Mun and in 1522 at the Battle of Sai Tso Wan on modern-day Lantau Island, Hong Kong. The Portuguese then shifted their search for a potential port westwards, and finally in 1535 landed on a tiny peninsula known as Haojingao ("oyster mirror inlet"), administered by the Cantonese county of Xiangshan, about sixty kilometers from Hong Kong. Haojingao had only a few hundred local inhabitants.[79] It is widely believed that the first Portuguese settlers mistook the name of Ma Kok Temple, a major sanctuary honoring the sea goddess Mazu, for the entire peninsula, and named the latter "Macau."[80] As Portuguese–Ming diplomatic relations improved, Lionel de Souza, commander of the Portuguese enterprise in East Asia, managed to secure the Ming Emperor's consent to set up a trading base on Macau. Macau quickly became a prosperous *entrepôt*, which, from about the 1550s onwards, facilitated the Portuguese monopoly

74 Sino–British Joint Declaration, art. 3(10).

75 Basic Law, art. 3(12).

76 Tsang, *supra* note 12, at 19.

77 Gungwu Wang & John Wong, *After Smooth Handover, Now the Hard Part, in* Hong Kong under Chinese Rule Economic Integration and Political Gridlock 3, 13 (Yongnian Zheng & Chiew Ping Yew eds., 2013).

78 Zhidong Hao, Macau: History and Society 10–11 (2011).

79 Herbert S. Yee, Macau in Transition: From Colony to Autonomous Region xvi (2001).

80 Hao, *supra* note 78, at 12–13.

of European trade with China,[81] and became one of the most important players in the Maritime Silk Route.[82] In 1573, the Portuguese signed a land-lease with the Ming court, agreeing to pay an annual rent of 500 taels of silver for Macau, symbolically to affirm China's sovereignty over the enclave.[83][84] The closure of all coastal ports to foreign trade by the Qing Empire in 1777 reinforced Portuguese Macau in its role as middleman between East and West, until the founding of Hong Kong in 1841.[85]

In its early days, Portuguese Macau had no Governor as such,[86] but was steered by a Senado founded in 1583, a relic of the medieval Portuguese governing tradition of local autonomy, and consisting of three leading citizens, two judges, and one procurator, elected triennially by the Portuguese residents.[87] In this sense, Macau may be regarded as the first jurisdiction in all of East Asia to adopt representative democratic institutions.[88] In the seventeenth and eighteenth centuries, a military commander acted as Governor who deferred administrative matters to the Senado, and whose influence declined continually during the nineteenth century.[89] In 1849, riding the tide of the British victory over the Qing in the First Opium War, Governor João Maria Ferreira do Amara succeeded in turning Macau into a de facto Portuguese colony by expelling the Chinese Imperial customs officials[90] who had had jurisdiction over Chinese residents in Macau.[91] In 1887, the Qing ended up conceding to the Portuguese a right of "perpetual occupation" in the Protocol of Lisbon and the Sino–Portuguese Treaty of Peking, a principle that was reaffirmed in the Sino–Portuguese Treaty of Friendship and Commerce of 1928.[92] During the Second World War, Portugal's neutrality spared Macau

81 Mary-Ann Gallagher, *Macau (Macao)*, *in* COLUMBIA CHRONOLOGIES OF ASIAN HISTORY AND CULTURE 244, 245 (John Brown ed., 2000).
82 Fok, *supra* note 50, at 23.
83 HAO, *supra* note 78, at 35–37.
84 Fok, *supra* note 50, at 24.
85 VICTOR F.S. SIT ET AL., ENTREPRENEURS AND ENTERPRISES IN MACAU: A STUDY OF INDUSTRIAL DEVELOPMENT 11 (1991).
86 Dom Francisco Mascarenhas, the first Governor, was not appointed to a three-year term until 1623. C.R. BOXER, THE AFFAIR OF THE MADRE DE DEUS: A CHAPTER IN THE HISTORY OF THE PORTUGUESE IN JAPAN 27 (2010).
87 Paulo Cardinal, *Macau: Transformation of an Historic Autonomy*, *in* PRACTISING SELF-GOVERNMENT: A COMPARATIVE STUDY OF AUTONOMOUS REGIONS 383, 385 (Yash Ghai & Sophia Woodman eds., 2013).
88 YUFAN HAO ET AL., POLITICAL ECONOMY OF MACAO SINCE 1999: THE DILEMMA OF SUCCESS 160 (2017).
89 Cardinal, *supra* note 87, at 385.
90 YEE, *supra* note 79, at xvii.
91 HAO, *supra* note 78, 45.
92 Cardinal, *supra* note 87, at 385–86.

a Japanese invasion.[93] In July 1955, despite opposition from the new government of the People's Republic of China, Lisbon designated Macau an "Overseas Province," giving it a constitution *de jure* to reinforce its claims to sovereignty over the territory. Indeed, the Estado Novo, the corporatist authoritarian regime then in power in Portugal, had never recognized the People's Republic as the legitimate government of China.[94]

Lisbon's Macau policy changed considerably after the coup of April 25, 1974, later known as the Carnation Revolution, which overthrew the Estado Novo. A new Portuguese Constitution was promulgated two years later, on April 25, 1976, under which Lisbon officially relinquished its claim on Macau and reclassified it a "Chinese territory under Portuguese administration."[95] Reflecting the political climate, on February 17, 1976, Lisbon then ratified the Estatuto Orgânico de Macau (Organic Statute of Macau), the territory's new constitutional instrument, which set up an unelected Governor as the incontestable center of power and head of the Portuguese administration, representing the Portuguese state at a rank equivalent to that of a minister in the central government.[96] Served also by a Consultative Council, he governed through Under-Secretaries and had notably wide-ranging legislative powers except on matters expressly reserved to the Government of Portugal, or to the Macau Legislative Assembly.[97] The Governor was, in practice, appointed and dismissed by the President of the Portuguese Republic, after consulting with the Legislative Assembly and interest groups representing corporate interests,[98] but also frequently as a reward by the President for his political allies in Lisbon.[99]

The Legislative Assembly established by the Estatuto Orgânico consisted of but seventeen members, six popularly elected, six elected by corporatist functional constituencies, and five appointed by the Governor.[100] The direct election of one-third of the Assemblymen reflected Lisbon's decolonization policy.[101] Its semi-democratic pedigree notwithstanding, the Legislative

93 Ming K. Chan, *Different Roads to Home. The Retrocession of Hong Kong and Macau to Chinese Sovereignty*, 12(36) J. CONTEMP. CHINA 493, 498 (2003).

94 Moisés Silva Fernandes, *The Normalisation of Portuguese-Chinese Relations and Macao's Handover to Mainland China*, 1974–79, 13(1) China: An Int'l J. 3, 3 (2015).

95 SIT ET AL., *supra* note 85, at 175.

96 YEE, *supra* note 79, at 22.

97 Paulo Cardinal, *Macau: The Internationalization of an Historical Autonomy*, 122 BOLETIN: MEXICANO DE DERECHO COMPARADO 637, 645 (2008).

98 *Id.* at 644.

99 YEE, *supra* note 79, at 22.

100 *Id.* at xviii.

101 SONNY SHIU-HING LO, POLITICAL DEVELOPMENT IN MACAU 245 (1995).

Assembly was never able to function as a politically significant parliament, for three reasons.[102] First, the Governor was given competence to issue Decree Laws that had the same legal status as primary legislation enacted by the Legislative Assembly. Second, the government did not supply enough expert legal personnel to the Legislative Assembly, and only a small number of Assemblymen possessed the requisite technical skills to draft statutes.[103] Third, most Assemblymen conceived of their status more as social prestige than real political responsibility to debate public policy on behalf of a constituency.[104] The Estatuto Orgânico did not create a system of courts for Macau; the Portuguese judiciary retained jurisdiction well into the 1990s, and the judges who heard cases from Macau had been appointed in Portugal, and were separate from the Macau government.[105] The Portuguese language remained the official language in court proceedings;[106] legal practitioners, procurators, judges and other legal officials were predominantly of Portuguese descent; and a cohort of sixteen students graduated in 1994 from the first Portuguese law degree program at the University of Macau.[107]

Portugal and China reestablished diplomatic relations on February 8, 1979. Both sides agreed to Lisbon's formulation that Macau was a "Chinese territory currently under Portuguese administration," and that the future of the territory should be resolved through friendly consultations.[108] In contrast to the tribal wars, bloody riots, and guerrilla warfare that plaguing Portugal's decolonization, Macau's transition to Chinese rule was characterized by absence of conflict between pro-Beijing locals and the colonial government.[109] The Portuguese simply continued their centuries-long tradition of ruling with the consent of the Chinese, and did not hesitate to collaborate with pro-

102 Hao et al., *supra* note 88, at 166. Between 1976 and 1984, the Portuguese-appointed Governor and the local Macanese-dominated Legislative Assembly were iteratedly in tension.

103 Yee, *supra* note 79, at 23–25.

104 Arnaldo Gonçalves, *Macau's Autonomy: Looking for a Fresh Awakening?*, *in* One Country, Two Systems, Three Legal Orders – Perspectives of Evolution: Essays on Macau's Autonomy after the Resumption of Sovereignty by China 733, 737 (Jorge Oliveira & Paulo Cardinal eds., 2009).

105 Yee, *supra* note 79, at 26.

106 Bill Chou, *Local Autonomy in Action: Beijing's Hong Kong and Macau Policies*, 42(3) J. Current Chinese Aff. 29, 38 (2013).

107 Yee, *supra* note 79, at 60.

108 Ming K. Chan & Shiu-Hing Lo, The A to Z of the Hong Kong SAR and the Macao SAR 269 (2010).

109 Yee, *supra* note 79, at 153. Chief Executive Edmund Ho's new Government decisively cracked down on organized triad crime, ending a decade of routine car explosions, kidnappings, attempted assassinations, and armed assault. Ian Scott, *Social Stability and Economic Growth*, *in* Gaming, Governance and Public Policy in Macao 1, 7 (Newman M.K. Lam & Ian Scott eds., 2011).

China groups to ease local governance.[110] Pro-China elites eventually replaced Portuguese and Macanese to become the most powerful force in the Legislative Assembly.[111] Furthermore, rapid growth in the economy starting in the late 1970s and 1980s facilitated recovery of the Portuguese administration from the 1966 anti-government Maoist riots.[112] Legalized gambling, first introduced in 1847 and rebooted in 1961 when the new and energetic syndicate Sociedade de Turismo e Diversões de Macau won the gambling franchise, emerged to become Macau's staple industry by the dawn of the Sino–Portuguese entente.[113] Given Portugal's rapprochement to China after the Carnation Revolution and Macau's tiny geographical and demographical size, it seems counterintuitive that Macau's retrocession to Chinese sovereignty should occur later than Hong Kong's; however, there were fears in Beijing that if Macau were reunited to the mainland first, Hong Kong's confidence might collapse, precipitating a massive financial and human capital flight – an exodus of valuables that Beijing could not have afforded.[114] Undeniably, in spite of its anti-imperial rhetoric against "unequal treaties," Beijing had continuously abided by a pragmatic approach of tolerance in its relations with British Hong Kong and Portuguese Macau in exchange for economic advantages, on the condition that these two dependencies would not credibly threaten the internal security of the Communist regime.[115]

In May 1985, less than half a year after the Sino–British Joint Declaration, the Sino–Portuguese Joint Communiqué committed the parties to bilateral negotiations on the "Question of Macau."[116] On April 13, 1987, after eight months and four rounds of fairly collegial discussions – in contrast to the thirteen months and twenty-two rounds of bargaining that the Sino–British Joint Declaration needed – the People's Republic of China and Portugal had converged sufficiently to issue the Joint Declaration on the Question of Macau, also without the participation of the people of Macau, which mandated China to resume sovereignty over the Portuguese dependency on December 20, 1999. China was unconcerned with the historical and

110 YEE, *supra* note 79, 4.

111 Bill K.P. Chou, *Interest Group Politics in Macau after Handover*, 14(43) J. CONTEMP. CHINA 191, 193 (2005).

112 YEE, *supra* note 79, at xxi.

113 VICTOR ZHENG & PO-SAN WAN, GAMBLING DYNAMISM: THE MACAO MIRACLE 44045 (2014).

114 Yash Ghai, *The Basic Law of the Special Administrative Region of Macau: Some Reflections*, 49(1) INT'L & COMP. L. Q. 183, 183 (2000).

115 Fok, *supra* note 50, at 21.

116 CHAN & LO, *supra* note 108, 269.

political variations between Hong Kong and Macau, both of which had been "lost" to foreign imperial rule.[117] To a large extent, then, the Sino–British Joint Declaration served as a "template" for the Sino–Portuguese Joint Declaration.[118] The constitutional infrastructure of post-1999 Macau "seems almost blindly copied from the legal framework designed for Hong Kong,"[119] which had sought to conserve British Hong Kong's political way of life.[120] Paradoxically, the Macau SAR would enjoy even more autonomy after 1999 than before, especially in external relations.[121]

The Sino–Portuguese Joint Declaration,[122] repeating much of the Sino–British Joint Declaration, provides for the establishment of a Macau SAR, consisting of the Macau Peninsula, Taipa Island, and Coloane Island[123] under Chinese sovereignty,[124] to enjoy "a high degree of autonomy, except in foreign and defence affairs,"[125] and "vested with executive, legislative and independent judicial power, including that of final adjudication."[126] As with Hong Kong, not only the executive, but also the Legislative Assembly of the SAR was to be made up of local inhabitants;[127] as in Hong Kong, too, the Chief Executive was to be locally nominated by "elections or consultations," then nominate Principal Officials of the Government, all to be confirmed by the State Council's appointment.[128] Macau was to maintain "unchanged" in its pre-existing "life-style,"[129] "social and economic systems,"[130] laws, "rights and freedoms[131] [of] inhabitants and other persons,"[132] encompassing "those of the person, of speech, of the

117 Carmen Amado Mendes, Portugal, China and the Macau Negotiations 1986–1999 37 (2013).
118 *Id.* at 61.
119 Cardinal, *supra* note 87, at 408.
120 Kevin K.S. Tso, *Fundamental Political and Constitutional Norms: Hong Kong and Macau Compared*, 13(1) Australian J. Asian L. 1, 15 (2012).
121 Eric C. Ip, *Comparative Subnational Foreign Relations Law in the Chinese Special Administrative Regions*, 65 Int'l & Comp. L. Q. 953, 967 (2016).
122 Joint Declaration of the Government of the People's Republic of China and the Government of the Republic of Portugal on the Question of Macao, Apr. 13, 1987 [hereinafter "Sino–Portuguese Macao Joint Declaration"].
123 Sino–Portuguese Joint Declaration, art. 1.
124 Sino–Portuguese Joint Declaration, art. 2(1).
125 Sino–Portuguese Joint Declaration, art. 2(2).
126 Sino–Portuguese Joint Declaration, art. 2(2).
127 Sino–Portuguese Joint Declaration, art. 2(3).
128 Sino–Portuguese Joint Declaration, art. 2(3).
129 Sino–Portuguese Joint Declaration, art. 2(4).
130 Sino–Portuguese Joint Declaration, art. 2(4).
131 Sino–Portuguese Joint Declaration, art. 2(4).
132 Sino–Portuguese Joint Declaration, art. 2(4).

press, of assembly, of association, of travel and movement, of strike, of choice of occupation, of academic research, of religion and belief, of communication and the ownership of property."[133] Unlike the Sino–British Joint Declaration, the Sino–Portuguese one included a clause guaranteeing to the Region competence to "decide policies in the fields of culture, education, science and technology and protect cultural relics,"[134] and to affirm the official use of the Portuguese language as well as Chinese in the government, the Legislative Assembly, and the courts.[135] The Macau SAR was empowered to "establish mutually beneficial economic relations with Portugal and other countries";[136] "maintain and develop economic and cultural relations and in this context conclude agreements with states, regions and relevant international organizations";[137] and issue its own travel documents.[138] It conserved Macau's free port,[139] separate customs territory,[140] legal tender,[141] taxation system,[142] and public security forces,[143] separate from those of mainland China. And it was to be endowed with its own flag and emblem on top of China's.[144] All the foregoing "basic policies" were to be codified into a "Basic Law of the Macao Special Administrative Region of the People's Republic of China [and] remain unchanged for 50 years."[145] The Joint Declaration's stress on conserving Macau's Portuguese heritage reflected Lisbon's calculation that it had little to lose and much to gain by releasing Macau to become a prosperous Chinese city-state that would continue to develop ties with Portugal and the rest of the Lusophone world, and that Beijing would be willing to acquiesce in a strong Portuguese cultural presence in post-1999 Macau insofar as it posed no threat to China's sovereignty.[146]

133 Sino–Portuguese Joint Declaration, art. 2(4).
134 Sino–Portuguese Joint Declaration, art. 2(5).
135 Sino–Portuguese Joint Declaration, art. 2(5).
136 Sino–Portuguese Joint Declaration, art. 2(6).
137 Sino–Portuguese Joint Declaration, art. 2(7).
138 Sino–Portuguese Joint Declaration, art. 2(7).
139 Sino–Portuguese Joint Declaration, art. 2(8).
140 Sino–Portuguese Joint Declaration, art. 2(8).
141 Sino–Portuguese Joint Declaration, art. 2(8).
142 Sino–Portuguese Joint Declaration, art. 2(9).
143 Sino–Portuguese Joint Declaration, art. 2(10).
144 Sino–Portuguese Joint Declaration, art. 2(11).
145 Sino–Portuguese Joint Declaration, art. 2(12).
146 Richard Louis Edmonds & Herbert S. Yee, *Macau: From Portuguese Autonomous Territory to Chinese Special Administrative Region*, 160 CHINA Q. 801, 803 (1999).

THE STRATEGIC STRUCTURE OF HYBRID SUBNATIONAL CONSTITUTIONS

Drafting the Basic Law and the Lei Básica

The Joint Declarations' resolution to elaborate on and codify the People's Republic of China's "basic policies" for Hong Kong and Macau in the Basic Law and the Lei Básica, respectively, implicated the commitment problem that plagues authoritarian regimes, including Communist China. The aptitude of regimes credibly to commit to their own promises, such as China's in the Joint Declarations guaranteeing "a high degree of autonomy" for the SARs, is an invaluable asset that benefits all domestic and international stakeholders.[147] Autocratic commitments are not automatically credible. A problem arises if the Chinese government's preferences evolve divergently from those of the Joint Declarations' beneficiaries, notably the residents of Hong Kong and Macau.[148] The Joint Declarations exhibit just this credibility problem, embittered by the cynicism that nowadays confronts promises made by the Chinese Party-state, after so many times that they have considered themselves bound for only so long as they find it advantageous in one instance.[149] The elaboration of the Joint Declarations' promises in comprehensive constitutional instruments renders as credible as they will ever be the practicably unenforceable commitments of Beijing.[150] Ideally, the Hong Kong Basic Law and the Lei Básica de Macau would operate as precommitment devices inhibiting any defection by Beijing from its declared promises even if its preferences do evolve, so as to limit substantially the costs it could impose on the SARs.[151]

Convening in June 1985 under the auspices of paramount leader Deng Xiaoping, the Hong Kong Basic Law Drafting Committee had fifty-nine members, most of them from the mainland and all handpicked by the

[147] Stefan Voigt, *Constitutional Political Economy: Analyzing Formal Institutions at the Most Elementary Level*, *in* New Institutional Economics: A Guidebook 363, 368 (Éric Brousseau & Jean-Michel Glachant eds., 2008).

[148] Daron Acemoglu & James A. Robinson, Economic Origins of Dictatorship and Democracy 133 (2007).

[149] Peter Wesley-Smith, *Comment: The SAR Constitution: Law or Politics*, 27 Hong Kong L. J. 125, 125–26 (1997).

[150] Michael Albertus & Victor Menaldo, *The Political Economy of Autocratic Constitutions*, *in* Constitutions in Authoritarian Regimes 53, 59 (Tom Ginsburg & Alberto Simpser eds., 2014).

[151] Tom Ginsburg, *The Design of Constitutions*, *in* The Oxford Handbook of Law and Economics: Volume III: Public Law & Legal Institutions 28, 29 (Francesco Parisi ed., 2017).

Communist Party and ratified by the Standing Committee of the National People's Congress.[152] Only twenty members were Hong Kong residents. Most of the Hong Kong members could be identified as eminences in business, twelve of whom were so-called "big capitalists," among the richest men in the world.[153] Only two were unambiguous democrats: Martin Lee QC and Szeto Wah, both of whom were to resign right after the Tiananmen Square crackdown of 1989, and they emerged as leaders of the pan-democratic movement. This make-up embodied "the political absorption of economics" that positioned China credibly to promise the Hong Kong business elite, in exchange for their political loyalty, that they might dominate the polity after 1997.[154] None was ever meant to be representative of the general public;[155] indeed, Hong Kong residents were given no chance to grant or withhold consent to the Basic Law.[156] The Drafting Committee epitomized the rising influence of Hong Kong's ethnic Chinese business elite, as Beijing was aware, who were hastening to expand their dynasties and undertake large-scale projects in the wake of the gradual exodus of British capital.[157] To stabilize the territory and prepare for new partnerships in the post-1997 epoch, Beijing turned for support to capitalists who stood to benefit from the arrangement economically and politically.[158] In return, business leaders accepted that Hong Kong's reversion was irreversible, and that their only realistic option in order to protect their vested interests was to coalesce into a pro-China bloc, also known later as the "Establishment Coalition." Supplementing the Drafting Committee was a 180-person Basic Law Consultative Committee, whose members, all from Hong Kong, represented the corporatist views of the commercial sector, the financial sector, the legal profession, other professionals, the media, labour unions and grassroots associations, the organized religions,

152 Cindy Yik-yi Chu, Chinese Communists and Hong Kong Capitalists: 1937–1997 71 (2010).

153 *Id.* at 19.

154 Ambrose Y.C. King, *The Hong Kong Talks and Hong Kong Politics*, *in* Hong Kong. A Chinese and International Concern 42, 54 (Jürgen Domes & Yu-ming Shaw eds., 1988).

155 Yiu-chu Liu, *Interpretation and Review of the Basic Law of the Hong Kong Special Administrative Region*, 2 J. Chinese L. 49, 51 (1988).

156 Scott, *supra* note 54, at 89.

157 *See* Tai-lok Lui & Stephen S.W. Chiu, *Governance Crisis and Changing State-Business Relations: A Political Economy Perspective*, *in* Repositioning The Hong Kong Government: Social Foundations and Political Challenges 91 (Stephen W. K. Chiu & Siu Lune eds., 2012).

158 Matthew Y.H. Wong, Comparative Hong Kong Politics: A Guidebook for Students and Researchers 228 (2017).

and expatriates.[159] Given the prominence of the business elite in the drafting process, it is unsurprising that the Basic Law has become "unique among contemporary national constitutions in [that it] enshrines general principles and concrete policies to preserve individual economic freedom."[160] To establish legal certainty that the libertarian-capitalist Basic Law will not be construed as contradicting the Chinese Constitution's mandate that the socialist system shall prevail in China nationwide, the Standing Committee of the National People's Congress issued a Decision on the date that the Basic Law was enacted, which authoritatively declared its compatibility with the Constitution.[161]

Amid the Hong Kong Basic Law's drafting, the Lei Básica Drafting Committee, with forty-eight members – twenty-nine mainland Chinese and nineteen Macau residents – was inaugurated on October 25, 1988 and, on May 28, 1989, the Lei Básica Consultative Committee, consisting of ninety Macau members, was set up. The make-up of the Lei Básica Drafting Committee mirrored its Hong Kong counterpart, in that all members were handpicked by Beijing; the majority were mainland Chinese; Macau members were businessmen and professionals disproportionately; and the entire Committee was insulated from local public opinion.[162] Unlike Martin Lee and Szeto Wah in Hong Kong, key Macau Pro-Democracy figures such as António Ng and Au Kam Sun were barred from participation in the Drafting Committee in the first place, only to be co-opted into the Consultative Committee later.[163] The Lei Básica's drafting was characterized by lack of controversy and disagreement compared with the position in Hong Kong, owing in part to apathy across society over politics,[164] and in part to the harmonious relations between Lisbon and Beijing – in sharp contrast to the deep tensions between the United Kingdom and China during the same time frame.[165] In particular, Portugal refrained from criticizing China's human rights record, and the last two Governors, Carlos Montez Melancia and Vasco Rocha Vieira, were largely indifferent to Macau's democratizing prospects. In return, Beijing rewarded Lisbon's friendliness with concessions on the dual

159 CHU, *supra* note 152, at 75.

160 Alvin Rabushka, *A Free-Market Constitution for Hong Kong: A Blueprint for China*, 8 CATO J. 641, 643 (1989).

161 Decision of the National People's Congress on the Basic Law of the Hong Kong Special Administrative Region of the People's Republic of China (adopted at the Third Session of the Seventh National People's Congress on April 4, 1990).

162 LO, *supra* note 101, at 210.

163 *Id.*

164 *Id.* at 242.

165 YEE, *supra* note 79, at xx.

nationality of Macau residents, many of whom – including ethnic Chinese – were also full citizens of Portugal, and, by extension, the European Union – not to mention the deliberate constitutionalized protection of Portuguese culture and language in the future SAR.[166] The Lei Básica was enacted by the First Session of the Eighth National People's Congress and officially promulgated by President Jiang Zemin on March 31, 1993.[167]

Constitutionally Entrenched Corporatist Hybrid Regimes

The Basic Law and the Lei Básica converge on being identical documents, even in basic structure:[168] both contain exactly nine chapters and three annexes. It could be said that much of the Basic Law's content was cloned into the Lei Básica at the expense of Macau's political tradition.[169] Consider two epitomes. First, the Basic Law, harking back to the English tradition of Orders in Council, empowers the Chief Executive to issue "executive orders";[170] this rule was reproduced in Article 50(4) of the Lei Básica, even though "executive orders" were "completely unknown" in Macau's civil law tradition.[171] Second, following the dualist tradition of English common law,[172] Article 39(1) of the Basic Law provides that international treaties "shall remain in force and shall be implemented through the laws of the Hong Kong Special Administrative Region." Perplexingly, this provision was recapitulated verbatim in the Lei Básica, Article 40 in the teeth of Macau's Portuguese tradition with its monist approach to international law that enforces treaties directly without domesticating them in local statutes first, before they can be given effect.[173]

166 *Id.* at xxi.
167 Lo, *supra* note 101, at 197.
168 This by no means suggests that the Basic Law and the Lei Básica are perfectly identical documents. For a list of differences, *see* Ghai, *supra* note 114, at 191–195.
169 Gonçalves, *supra* note 104, at 737.
170 Basic Law, art. 48(4).
171 Cardinal, *supra* note 87, at 408.
172 Jan Klabbers, International Law 289 (2013) ("Under dualism, international law and domestic law are regarded as two distinct legal spheres which, moreover, have very little to do with one another . . . For an international rule to become effective in the domestic legal order, it needs to be transformed into the sort of rule recognized by that legal order. If a legal order recognizes only, for instance, Acts of Parliament as valid law, then the international law rule can only enter that legal order if it is given the form of such an Act of Parliament.")
173 *Id.* at 290. ("The critique of dualism culminated in the work of Hans Kelsen, under the label monism. Monism, as the label suggests, thinks of international law and domestic law (regardless of which domestic system) as different branches of what is fundamentally the same tree . . . under monism, international law usually prevails over a conflicting rule of domestic law.")

Both documents contain important provisions to reinforce the apparently liberal outlook of the SAR polities. Their purpose was "to ensure the implementation of the basic policies of the People's Republic of China regarding [Hong Kong or Macao]," as "elaborated by the Chinese Government in the [Sino–British or Sino–Portuguese] Joint Declaration."[174] Both identically guarantee the Chinese SARs would retain "a high degree of autonomy and enjoy executive, legislative and independent judicial power, including that of final adjudication";[175] that "[t]he socialist system and policies shall not be practised in [either Region], and the previous capitalist system[s] and way[s] of life shall remain unchanged for 50 years";[176] and that "[n]o department of the Central People's Government and no province, autonomous region, or municipality directly under the Central Government may interfere in the affairs which [either Region] administers, on its own, in accordance with the [Basic Law or Lei Básica]." It is not far-fetched to infer that both Joint Declarations, whence both constitutions derive their content, broadly conform to the liberal constitutionalist paradigm entailing substantial protections of human rights and the rule of law.[177] Hence the fingerprints of some crucial principles of constitutional government are found all over the constitutions of the SARs – for instance, the obligation to safeguard the rights and freedoms of persons within their territories;[178] equal justice under law;[179] the government itself subject to law;[180] judicial control of administrative action;[181] and judicial independence.[182] Each document contains in its Chapter III an elaborate bill of rights that expands on the above-mentioned rights and freedoms enshrined in the Joint Declarations. Interestingly, the two bills of rights have different emphases.[183] The Basic Law contains rights that clearly stem from the English common law tradition: prohibition of unlawful deprivation of

174 Basic Law, Preamble; Lei Básica, Preamble.

175 Basic Law, art. 2; Lei Básica, art. 2.

176 Basic Law, art. 5; Lei Básica, art. 5.

177 Michael C. Davis, *Constitutionalism in Hong Kong: Politics versus Economics*, 18(1) U. PA. INT'L ECON. L. 157, 159 (1997).

178 Basic Law, art. 4; Lei Básica, art. 4.

179 Basic Law, art. 25; Lei Básica, art. 25.

180 Basic Law, art. 64; Lei Básica, art. 65.

181 Basic Law, art. 35(2); Lei Básica, art. 36(2).

182 Basic Law, art. 2; Lei Básica, art. 2.

183 For a thorough discussion of the different emphases, *see* Simon N.M. Young, *Fundamental Rights and the Basic Laws of the Hong Kong and Macau Special Administrative Regions, in* ONE COUNTRY, TWO SYSTEMS, THREE LEGAL ORDERS – PERSPECTIVES OF EVOLUTION: ESSAYS ON MACAU'S AUTONOMY AFTER THE RESUMPTION OF SOVEREIGNTY BY CHINA 681, 685 (Jorge Oliveira & Paulo Cardinal eds., 2009).

life;[184] the right to fair trial;[185] the principle of trial by jury;[186] and rights to confidential legal advice and choice of lawyers for timely protection of lawful rights and interests.[187] In turn, the Lei Básica contains rights absent from the Basic Law, which reflect the Continental legal tradition of Portugal, such as freedom from discrimination based on "nationality descent, race, sex, language, religion, political persuasion or ideological belief, educational level, economic status or social conditions";[188] prohibition of torture or inhuman treatment;[189] inviolability of human dignity and prohibition of humiliation, slander, and false accusation;[190] rights to personal reputation, privacy of personal and family life;[191] rights to obtain travel documents and to leave the Region without special authorization, unless restricted by law;[192] protection of the legitimate rights and interests of women;[193] protection of minors, the aged, and the disabled;[194] and protection of the interests, customs, and cultural traditions of residents of Portuguese descent.[195] The Macau Lei Básica is clear on the point that children born outside Macau of a Chinese national parent who is a permanent resident of Macau do not become permanent residents by virtue of that connection unless they were born after the parent had secured the right of abode (art. 24(2)). This issue has been strongly contested in Hong Kong, and has been the subject of much litigation.[196]

Not unexpectedly, the design of the Basic Law and the Lei Básica retain many vestiges of colonial government,[197] especially the legal and political predominance of the Governor[198] over against the Legislative Council or the Legislative Assembly, which were known for their deference to government bills and respect for officials attending legislative sessions.[199] It is thus no surprise that the Chief Executive – the colonial-era Governor's

184 Basic Law, art. 28(2).
185 Basic Law, art. 87(2).
186 Basic Law, art. 86.
187 Basic Law, art. 35(1)
188 Lei Básica, art. 25.
189 Lei Básica, art. 28(4).
190 Lei Básica, art. 30(1).
191 Lei Básica, art. 30(2).
192 Lei Básica, art. 33.
193 Lei Básica, art. 38(2).
194 Lei Básica, art. 38(3).
195 Lei Básica, art. 42.
196 Ghai, *supra* note 114, at 196.
197 Eliza W.Y. Lee & Rikkie L.K. Yeung, *The "Principal Officials Accountability System": Its Underdevelopment as a System of Ministerial Government*, 39(2) ASIA PAC. J. PUB. ADMIN. 120, 122 (2017).
198 HAO ET AL., *supra* note 88, at 167.
199 LO, *supra* note 101, at 242.

successor[200] – functions as the "linchpin"[201] of each SAR. China, if it would influence SAR politics, should find it more convenient to vest power in a single trusted agent rather than disperse it among many agents. Indeed, the parceling out of legislative, executive, and judicial powers between independent branches, with or without overlap, raises the transaction cost of authoritarian governance.[202] One strong Chief Executive in each SAR relieves Beijing of any necessity of dealing with multiple disagreeing agents, affording a way of lowering its political transaction cost if circumstances demand.[203] The drafters' fixation with the formal legal structure of central–local relations had, rather problematically, caused them to omit the reality of ceaseless negotiations between London and Victoria City, and the wide array of political tactics available to Governors vis-à-vis Whitehall, in withholding information, mobilizing local opinion, and lobbying local resistance against imperial encroachments.[204]

The Chief Executive in each SAR is selected by an electoral college,[205] called the "Election Committee," for a five-year, once-renewable term,[206] and appointed by the State Council in Beijing.[207] Despite the Chief Executive's constitutional status as the head and representative of the SAR,[208] the office is more akin to a Chinese prefect in charge of SAR affairs, armed with most of the autocratic powers wielded by the former Governor.[209] He has power to grant or withhold assent to bills and budgets passed by the Legislative Council or the Legislative Assembly;[210] make government policies and issue executive

200 Bruce K.K. Kwong, *Patron-Clientelism and Elections in Macao: The 2009 Chief Executive Election, in* China's Macao Transformed: Challenge and Development in the 21st Century 55, 58 (Eilo W.Y. Yu & Ming K. Chan eds., 2014).

201 Yash Ghai, *The Rule of Law and Capitalism: Reflections on the Basic Law, in* Hong Kong, China and 1997: Essays in Legal Theory 365 (Raymond Wacks ed., 1993).

202 Richard A. Posner, *The Constitution as an Economic Document*, 56 Geo. Wash. L. Rev. 4, 39 (1987).

203 Tai Wei Lim & Xiaojuan Ping, Contextualizing Occupy Central in Contemporary Hong Kong 83 (2015).

204 Ray Yep, *A Historical Perspective on Hong Kong Autonomy: Traditions of British Imperialism, Maritime Enclave and Contending Views of British Interest', in* Hong Kong 20 Years after the Handover: Emerging Social and Institutional Fractures after 1997 231, 234 (Brian C.H. Fong & Tai-lok Lui eds., 2018).

205 The first Chief Executive in each Region was selected by a "Selection Committee," because the Election Committee has not yet been formed. The Selection Committees were established by Preparation Committees under the Standing Committee of the National People's Congress.

206 Basic Law, annex I; Lei Básica, annex I.

207 Basic Law, art. 45(1); Lei Básica, art. 47(1).

208 Basic Law, art. 43; Lei Básica, art. 45.

209 Ian Scott, The Public Sector in Hong Kong 29 (Hong Kong Univ. Press 2010).

210 Basic Law, 49; Lei Básica, art. 51.

orders;[211] nominate Principal Officials for the State Council to appoint;[212] appoint or remove judges "in accordance with legal procedures";[213] conduct external affairs;[214] appoint or remove members of the Executive Council on his own, without the need to consult the State Council,[215] and other public officers;[216] pardon criminal convicts or commute their sentences;[217] and hear and try petitions and complaints.[218] The Chief Executive of Macau also has the constitutional authority to formulate and enact administrative regulations;[219] appoint the Appointed Members of the Legislative Assembly;[220] and confer medals and titles of honor.[221] Significantly, both Chief Executives wield veto power at more than one point in the legislative process. No bill related to "government policies" may be introduced for legislative consideration without his "written consent."[222] No one but the Chief Executive himself may introduce bills related to "public expenditure," or "political structure," or the "operation of the government."[223] No government official may testify before the Legislative Council or the Legislative Assembly without his permission "in the light of security and vital interests."[224] The advice of his handpicked Executive Council is not binding on him,[225] even if unanimous.[226] Yet nothing makes him politically accountable to either the Legislative Council or the citizenry. Formally speaking, then, the Chief Executive is accountable to no one in matters not directly affecting China's national interests.[227] According to one comparative empirical study, both Chief Executives are more powerful than most of the world's presidents.[228]

211 Basic Law, 48(4); Lei Básica, art. 50(4).
212 Basic Law, 48(5); Lei Básica, art. 50(6).
213 Basic Law, 48(6); Lei Básica, art. 50(9).
214 Basic Law, 48(9); Lei Básica, art. 50(13).
215 Basic Law 55; Lei Básica, art. 50(8).
216 Basic Law 48(7); Lei Básica, art. 50(11).
217 Basic Law 48(12); Lei Básica, art. 50(17).
218 Basic Law 48(13); Lei Básica, art. 50(18).
219 Lei Básica, art. 50(5).
220 Lei Básica, art. 50(7).
221 Lei Básica, art. 50(16).
222 Basic Law, art. 74; Lei Básica, art. 75.
223 Basic Law, art. 74; Lei Básica, art. 75.
224 Basic Law, art. 48(11); Lei Básica, art. 50(15).
225 Basic Law, art. 55(1); Lei Básica, art. 57(1).
226 Basic Law, art. 56(2); Lei Básica, art. 58(2).
227 Steve Tsang, *China and Political Reform in Hong Kong*, 2(1) PAC. REV. 68, 72 (1989).
228 NGOK MA, POLITICAL DEVELOPMENT IN HONG KONG: STATE, POLITICAL SOCIETY, AND CIVIL SOCIETY 129 (2007).

The term "election" in the Joint Declarations, which can mean nearly anything in Chinese political parlance, did not prevent Beijing from using the SAR constitutions to set up candidly hybrid regimes in Hong Kong and Macau.[229] In his speech to the Basic Law Drafting Committee of April 16, 1987, no less applicable to the future Lei Básica Drafting Committee, Deng Xiaoping, the "chief architect of the 'One Country, Two Systems' precept,"[230] stated that "Hong Kong's system of government should not be completely Westernized," meaning that its political structure must not replicate "Western democracy," understood as "includ[ing], among other features, the separation of the three powers and multiparty elections."[231] Deng continued, "I am afraid it would not be appropriate for [the Hong Kong] system to be a total copy of ... the separation of the three powers and a British or American parliamentary system," "[n]or would it be appropriate for people to judge whether Hong Kong's system is democratic on the basis of whether it has those features."[232] This was a telling admission that the Basic Law (hence the Lei Básica) was not originally meant to provide for transition to fully fledged liberal democracy featuring uninhibited interbranch, interparty competition. Beijing's stance was that if the Chief Executive and all members of the Legislative Council were directly elected, then Beijing would have no way of effectively controlling the Region.[233] Democratization in the SARs might open the floodgates to other rich coastal cities on the mainland demanding the same.[234] There is a widespread belief that excessive devolution would destabilize China politically and ultimately subvert the legitimacy of the central Party-state.[235]

229 Alvin Y. So, *Hong Kong's Problematic Democratic Transition: Power Dependency or Business Hegemony?*, 59(2) J. Asian Stud. 359, 367 (2000).

230 Yahong Li, *The Central-HKSAR Legislative Relationship: A Constitutional Assessment*, *in* The New Legal Order in Hong Kong 163, 165 (Raymond Wacks ed., 1999).

231 Deng Xiaoping, *Speech at a Meeting with the Members of the Committee for Drafting the Basic Law of the Hong Kong Special Administrative Region*, Apr. 16, 1987, https://dengxiaopingworks.wordpress.com/2013/03/18/speech-at-a-meeting-with-the-members-of-the-committee-for-drafting-the-basic-law-of-the-hong-kong-special-administrative-region/

232 *Id.*

233 Jorge Godinho, *Electoral Reform and Political Representation in Macao*, *in* China's Macao Transformed: Challenge and Development in the 21st Century 43, 45 (Eilo W.Y. Yu & Ming K. Chan eds., 2014).

234 Eric C. Ip, *The High Court of the People: Popular Constitutionalism in Hong Kong under Chinese Sovereignty*, 36(3) Law & Pol'y 314, 319 (2014); *see* Peter T.Y. Cheung, *Who's Influencing Whom? Exploring the Influence of Hong Kong on Politics and Governance in China*, 51(4) Asian Surv. 718 (2011).

235 Bill K.P. Chou, *Local Autonomy Matters: One-Country Two-System Policy in Macao and its Implications to China's Policies towards Borderlands*, *in* China's Policies on its Borderlands and International Relations 225, 226 (Yufan Hao & Bill K P Chou eds., 2010).

As the Basic Law was being drafted, Hong Kong's ethnic Chinese major business leaders tactfully joined forces with their traditional adversaries, the Leftist trade unions, to lobby for a corporatist regime that would cement their dominance of the political and economic future.[236] Opposition to universal suffrage by sectoral vested interests is explained by the virtue of universal suffrage in reducing rent seeking, given that the larger the electorate, the costlier it is for prospective rent seekers to forge coalitions to exploit vulnerable constituencies.[237] Thus, the mere fact that the Basic Law included "sunrise clauses"[238] postponing universal suffrage to an unspecified date[239] does not indicate any intention on the part of Beijing to establish a liberal democratic government in the Region, even in the distant future. Note that the relevant provision qualifies "the ultimate aim" of selecting the Chief Executive "by universal suffrage" by subordinating it to the candidates' "nomination by a broadly representative nominating committee in accordance with democratic procedures."[240] Such a nominating committee contrasts with other nomination methods, such as civic nomination or nomination by parties. The divisive August 31, 2014 decision of the Standing Committee of the National People's Congress also confirmed that all prospective candidates for any Chief Executive election submitted to universal suffrage, in order to qualify, must be vetted by a 1,200-member Nomination Committee whose make-up will be subject to Beijing's approval.[241] The Standing Committee further decided that the Nomination Committee may nominate no more than three candidates enjoying the consent of more than half the

[236] Ma, *supra* note 228, at 41.

[237] Richard A. Posner, Economic Analysis of Law 750 (9th ed. 2014).

[238] Ginsburg, *supra* note 151, at 34.

[239] Basic Law, art. 45(2): "The method for selecting the Chief Executive shall be specified in the light of the actual situation in the Hong Kong Special Administrative Region and in accordance with the principle of gradual and orderly progress. The ultimate aim is the selection of the Chief Executive by universal suffrage upon nomination by a broadly representative nominating committee in accordance with democratic procedures." Basic Law, art. 45(2): "The method for forming the Legislative Council shall be specified in the light of the actual situation in the Hong Kong Special Administrative Region and in accordance with the principle of gradual and orderly progress. The ultimate aim is the election of all the members of the Legislative Council by universal suffrage."

[240] Basic Law, art. 45(2).

[241] Decision of the Standing Committee of the National People's Congress on Issues Relating to the Selection of the Chief Executive of the Hong Kong Special Administrative Region by Universal Suffrage and on the Method for Forming the Legislative Council of the Hong Kong Special Administrative Region in the Year 2016 (adopted at the Tenth Session of the Standing Committee of the Twelfth National People's Congress on Aug. 31, 2014).

TABLE 3.1 *Composition of the Hong Kong SAR Election Committee according to Annex I, Art. 2, Hong Kong Basic Law*

	Number of electors (1998–2012)	Number of electors (2012–present)
Industrial, commercial, and financial sectors	200	300
The professions	200	300
Labour, social services, religious, and other sectors	200	300
The political sector	200	300

Committee's members.[242] In Macau, the Lei Básica does not promise to implement universal suffrage in Chief Executive and Legislative Assembly elections. It merely permits the Region to review its selection methods after 2009.[243] In a similar vein, it differs from its Hong Kong counterpart in not guaranteeing a Legislative Assembly "constituted by elections,"[244] but merely providing that the Assembly should have a "majority,"[245] as distinct from a totality, of elected members.[246]

A former Vice-Chairman of the Basic Law Drafting Committee has hinted that Deng's "Hong Kong People Governing Hong Kong" precept meant the dictatorship of the Hong Kong capitalists and no other classes.[247] A Drafting Committee manned by business and professional interests could hardly be expected to furnish anything other than a corporatist regime controlled by a rarefied Election Committee and a motley crew of functional constituencies preempting no less than half the Legislative Council. This model was of course replicated in Macau. Both Election Committees were to be made up of four corporate blocs: commercial and financial; the professions; labour, social services, and religious; and political (Tables 3.1 and 3.2). Since 2012, the

242 Explanations on the Draft Decision of the Standing Committee of the National People's Congress on Issues Relating to the Selection of the Chief Executive of the Hong Kong Special Administrative Region by Universal Suffrage and on the Method for Forming the Legislative Council of the Hong Kong Special Administrative Region in the Year 2016 (adopted at the Tenth Session of the Standing Committee of the Twelfth National People's Congress on Aug. 27, 2014).

243 Lei Básica, annex I, s. 7; annex II, s. 3.

244 Basic Law, art. 68.

245 Lei Básica, 68(2).

246 Cardinal, *supra* note 87, at 409.

247 CHU, *supra* note 152, at 69.

TABLE 3.2 *Composition of the Macau SAR Election Committee according to Annex I, Art. 2, Lei Básica de Macau*

	Number of Electors (1999–2014)	Number of Electors (2014–present)
Industrial, commercial, and financial sectors	100	120
The professions	80	115
Labour, social services, religious, and other sectors	80	115
The political sector	40	50

Hong Kong Election Committee has comprised 1,200 Electors and, since 2014, the Macau Election Committee has comprised 400 Electors. Aspiring candidates for Chief Executive must secure nominations from one-eighth of the Committee in Hong Kong (or 150 Electors), and one-sixth of the Macau Committee (or 66 Electors). The Election Committee en bloc chooses between the nominees in a one-round plurality vote.[248] The nomination threshold is very difficult to clear. In Hong Kong, only one candidate received sufficient nominations in two out of five Chief Executive elections in the twenty years between 1997 and 2017; and, in Macau, only one candidate in all three Chief Executive elections held between the Handover in 1999 and 2017 (Tables 3.3 and 3.4).

As at March 2017, the 1,200 Electors of the Hong Kong Election Committee are selected from and by a small franchise of 250,000 persons in a total electorate of circa 3,800,000[249] under a system that is "anything but proportional and representative."[250] Not all Electors are returned by one-person-one-vote: Hong Kong deputies to China's National People's Congress, cautiously selected by Beijing, are ex officio Electors of the political sector.[251] Corporations or associations in sectors such as tourism, insurance, catering, financial services, import and export, wholesale and retail trade, transport, textiles and garments, real estate and construction, and agriculture and fisheries elect their representatives by corporate suffrage.[252] But these corporations

248 WONG, *supra* note 158, at 43.

249 Voter Registration, The Government of the Hong Kong Special Administrative Region, *Voter Registration Statistics: Geographical Constituency*, www.voterregistration.gov.hk/eng/statistic20171.html#1

250 WONG, *supra* note 158, at 253.

251 *Id.* at 253.

252 Ma, *supra* note 37, at 251.

TABLE 3.3 *Composition of the Legislative Council of Hong Kong (1985–2020)*

Session	Official Members	Appointed Unofficial Members	Electoral College/ Election Committee/ Selection Committee	Functional Constituencies (Indirectly Elected)	Geographical Constituencies (Directly Elected)	Total
1985–88	10	22	12	12	0	56
1988–91	10	20	12	14	0	56
1991–95	3	18	0	21	18	60
1995–97	0	0	10	30	20	60
1997–98	0	0	60	0	0	60
1998–2000	0	0	10	30	20	60
2000–04	0	0	6	30	24	60
2004–08	0	0	0	30	30	60
2012–16	0	0	0	35	35	70
2016–20	0	0	0	35	35	70

Source: Percy Luen-tim Lui, *The Legislature, in* CONTEMPORARY HONG KONG GOVERNMENT AND POLITICS 45, 47 (Wai-man Lam et al. eds., Hong Kong Univ. Press, 2nd ed. 2012)

TABLE 3.4 *Composition of the Legislative Assembly of Macau (1976–2021)*

Session	Appointed	Indirectly elected	Directly elected	Total
1976–80	5	6	6	17
1980–84	5	6	6	17
1984–88	5	6	6	17
1988–92	7	8	8	23
1992–96	7	8	8	23
1996–2001	7	8	8	23
2001–05	7	10	10	27
2005–09	7	10	12	29
2013–17	7	12	14	33
2017–21	7	12	14	33

Source: Yufan Hao et al., Political Economy of Macao since 1999: The Dilemma of Success 163 (Palgrave Macmillan 2017).

or associations are themselves undemocratically organized. For instance, licensed banks can vote, but not banking employees; agricultural associations can vote, but not fishermen or farmers.[253] Nor do all votes carry equal weight: the education subsector comprises a sizeable pool of 100,000 voters who can pick only 30 Electors, whereas the Hong Kong Employer's Federation's one hundred corporations select sixteen Electors, over half of the thirty representing 1,000 times more.[254] This carefully engineered process naturally yields outcomes such as that roughly a third of the Election Committee's seats were uncontested in 2006 and 2011.[255] As a result, a handful of conglomerates could aggregately control large voting blocs of corporate agents.[256]

Individual voting does not exist in the constitution of the Macau Election Committee: all of the Electors are selected by the directors or administrators of interest groups known as "associations," meaning that they are recognized by the government as corporate voters.[257] The government has wide discretion to appoint corporate voters to the various sectors or subsectors that make up the

253 *Id.*

254 Wong, *supra* note 158, at 42.

255 *Id.* at 42–43.

256 Chiew Ping Yew, *Political Reform and Dilemma*, *in* Hong Kong under Chinese Rule Economic Integration and Political Gridlock 209, 215 (Yongnian Zheng & Chiew Ping Yew eds., 2013).

257 Bill K.P. Chou, *Politics and Social Organisations in Macao: A Historical Institutionalist Analysis*, 13(1) China: An Int'l J. 22, 28 (2015). *See* Chief Executive Election Law, Law No. 3/2004 (Macau); Voter Registration Law, Law No. 12/2000 (Macau).

Committee.[258] This has allowed Establishment interests to monopolize the Committee seats;[259] consequently, for all practical purposes, selection of Electors happens behind the scenes in negotiations controlled by the Establishment, rendering public campaigns useless.[260] Electorships lie uncontested, as the candidates "know better": the number running rarely or never exceeds the number of available seats.[261] In brief, anyone who has garnered enough nominations from interest groups automatically gets to be an Elector.[262] This system ensures that Beijing's preferences will prevail in all elections in Macau, while their commercial interests in China ensure that the corporate Electors stay part of the Establishment Coalition. Chosen by loyalists to mainland interests, the Chief Executive's policy preferences are virtually guaranteed substantially to reflect Beijing's. Hence, for all practical purposes, Beijing maintains a hammerlock on the electoral processes of both SARs, controlling both who can run for Chief Executive and who can win.[263]

Corporatist "functional constituencies" in the Legislative Council of Hong Kong and Legislative Assembly of Macau were, not without a certain grim irony, introduced by the Western European colonial governments of both territories in the 1970s and 1980s as a threshold to representative government. Functional constituencies featured preeminently in the design of the Hong Kong Legislative Council. As in the Election Committee, they are a small fraction of registered voters and consist of designated corporate persons and incorporated professions[264]: doctors, lawyers, accountants, social workers, and teachers, but also banks, mega-companies, and corporate members of chambers of commerce and industry bodies, plus a handful of trade unions.[265]

258 Eilo Wing-Yat Yu, *Formal and Informal Politics in Macao Special Administrative Region Elections 2004–2005*, 16(52) J. CONTEMP. CHINA 417, 422 (2007).

259 Sonny S.H. Lo & Herbert S. Yee, *Legitimacy-Building in the Macau Special Administrative Region: Colonial Legacies and Reform Strategies*, 13(1) ASIAN J. POL. SCI. 51, 53 (2005).

260 Eilo Wing-yat Yu, *Macao's "One Country, Two Systems": High Autonomy or Intervention?*, *in* NEGOTIATING AUTONOMY IN GREATER CHINA: HONG KONG AND ITS SOVEREIGN BEFORE AND AFTER 1997 207, 211 (Ray Yep ed., 2013).

261 Chou, *supra* note 257, at 30.

262 Yu, *supra* note 258, at 423.

263 Chou, *supra* note 106, at 33.

264 In the 2013–17 Legislative Assembly of Macau, Functional Constituency Members were returned from four constituencies: Employee Interests; Business Interests; Professional Interests; and Charity, Culture, Education, and Sports Interests.

265 In the 2012–16 Legislative Council of Hong Kong, Functional Constituency Members were returned from twenty-nine constituencies: Heung Yee Kuk (Rural Council); Agriculture and Fisheries; Insurance; Transport; Education; Legal; Accountancy; Medical; Health Services; Engineering; Architectural, Surveying and Planning; Labour; Social Welfare; Real Estate and Construction; Tourism; Commercial (First); Commercial (Second); Industrial (First); Industrial (Second); Finance; Financial Services; Sports; Performing Arts; Culture and

Representatives popularly elected by "geographical constituencies" occupied no more than a third of the sixty legislative seats before 2004, and so could not win passage of any bill without the cooperation of the functional constituencies.[266] The official justification for the continuance of corporatism in the post-Handover era was that functional constituencies could strike a better "balance" between diverse societal interests, ostensibly to accommodate a vague ideal known as "balanced participation."[267] In reality, functional constituencies decisively empower the Establishment Coalition to hang on to a majority in the Legislative Council, any number of defeats in the popular vote notwithstanding.

As with the Election Committee, corporatism defines Macau's Legislative Assembly elections: "overrepresented"[268] interest groups coordinate internally to nominate and elect only Establishment Coalition candidates.[269] The domination of pro-Beijing elites – industrialists, wealthy businessmen, entrepreneurs of the Business and Labor functional constituencies[270] – is so complete that even casino capitalists, with all their influence on the economy, must seek political representation in the professional, welfare and education, and culture and sports constituencies.[271] Seven of thirty-three Assemblymen (or 21.2 percent) are appointed by the Chief Executive, a mechanism "whereby someone at the stroke of a pen is moved from more or less obscurity to a seat in the Assembly without having to go through the rigors of an election campaign."[272] This kind of entrenchment cements the unity of legislative and executive branches under Chief Executive leadership. In Hong Kong or in Macau, changes to the Election Committee or the functional constituencies, let alone abolition, pivotally depend on the consent of the functional

Publication; Import and Export; Textiles and Garment; Wholesale and Retail; Information Technology; Catering; District Council (First); and District Council (Second).

266 As stipulated in Basic Law, annex II, bills or amendments to government bills introduced by individual members to be passed require a separate majority in both orders of constituency. This allows half the legislators from either the Geographical Constituencies or Functional Constituencies (or one-quarter of the whole) to block any such bill or amendment. This amplifies the influence of narrow functional constituencies, empowering them to veto bills with wide societal support indefinitely. *See* WONG, *supra* note 158, at 46.

267 Ming Sing, *To What Extent Have Members of the Functional Constituencies Performed the "Balancing Role" in Hong Kong?*, *in* THE HONG KONG SPECIAL ADMINISTRATIVE REGION IN ITS FIRST DECADE 109, 110 (Joseph Y.S. Cheng ed., 2007).

268 Bill K.P. Chou, *Legitimacy-Building and Public Sector Reform in Macao: Administrative Measures to Address Political Problems*, 10(3) CHINA: AN INT'L J. 133, 144 (2012).

269 Chou, *supra* note 111, at 199.

270 HAO ET AL., *supra* note 88, at 164.

271 HAO ET AL., *supra* note 88, at 165.

272 Godinho, *supra* note 233, at 47.

constituencies within the Legislative Council or the Legislative Assembly, in light of their de facto veto power over proposals originating in the SARs to amend the Basic Law or the Lei Básica.[273] This practically functions as a self-defence mechanism for corporatist interests to ward off challenges to the status quo.[274]

Constitutional Enforcement

Hong Kong's Basic Law and Macau's Lei Básica contain provisions that uphold their constitutional supremacy in their respective jurisdictions.[275] Both formally obligate the Chief Executive to see to their implementation,[276] but it is hard to imagine any Chief Executive enforcing it against decisions of his own Government or the State Council or the Standing Committee of the National People's Congress. Nor does either Basic Law encompass any mechanism to rectify breaches of itself by legislative enactments relating to matters wholly within the autonomy of the Region other than for the Legislative Council or the Legislative Assembly to amend or repeal its own statutes, if in its sole discretion it comes to believe itself in the wrong.[277] Moreover, the State Council may issue administrative directives to the Chief Executive,[278] and the Standing Committee of the National People's Congress may invalidate acts of the Legislative Council or the Legislative Assembly that pertain to matters not wholly inside SAR autonomy, which the former deems contrary to the Basic Law or the Lei Básica;[279] although these options have never been used as of the time of writing. At the end of the day, nothing in either Basic Law obligates the National People's Congress or its

[273] Johannes Chan, *Hong Kong's Constitutional Journey, 1997–2011*, *in* CONSTITUTIONALISM IN ASIA IN THE EARLY TWENTY-FIRST CENTURY 169, 190 (Albert H.Y. Chen ed., 2014).

[274] WONG, *supra* note 158, at 229.

[275] Basic Law, art. 8: "The laws previously in force in Hong Kong, that is, the common law, rules of equity, ordinances, subordinate legislation and customary law shall be maintained, except for any that contravene this Law, and subject to any amendment by the legislature of the Hong Kong Special Administrative Region." Basic Law, art. 11(2): "No law enacted by the legislature of the Hong Kong Special Administrative Region shall contravene this Law." Lei Básica, art. 8: "The laws, decrees, administrative regulations and other normative acts previously in force in Macao shall be maintained, except for any that contravenes this Law, or subject to any amendment by the legislature or other relevant organs of the Macao Special Administrative Region in accordance with legal procedures." Lei Básica, art. 11(2): "No law, decree, administrative regulations and normative acts of the Macao Special Administrative Region shall contravene this Law."

[276] Basic Law, art.48(2); Lei Básica, art. 50(2).

[277] Basic Law, art.160(1); Lei Básica, art. 145(1).

[278] Basic Law, art. 48(8); Lei Básica, art. 50(12).

[279] Basic Law, art. 17(3); Lei Básica, art. 17(3).

Standing Committee to guarantee that any amendment to them is consistent with the Sino–British or the Sino–Portuguese Joint Declaration, respectively, as mandated by these documents themselves.[280]

The lack of any independent enforcement authority in the constitutional texts of the Chinese SARs is hardly surprising; as Wu Jianfan, law professor and member of the Hong Kong Basic Law Drafting Committee for the mainland, admitted in 1988: "[The Sino–British Joint Declaration] says nothing about who decides whether the laws enacted are in accordance with the Basic Law and the Legal procedures or how to handle laws which do not accord with the Basic Law and the Legal procedures."[281] It should surprise no one familiar with contemporary Chinese constitutional law, which affords no realistic legal remedy for breaches of the Constitution, if the Basic Law and the Lei Básica somehow empower the SARs' major political actors to be judges in their own causes.[282] It is a fact that constitutional rights "do not have primacy" in the mainland Chinese legal system; the Constitution "has not become the standard for judging the behaviour of state organs or citizens,"[283] and the People's courts rarely if ever cite constitutional provisions in either criminal or civil judgments.[284] It follows that, apart from the goodwill and self-restraint of the SAR regimes and of the Chinese central authorities, there is no formal mechanism in either Region checking a Chief Executive who would veto a judicial nominee, even if recommended by the relevant independent commission.[285] Nor does any firewall prevent the government declaring virtually any government act under constitutional challenge to be a non-justiciable "act of state" according to the vaguely worded Article 19(3), nullifying the jurisdiction of the courts;[286] or the Hong Kong Legislative

280 Basic Law, art.159(4); Lei Básica, art. 144(4).

281 Jianfan Wu, *Several Issues Concerning the Relationship between the Central Government of the People's Republic of China and the Hong Kong Special Administrative Region*, 2(1) J. CHINESE L. 65, 75 (1988).

282 Albert H.Y. Chen, *The Court of Final Appeal's Ruling in the "Illegal Migrant" Children Case: Congressional Supremacy and Judicial Review*, *in* HONG KONG'S CONSTITUTIONAL DEBATE: CONFLICT OVER INTERPRETATION 73, 77 (Johannes M.M. Chan et al. eds., 2001).

283 Jihong Mo, *The Constitutional Law of the People's Republic of China and its Development*, 23 COLUM. J. ASIAN L. 137, 182 (2009).

284 Zhenmin Wang & Kai Tu, *Chinese Constitutional Dynamics: A Decennial Review*, *in* CONSTITUTIONALISM IN ASIA IN THE EARLY TWENTY-FIRST CENTURY 118, 122 (2014).

285 Basic Law, art. 88; Lei Básica, art. 87(1).

286 Basic Law, art. 19(3): "The courts of the Hong Kong Special Administrative Region shall have no jurisdiction over acts of state such as defence and foreign affairs. The courts of the Region shall obtain a certificate from the Chief Executive on questions of fact concerning acts of state such as defence and foreign affairs whenever such questions arise in the adjudication of cases. This certificate shall be binding on the courts. Before issuing such a certificate, the Chief Executive shall obtain a certifying document from the Central People's Government." Lei

Council conducting potentially intimidating hearings on an appointee to or judge of the CFA;[287] or Macau's Legislative Assembly charging a review committee to support the Chief Executive's decision to remove defiant judges from the TUI;[288] or either SAR's authorities passing a budget slashing the judicial budget, no matter how contradictory to the spirit of the constitutions' guarantees of the exercise of independent judicial power[289] according to the law and the law only;[290] of the legal immunity of judges;[291] of the recruitment of judges on the basis of their professional qualities;[292] and of the security of their tenure.[293] Nothing in the constitutions of either SAR intrinsically stops their descent to "nominal" instruments that function "partly as propaganda and partly as camouflage," much like the Chinese Constitution itself.[294]

Contrary to conventional wisdom, neither constitution expressly clarifies whether the SAR courts, headed by the CFA in Hong Kong and the TUI in Macau, are entitled even to review, let alone strike down legislation on constitutional grounds.[295] In the same vein, neither text addresses a word on the types of disputes in which Chapter III rights may be invoked; who may invoke Chapter III rights in court; on what grounds courts may justify infringements of Chapter III rights; or what may be the remedies available in case a Chapter III right is breached.[296] In fact, prominent drafters of the Basic Law warned against such issues being brought up before the courts. Hong Kong drafter Liu Yiu-chu decried that to vest in the CFA "the power of final adjudication over disputes which concern the 'constitutionality' of Special Administrative Region legislation" would be not only "weird," but also tantamount to "establishing [judicial] supremacy" over the Hong Kong and

Básica, art. 19(3): "The courts of the Macao Special Administrative Region shall have no jurisdiction over acts of state such as defence and foreign affairs. The courts of the Region shall obtain a certificate from the Chief Executive on questions of fact concerning acts of state such as defence and foreign affairs whenever such questions arise in the adjudication of cases. This certificate shall be binding on the courts. Before issuing such a certificate, the Chief Executive shall obtain a certifying document from the Central People's Government."

287 Basic Law, art. 90(2).

288 Lei Básica, art. 87(3).

289 Basic Law, art. 85; Lei Básica, art. 83.

290 Basic Law art. 84; Lei Básica, art. 83.

291 Basic Law art. 85; Lei Básica, art. 89(2).

292 Basic Law, art. 92; Lei Básica, art. 87(1).

293 Basic Law, art. 89(1); Lei Básica, art. 87(2).

294 Peter Wesley-Smith, Constitutional and Administrative Law in Hong Kong 48 (2d ed. 1994).

295 Albert H.Y. Chen, *The Relationship between the Central Government and the SAR*, *in* The Basic Law and Hong Kong's Future 107, 124 (Peter Wesley-Smith & Albert H.Y. Chen eds., 1988).

296 Young, *supra* note 183, at 685.

Chinese Governments "in all matters covered by the Basic Law."[297] Xiao Weiyun prescribed that "the power to review whether the laws enacted by the Hong Kong legislature were consistent with the Basic Law was vested in the National People's Congress Standing Committee and not in the Court of Final Appeal."[298]

Both the Basic Law and the Lei Básica do formally debar "strong-form review," the kind of judicial review that originated in the United States and spread to Western Europe after 1945, and from the late 1980s onwards to the former Soviet bloc, Latin America, Africa, and Asia.[299] Strong-form review, also known as judicial supremacy, refers to the constitutional arrangement under which the apex or constitutional court is empowered to pronounce final interpretations of an entrenched constitution[300] that cannot be amended by simple legislative majority;[301] just as judicial invalidations of statutes on constitutional grounds cannot be overturned by simple majority.[302] In contrast with countries with strong-form review (including many hybrid regimes), the plenary National People's Congress may, upon the initiative of the Standing Committee, the State Council, or the respective Region,[303] by a simple majority amend the Basic Law or the Lei Básica to nullify not only the judicial interpretations of the CFA or the TUI but even the elaborate formal guarantees of judicial independence in either constitutional instrument.[304] Moreover, a constitutional amendment proposal originating from an SAR is much more difficult to carry than one from Beijing: it requires a two-thirds majority of the SAR's deputies to the National People's Congress, plus two-thirds of the Legislative Council or the Legislative Assembly, and finally the assent of the respective Chief Executive.[305] Compared with Standing Committee Interpretations, amendments are costly in terms of political transactions. First, the National People's Congress convenes only three weeks

297 Yiu-Chu Liu, *Interpretation and Review of the Basic Law of the Hong Kong Special Administrative Region*, 2(1) J. CHINESE L. 49, 56 (1988).

298 Weiyun Xiao et al., *Why the Court of Final Appeal Was Wrong: Comments of the Mainland Scholars on the Judgment of the Court of Final Appeal*, *in* HONG KONG'S CONSTITUTIONAL DEBATE: CONFLICTS OVER INTERPRETATION 53, 56 (Johannes M.M. Chan et al. eds., 2000).

299 STEPHEN GARDBAUM, THE NEW COMMONWEALTH MODEL OF CONSTITUTIONALISM: THEORY AND PRACTICE 6 (2013).

300 *Id.* at 62.

301 *Id.* at 6.

302 Mark Tushnet, *The Rise of Weak-Form Judicial Review*, *in* COMPARATIVE CONSTITUTIONAL LAW 321, 323 (Tom Ginsburg & Rosalind Dixon eds., 2011).

303 Basic Law, art. 159(2); Lei Básica, art. 144(2).

304 Basic Law, art. 159(1); Lei Básica, art. 144(1).

305 Basic Law, art. 159(2); Lei Básica, art. 144(2).

a year, capping the practical frequency of amendment; second, a proposed amendment that is deemed to contradict the "established basic policies of the People's Republic of China regarding Hong Kong [or Macau],"[306] reflected in the Joint Declarations,[307] imposes a "basic structure"[308] in theory constraining the kind of amendment that may be attempted.

Of far more consequence in practice is to have vested in a parliamentary body – the Standing Committee of the National People's Congress – the power to enact prepotent legal instruments bearing the label "Interpretations" of the SAR constitutional documents.[309] Such competence has been described as a Stalinist institution[310] that is designed to facilitate the Leninist Party-state's control of all politico-legal questions that it considers important.[311] It is integral to the Socialist law tradition, which differs from both the common law and civil law legal families in critical ways.[312] The People's Republic of China does not practice checks and balances; however, it does practice a "separation of functions" under which state power is distributed to different bodies.[313] The Standing Committee exercises legislative, not executive or judicial, power;[314] indeed, "Legislative Interpretation" is the formal designation of its handiwork, and is analogous to a constitutional amendment in other jurisdictions.[315] If an Interpretation is a legislative act, then it must be subject to the ordinary procedures of legislation such as committee deliberation and majoritarian voting.[316] In fact, China's Legislation Law,[317] which

306 Basic Law, art. 159(4); Lei Básica, art. 144(4).

307 Basic Law, Preamble; Lei Básica, Preamble.

308 Yaniv Roznai, Unconstitutional Constitutional Amendments: The Limits of Amendment Powers 28–29 (2017).

309 Basic Law, arts. 158(1) & 158(4); Lei Básica, arts. 143(1) & 143(4).

310 Sophia Woodman, *Legislative Interpretation by China's National People's Congress Standing Committee: A Power with Roots in the Stalinist Conception of Law*, *in* Interpreting Hong Kong's Basic Law: The Struggle for Coherence 229, 236 (2007).

311 Xiaonan Yang, *Legislative Interpretations by the Standing Committee of the National People's Congress in China*, 38(1) Hong Kong L. J. 255, 258 (2008).

312 Eric C. Ip, *Interpreting Interpretations: A Methodology for the Judicial Enforcement of Legislative Interpretations of the Hong Kong Basic Law*, 2017 Pub. L. 552, 554 (2017).

313 Charles R. McElwee, Environmental Law in China: Mitigating Risk and Ensuring Compliance 33 (2011).

314 Jian-guo Gong, *Interpretation of the Constitution and Statutes of the People's Republic of China*, 14(2) Crim. Just. Rev. 166, 169 (1989).

315 Albert H.Y. Chen, An Introduction to the Legal System of the People's Republic of China 155 (4th ed. 2011).

316 Dingjian Cai, *The Mechanism for Resolving the Conflict of Laws in China: Ratifying, Recording and Interpreting Law*, *in* Hong Kong's Constitutional Debate 45, 49 (Johannes M.M. Chan & Lison Harris eds., 2005).

317 Legislation Law of the People's Republic of China (adopted at the Third Session of the Ninth National People's Congress on Mar. 15, 2000 and amended in accordance with the Decision

makes no part of Hong Kong or Macau law,[318] does provide for the process of enacting Interpretations generally. Consolidating earlier rules, Section 45 authorizes the Standing Committee to give out an Interpretation whenever "the specific meaning of a legislative provision requires further clarification and/ or a new situation arises after enactment of such legislation, thereby requiring clarification of the basis of its application." In sum, an Interpretation is "a new gloss on an old law."[319] Nevertheless, the Standing Committee has never promulgated any method for arriving at Interpretations.[320] Nothing therefore prevents mainland Chinese legal concepts from being injected into SAR law through such supplementary legislation.[321] This power is the "most powerful and effective tool"[322] Beijing has for intervening in SAR politics and law. The Standing Committee's final interpretative authority[323] entails that any interpretation of the Basic Law or Lei Básica by the CFA or the TUI cannot be regarded as final, but rather subject to approval or acquiescence by the Standing Committee. In brief, judicial interpretations may be reversed by Standing Committee Interpretations without resort to formal procedures for amending constitutions.

While the Standing Committee is obligated to delegate to courts of the Region the independent interpretation, in the course of adjudication, of any provisions "which are within the limits of the autonomy of the [Regions],"[324] the two SAR constitutions, by limiting the competence of courts to "adjudication," may be read as implying that they have no jurisdiction but to resolve concrete disputes in cases at bar, not reviewing and invalidating statutes for unconstitutionality.[325] The SAR courts are authorized to interpret collateral

on Amending the Legislation Law of the People's Republic of China adopted at the Third Session of the Twelfth National People's Congress on Mar. 15, 2015).

318 Basic Law, art.18(2).

319 Qianfan Zhang, The Constitution of China: A Contextual Analysis 136 (2012).

320 Xiaonan Yang, *Two Interpreters of the Basic Law*, *in* Hong Kong's Court of Final Appeal: The Development of the Law in China's Hong Kong 69, 86–87 (Simon N.M. Young & Yash Ghai eds., 2014).

321 Chen, *supra* note 315, at 159.

322 Yang, *supra* note 320, at 78.

323 Contrary to conventional wisdom, the Standing Committee's legislative authority to enact Interpretations is incommensurable with the competence of courts of the Regions to judicially interpret the Basic Law and the Lei Básica in the ordinary course of adjudication. Basic Law. Although the Standing Committee is a higher constitutional authority, it is not a court and cannot set judicial precedents. Legislative Interpretations are general, rather than "question-specific" as with judicial decisions. Yang, *supra* note 320, at 78. The CFA and the TUI remain the sole bodies the SAR constitutions have endowed with final authority to adjudicate in concrete disputes on constitutional issues.

324 Basic Law, art. 158 (2); Lei Básica, art. 143(2).

325 P.Y. Lo, The Hong Kong Basic Law 468 (2011).

provisions in the course of adjudication, but if their interpretations concern "affairs which are the responsibility of the Central People's Government, or concerning the relationship between the Central Authorities and the Region," in cases that cannot be appealed, they are obligated to apply for the CFA or the TUI to elicit an Interpretation of the affected provisions from the Standing Committee.[326] Interpretations are all binding on the courts, although they cannot retroactively affect "judgments previously rendered."[327] Nevertheless, a power in the Standing Committee to override the precedential value of previous court judgments implies the power to determine what the constitutional rules in the SAR will ultimately be, and hence "secure the total subordination of Hong Kong to China."[328]

From the foregoing it must follow that if the Basic Law or the Lei Básica establishes any system of constitutional review in the SARs, it would have to be one of "weak-form review" at best.[329] In a nutshell, weak-form review contrasts with strong-form review in permitting independent courts to express their view that an impugned statute is incompatible with constitutional or human rights norms, but also enables the regime to override the court if it concludes otherwise.[330] Of course, the variant of weak-form review in the SARs differs from those prevalent in Canada, New Zealand, the United Kingdom, the Australian Capital Territory, or the Australian State of Victoria since the 1980s and 1990s, in that Hong Kong or Macau political authorities themselves cannot override disfavored judicial invalidations; they have to invite the Standing Committee to intervene. Nevertheless, whether in the SARs or in the Commonwealth countries above, weak-form judicial review realizes the arrangement that final appellate courts do not automatically enjoy ultimate authority to resolve constitutional issues.[331] Hong Kong and Macau have the distinction of being the only jurisdictions that practice weak-form review without being liberal democracies;[332] as, clearly, the rationale for adopting weak-form review in both SARs was

326 Basic Law, art. 158 (3); Lei Básica, art. 143(3).
327 Basic Law, art.158(4); Lei Básica, art. 143(4).
328 Ghai, *supra* note 47, at 345.
329 Mark Tushnet & Rosalind Dixon, *Weak-Form Review and Its Constitutional Relatives: An Asian Perspective*, in COMPARATIVE CONSTITUTIONAL LAW IN ASIA 102, 105 (Rosalind Dixon & Tom Ginsburg eds., 2014).
330 Tushnet, *supra* note 302, at 323.
331 Stephen Gardbaum, *Are Strong Constitutional Courts Always a Good Thing for New Democracies?*, 53 COLUM. J. TRANSNAT'L L. 285, 289 (2015).
332 *Id.* at 293.

not to guarantee the primacy of the electorate and their representatives in constitutional interpretation but to safeguard the sovereign paramountcy of China's authoritarian regime over them.

CONCLUSION

This chapter explored the strategic structure of Hong Kong's Basic Law and Macau's Lei Básica from both historical and institutional design perspectives. In analogizing their constitutions to political bargains reached in the context of the colonial histories of the two SARs, this chapter endeavored to evidence that many important provisions of the Basic Law and the Lei Básica were designed, subject to the Joint Declaration's constraints, to serve the political and economic interests of elite classes, namely the Chinese Party-state authorities in Beijing and influential business tycoons and professionals in Hong Kong and Macau. Final constitutional authority over the SARs has been placed firmly in the hands of the mainland Party-state, acting through the Standing Committee of the National People's Congress, delegating it where it prefers and reserving it where it does not.[333] Since the late 1980s and early 1990s, the fear that reforms relaxing the Party's grip on political power would trigger nationwide political turmoil has hardened into an adamantine consensus in elite mainland circles.[334] The central authorities are prepared to suppress the SARs' democratization in order to avoid political challenges.[335]

The political systems provided for in the Basic Law and the Lei Básica are indisputably authoritarian in character, as witness the entrenchment of corporatism in the selection of the Chief Executives and a large part of the Legislative Council or the Legislative Assembly. In sum, by constituting the SARs as condominiums of corporate bodies and functional sectors, China can claim to have had people from all walks of life represented, while at the same time ensuring that political loyalists cementing two Establishment Coalitions would dominate both SARs' executives and legislatures.[336] Unified government is a virtual certainty under both constitutions, especially because of a powerful Chief Executive unhindered by competitive elections or rigorous

333 Peter W. Preston, The Politics of China-Hong Kong Relations: Living with Distant Masters 83 (2016).

334 Timothy R. Heath, China's New Governing Party Paradigm: Political Renewal and the Pursuit of National Rejuvenation 11–12 (2014).

335 Alvin Y.H. Cheung, *Road to Nowhere: Hong Kong's Democratization and China's Obligations under Public International Law*, 40(2) Brook. J. Int'l L. 465, 543–44 (2014).

336 Bill K.P. Chou, *Elections in Hong Kong: International Perspectives and Implications for China, in* China and East Asia: After the Wall Street Crisis 75, 90 (Peng Er Lam et al. eds., 2013).

legislative checks. Both constitutions, however, also exhibit liberal, even neoliberal characteristics, and the SAR regimes are structurally liberal autocracies rather than illiberal democracies. Both Hong Kong and Macau constitutions contain important guarantees of personal rights and freedoms as well as judicial independence and government accountability, all of which essentially constrain the SAR regimes to devising policies that avoid negative externalities and incur positive ones. On the dark side, de facto permanently limited suffrage and enduring corporatism radically limit the degree to which citizens can use elections to check, let alone replace, unwanted incumbents and thereby hold the government accountable for its performance.[337] It is therefore safe to conclude that the subnational regimes of the SARs are hybrid by design.

Regarding the problem of constitutional enforcement, the Basic Law and the Lei Básica certainly place heavier emphasis on the roles of political institutions such as the Chief Executive, the Legislative Council or the Legislative Assembly, and the Standing Committee of the National People's Congress, than on the Hong Kong CFA or the TUI. Interpretations by the Standing Committee of the National People's Congress, constituting supplementary legislation that may "interpret" the Basic Law or the Lei Básica, can up-end the "game" of constitutional interpretation by overriding judgments of the CFA or the TUI (up to a point) without engaging the formal amendment process. Had the Basic Law and the Lei Básica been followed by rote, no meaningful constitutional review could have arisen. Both Court and Tribunal could easily abdicate their review competence by ruling that such competence is vested in the Standing Committee exclusively; thus all local legislation not so repealed is to be presumed constitutional, and is bound to be enforced by the courts.[338] And either SAR regime or Beijing could easily whip the courts back into line by using the latent authoritarianism and judicial minimalism of the two Basic Laws by formal or informal means, ranging from amendment to court curbing. Above all, given the vast similarities between Hong Kong's Basic Law and Macau's Lei Básica in terms of constituting unified corporatist governments and weak-form review, any major, persistent divergence between the two SARs in terms of political transaction costs or the antithesis between high-energy and low-energy constitutional review must be explained by appealing to other variables.

337 Bush, *supra* note 49, at 48.

338 Chen, *supra* note 295, at 124.

4

Comparative Constitutional Review in the Chinese Special Administrative Regions

INTRODUCTION

In contrast to the near-identity of formal design in the Hong Kong Basic Law[1] and the Lei Básica de Macau,[2] the practice of hybrid constitutionalism arising from the two constitutional documents of the Hong Kong and Macau Special Administrative Regions (SARs) diverges fundamentally, as witness the antithetical jurisprudence of the Hong Kong Court of Final Appeal (CFA) and the Tribunal de Última Instância de Macau (TUI).[3] The CFA has adopted for itself, and for the courts below it, a "constitutional jurisdiction" to invalidate legislative and administrative acts *erga omnes* on the ground of incompatibility with the Basic Law.[4] In pursuance of these implied powers, but in the absence of explicit constitutional mandates, it has radically extended the franchise in Village Representative elections in the myriad indigenous villages of the Region;[5] imposed on the Hong Kong police a "positive duty" to assist peaceful demonstrators;[6] ordered the Legislative Council to revise covert surveillance statutes to accommodate privacy rights;[7] "read down" primary legislation to save it from being found unconstitutional;[8] struck down admittedly

[1] Basic Law of the Hong Kong Special Administrative Region of the People's Republic of China (adopted at the Third Session of the Seventh National People's Congress on Apr. 4, 1990, effective on Jul. 1, 1997).

[2] Lei Básica da Região Administrativa Especial de Macau da República Popular da China (Basic Law of the Macao Special Administrative Region of the People's Republic of China) (adopted by the First Session of the Eighth National People's Congress on Mar. 31, 1993, effective Dec. 20, 1999).

[3] Paulo Cardinal, *Autonomy as a Tool for Peace: Some Topics Using as a Reference Point the Chinese SARs Seasoned with a Kantian Perpetual Peace Fragrance*, 89 Bol. Fac. Direito U. Coimbra 925, 939 (2013).

[4] P.Y. Lo, The Judicial Construction of Hong Kong's Basic Law: Courts, Politics and Society after 1997 209 (2014).

[5] Sec'y for Justice v. Chan Wah (2000) 3 H.K.C.F.A.R. 459 (H.K.C.F.A.).

[6] Leung Kwok Hung v. H.K.S.A.R. (2005) 8 H.K.C.F.A.R. 229 (H.K.C.F.A.).

[7] Koo Sze Yiu v. Chief Exec. of the H.K.S.A.R. (2006) 9 H.K.C.F.A.R. 441 (H.K.C.F.A.).

[8] H.K.S.A.R. v. Hung Chan Wa (2006) 9 H.K.C.F.A.R. 614 (H.K.C.F.A.).

constitutional statutory provisions, the better to achieve transcendent constitutional ends;[9] deployed defunct colonial laws as additional grounds for invalidating impugned statutory provisions retrospectively as being disproportionate;[10] quashed statutory limits enacted by the Legislative Council on final appellate challenges to virtually any electoral result;[11] entitled post-operative transsexuals to marry in their reassigned sex;[12] prohibited public agencies from imposing "unacceptably harsh burdens on the individual" even when pursuing undisputed "societal interests."[13] These decisions have led scholars to conclude that the CFA has been playing an "activist" role,[14] as an "independent"[15] and "pivotal"[16] "custodian of the constitution,"[17] notwithstanding the continued denial of democratic self-rule by China's authoritarian party-state.[18] Remarkably, the CFA had held impugned statutory provisions to be unconstitutional in more than half – 52.9 percent – of all decisions in which it reviewed the constitutionality of primary legislation between 1997 and 2017 (see Table 4.3).

By contrast, the TUI has neither invalidated any act of primary legislation by the Legislative Assembly nor fashioned any elaborate jurisprudence on the rights and liberties enumerated in Chapter III of the Lei Básica.[19] Indeed, the Tribunal has developed no "in-depth"[20] practice of constitutional review whatever; carefully eschewing the European doctrine of structured proportionality, for example, to scrutinize curtailments of constitutional rights; a jurisprudence that might best be described as "moderate or shy."[21] Its role

9 Koon Wing Yee v. Insider Dealing Tribunal (2008) 11 H.K.C.F.A.R. 170 (H.K.C.F.A.).

10 A Solicitor v. Law Soc'y of Hong Kong (2003) 6 H.K.C.F.A.R. 570 (H.K.C.F.A.).

11 Mok Charles v. Tam Wai Ho (2010) 13 H.K.C.F.A.R. 762 (H.K.C.F.A.)

12 W v. The Registrar of Marriages (2013) 16 H.K.C.F.A.R. 112 (H.K.C.F.A.).

13 Hysan Development Co. Ltd. v. Town Planning Bd. (2016) 19 H.K.C.F.A.R. 372, at 424 (H.K.C.F.A.).

14 Laifan Lin & Mingkang Gu, *Can Courts in Hong Kong Examine the Constitutionality of the Legislative Conduct of the PRC?*, *in* Hong Kong in Transition: One Country, Two Systems 175, 188 (Robert Ash et al. eds., 2003).

15 Eric C. Ip, *The Evolution of Constitutional Adjudication in the Chinese Special Administrative Regions: Theory and Practice*, 61 Am. J. Comp. L. 799, 801 (2013).

16 Johannes Chan, *Hong Kong's Constitutional Journey, 1997–2011*, *in* Constitutionalism in Asia in the Early Twenty-First Century 169, 179 (Albert H.Y. Chen ed., 2014).

17 Albert H.Y. Chen & P.Y. Lo, *The Basic Law Jurisprudence of the Court of Final Appeal*, *in* Hong Kong's Court of Final Appeal: The Development of the Law in China's Hong Kong 352, 390 (Simon N.M. Young & Yash Ghai eds., 2014).

18 Martin S. Flaherty, *Hong Kong Fifteen Years after the Handover: One Country, Which Direction?*, 51 Colum. J. Transnat'l L. 275, 276 (2013).

19 Paulo Cardinal & Yihe Zhang, *Subnational Constitutionalism in the SARS of the People's Republic of China: An Exceptional Tailored Suit Model?*, 4(2) Persp. on Fed. 101, 128 (2012).

20 *Id.* at 129.

21 *Id.* at 128.

in protecting rights has been criticized as suffering from a "deficit"[22]: in some of its earliest cases[23] the TUI dealt a "deadly blow" to the *amparo*,[24] a judicial procedure widely used in Latin America, among other regions of the world, to uphold constitutional rights against the state.[25] Thus, Macau has become an outlier in the global rise of *amparo* mechanisms across the civil law world,[26] having closed off all procedural avenues for addressing issues of constitutionality before the Macau judiciary in general, let alone the TUI.[27] The latter has consistently diverged from the CFA in declining to review legislation or on any grounds to declare it null and void with general, prospective, and retrospective effect,[28] while affirming the competence of the Chief Executive to legislate de facto in the guise of administrative regulations independently of the Legislative Assembly.[29] Contrary to the established opinion of the United Nations Human Rights Committee,[30] the TUI has repeatedly rejected the right of senior officials convicted at trial before the TUI to appeal their convictions, as guaranteed by the International Covenant on Civil and Political Rights (ICCPR) incorporated by reference in the Lei Básica.[31] More recently, the Tribunal has declined to exercise jurisdiction over an appeal from the organizers of an unofficial Civil Referendum on democratization against the decision of the Instituto para os Assuntos Cívicos e Municipais (Civil and Municipal Affairs Bureau) to suppress their movement, on the ground that the nature of such a Referendum is unclassifiable under current law, and thus cannot be protected by Article 27 of the Lei Básica, which guarantees the freedoms of association and assembly.[32]

22 Jorge Godinho & Paulo Cardinal, *Macau's Court of Final Appeal, in* HONG KONG'S COURT OF FINAL APPEAL: THE DEVELOPMENT OF THE LAW IN CHINA'S HONG KONG 608, 634 (Simon N.M. Young & Yash Ghai eds., 2014).

23 Case 1/2000 (T.U.I.M.); Case 2/2000 (T.U.I.M.).

24 Paulo Cardinal, *The Judicial Guarantees of Fundamental Rights in the Macau Legal System:* A Parcours *Under the Focus of Continuity and of Autonomy, in* ONE COUNTRY, TWO SYSTEMS, THREE LEGAL ORDERS – PERSPECTIVES OF EVOLUTION 221, 261 (Jorge Costa Oliveira & Paulo Cardinal et al. eds., 2009).

25 ALLAN R. BREWER-CARÍAS, CONSTITUTIONAL PROTECTION OF HUMAN RIGHTS IN LATIN AMERICA: A COMPARATIVE STUDY OF AMPARO PROCEEDINGS 1 (2009).

26 *See* Paulo Cardinal, *The Writ of Amparo: A New Lighthouse for the Rule of Law in the Philippines*, 87 PHIL. L.J. 229 (2012)

27 Godinho & Cardinal, *supra* note 22, at 621.

28 LO, *supra* note 4, at 209.

29 Case 28/2006 (T.U.I.M.).

30 Human Rights Committee, *General Comment No. 32. Article 14: Right to equality before courts and tribunals and to a fair trial, doc.*, C.C.P.R./C./G.C./32 (2007).

31 Lei Básica, art. 40(1).

32 Case 100/2014 (T.U.I.M.).

This chapter compares and contrasts the high-energy constitutional review of the CFA from 1997 to 2017 with the TUI's low-energy constitutional review between 1999 and 2017, as expressed in the judicial doctrines they evolved in the first two decades of their existence. The reason for focusing on judicial doctrine is because it is "the currency of the law,"[33] the abstract of legal rules and standards espoused in particular judgments, making up the core of judges' acts.[34] On the one hand, it sets boundaries on the conduct of judges; on the other, it equips them with stratagems *qua* decisional principles for reaching preferred legal outcomes.[35] Legal scholars have studied doctrine from a normative perspective, but have yet to give proper attention to its practical functioning. Oddly, many of the same social scientists who have conducted significant explanatory or descriptive research into law and courts, uncritically assume legal doctrine, the corpus of detailed justificatory arguments that judges craft, to be irrelevant.[36] Even less is it appreciated how doctrine affects politics.[37] But groundbreaking empirical or behavioral studies of law and courts will not be feasible until first the phenomenon in question is fully fathomed.[38] This chapter is organized as follows. The next section describes the institutional properties of the CFA and the TUI: their organizational structure, appellate jurisdiction, and personnel composition. Though hailing from different legal traditions, the apex courts' outfits are not near as far removed from each other as are their diametrically opposite principles of constitutional adjudication. Both courts dispose of considerable institutional independence and security whenever they might want to avail themselves, as both wield power to adjudicate with finality. Most importantly, appointments to both Courts have not been politicized, and their judges have been confirmed in no identifiable partisan tendencies.[39] The third section contrasts the constitutional jurisprudence of the CFA and the TUI in the following five dimensions: constitutional review jurisdiction, interpretive methodology,

33 Emerson H. Tiller & Frank B. Cross, *What is Legal Doctrine?*, 100(1) Nw. U. L. Rev. 517, 517 (2006).

34 David Robertson, The Judge as Political Theorist: Contemporary Constitutional Review 21 (2010).

35 Emerson H. Tiller, *The "Law" and Economics of Judicial Decision-Making: A Positive Political Theory Perspective*, *in* The Oxford Handbook of Law and Economics: Volume 1: Methodology and Concepts 222, 242 (Francesco Parisi ed., 2017).

36 Robertson, *supra* note 34, at 24.

37 Tiller & Cross, *supra* note 33, at 518.

38 Jan M. Smits, *What Is Legal Doctrine? On The Aims and Methods of Legal-Dogmatic Research*, *in* Rethinking Legal Scholarship: A Transatlantic Dialogue 207, 227 (Rob van Gestel et al. eds., 2017).

39 Simon N.M. Young, *Constitutional Rights in Hong Kong's Court of Final Appeal*, 27 Chinese (Taiwan) Y. B. Int'l L. & Aff. 67, 93 (2011).

abstract review, standards of review, and judicial petition. It demonstrates how the constitutional doctrines of the two apex tribunals are nearly perfectly opposed to each other. The final section concludes with the findings of this chapter.

INSTITUTIONAL COMPARISON

The CFA and the TUI as formal institutions mirror each other. Common Article 2 of the Basic Law and the Lei Básica authorizes the SARs of both Hong Kong and Macau to "exercise a high degree of autonomy and enjoy executive, legislative and independent judicial power, including that of final adjudication." In both constitutions, Article 11 establishes their supremacy over all other legal norms in both SARs. Common Article 19 vests in both judiciaries "independent judicial power, including that of final adjudication," and "jurisdiction over all cases," except for "acts of state such as defence and foreign affairs." Article 82 of the Basic Law and Article 84 of the Lei Básica provide that "the power of final adjudication" is "vested" in the CFA and the TUI, respectively. Although Macau's civil law system knows no doctrine of precedent, the TUI's statutory competence to harmonize jurisprudence binds lower courts across all domains of law constitutional and non-constitutional,[40] and is comparable to the precedential effect of common law judgments.[41] The fact that the three-member TUI possesses the smallest possible number of judges entails that, for most practical purposes, it would follow its own decisions in comparable future cases, simply because the same judges who determined the former would also determine the later.[42] Neither the Sino–British or Sino–Portuguese Joint Declaration, nor either SAR constitutional document contains detailed provisions on the composition and structure of either apex court, placing considerable discretion in the hands of the Legislative Council and the Legislative Assembly to design the organization of the CFA and the TUI by way of the Hong Kong Court of Final Appeal Ordinance[43] and the Lei de

[40] Jorge A.F. Godinho, Macau Business Law & Legal System 20 (2007).

[41] Paulo Cardinal & Pereira Vidal, *An Outline of the Macau Legal System*, 23 Hong Kong L.J. 358, 363 (1993).

[42] Godinho & Cardinal, *supra* note 22, at 609–610.

[43] Hong Kong Court of Final Appeal Ordinance, Cap. 484 (Hong Kong) [hereinafter "CFA Ordinance"]. For a historical overview of the process leading to the enactment of the Ordinance, *see* Simon N.M. Young et al., *Genesis of Hong Kong's Court of Final Appeal, in* Hong Kong's Court of Final Appeal: The Development of the Law in China's Hong Kong 121, 141–42 (Simon N.M. Young & Yash Ghai eds., 2014) ("The establishment of the CFA was a tumultuous process consumed by politics and negotiations between the

Bases da Organização Judiciária (Fundamental Law on Judicial Organization).[44]

The Hong Kong Court of Final Appeal

The Hong Kong Court of Final Appeal Ordinance establishes the CFA as a superior court of record[45] to hear appeals from the Court of Appeal and the High Court[46] and vests in its power to "confirm, reverse or vary the decision of the court from which the appeal lies or may remit the matter with its opinion thereon to that court."[47] The CFA has no specific constitutional jurisdiction, just like the TUI: cases of constitutional importance reach the court by way of civil or criminal appeals. Constitutional cases channeled through the route of civil appeals take the form of appeals for judicial review[48] or other civil decisions which rely on a collateral constitutional challenge to the High Court. The Court of Appeal has accepted that the constitutionality of legislation may be challenged even if the applicant has not been affected by an administrative act made pursuant to a legislative provision alleged to be unconstitutional, if the applicant can establish that the provision would infringe his fundamental rights were it enforced by agencies of the executive.[49] This acceptance is not questioned by the CFA, whence all civil appeals are now within the discretion of the Court of Appeal or the CFA if "the question involved in the appeal is one which [has] great general or public importance," or if otherwise the issue at bar ought to be submitted to the Court

Chinese and British governments as well as the legislature of Hong Kong. It highlighted how much Hong Kong people at that time valued the importance of having distinguished overseas judges sitting on the final court. It also highlighted the mistrust that Hong Kong people felt about China, especially after the events of 4 June 1989. In the end, the shape of the CFA reflected much Chinese thinking, probably more so than British or Hong Kong aspirations for the Court.")

44 Lei de Bases da Organização Judiciária, Law 9/1999 (Macau) [hereinafter "Lei de Bases da Organização Judiciária"].

45 CFA Ordinance, s. 3.

46 The High Court of Justice was officially renamed the "Court of First Instance of the High Court" on July 1, 1997.

47 CFA Ordinance, s. 17(1).

48 Lee Yee Shing Jacky v. Inland Revenue Bd. of Rev. [2011] 6 H.K.C. 307, at [74] (H.K.C.F.I.) (Lam J: "In the exercise of its supervisory jurisdiction, the High Court through the mechanism of judicial review ensures all administrative bodies and inferior tribunals observe the rule of law. Legality, rationality and fairness are the touchstones of this jurisdiction. It is described as 'one of the great historic artefacts of the common law' and it stems from 'the constitutional role of the High Court as the guardian of standards of legality and due process."

49 Johannes M.M. Chan & Kemal Bokhary, Halsbury's Laws of Hong Kong: Constitutional and Human Rights Law 199 (2015).

for decision.[50] Merit, rather than the satisfaction of an arbitrary pecuniary threshold, is now the primary factor determining the fate of civil appeals to the CFA. Regarding criminal matters, the CFA may in its own discretion hear appeals from the Court of Appeal or the High Court relating to decisions other than jury verdicts or findings, such as appeals from Magistrates' Courts.[51] The accused in a criminal case is normally entitled to raise constitutional challenges, often against legislation, collaterally.[52]

The CFA has always jealously guarded its power of final adjudication under the Sino–British Joint Declaration and the Basic Law. In *Solicitor v. Law Society of Hong Kong*,[53] the Court invalidated a ban on appeals to itself from the Court of Appeal concerning orders of the Solicitors Disciplinary Tribunal, as set forth in Section 13(1) of the Legal Practitioners Ordinance;[54] statutory limitations of this kind "cannot be imposed arbitrarily . . . there must be reasonable proportionality between the limitation and the [legitimate] purpose sought to be achieved."[55] Similarly, in *Mok Charles Peter v. Tam Wai Ho*[56] the Court invalidated Section 67(3) of the Legislative Council Ordinance[57] that prohibited appeals to the Court from determinations of the High Court at trials of election petitions. The Legislative Council responded favorably and in 2011 amended legislation to extend the Court's jurisdiction to settle disputes in elections for the Legislative Council itself, the eighteen District Councils, and Village Representatives from roughly 700 villages.[58]

The current arrangements for judicial appointments to the CFA appear designed to minimize the Chief Executive's influence. The Judicial Officers Recommendation Commission, chaired by the

50 CFA Ordinance, s. 22(1)(b).

51 CFA Ordinance, s. 31.

52 Richard Gordon & Johnny Mok, Judicial Review in Hong Kong 324 (LexisNexis, 2d ed. 2014).

53 A Solicitor v. Law Soc'y of Hong Kong (2003) 6 H.K.C.F.A.R. 570 (H.K.C.F.A.).

54 Legal Practitioners Ordinance, Cap. 159 (Hong Kong).

55 A Solicitor v. Law Soc'y of Hong Kong (2003) 6 H.K.C.F.A.R. 570, at 584–85 (H.K.C.F.A.).

56 Mok Charles Peter v. Tam Wai Ho (2010) 13 H.K.C.F.A.R. 762 (H.K.C.F.A.).

57 Legislative Council Ordinance, Cap. 542 (Hong Kong) [hereinafter "Legislative Council Ordinance"].

58 Yu Chi Shing Paul v. Or Sin Yi Windy [2013] 5 H.K.L.R.D. 326, 330–31 (H.K.C.A.) (Cheung, C.J.H.C.) ("Following these cases [e.g., Mok Charles v. Tam Wai Ho (2010) 13 H.K.C.F.A.R. 762 (H.K.C.F.A.)], the Administration introduced the Electoral Legislation (Miscellaneous Amendments) Bill 2011 to provide for an appeal mechanism under which a party to an election petition concerning a Legislative Council election, District Councils election or Village Representative election may lodge an appeal to the Court of Final Appeal against the determination of the election petition by the Court of First Instance, subject to leave being granted by the Appeal Committee of the Court of Final Appeal.")

Chief Justice,[59] consists of the Secretary for Justice (*viz.* Attorney General),[60] two judges, one barrister, one solicitor, and three lay members[61] appointed by the Chief Executive on the Law Society Council's and the Bar Council's recommendation.[62] To appoint or dismiss the judges of the CFA requires the Legislative Council's endorsement.[63] By convention, the Chief Executive appoints every candidate for judicial office recommended by the Commission, and the Legislative Council endorses these appointments. American-style, politicized confirmation hearings of judges have never occurred in Hong Kong.

The Chief Justice of the CFA doubles as Head of the Judiciary, and is charged with administering the court system as a whole.[64] He has power to appoint and dismiss deputy High Court judges,[65] deputy District judges,[66] deputy magistrates and deputy special magistrates,[67] and to invite a High Court judge to sit on the Court of Appeal as an additional judge.[68] The Chief Justice is spokesman for the judiciary[69] and defender of its independence versus the Government and Legislative Council.[70] As the CFA's President,[71] he is responsible for conducting the Court's business,[72] as by selecting which local or overseas non-permanent judges will sit in a given case.[73] The Chief Justice also has power to make subsidiary legislation under a plethora of statutes.[74] To be appointed Chief Justice,

59 Judicial Officers Recommendation Commission Ordinance, Cap. 92 (Hong Kong), s. 3(1)(a) [hereinafter "JORC Ordinance"].

60 JORC Ordinance, s. 3(1)(b).

61 JORC Ordinance, s. 3(1)(c).

62 JORC Ordinance, s. 3(1A).

63 Basic Law, art. 90(2).

64 CFA Ordinance, s. 6(2).

65 High Court Ordinance, Cap.4 (Hong Kong) [hereinafter "High Court Ordinance"], s. 10(1) & s. 10(4).

66 District Court Ordinance, Cap.336 (Hong Kong), s. 7(1) & s. 7(4).

67 Magistrates Ordinance, Cap.227 (Hong Kong), s.5A(1) & s. 5A(3).

68 High Court Ordinance, s. 5(2).

69 Simon N.M. Young et al., *Role of the Chief Justice*, *in* Hong Kong's Court of Final Appeal: The Development of the Law in China's Hong Kong 225, 248 (Simon N.M. Young & Yash Ghai eds., 2014).

70 Farewell Sitting for the Honourable Mr Justice Andrew Li CJ (2010) 13 H.K.C.F.A.R. 128, at 128–29 (H.K.C.F.A.).

71 CFA Ordinance, s. 16(2).

72 CFA Ordinance, s. 47.

73 CFA Ordinance, s. 16(1)(c).

74 P.Y. Lo, The Hong Kong Basic Law 507 (LexisNexis 2011). Examples include the Bankruptcy Ordinance, Cap. 6 (Hong Kong); Probate and Administration Ordinance, Cap. 7 (Hong Kong); Labour Tribunal Ordinance, Cap.25 (Hong Kong); the Trustee Ordinance, Cap.29 (Hong Kong);fcdcc Mental Health Ordinance (Cap.155); the Legal Practitioners

a candidate must be a permanent resident of the Hong Kong Special Administrative Region of Chinese nationality, with no right of abode in any foreign state,[75] and be either a superior court judge[76] or a barrister having practiced as a barrister or solicitor in Hong Kong for a period of no less than ten years.[77] A Chief Justice's tenure is slightly more secure than other judges': he may be removed from office by the Chief Executive only after an investigation that will have vindicated an allegation of inability to discharge his duties or misbehavior, by a tribunal appointed by the latter and consisting of no less than five local judges, plus the endorsement of the Legislative Council.[78] The CFA's inaugural Chief Justice was Andrew Li QC, then forty-nine years old, who specialized in commercial law but lacked judicial experience apart from serving as a part-time deputy High Court judge, and had being appointed to the Executive Council of Governor Chris Patten at the same time as C. H. Tung, the future Chief Executive, in 1992.[79]

In addition to the Chief Justice, the CFA has three full-time permanent judges.[80] The qualifications required of an appointee to a permanent judgeship are identical to those of an appointee to the Chief Justiceship,[81] except that one may hold a right of abode in a foreign state. Between 1997 and 2017, all seven persons appointed to be permanent judges of the CFA had served as judges of the Court of Appeal; each had also been a barrister in private practice before joining the bench. Sixty-five years is the ordinary retirement age of Chief Justices and permanent judges;[82] with the Chief Executive's approval, either may have their time in office extended for a maximum of two periods of three years beyond that age.[83] The Basic Law offers no express protection of judges' income security except the guarantee that all colonial judges might retain seniority with salaries and benefits "no less favourable than before [the

Ordinance, Cap.159 (Hong Kong); and Domestic and Cohabitation Relationships Violence Ordinance, Cap.189 (Hong Kong).

75 Basic Law, art. 90.

76 CFA Ordinance, s. 12(1)(a) & s. 12(1A)(a).

77 CFA Ordinance, s. 12(1).

78 Basic Law, art. 89(2).

79 Young et al., *supra* note 43, at 140–41.

80 Simon N.M. Young & Antonio Da Roza, *The Judges*, *in* HONG KONG'S COURT OF FINAL APPEAL: THE DEVELOPMENT OF THE LAW IN CHINA'S HONG KONG 253, 261 (Simon N.M. Young & Yash Ghai eds., 2014).

81 CFA Ordinance, s.12(1)(1A).

82 Pension Benefits (Judicial Officers) Ordinance, Cap.401 (Hong Kong), s. 6.

83 CFA Ordinance, s. 14(2)(a). Kang-chung Ng, *Former Judge Bokhary: "I was Ousted for Being Too Liberal,"* SOUTH CHINA MORNING POST, Nov. 4, 2012, www.scmp.com/news/hong-kong/article/1075186/former-judge-bokhary-i-was-ousted-being-too-liberal

Handover]."[84] Judicial remuneration is rather determined by the Chief Executive from year to year after considering the non-binding recommendation of the Standing Committee on Judicial Salaries and Conditions of Service, a non-statutory body.[85] By convention, rather than statute, judicial salaries are secure.

The non-permanent judges of the Court are chosen by the Chief Justice case by case from two lists comprising at most thirty judges,[86] each appointed for three years at a time. One list consists of sitting or retired Hong Kong judges; the other, sitting or retired judges from outside the Region with experience on courts of final appeal or judicial administration elsewhere in the common law world.[87] There is no mandatory retirement age for either category of non-permanent judge; they may serve an unlimited number of three-year terms so long as they continue to be reappointed by the Chief Executive on the Chief Justice's recommendation and with the Legislative Council's endorsement.[88] The institution of overseas non-permanent judges originated as continuity in the provision of world-class legal expertise and judicial independence for the Hong Kong legal system after the abolition of appeals to the Privy Council in London in 1997.[89] As of December 2017, four Chief Justices of Australia, three Justices of the High Court of Australia, one Justice of the Supreme Court of Fiji, one Chief Justice of New Zealand, two Judges of the Supreme Court of New Zealand, two Presidents of the Supreme Court of the United Kingdom, and ten Law Lords or Justices of the latter Court had among others been appointed to serve as overseas non-permanent judges. They fly into Hong Kong to sit on the Court's five-judge panel, as scheduled, in one-month stints, and usually spend the first two weeks of their stint in hearings, while reserving the balance of it for writing judgments.[90] The availability of active foreign judges is limited by their domestic judicial duties.[91] The Court under Chief Justice Andrew Li developed a policy to invite an overseas judge to be the fifth judge in every substantive case.[92]

84 Basic Law, art. 93.

85 Billy S.K. Wong, *Hong Kong Judges See Lowest Pay Rise in Eight Years Amid Manpower Crunch*, SOUTH CHINA MORNING POST, Oct. 4, 2017, www.scmp.com/news/hong-kong/law-crime/article/2114030/hong-kong-judges-see-lowest-pay-rise-eight-years-amid

86 CFA Ordinance, s. 10.

87 Basic Law, art. 82.

88 Young & Da Roza, *supra* note 80, at 256–57.

89 *Id.* at 263.

90 Young et al., *supra* note 43, at 142.

91 David S. Law, *Judicial Comparativism and Judicial Diplomacy*, 163 U. PA. L. REV. 927, 993–94 (2015).

92 Young et al., *supra* note 43, at 143.

The presence of a diverse mix of distinguished jurists on the Court has greatly enhanced the CFA's global standing and reputation.[93]

Tribunal de Última Instância de Macau

The principle of judicial independence did not become officially enshrined in Macau until after the Carnation Revolution of 1974. The Constitution of Portugal of 1976 introduced to Macau a "mixed" system of constitutional review through the Estatuto Orgânico de Macau 1976,[94] which was deployed as an instrument to establish an autonomous judiciary in the dependency.[95] In this system, centralized constitutional review in the Tribunal Constitucional in Lisbon coexisted with decentralized review in the local courts that had jurisdiction in Macau cases.[96] The courts of Macau fit in as comarca (county) courts into the metropolitan system of the Portuguese judiciary, and had no power of final adjudication.[97] Because of their direct subordination to superiors in Lisbon, the Macau Governor and Government had little room for maneuver in influencing judicial decision-making.[98] It was not until the 1991 that the Portuguese Parliament gave the Macau judiciary autonomy from Portugal.[99] In the years leading up to the Handover in 1999, the Government of Macau took positive steps to develop and strengthen the local judicial system in preparation for Chinese rule.[100] In 1993, a Tribunal Superior de Justiça was established as the de facto final appellate court of Macau over matters civil, criminal, administrative, fiscal and customs related.[101] Judges were appointed by the Governor on the recommendation of the Supreme Council of Justice and the Judicial Council.[102] That said, in

93 Albert H.Y. Chen & P.Y. Lo, *Hong Kong's Judiciary under "One Country, Two Systems," in* ASIA-PACIFIC JUDICIARIES: INDEPENDENCE, IMPARTIALITY AND INTEGRITY 131, 135 (H.P. Lee ed., 2018).

94 CHIEN-HUEI WU, WTO AND THE GREATER CHINA: ECONOMIC INTEGRATION AND DISPUTE RESOLUTION 240 (2012).

95 YUFAN HAO ET AL., POLITICAL ECONOMY OF MACAO SINCE 1999: THE DILEMMA OF SUCCESS 171 (2017).

96 Sofia Amaral-Garcia et al., *Judicial Independence and Party Politics in the Kelsenian Constitutional Court: The Case of Portugal*, 6(2) J. EMPIRICAL LEGAL STUD. 381, 385 (2009).

97 GODINHO, *supra* note 40, at 10.

98 Cardinal & Vidal, *supra* note 41, at 375.

99 MAN LENG MAI & WAI NENG HO, ADMINISTRATIVE LITIGATION IN MACAO: SYSTEM, LEGISLATION AND CASES 4 (2011).

100 HAO ET AL., *supra* note 95, at 170.

101 GODINHO, *supra* note 40, at 10.

102 U.S. Department of State, *Macau*, 24 ANN. HUM. RTS. REP. SUBMITTED TO CONG. 1089, 1090 (1999).

cases involving the "basic rights of the citizen," defendants could still appeal to Portugal's Tribunal Constitucional, which could overturn all lower court rulings.[103] The election of Jorge Sampaio as President of Portugal in 1996 added further momentum to the consolidation of Macau's judicial institutions as guardians of its autonomy and identity.[104] In light of a dearth of qualified personnel to speed legal proceedings,[105] the Portuguese Macau government instituted a scheme to supply future judges by recruiting graduates of Chinese universities, sending them to Portugal for two years' training in law, followed by a year of further judicial studies at the University of Macau.[106] In June 1999, six months prior to the Handover, President Sampaio signed a decree devolving all judicial power to the Macau judiciary.[107]

The Tribunal de Última Instância was established on December 20, 1999, the date of the Handover, under the Fundamental Law on Judicial Organization 1999, which made the Tribunal "the highest organ in the hierarchy of courts,"[108] vested with final appellate jurisdiction over all cases in the Macau Special Administrative Region,[109] and competence to interpret the Lei Básica according to Article 143 of the latter;[110] and with jurisdiction inter alia to issue "unified judicial opinions" or to uniformizar a jurisprudência in a way that binds all inferior courts (despite lack of a formal doctrine of precedent);[111] hear civil and criminal appeals from the intermediate appellate court, Tribunal de Segunda Instância (TSI);[112] adjudicate cases arising from the official acts of the Chief Executive, of the President of the Legislative Assembly, of the President of the TUI, of the Procurator General, and of other high officials of the Government;[113] try criminal cases pertaining to offences committed by these officials;[114] hear habeas corpus

[103] U.S. Department of State, *Macau*, 19 ANN. HUM. RTS. REP. SUBMITTED TO CONG. 922, 926 (1994).

[104] CARMEN AMADO MENDES, PORTUGAL, CHINA AND THE MACAU NEGOTIATIONS 1986–1999 71 (2013).

[105] HAO ET AL., *supra* note 95, at 175.

[106] *Id.* at 172.

[107] Chaoyang Jiang & Feng Yang, *The Administrative Litigation System in Macao*, *in* ADMINISTRATIVE LITIGATION SYSTEMS IN GREATER CHINA AND EUROPE 73, 77 (Yuewen Li ed., 2016).

[108] Lei de Bases da Organização Judiciária, s. 44(1).

[109] Lei de Bases da Organização Judiciária, s. 16(1).

[110] Lei de Bases da Organização Judiciária, s. 16(2).

[111] Lei de Bases da Organização Judiciária, s. 44(2)(1).

[112] Lei de Bases da Organização Judiciária, s. 44(2)(2) & s. 44 (2)(3).

[113] Lei de Bases da Organização Judiciária, s. 44(2)(5) & s. 44(2)(7).

[114] Lei de Bases da Organização Judiciária, s. 44(2)(6) & s. 44(2)(8).

applications;[115] and resolve jurisdictional conflicts between lower courts,[116] and between the lower courts and executive authorities.[117]

In notable contrast to the CFA, which acquiesced in the High Court's incremental expansion of its jurisdiction to review legislative acts, the TUI has proactively suppressed moves to initiate litigation for the purpose of testing the constitutionality of legislative or administrative acts.[118] In Case 1/2000[119] the TUI affirmed that the Lei Básica has instituted no dedicated constitutional review procedure. The claimant had applied for a concrete review appeal before the Tribunal Constitucional of Portugal against a decision of Macau's Tribunal Superior de Justiça, which in reaching its judgment had relied on legislation that should, it was argued, be struck down as contrary to the Portuguese Constitution. The Tribunal Constitucional, however, did not render a decision before the end of Portuguese rule in 1999. After the lower courts of Macau dismissed his case under Section 70(2)(3) and (4) of the new Fundamental Law of Judicial Organization which, entering into effect on the date of the Handover, obligated the courts to cease adjudicating cases invoking application of the Constitution of Portugal, the claimant applied to the TUI to impugn the original decision as contrary to the Lei Básica instead, arguing that the TUI should entertain his appeal because, otherwise, two statutory norms alleged incompatible with the Lei Básica would be continuously effective, "undermining the spirit of a rule of law state system."[120] The TUI dismissed the appeal. Judge Chu Kin, writing for a unanimous Tribunal, ruled that no right of appeal against a court judgment issued prior to the Handover could be grounded on the Lei Básica, which entered into force on the date of the Handover. To recognize such a right would be "tantamount to establishing a species of appeal that does not exist under ... current law"; thus "after the cessation of the litigation process of the instant case, it is not permissible to invoke incompatibility with the Lei Básica da Região Administrativa Especial de Macau as a ground to re-open the litigation process to review the effectiveness of statutory norms applied in the course of judicial adjudication."[121]

The TUI is made up of three judges,[122] headed by a President appointed by the Chief Executive from incumbent judges, who all serve renewable three-

[115] Lei de Bases da Organização Judiciária, s. 44(2)(10).

[116] Lei de Bases da Organização Judiciária, s. 44(2)(14).

[117] Lei de Bases da Organização Judiciária, s. 44(2)(15).

[118] Chaoyang Jiang, A Study on the Basic Law of Macau and the Rule of Law of the Macau Special Administrative Region 180 (2016).

[119] Case 1/2000 (T.U.I.M.); *see* Case 2/2000 (T.U.I.M.) & Case 4/2000 (T.U.I.M.).

[120] Case 1/2000, at 2 (T.U.I.M.).

[121] Case 1/2000, at 4 (T.U.I.M.).

[122] Lei de Bases da Organização Judiciária, Annex, Table III.

year terms.[123] Under the Uniformização de Jurisprudência (Fixation of Jurisprudence) procedure, the TUI may convene as an expanded panel of five judges to resolve conflicts between its own decisions, or between itself and the TSI, the additional two judges being the TSI's President and its most senior judge.[124] The President of the TUI is the representative of the Macau judiciary;[125] he convenes and presides over the TUI's hearings,[126] and administers its work, including assigning judicial duties.[127] The President is assisted by a permanent and autonomous Office of the President of the Tribunal in coordinating the various levels of courts, providing them with administrative, technical and fiscal support.[128] The President of the TUI must be a Chinese citizen who is a permanent resident of Macau; however, no express provision exists in the Lei Básica requiring forfeiture of his right of abode in foreign states, as there is in Hong Kong's Basic Law.[129] As in many civil law jurisdictions,[130] a Judicial Council exists in Macau, under the Chairmanship of the President, to oversee the management and discipline of judiciary officers and supporting staff.[131]

TUI judges are appointed by the Chief Executive upon the recommendation of a Comissão Independente para a Indigitação de Juízes (Independent Commission for the Recommendation of Judges), made up of one judge (currently the President of the TUI), one lawyer, and five prominent members of the community.[132] The President of the TUI, unlike the Chief Justice of the CFA, is not the Commission's chairman, nor is there a Macau government

[123] Lei de Bases da Organização Judiciária, s. 49(1); s. (2); & s. (3).

[124] Case 60-A/2015, at 4 (T.U.I.M.) (Lima, J.: "Under the circumstances of Uniformização de Jurisprudência, that is, on the same legal question, the Tribunal de Última Instância had issued two conflicting decisions, or a decision of the Tribunal de Segunda Instância is in conflict with a decision of the Tribunal de Última Instância, it is indeed possible to lodge an appellate application with the Tribunal de Última Instância, to have an expanded collegial bench made up of five judges to take part in adjudication; for this reason, the President of the Tribunal de Segunda Instância and the most senior judge of that Tribunal, together with the three judges of the Tribunal de Última Instância, would be summoned [to form the expanded bench] according to Lei de Bases da Organização Judiciária, s. 44(2)(1) & s. 46, and Código de Processo Penal (Code of Criminal Procedure), s. 419 & s.425.") [author's translation].

[125] Lei de Bases da Organização Judiciária, s. 51(1) & s. (2).

[126] Lei de Bases da Organização Judiciária, s. 51(5) & s. (6)

[127] Lei de Bases da Organização Judiciária, s. 51(4) & s. 9.

[128] Lei de Bases da Organização Judiciária, s. 51.

[129] Lei Básica, art. 88(2).

[130] *See* Nuno Garoupa & Tom Ginsburg, *The Comparative Law and Economics of Judicial Councils*, 27 BERKELEY J. INT'L LAW. 53 (2009).

[131] Estatuto dos Magistrados (General Rules of the Magistrates), Law 10/1999 (Macau), s. 93(3) [hereinafter "Estatuto dos Magistrados"].

[132] Comissão Independente para a Indigitação de Juízes (CIIJ), *Lista dos Membros*, TRIBUNALS DA RAEM, www.court.gov.mo/pt/subpage/ciij

representative on it such as Hong Kong's Secretary for Justice. But like their Hong Kong counterparts judges are selected on the basis of professional qualifications; plus, the Macau Commission may recommend "qualified judges of foreign nationality" for appointment, including to the TUI.[133] Indeed, appointment of overseas judges is not anathema to the civil law tradition.[134] To qualify for the TUI, a prospect must hold a recognized law degree, "familiarity with the Macau legal system,"[135] and have completed relevant courses, trainee programs, and examinations for judges and procurators.[136] Nothing requires judicial appointees to the TUI to be confirmed by the Legislative Assembly, although removal of judges does require the Chief Executive to render a decision on the recommendation of a review committee comprising Members of the Legislative Assembly.[137] TUI judges enjoy life tenure,[138] and may not be transferred, suspended, forced into retirement, or removed contrary to law.[139] Unlike Hong Kong, judicial salaries in Macau are regulated by legislation: the salaries of the President and other judges of the TUI are statutorily fixed at 80 percent[140] and 75 percent[141] of the Chief Executive's, respectively.

From its creation in 1999 up until 2011, the TUI had the same three judges: President Sam Hou Fai, Judge Viriato Lima, and Judge Chu Kin. All three judges were recruited from the Tribunal Judicial de Base, the first instance court of Portuguese Macau, none from the appellate Tribunal Superior de Justiça.[142] Chu Kin died at forty-two years of age on November 22, 2011 in a car accident in mainland China. He was replaced by the first female judge, Song Man Lei, formerly an Assistant Procurator General.[143] In 1999 President Sam was thirty-seven years of age. His colleagues were young too: thirty-year-old Chu Kin had only five years of experience, and forty-five-year-old Viriato Manuel Pinheiro de Lima was

133 Lei Básica art. 87(1).

134 *See* Joseph Marko, *Foreign Judges: A European Perspective*, *in* HONG KONG'S COURT OF FINAL APPEAL: THE DEVELOPMENT OF THE LAW IN CHINA'S HONG KONG 637 (Simon N.M. Young & Yash Ghai eds., 2014).

135 Estatuto dos Magistrados, s. 13(1).

136 Estatuto dos Magistrados, s. 14(1).

137 Lei Básica, art. 87(3)

138 LINLIN ZHAO, A NEW STUDY ON MACAU JUDICIAL SYSTEM 18 (2015).

139 Estatuto dos Magistrados, s. 5.

140 Regime Remuneratório dos Magistrados, s. 3 & s. 4(1).

141 Regime Remuneratório dos Magistrados, at s. 4(1).

142 Godinho & Cardinal, *supra* note 22, at 615.

143 MacauNews/Politics, *Former Public Prosecutor Sworn in as Macau's First Top Female Judge*, MACAU NEWS, Jan. 5, 2012, https://macaunews.mo/former-public-prosecutor-sworn-macaus-first-top-female-judge/

the most experienced, with twenty years.[144] Except for Lima, the three had no more than a couple of years of experience as judges in Macau.

COMPARATIVE CONSTITUTIONAL REVIEW

The formal supremacy of constitutional law does nothing in itself to establish judicial supremacy over constitutional questions.[145] In principle, the Hong Kong Basic Law provides that "[n]o law enacted by the legislature of the Hong Kong Special Administrative Region shall contravene this Law,"[146] and the Lei Básica de Macau similarly admonishes that "[n]o law, decree, administrative regulations and normative acts of the Macao Special Administrative Region shall contravene this Law."[147] Neither constitution mandates judicial invalidation of an inconsistent act, however; and non-judicial actors such as the Chief Executive and the Legislative Council or the Legislative Assembly are given considerable constitutional authority. It is not absurd for them to lay claim to interpretive authority on a par with courts, at least in discharging their constitutional duties.[148] As the findings of Chapter 3 hereinabove indicate, whatever system of judicial review the Basic Law or the Lei Básica established in either SAR, it was at best a "weak-form."[149] The CFA and the TUI could easily have abdicated the power to review legislative and administrative acts and to invalidate acts inconsistent with the Basic Law or the Lei Básica, by holding that such jurisdiction is vested exclusively in the Standing Committee of the National People's Congress, and any legislation not vetoed by it must be presumed consistent with the Basic Law, and bound to be enforced by the courts.[150] For that matter, the SARs' hybrid regimes or the Standing Committee of the National People's Congress could either one have whipped the Court and Tribunal back into line with the latent authoritarianism and judicial minimalism of the Basic Law and the Lei

144 Sonny Shiu-Hing Lo, Political Change in Macao 11 (2008).

145 *See* Keith E. Whittington, Political Foundations of Judicial Supremacy: The Presidency, the Supreme Court, and Constitutional Leadership in U.S. History 9 (2007).

146 Basic Law, art. 11(2).

147 Lei Básica, art. 11(2).

148 Po Jen Yap, *Interpreting the Basic Law and the Adjudication of Politically Sensitive Questions*, 6 Chinese J. Int'l L. 543, 563 (2007).

149 Mark Tushnet & Rosalind Dixon, *Weak-Form Review and Its Constitutional Relatives: An Asian Perspective*, *in* Comparative Constitutional Law in Asia 102, 105 (Rosalind Dixon & Tom Ginsburg eds., 2014).

150 Albert H.Y. Chen, *The Relationship between the Central Government and the SAR*, *in* The Basic Law and Hong Kong's Future 107, 124 (Peter Wesley-Smith & Albert H.Y. Chen eds., 1988).

Básica by formal or informal means, ranging from amendment to court-curbing.

Constitutional Jurisdiction

In January 1999, the CFA, still new, seized the opportunity of its first major case, *Ng Ka Ling v. Director of Immigration*,[151] concerning the right of abode of mainland China-born children of Hong Kong permanent residents, to dispel all doubts about the constitutional jurisdiction of the post-British common law courts of Hong Kong and their interpretive supremacy over the Basic Law. In a sort of "big bang" moment for constitutional review under the Basic Law, the CFA intoned:

> In exercising their judicial power conferred by the Basic Law, the courts of the Region have a duty to enforce and interpret that Law. They undoubtedly have the jurisdiction to examine whether legislation enacted by the legislature of the Region or acts of the executive authorities of the Region are consistent with the Basic Law and, if found to be inconsistent, to hold them to be invalid. The exercise of this jurisdiction is a matter of obligation, not of discretion so that if inconsistency is established, the courts are bound to hold that a law or executive act is invalid at least to the extent of the inconsistency. Although this has not been questioned, it is right that we should take this opportunity of stating it unequivocally. In exercising this jurisdiction, the courts perform their constitutional role under the Basic Law of acting as a constitutional check on the executive and legislative branches of government to ensure that they act in accordance with the Basic Law.[152]

Even most significantly, the CFA asserted its constitutional primacy over against the National People's Congress and its Standing Committee:

> Like other constitutions, it distributes and delimits powers, as well as providing for fundamental rights and freedoms. As with other constitutions, laws which are inconsistent with the Basic Law are of no effect and are invalid. Under it, the courts of the Region have independent judicial power within the high degree of autonomy conferred on the Region. It is for the courts of the Region to determine questions of inconsistency and invalidity when they arise. It is therefore for the courts of the Region to determine whether an act of the National People's Congress or its Standing Committee is inconsistent with the Basic Law, subject of course to the provisions of the Basic Law itself.[153]

[151] Ng Ka Ling v. Dir. of Immigration (1999) 2 H.K.C.F.A.R. 4 (H.K.C.F.A.).
[152] Ng Ka Ling v. Dir. of Immigration (1999) 2 H.K.C.F.A.R. 4, 25 (H.K.C.F.A.) (Li, C.J.).
[153] Ng Ka Ling v. Dir. of Immigration (1999) 2 H.K.C.F.A.R. 4, 26 (H.K.C.F.A.) (Li, C.J.).

The CFA did not back down even when obliged by leading mainland Chinese drafters of the Basic Law, as well as local pro-China political heavyweights, to "clarify" its provocative assertions. In *Ng Ka Ling v Director of Immigration (No. 2)*,[154] a short, six-paragraph statement issued in February 1999, presumably in response to the critics, the Court merely reiterated its position that it would never challenge the authority of the Congress or its Standing Committee so long as their acts were "in accordance with the provisions of the Basic Law and the procedure therein"[155] without stating whether or how it would challenge their authority if their acts were *not* in accordance with the Basic Law. In short, the clarification "clarifies nothing," for what was "clarified" was already said in the original judgment.[156] Chinese officials nonetheless composed their disagreements, stating the Clarification had adequately resolved the controversy.[157]

Of the four applicants in *Ng Ka Ling*, three reached the Region on July 1, 1997, having been born out of wedlock to a Chinese father who had resided in Hong Kong continuously for the legal period of at least seven years. The fourth, born out of wedlock to a Hong Kong Permanent Resident, entered Hong Kong in December 1994 and overstayed. Each applicant had reported to the Immigration Department only after the Handover. They alleged that the Immigration (Amendment) (No. 2) Ordinance (No. 2 Ordinance)[158] and the Immigration (Amendment) (No. 3) Ordinance (No. 3 Ordinance),[159] both enacted by the Provisional Legislative Council, an unelected body handpicked by the Standing Committee of the National People's Congress to replace the last, largely popularly elected, British Hong Kong legislature, impermissibly imposed a heavier burden on immigrants seeking permanent

154 Ng Ka Ling v. Dir. of Immigration (No. 2) (1999) 2 H.K.C.F.A.R. 141 (H.K.C.F.A.).

155 Ng Ka Ling v. Dir. of Immigration (No. 2) (1999) 2 H.K.C.F.A.R. 141, 142 (H.K.C.F.A.) (Li, C.J.).

156 Johannes M.M. Chan, *Clarified in Its Clarification: Jurisdiction and Amicus Intervention, in* HONG KONG'S CONSTITUTIONAL DEBATE: CONFLICT OVER INTERPRETATION 171, 180 (2000).

157 When asked whether Beijing would take any further action against the CFA, Vice Premier Qian Qishen merely replied, "Let us leave [the Court's clarification] as it is." *See* TAMMY LI, THE CONTACT BETWEEN LEGAL INTERPRETIVE INSTITUTIONS OF THE HONG KONG SPECIAL ADMINISTRATIVE REGION BASIC LAW 154 (2011). Tsang Hin-Chi, Member of the Standing Committee of the National People's Congress, similarly agreed that, after the Clarification, there was no necessity for the NPCSC to reinterpret or amend the Basic Law's provisions on constitutional interpretation. *See* Emily Johnston Barton, *Pricing Judicial Independence: An Empirical Study of Post-1997 Court of Final Appeal Decisions in Hong Kong*, 43(2) HARV. INT'L L.J. 361, 382–83 (2002).

158 Immigration (Amendment) (No. 2) Ordinance, No. 122 of 1997 (Hong Kong).

159 Immigration (Amendment) (No. 3) Ordinance, No. 124 of 1997 (Hong Kong).

residency, contrary to the Basic Law, which expressly grants the children of Permanent Residents the right to reside in Hong Kong. Article 24(2) provides that a person of Chinese nationality born outside Hong Kong to a Permanent Resident is a permanent resident automatically, but the drafters did not foresee the proliferation of mainland-born children whose father, mother or both would have Permanent Resident status. The No. 2 Ordinance was thus enacted to exclude illegitimate children born outside Hong Kong from permanent residency, while the No. 3 Ordinance retroactively restricted the right of abode to those mainland Chinese children whose parents were married and had permanent resident status at the time of their birth, and provided that even persons having a right of abode under the Basic Law, both before or after enactment, reside in Hong Kong subject to a strict quota enforced through a "Certificate of Entitlement" system.[160]

The CFA unanimously invalidated portions of the No. 3 Ordinance on grounds of retroactivity and its requirement that the one-way permit issued at the discretion of mainland Chinese authorities was a condition for entry to Hong Kong, contrary to Article 24(3) of the Basic Law.[161] The Court also struck down the No. 2 Ordinance's requirement that the parent must have been a Hong Kong Permanent Resident at the time of birth for the child to claim a right of abode under Article 24(2)(3).[162] The importance of political transaction costs to the survival of high-energy constitutional review under authoritarianism cannot be overstated. The government retracted its acquiescence in the CFA's judgment in light of its growing fear, shared by public opinion, that the decision would trigger an inundation of children from mainland China in the next ten years, estimated at 1.675 million,[163] precipitating a severe social and economic crisis.[164] In June 1999, the Chief Executive took the constitutionally dubious shortcut, nowhere mentioned in the Basic Law, of inviting the Standing Committee to reverse the Court's decision with a binding Interpretation through petitioning the State Council. Noticeably, in its first

160 *See* Albert H.Y. Chen & Anne S.Y. Cheung, *Debating Rule of Law in the Hong Kong Special Administrative Region, 1997–2002*, *in* Asian Discourses of Rule of Law 250, 255 (Randall Peerenboom ed., 2004).

161 Ng Ka Ling v. Dir. of Immigration (1999) 2 H.K.C.F.A.R. 4, 36 (H.K.C.F.A.) (Li, C.J.).

162 Ng Ka Ling v. Dir. of Immigration (1999) 2 H.K.C.F.A.R. 4, 41 (H.K.C.F.A.) (Li, C.J.).

163 Government of the Hong Kong Special Administrative Region, *Assessment of Service Implication in Relation to the Judgment of the Court of Final Appeal on the Right of Abode Issue Tabled at the Legislative Council*, May 6, 1999, www.info.gov.hk/gia/general/199905/06/0506104.htm

164 Johannes M.M. Chan, *Immigration Policies and Human Resources Planning*, *in* Hong Kong Mobile: Making a Global Population 149, 188 (Helen F. Siu & Agnes S. Ku eds., 2008).

Basic Law Interpretation,[165] delivered solely to reinstate anti-immigration policies on behalf of the Chief Executive, the Standing Committee did not harshly criticize the Court's self-aggrandizement. Notwithstanding that the Chief Executive's initiative to refer in the absence of pressure from Beijing has been castigated as a self-inflicted wound to Hong Kong's autonomy and the rule of law,[166] the Standing Committee has exercised considerable self-restraint in pursuing any rivalry with the CFA on the issue of constitutional review. Its Interpretation was a non-retrospective decision that did not purport to overturn the *Ng Ka Ling* judgment's finality and applicability to the parties concerned, or resurrect all other statutory provisions struck down by the Court, or question the competence of the courts to nullify acts of the Legislative Council, or even impugn the CFA's claim to power to review decisions of the National People's Congress and its Standing Committee regarding the Basic Law.[167] The Interpretation did not set back consolidation of the doctrine of Basic Law supremacy, which in many contexts, especially if Beijing's political interests are not engaged,[168] is tantamount to de facto judicial supremacy. This doctrine is the most fundamental of constitutional common law doctrines in the SAR, without which the CFA could hardly, most of the time, equate its reading of the Basic Law with the thing itself. Fortunately for the Court, the alliance of popular opinion, the SAR regime, and the Standing Committee, which would entail a drastic decrease in political transaction costs, proved to be short lived. By the same token, the almost complete absence of constitutional adjudication throughout much of the British era can be explained by extremely low levels of political transaction costs back then, when elite cohesion was high and systemic popular resistance was non-existent.[169]

Meanwhile, the dénouement of this "rabid chastisement"[170] saw the CFA admit in *Lau Kong Yung v. Director of Immigration*[171] that the Standing

165 Interpretation of Articles 22(4) and 22(2)(3) of the Basic Law of the Hong Kong Special Administrative Region of the People's Republic of China (adopted by the Tenth Session of the Standing Committee of the Ninth National People's Congress at its Tenth Session on Jun. 26, 1999).

166 Albert H.Y. Chen, *The Constitution and the Rule of Law*, *in* The First Tung Chee-hwa Administration: The First Five Years of the Hong Kong Special Administrative Region, 69, 78 (Siu-kai Lau ed., 2002).

167 Tahirh V. Lee, 2001. *"Apres Moi Le Deluge?" Judicial Review in Hong Kong since Britain Relinquished Sovereignty*, 11(2) Ind. Int'l & Comp. L. Rev. 319, 323 (2001).

168 Po Jen Yap, Courts and Democracies in Asia 48 (2017).

169 Eric C. Ip, *The Economic Structure of Hong Kong Administrative Law*, 12(2) Wash. U. Global Stud. L. Rev. 227, 235–36 (2013).

170 Po Jen Yap, 10 *Years of the Basic Law: The Rise, Retreat and Resurgence of Judicial Power in Hong Kong*, 36(2) Common L. World Rev. 166, 174 (2007).

171 Lau Kong Yung v. Dir. of Immigration (1999) 2 H.K.C.F.A.R. 300 (H.K.C.F.A.).

Committee's power to interpret the Basic Law is "plenary in that it covers all the provisions of the Basic Law [and] may be exercised in the absence of litigation."[172] Nowhere in *Lau Kong Yung*, however, did the CFA retract its strictures in *Ng Ka Ling* against acts of the National People's Congress or its Standing Committee that may be incompatible with the Basic Law.[173] In *HKSAR v. Ng Kung Siu*,[174] issued twelve days after *Lau Kong Yung*, the Court rejected the claim by convicted street activists that a statute criminalizing flag desecration unnecessarily restricted freedom of expression contrary to Article 19 of the ICCPR. The impugned provisions – Sections 7 of the National Flag and National Emblem Ordinance[175] and the Regional Flag and Regional Emblem Ordinance[176] – were enacted by the Provisional Legislative Council to localize China's National Flag Law,[177] of which Article 19 bans "publicly and wilfully burning, mutilating, scrawling on, defiling or trampling upon" the flag. The National Flag Law was listed by the Standing Committee in Annex III of the Basic Law to ensure that it became part of Hong Kong's body of law, beyond the reach of local politicians, though it had to be domesticated first in order to take local legal effect. While deferring to China's interest in privileging the symbol of its sovereignty over Hong Kong, the CFA asserted jurisdiction to review local legislation domesticating Chinese national law nonetheless,[178] and so contain, albeit imperfectly, the impact of Annex III national laws that can be added by the Standing Committee at will.[179] Note that its judgment neither fined nor imprisoned the defendants but merely bound them over to keep the peace for one year. The Court softened the impact even further by expatiating on freedom of expression as "a fundamental freedom in a democratic society," which "includes the freedom to express ideas which the majority may find disagreeable or offensive and the freedom to criticize government institutions and the conduct of public officials."[180]

172 Lau Kong Yung v. Dir. of Immigration (1999) 2 H.K.C.F.A.R. 300, 324 (H.K.C.F.A.) (Li, C.J.).
173 Yap, *supra* note 170, at 175.
174 HKSAR v. Ng Kung Siu (1999) 2 H.K.C.F.A.R. 442 (H.K.C.F.A.).
175 National Flag and National Emblem Ordinance, No. 116 of 1997 (Hong Kong).
176 Regional Flag and Regional Emblem Ordinance, No. 117 of 1997 (Hong Kong).
177 National Flag Law of the People's Republic of China (adopted at the Fourteenth Meeting of the Standing Committee of the Seventh National People's Congress on Jun. 28, 1990, effective as of Oct. 1, 1990).
178 HKSAR v. Ng Kung Siu (1999) 2 H.K.C.F.A.R. 442, 447 (H.K.C.F.A.).
179 Chen, *supra* note 166, at 81.
180 HKSAR v. Ng Kung Siu (1999) 2 H.K.C.F.A.R. 442, 455 (H.K.C.F.A.).

Integral to the doctrine are credible judicial remedies for breaches of the Basic Law as defined by the courts. Remedies embody the collision between competing and sometimes irreconcilable public goods: the vindication of the constitution, the injured party's right to effective redress, and the state's power to restrict conduct it deems to be harmful.[181] The CFA has given the leading role to its two main remedies: remedial interpretation and declarations of invalidity.[182] Although less dramatic than invalidation, remedial interpretation is if anything more consequential, for it empowers the Court to save a statute "in an altered form"[183] of its own choosing, using "judicial techniques such as reading down and reading in."[184] To justify this proceeding the Court imputes to the Legislative Council the intention that it would rather "its legislative provision to have a valid, even if reduced, operation than to have no operation at all."[185] Only if an impugned provision admits of no remedial interpretation that is not "fundamentally at odds with the intent of the legislation in question"[186] must it be invalidated.[187] One commentator noted that remedial interpretation enables the Court "to make choices on how best to deal with the unconstitutionality"[188] of statutes, and thereby "to legislate."[189] Invalidation formally excises the impugned provision from an Ordinance, subsidiary legislation, and other legal instruments such as an Order in Council once for all,[190] and is rightly called "a course of last resort in the fullest sense."[191] Accordingly, the CFA has asserted the competence of courts to suspend invalidations and remedial interpretations temporarily. In *Koo Sze Yiu v. Chief Executive of the HKSAR*,[192] weighing up the pragmatic value of covert surveillance "in

181 Aharon Barak, *A Research Agenda for the Future*, *in* PROPORTIONALITY: NEW FRONTIERS, NEW CHALLENGES 322, 337 (Vicki C. Jackson & Mark Tushnet eds., 2017).

182 KEMAL BOKHARY, HUMAN RIGHTS: SOURCE, CONTENT AND ENFORCEMENT 37 (2015).

183 HKSAR v. Lam Kwong Wai (2006) 9 H.K.C.F.A.R. 574, 610 (H.K.C.F.A.) (Sir Anthony Mason, N.P.J.).

184 HKSAR v. Ng Po On (2008) 11 H.K.C.F.A.R. 91, 108 (H.K.C.F.A.) (Ribeiro, P.J.).

185 HKSAR v. Lam Kwong Wai (2006) 9 H.K.C.F.A.R. 574, 610 (H.K.C.F.A.) (Sir Anthony Mason, N.P.J.).

186 HKSAR v. Ng Po On (2008) 11 H.K.C.F.A.R. 91, 109 (H.K.C.F.A.) (Ribeiro, P.J.).

187 W v. The Registrar of Marriages (2013) 16 H.K.C.F.A.R. 112, 186 (H.K.C.F.A.).

188 Simon N.M. Young, *Human Rights*, *in* HONG KONG'S COURT OF FINAL APPEAL: THE DEVELOPMENT OF THE LAW IN CHINA'S HONG KONG 391, 408 (Simon N.M. Young & Yash Ghai eds., 2014).

189 *Id.*

190 LO, *supra* note 4, at 209.

191 W v. The Registrar of Marriages (2013) 16 H.K.C.F.A.R. 112, 186 (H.K.C.F.A.).

192 Koo Sze Yiu v. Chief Exec. of the HKSAR (2006) 9 H.K.C.F.A.R. 441 (H.K.C.F.A.).

the detection and prevention of crime and threats to public security,"[193] the Court suspended for a grace period of six months its judgment condemning a statutory provision as well as an Executive order that had authorized covert surveillance by law enforcement agencies, to give time for the political authorities to revisit the legal framework to align it with constitutional guarantees of privacy and communication rights. This "breakthrough in judicial creativity"[194] was so unprecedented that Sir Anthony Mason of the *Koo Sze Yiu* Court conceded that it might raise "fundamental doctrinal questions relating to the separation of powers, the role of the courts, the relationship between the courts and the legislative branch of government."[195] The Legislative Council complied anyway.

In *Mok Charles Peter v. Tam Wai Ho*,[196] a differently constituted CFA under a new Chief Justice struck down Section 67(3) of the Legislative Council Ordinance on the basis that "while the views of the legislature are to be considered, it is the court that has the ultimate responsibility to determine whether legislation is constitutional. This is a matter of law, only for the courts to determine."[197] Going a step further in *W v. Registrar of Marriages*,[198] the Court interpreted statutory marriage provisions remedially that had unconstitutionally in its view excluded postoperative male-to-female transsexuals from the meaning of "woman" and "female," but suspended its orders for twelve months. It additionally ruled that even if "such legislation does not eventuate," the courts below would still be bound to decide in accord with its judgment "questions regarding the implications of recognising an individual's acquired gender for marriage purposes as and when any disputed questions arise."[199] Subsequently, the Legislative Council's failure to agree a response before expiry of the suspension period did not prevent the Court granting the appellant's prayer for relief.[200]

The jurisprudence of the Tribunal de Última Instância de Macau on its constitutional jurisdiction presents a radically different picture. As late as

193 Koo Sze Yiu v. Chief Exec. of the HKSAR (2006) 9 H.K.C.F.A.R. 441, 449 (H.K.C.F.A.) (Bokhary, P.J.).

194 Chen & Lo, *supra* note 17, at 377.

195 Koo Sze Yiu v. Chief Exec. of the HKSAR (2006) 9 H.K.C.F.A.R. 441, 460 (H.K.C.F.A.) (Sir Anthony Mason, N.P.J.).

196 Mok Charles Peter v. Tam Wai Ho (2010) 13 H.K.C.F.A.R. 762 (H.K.C.F.A.)

197 Mok Charles v. Tam Wai Ho (2010) 13 H.K.C.F.A.R. 762, 787 (H.K.C.F.A.) (Ma, C.J.).

198 W v. The Registrar of Marriages (2013) 16 H.K.C.F.A.R. 112 (H.K.C.F.A.).

199 W v. The Registrar of Marriages (2013) 16 H.K.C.F.A.R. 112, 171 (H.K.C.F.A.) (Ma, C.J. & Ribeiro, P.J.).

200 Johannes M.M. Chan, *Right to Judicial Remedies*, *in* LAW OF THE HONG KONG CONSTITUTION 1109, 1129 (Johannes M.M. Chan & C.L. Lim eds., 2d ed. 2015).

2007, eight years after the Handover, one commentator could note that it is not absolutely certain whether the courts of Macau can in the ordinary course of adjudication decline to enforce enactments in conflict with the Lei Básica.[201] And as late as 2015, sixteen years after the Handover in 1999, another commentator could still observe that "the main interpretive dilemma" in Macau is whether the Lei Básica should be interpreted in line with the Socialist legal standards of the National People's Congress that legislated it in the first place, or with the civil law tradition of Macau's Portuguese heritage.[202] "So far," noted the commentator, "this dilemma has not been entirely settled."[203] In the event, the TUI early on took exactly the opposite stance to the CFA regarding the scope of its competence to invalidate statutes. In Case 7/2001,[204] one of the Tribunal's earliest, concerning the pension of a retired public servant of Portuguese Macau, in the context of the transition of previous laws into the post-Handover era, Judge Chu Kin affirmed that:

> The Lei Básica was enacted by the National People's Congress in accordance with Article 31 of the Constitution of the People's Republic of China, is by nature a constitutional law of the Macau Special Administrative Region, and is the foundation of the various systems and policies of the Special Administrative Region. Any law, decree, administrative regulation and other normative document of the Macau Special Administrative Region shall not contradict the Basic Law.[205]

Notwithstanding this avowal, the TUI declined to declare, or even discuss whether the Macau courts have any authority to strike down unconstitutional laws; contenting itself with affirming, rather non-controversially, the principle that "if previous laws of pre-Handover Macau contradict with the Lei Básica, in principle they would not be preserved by the Macau Special Administrative Region for implementation."[206] In the end, the Tribunal ruled in favor of the Government and rejected the claim that a civil servant of Portuguese Macau

201 *See* Vitalino Canas, *The General Regime of Fundamental Rights in the Basic Law and the International Instruments*, *in* One Country, Two Systems, Three Legal Orders – Perspectives of Evolution 655, 674 (Jorge Costa Oliveira & Paulo Cardinal et al. eds., 2009).

202 Denis de Castro Halis, *"Post-Colonial" Legal Interpretation in Macau, China: Between European and Chinese Influences*, *in* East Asia's Renewed Respect for the Rule of Law in the 21st Century: The Future of Legal and Juridical Landscapes in East Asia 68, 80 (Setsuo Miyazawa ed., 2015).

203 *Id.*

204 Case 7/2001 (T.U.I.M.).

205 Case 7/2001, 17 (T.U.I.M.) (Chu, J.).

206 Case 7/2001, 18 (T.U.I.M.) (Chu, J.).

who retired before the Special Administrative Region was founded enjoys the Lei Básica's guarantee of a pension.

The TUI's unprecedented decision in Case 2/2004[207] to suspend the effect of Section 1(3) of the Código Civil (Civil Code)[208] could not be interpreted as an assertion of review power, let alone the striking down of a legislative provision by an activist court. The purpose of Section 1(3) was to confer on international treaties a legal status superior to ordinary laws in Macau's legal system. The problem, the Tribunal believed, was that Section 1(3) was illogical, because "no norm can confer on another norm a status superior to the former's place in the legal hierarchy": ordinarily legislated "laws possess an effect that is inferior to the status of constitutional laws, and only the latter could confer on international conventions a legal status that is superior to [ordinarily legislated] laws."[209] Yet the Tribunal refused to strike down the impugned provision, even commending it as "an expression of the Legislator's goodwill."[210] What it did do was to appeal to the Lei Básica to uphold essentially the same principle as contained in the impugned Section 1(3). Ironically, Case 2/2004 actually reinforces the position that the courts are not entitled to strike down ordinary legislation in their judgments, for their judgments as normative acts are undoubtedly inferior to ordinary legislation.

Not until almost eight years after the Handover did the TUI lay out in relatively comprehensive form its philosophy of constitutional review, in its July 2007 judgment in Case 28/2006, a case concerning the Secretary for Security's refusal to permit the extension of stay of two foreign workers. It explained the doctrine of disapplication of Lei Básica-incompatible legal norms in these terms:

> If a court shall interpret the Lei Básica in adjudicating a case, and is certain that it could reach a conclusion that certain legal provisions or administrative regulations are in contradiction with the Lei Básica, under this circumstance, it must enforce the provisions of Article 11 of the Lei Básica: therefore, it shall not apply those regulations that contradict the provisions or general principles of the Lei Básica, without prejudice to Article 143 of that Law.[211]

As will be explained below, disapplication in no way affects the validity of legislation, and thus is by nature incomparable to the declarations of invalidity issued by the CFA, which nullifies impugned statutory provisions both

207 Case 2/2004 (T.U.I.M.).
208 Código Civil de Macau (approved by Decree Law 39/99/M, Aug. 3, 1999) (Macau).
209 Case 2/2004, 6 (T.U.I.M.) (Lima, J.).
210 Case 2/2004, 7 (T.U.I.M.) (Lima, J.).
211 Case 28/2006, 31 (T.U.I.M.) (Lima, J.).

retrospectively and prospectively, with *erga omnes* effect. As the Tribunal unequivocally disclaimed in the administrative law decision in Case 8/2007, delivered in April 2008:

> Nonetheless, it shall be noted that the judgment here that a norm is in violation of a rule of higher hierarchy is nothing more than an integral part of the courts' reasoning, that is, one step within the logical process that results in the final determination, which in itself does not form part of the judgment. The court cannot use this as a basis to judge that a norm is illegal with a concrete and binding force. The judgment is only valid in the case itself, and does not yield any effect towards other cases or even other courts; the norm deemed illegal does not become invalid because of this judgment.[212]

Case 16/2010 represented a slightly more assertive tendency by the TUI regarding the freedom of assembly and the right to demonstrate free from administrative interference.[213] In that decision, the Tribunal quashed the decision of the Civil and Municipal Affairs Bureau to exploit a loophole in Law 2/9/M[214] to impose spatial limits on a public procession organized by the applicant on the basis that other assemblies would also take place in the same location. Judge Chu Kin, writing for the TUI, affirmed that pursuant to Article 40(2) of the Lei Básica, the rights and freedoms enjoyed by Macau residents cannot be restricted except by law.[215] While the TUI did not cast doubt on any statutory provision, it indirectly criticized the Legislative Assembly for "inappropriately" failing to address the potential conflict of rights of assembly and demonstration in the same location through "legitimate and proportionate" fundamental principles.[216] On the other hand, in Case 25/2011,[217] the TUI declined an opportunity to nullify a statutory provision as unconstitutional. This case raised the question of whether Section 5 of Law 2/93/M, which

212 Case 8/2007, 9 (T.U.I.M.) (Chu, J.) ("No entanto, é de salientar que o juízo aqui falado de que uma norma viola outra de hierarquia superior é apenas uma parte integrante da fundamentação da sentença, ou seja, um passo de todo o raciocínio lógico-jurídico da decisão final, não constituindo o conteúdo da decisão da sentença. O tribunal não pode server deste juízo para proferir uma sentença de que uma norma seja ilegal e com força obrigatória geral. Tal juízo é válido apenas no próprio processo, já não em relação a outros processos ou até outros tribunais. A norma que se considera ilegal não se torna inválida por causa deste juízo.")

213 Most recently, in Case 57/2017 (T.U.I.M.), delivered on September 11, 2017, the TUI quashed a decision of the Civil and Municipal Affairs Bureau to ban a Legislative Assembly election rally by a pro-democracy politician on the ground of error in statutory interpretation, rather than incompatibility with a specific provision of the Lei Básica.

214 Law 2/93/M (Macau) was subsequently amended and re-enacted into Law 16/2008 (Macau).

215 Case 16/2010, 6 (T.U.I.M.) (Chu, J.).

216 Case 16/2010, 10 (T.U.I.M.) (Chu, J.).

217 Case 25/2011 (T.U.I.M.).

requires three organizers of any public protest to sign a letter of notification about the details of the event beforehand, was compatible with Article 27 of the Lei Básica, which guarantees the rights of individuals to assemble and demonstrate. The TUI admitted that a literal reading of the impugned Section does suggest unconstitutionality, yet in the end it refused to suspend the Section but adopted instead an interpretation that rendered the Section consistent with the Lei Básica.[218] Judge Lima concluded his judgment with the following words: "As is well known, the interpretation of ordinary legislation should privilege an interpretation that is compatible with the Basic Law (interpretação que se compatibilize com a Lei Básica), subject to the canons of legal interpretation."[219] It must be noted that this doctrine is worlds apart from the power of remedial interpretation asserted by the CFA, in that it does not permit the TUI to ignore expressed words in statutory provisions or creatively modify their meaning; it merely obligates the TUI to select the interpretation that is most consistent with the Lei Básica when the statutory language in question has given rise to multiple equally plausible constructions.

The disapplication of Lei Básica-incompatible legal norms, unlike a declaration of the invalidity of Basic Law-incompatible legislative and administrative acts, affects neither the validity of the impugned law generally nor that of any of its particular provisions. If amid adjudication a Macau court finds an otherwise applicable norm to contradict a superior norm, it should directly apply the latter norm, or an earlier version of the former that does not contradict the latter, or a norm that is applicable in some supplementary manner, or some other lawful norm, but it must not apply the contradictory norm of inferior rank.[220] The impact of Macau's disapplication doctrine is especially minimal compared with invalidation in Hong Kong, because Macau courts lack any doctrine of precedent[221]: a lower court has no obligation at all to disapply a norm earlier disapplied by a higher court, and the higher court has no obligation either to disapply the same norm that it had disapplied in an earlier case. In other words, nothing prevents a provision disapplied in an earlier TUI judgment from being resurrected as fully applicable in a future judgment of any court in Macau. A TUI judgment cannot

218 Case 25/2011, 6 (T.U.I.M.) (Lima, J.).

219 Case 25/2011, 6 (T.U.I.M.) (Lima, J.).

220 Albert H.Y. Chen et al., *The Constitutional Orders of "One Country, Two Systems": A Comparative Study of Constitutional Review and Proportionality Analysis in the Hong Kong and Macau Special Administrative Regions*, *in* THE STUDY OF POLITICAL STRUCTURE OF THE HONG KONG SPECIAL ADMINISTRATIVE REGION 185, 208–09 (Guobin Zhu ed., 2017).

221 JIANG, *supra* note 118, at 181.

bind the lower courts unless the Tribunal itself follows the abovementioned Fixation of Jurisprudence procedure. But the TUI has yet to invoke this procedure in the context of constitutional review, let alone disapply a single legislative norm. Lack of precedent also means that nothing stops the Chief Executive or his Government to continue relying on a previously disapplied norm in hopes that the courts will ultimately concede its general applicability. Strictly speaking, no one can be faulted for relying on a provision disapplied in one case, even a TUI case. What is more, the TUI has acquiesced in Section 88(2) of the Código do Processo Administrativo Contencioso (Administrative Litigation Code),[222] which precludes the Tribunal to issue general, binding declarations of unconstitutionality in reviewing administrative regulations.[223] Yet this Section 88(2) is in deep tension with a combined reading of Article 11(2) and Article 143(2) of the Lei Básica.[224]

Interpretive Methodology

Neither the Basic Law nor the Lei Básica gives any explicit guidance on how each should be interpreted, nor has its final interpreter, the Standing Committee of the National People's Congress, ever attempted to provide any,[225] despite "considerable anxiety and debate," at least in Hong Kong.[226] Vague gestures to "stability and prosperity" have been invoked in lieu of clear legal propositions to justify the Interpretations.[227] In the Hong Kong legal system constitutional common law has filled the gap. Again in *Ng Ka Ling*, the CFA pronounced the Basic Law "a living instrument intended to meet changing needs and circumstances,"[228] the interpretation of which requires a "purposive approach" to ascertaining its "true meaning" by reference to "the purpose of the instrument and its relevant provisions as well as the

222 Administrative Litigation Code (approved by Decree Law 110/99/M, Dec. 13, 1999).

223 Jiang & Yang, *supra* note 107, at 90.

224 Mai & Ho, *supra* note 99, at 90.

225 Michael W. Dowdle, *Constitutionalism in the Shadow of the Common Law: The Dysfunctional Interpretive Politics of Article 8 of the Hong Kong Basic Law*, *in* Interpreting Hong Kong's Basic Law: The Struggle for Coherence 55, 72 (Hualing Fu et al. eds., 2007); Robert J. Morris, *The "Replacement" Chief Executive's Two-Year Term: A Pure and Unambiguous Common Law Analysis*, 35 Hong Kong L.J. 17, 23 (2005).

226 Bing Ling, *Subject Matter Limitation on the NPCSC's Power to Interpret the Basic Law*, 37 Hong Kong L.J. 619, 620 (2007).

227 Yash Ghai, *Hong Kong's Autonomy: Dialects of Powers and Institutions*, *in* Practising Self-Government: A Comparative Study of Autonomous Regions 315, 345 (Yash Ghai & Sophia Woodman eds., 2013).

228 Ng Ka Ling v. Dir. of Immigration (1999) 2 H.K.C.F.A.R. 4, 28 (H.K.C.F.A.) (Li, C.J.).

language of its text in the light of the context."[229] The courts "should give a generous interpretation" to the Basic Law's rights provisions so as to "give to Hong Kong residents the full measure of fundamental rights and freedoms so constitutionally guaranteed."[230]

This approach was elaborated in *Director of Immigration v. Chong Fung Yuen* in 2001.[231] At issue was whether, under Article 24(2)(1) of the Basic Law, a right of abode vests in children born in Hong Kong to mainlander parents not Hong Kong residents but merely sojourning in the Region temporarily or illegally resident in it. A literal reading would be that such a right does vest; however, both of the challenged statutory provisions implied otherwise. The Standing Committee had in its above-mentioned Interpretation vaguely and briefly mentioned that the original intent of Article 24(2) had already been "reflected" in the "Opinions" of the defunct Hong Kong Special Administrative Region Preparatory Committee – an *ad hoc* working committee of the Standing Committee – in 1996. The Opinions, some written as long as six years after the Basic Law's promulgation, purported to fill in a constitutional lacuna, the Basic Law's drafters had failed to give adequate thought to when drafting its citizenship provisions, without the need to embark on the costly and controversial path of amending the Basic Law.

The CFA had to decide between two alternatives: to uphold the Basic Law as a self-contained founding text standing on its own, or accept the Standing Committee's discretion to invent specious "original intents" ex post facto, even to the detriment of the Basic Law's integrity.[232] Orthodox Chinese legal doctrine held it unconstitutional for the CFA to interpret the Hong Kong Basic Law, which was "written in the spirit of continental civil law," exhaustively but with common law principles and methods.[233] This position, however, was rejected by the CFA; after all, it implied a loss of judicial authority, as the Court must follow the lead of mainland Chinese jurists in interpreting the Basic Law. The Court underscored the primacy of the common law in interpreting the Basic Law, that "the courts in Hong Kong are bound to apply the common law in exercising their power of interpretation," for "the Basic Law provides for a separate legal system in the HKSAR based on the

229 Ng Ka Ling v. Dir. of Immigration (1999) 2 H.K.C.F.A.R. 4, 28 (H.K.C.F.A.) (Li, C.J.).

230 Ng Ka Ling v. Dir. of Immigration (1999) 2 H.K.C.F.A.R. 4, 29 (H.K.C.F.A.) (Li, C.J.).

231 Dir. of Immigration v. Chong Fung Yuen (2001) 4 H.K.C.F.A.R. 211 (H.K.C.F.A.)

232 The Standing Committee of the National People's Congress is primarily a legislative body. Notwithstanding its misleading label, a Standing Committee Interpretation is, by nature, a statute on the mainland, and a "constitutional" statute in Hong Kong, which, as a matter of Chinese law, enjoys a status that is for all practical purposes equivalent to the Basic Law itself.

233 Norbert C.Y. Fan, The Electoral System of the Hong Kong Special Administrative Region 183 (2006).

common law."[234] The CFA decided that the Preparatory Committee's Opinions, having been delivered after the Basic Law was ratified, cannot reflect original intent even if made in a binding Interpretation which tramples down the distinction between *ratio decidendi* and *obiter dicta*. Chief Justice Andrew Li, tacitly contradicting the relevance of the Chinese legal doctrine that any output by the Standing Committee pursuant to Article 158 must have the force of constitutional law in Hong Kong, opined that:

> The courts' role under the common law in interpreting the Basic Law is to construe the language used in the text of the instrument in order to ascertain the legislative intent as expressed in the language. Their task is not to ascertain the intent of the lawmaker on its own. Their duty is to ascertain what was meant by the language used and to give effect to the legislative intent as expressed in the language. It is the text of the enactment which is the law and it is regarded as important both that the law should be certain and that it should be ascertainable by the citizen.[235]

Reiterating the components of the purposive rule of statutory construction, the Court held that only "pre-enactment materials, that is, materials brought into existence prior to or contemporaneous with the enactment of the Basic Law,"[236] are to be deemed permissible extrinsic aids in constitutional interpretation. This premise underlay the CFA's ruling for the appellants, arguably contrary to Article 158 which provides that, when the Standing Committee "makes an interpretation of the provisions concerned, the courts of the Region, in applying those provisions, shall follow the interpretation of the Standing Committee." Notably, in this case the Court also claimed for itself the further prerogative to judge the "character," rather than the practical effect of a Basic Law provision, to determine whether it is subject to the Standing Committee's Interpretation as concerning mainland ChinaHong Kong relations.

The Standing Committee, presumably being averse to costly constitutional collisions with the CFA only three years after the SAR was established, acquiesced in the *Chong Fung Yuen* decision in spite of the Court's assertiveness.[237] On the morning after *Chong Fung Yuen* was handed down,

[234] Dir. of Immigration v. Chong Fung Yuen (2001) 4 H.K.C.F.A.R. 211, 222 (H.K.C.F.A.) (Li, C.J.).

[235] Dir. of Immigration v. Chong Fung Yuen (2001) 4 H.K.C.F.A.R. 211, 223 (H.K.C.F.A.) (Li, C.J.).

[236] Dir. of Immigration v. Chong Fung Yuen (2001) 4 H.K.C.F.A.R. 211, 224 (H.K.C.F.A.) (Li, C.J.).

[237] Eric C. Ip, *Constitutional Competition between the Hong Kong Court of Final Appeal and the Chinese National People's Congress Standing Committee: A Game Theory Perspective*, 39(4) Law & Soc. Inquiry 824, 836 (2014).

the Standing Committee's Legislative Affairs Commission spokesperson did express concern over the Court's aggression, arguing that the ruling was "not consistent" with the Standing Committee's understanding of the Basic Law.[238] This statement, according to Albert Chen of the Standing Committee's Hong Kong Basic Law Committee, may be understood as expressing China's displeasure with the Court's subtle contempt of the Interpretation of 1999, which after all explicitly declared that the Preparatory Committee's opinion did embody the original intent of the Basic Law.[239] The Standing Committee did not pursue the matter any further. The SAR's political authorities tolerated *Chong Fung Yuen* no less. Ten years later, the ruling has been conducing ever more hostile public sentiment due to the strain on the Region's social and healthcare resources,[240] but there was no widespread public opposition to it at the time of its delivery. Even the government admitted in its submissions to the Court that no immediate threat of an immigration inundation existed. Consequently, the CFA managed to carve out the final authority to remould and circumscribe Interpretations of the Standing Committee to effectuate its own preferred understanding of the Basic Law in this case. Implicitly, the CFA let on that it would be sufficient for local common law judges to pay lip service to the formal obligation of an Interpretation; they would have no obligation to align their own understandings of an Interpretation with the actual intention of the Standing Committee.

What is more, in contrast to its cavalier attitude to mainland legal documents, the Court has laid extraordinary stress on the need to respect foreign and international jurisprudence when interpreting the Basic Law. In *Solicitor (24/07) v Law Society of Hong Kong*,[241] Chief Justice Andrew Li admonished:

> After 1 July 1997, in the new constitutional order, it is of the greatest importance that the courts in Hong Kong should continue to derive assistance from overseas jurisprudence. This includes the decisions of final appellate courts in various common law jurisdictions as well as decisions of supra-national courts, such as the European Court of Human Rights. Compared to many common law jurisdictions, Hong Kong is a relatively small jurisdiction. It is of great benefit to the Hong Kong courts to examine comparative

[238] Albert H.Y. Chen, *Another Case of Conflict between the CFA and the NPC Standing Committee?*, 31(1) HONG KONG L.J. 179, 179 (2001).

[239] Albert H.Y. Chen, *Constitutional Adjudication in Post-1997 Hong Kong*, 15 PAC. RIM L. & POL'Y J. 627, 649 (2006).

[240] Sharon LaFraniere, *Mainland Chinese Flock to Hong Kong to Give Birth*, NEW YORK TIMES. Feb. 22, 2012, www.nytimes.com/2012/02/23/world/asia/mainland-chinese-flock-to-hong-kong-to-have-babies.html

[241] Solicitor (24/07) v. Law Soc'y of Hong Kong (2008) 11 H.K.C.F.A.R. 117, 133 (H.K.C.F.A.) (Li, C.J.).

> jurisprudence in seeking the appropriate solution for the problems which come before them. This is underlined in the Basic Law itself. Article 84 expressly provides that the courts in Hong Kong may refer to precedents of other common law jurisdictions.[242]

Returning to W, the Court was asked to determine whether provisions in the Basic Law on "the freedom of marriage of Hong Kong residents"[243] protected the right of post-operative transsexuals to marry. When they drafted the Basic Law in the 1980s, its framers may well have intended to guarantee only the freedom of marriage of one born male with one born female, competent to procreate, excluding transsexuals. Yet the Court by a four-to-one majority claimed "the Basic Law (and the ICCPR as given constitutional effect by the Bill of Rights and art. 39 of the Basic Law) are living instruments intended to meet changing needs and circumstances."[244] Without purporting to change the legal meaning of marriage as a union between a male and female, the Court ruled that to deny a post-operative transsexual woman the right to marry a man is to "deny her right to marry at all [and to] impair the very essence of the right to marry."[245] The Court's message was clear: it is the common law that breathes life into the Basic Law, making a "living constitution" of it, not the other way round.[246] The Basic Law of Hong Kong is like other common law constitutions[247] that evolve, change with the times, adapting to circumstances without being formally amended.

Hong Kong's political system is often described as "executive-led." Neither the Basic Law nor the Letters Patent ever used such a term;[248] still, when the Basic Law was drafted, Deng Xiaoping explicitly rejected the "Western" principle of "separation of powers" as incompatible with the "national situation" of China and the "reality" of Hong Kong.[249] On this view, the Basic Law is to be read as envisaging some kind of collaboration between the three nominal branches of the constitution, requiring each to defer to other's

[242] Solicitor (24/07) v. Law Soc'y of Hong Kong (2008) 11 H.K.C.F.A.R. 117, 133 (H.K.C.F.A.) (Li, C.J.).
[243] Basic Law, art. 37.
[244] W v. The Registrar of Marriages (2013) 16 H.K.C.F.A.R. 112, 152 (H.K.C.F.A.) (Ma, C.J. & Ribeiro, P.J.).
[245] W v. The Registrar of Marriages (2013) 16 H.K.C.F.A.R. 112, 160 (H.K.C.F.A.) (Ma, C.J. & Ribeiro, P.J.).
[246] Eric C. Ip, *The Politics of Constitutional Common Law in Hong Kong under Chinese Sovereignty*, 25(3) Washington Int'l L. J. 565, 584 (2016).
[247] David A. Strauss, The Living Constitution 1 (2010).
[248] Swati Jhaveri et al., Administrative Law in Hong Kong 22 (2d ed. 2013).
[249] Michael C. Davis, Constitutional Confrontation in Hong Kong: Issues and Implications of the Basic Law 37 (1990).

institutional prerogatives when proper.[250] By contrast, the common law posits that checks and balances between separated powers are equally important, and definitive of the Hong Kong political system. The role of the courts, according to the Court of Final Appeal, is to act as "a constitutional check on the executive and legislative branches of government," so as "to ensure that they act in accordance with the Basic Law."[251] Constitutional review is not judicial self-aggrandizement, but "simply a matter of maintaining the separation of powers."[252] The issue ever at bar is "whether the approach chosen by the legislature is one permitted by the constitution," something that "does not involve deference to the legislature."[253]

Unlike the CFA, which strove to keep the influence of contemporary Chinese law out of its constitutional adjudication acts,[254] the TUI approached the Lei Básica not merely from the perspective of pre-Handover Portuguese civil law, but also within the interpretive framework of the socialist Constitution of the People's Republic of China.[255] In the abovementioned Case 28/2006, the Tribunal argued that, despite the Lei Básica's exhibiting certain formal characteristics related to the political constitution of states, "it does not have the form of a constitution."[256] And in spite of its conservation of Macau's previous legal system, for the TUI, the Lei Básica can and ought to be interpreted with reference to the socialist legal tradition of the mainland. In answering the question of whether the Chief Executive or Government may, independently of the Legislative Assembly and without statutory authorization, promulgate "administrative regulations,"[257] a source of law[258] unknown to Portuguese Macau, the TUI declared the Chinese Constitution to be effectively Macau's:

> To better understand the various aspects of the problem, it is of first priority to begin the analysis with the legislative system provided by the Chinese Constitution, especially from the point of view of the Chinese Constitution ... [because] Macau's Lei Básica was enacted by the National People's Congress – the same legislative organ that ratified the current Constitution of China ... [as well] many mainland members of the Lei

250 Yap, *supra* note 148, at 563.
251 Ng Ka Ling v. Dir. of Immigration (1999) 2 H.K.C.F.A.R. 4, 25 (H.K.C.F.A.) (Li, C.J.).
252 H.K.S.A.R. v. Ng Kung Siu (1999) 2 H.K.C.F.A.R. 442, 467 (H.K.C.F.A.) (Bokhary, P.J.).
253 H.K.S.A.R. v. Ng Kung Siu (1999) 2 H.K.C.F.A.R. 442, 467 (H.K.C.F.A.) (Bokhary, P.J.).
254 Chen & Lo, *supra* note 17, at 385.
255 Ignazio Castellucci, Rule of Law and Legal Complexity in the People's Republic of China 182 (2012).
256 Case 28/2006, 28 (T.U.I.M.) (Lima, J.).
257 Lei Básica art. 50(5) & art. 64.
258 Lei Básica art. 8 & art. 18(1).

> Básica Drafting Committee participated in the drafting and framing of the current Constitution of China, such that the Chinese constitutional thought of those legal personnel is certainly reflected in the current Constitution of China as well as the Macau Lei Básica.[259]

After an exhaustive comparison of Chinese legal documents and the work of mainland and Portuguese jurists on administrative regulations, the Tribunal concluded that the Chief Executive indeed had jurisdiction to "enact independent administrative legal regulations, even in the absence of concrete delegation – subject to the Lei Básica – by any law."[260] The contrast with the CFA's approach in *Chong Fung Yuen* could not have been starker: the TUI casually referenced extrinsic documents, largely uncritically, such as the now-repealed Chinese Constitutions of 1975 and 1978,[261] and the Legislation Law of 2000,[262] to determine the Lei Básica's meaning. The Tribunal then remanded the case back to the Tribunal de Segunda Instância for reconsideration. The TUI's deference to the Chief Executive's rule-making competence may have taken judicial restraint to a fault; the Chief Executive actually held a more moderate view than the TUI: that his rule-making powers were indeed unjustifiably wide. As Chapter 5 will discuss, the Legislative Assembly enacted Law 13/2009, which regulates the Chief Executive's judgment powers; effectively reversing the rule in Case 28/2006 – exposing it as too deferential. To top that off, the affinity of Macau's legal legacy to the continental European civil law tradition notwithstanding, the TUI rarely consults the decisions of international courts like the European Court of Human Rights, even in cases involving the ICCPR, which is directly applicable to Macau.[263] There is a tandem tendency of the Tribunal to use Chinese legal concepts and doctrine to justify its determinations, even in cases when the subject matter unambiguously lies within the SAR's autonomy, at the expense of Macau's autonomous legal identity.[264]

[259] Case 28/2006, 37–38 (T.U.I.M.) (Lima, J.) ("para melhor compreensão de todas as vertentes do problema, é importante e essencial, proceder à análise a partir do regime legislativo consagrado na Constituição da China, nomeadamente sob o ponto de vista da Constituição chinesa ... a feitura da Lei Básica resulta do mesmo órgão legislativo que elaborou a Constituição chinesa ... muitos membros da parte do Interior da China da Comissão da Lei Básica que se responsabilizaram pela feitura da Lei Básica de Macau tinham participado na redacção e elaboração da Constituição da China em vigor.")

[260] Case 28/2006, 100–01 (T.U.I.M.) (Lima, J.).

[261] Case 28/2006, 42 (T.U.I.M.) (Lima, J.).

[262] Case 28/2006, 55 (T.U.I.M.) (Lima, J.).

[263] Godinho & Cardinal, *supra* note 22, at 626.

[264] *Id.*

Abstract Review

A strict and narrow construction of Article 158 of the Basic Law and Article 143 of the Lei Básica would imply that the CFA and the TUI may only interpret constitutional provisions (not to mention review the constitutionality of enactments and administrative acts) in order to resolve *concrete disputes*; a broader understanding, however, implies that "cases" may not mean merely *concrete cases*, so that the Court and Tribunal may lawfully assert an *abstract* review competence. The CFA and the TUI have, once again, taken opposite positions. In more than one case the Tribunal has asserted that litigants "may not resort to incompatibility with the Lei Básica as a ground to reopen a judicial review litigation to scrutinize the validity of legal norms being applied."[265] It even admitted in Case 9/2006 that, although "[t]here is no constitutional court in the Macau SAR,"[266] its Código do Procedimento Administrativo (Code of Administrative Procedure) was originally enacted with the expectation that the TUI would use it to review the Lei Básica-compatibility of legislation. Yet just because the Fundamental Law on Judicial Organization had not provided[267] a "specialized litigation procedure for reviewing whether legal norms conform to the Lei Básica, hence the courts can only deal with [constitutional] issues in the proceedings of individual cases."[268] Thus, Case 9/2006: "in the legal order of Macao, there is no specific appellate channel route for reviewing whether laws are compatible with the Lei Básica, therefore the courts can consider whether laws are compatible with the Lei Básica only in applicable proceedings of concrete cases."[269]

By contrast, the Court of Final Appeal in Hong Kong never said a word against the High Court conferring upon itself competence to review legislative and executive acts for constitutionality even when no actual infringement of rights has transpired yet. In *Leung T.C. William Roy v. Secretary for Justice*,[270] for example, the Court of Appeal struck down provisions in the Crimes Ordinance[271] criminalizing certain homosexual acts at the instance of an applicant who was not facing prosecution. Geoffrey Ma, then President of the Court of Appeal, who became Chief Justice of the CFA in 2010, decided that:

265 Case 1/2000, 4 (T.U.I.M.) (Chu, J.).
266 Case 9/2006, 3 (T.U.I.M.) (Lima, J.).
267 Chen et al., *supra* note 220, at 205–06.
268 Case 9/2006, 3 (T.U.I.M.) (Lima, J.).
269 Case 9/2006, 3 (T.U.I.M.) (Lima, J.).
270 Leung T.C. William Roy v. Sec'y for Justice, [2006] 4 H.K.L.R.D. 211 (H.K.C.A.).
271 Crimes Ordinance, Cap. 200 (Hong Kong)

> It is of course up to the court on a case by case basis to determine whether sufficiently exceptional circumstances exist to enable it to exercise the discretion to hear cases notwithstanding that future conduct or a hypothetical situation is involved . . . In my judgment, another area in which the court may be more inclined to engage itself in determining issues is where constitutional challenges are made to legislation. Here, the courts in Hong Kong are duty bound to enforce and interpret the Basic Law so that if any legislation infringes the Basic Law (or the Bill of Rights), that law must be held invalid: – see *Ng Ka Ling & Others v Director of Immigration* (1999) 2 HKCFAR 4, at 25 G-J. This is all the more so where fundamental rights are involved and even more acute if a risk exists of a wrong prosecution.[272]

Ma's predecessor as Chief Justice, Andrew Li, praised the decision extrajudicially, writing, "The resolution of constitutional questions sooner rather than later is in the public interest."[273] The CFA itself has heard appeals where the issue was moot, meaning any concrete dispute was already extinct.[274]

Standards of Review

Nowhere in the Basic Law or Lei Básica is any standard of constitutional review cited. In most liberal democracies, the proportionality standard has become the "linchpin judicial test" for deciding whether a violation of right may be justified, and is widely seen as a tool that facilitates judicial activism.[275] The logic of proportionality stems from the tension between two premises: that rights and freedoms ought to be generally vindicated against limitations, but that the same rights and freedoms may sometimes be limited under certain justifying circumstances; yet such limitations, lest they be arbitrary, must be proportionate.[276] In Hong Kong since the British domesticated the ICCPR in 1991, the courts in cautious, incremental steps have been taking on board the proportionality standard of review when arguing the demerits of limitations to fundamental rights; expressly referencing foreign and international human rights case law, and affirming the competence of judges to nullify impugned

[272] Leung T.C. William Roy v. Sec'y for Justice, [2006] 4 H.K.L.R.D. 211, [28] (H.K.C.A.) (Ma, C.J.H.C.).

[273] Andrew Li, *Reflections on the Retrospective and Prospective Effect of Constitutional Judgments*, The Common Law Lecture Series 2010 45 (Jessica Young & Rebecca Lee, eds., 2011).

[274] *See, e.g.*, Sec'y for Security v. Sakthevel Prabakar (2004) 7 H.K.C.F.A.R. 187 (H.K.C.F.A.); Fok Chun Wa v. Hong Kong Hospital Auth. [2012] 2 H.K.C. 413 (H.K.C.F.A.).

[275] Po Jen Yap, Constitutional Dialogue in Common Law Asia 180–81 (2015).

[276] Bernard Schlink, *Proportionality in Constitutional Law: Why Everywhere But Here?*, 22 Duke J. Comp. & Int'l L. 291, 297 (2012).

legislation rather than set it aside for the nonce or leave it entirely up to the Legislative Council to determine the constitutionality of its own statutes.[277] The CFA, undaunted by the resumption of Chinese sovereignty, continues to invoke this cogent doctrine in order to review legislative and executive acts, and common law rules, on many occasions.[278]

Structured proportionality review comprises consecutive analytical steps[279] that require courts to scrutinize legislative and administrative acts with a more rigorous standard of review.[280] Consider *Leung Kwok Hung v. HKSAR*,[281] which concerned a public procession along Queensway[282] organized in May 2002 by prominent Pan-Democratic activist Leung Kwok Hung.[283] The protest itself was peaceful, but Leung and his aides had refused to comply with the notification procedure in Section 13A of the Public Order Ordinance,[284] which required them to give the police written notice of any procession attended by more than thirty people, along with a description of the purpose, time, route, and estimated number of attendees. Leung and two others were convicted at trial of holding an unlawful procession. On appeal, Leung challenged the provisions in the said Ordinance which authorized the Commissioner of Police to object to or impose conditions on a notified procession on the ground of *ordre public*. The CFA held that the Commissioner of Police must apply the proportionality test when exercising his statutory discretion to impose limits on the right of peaceful assembly, cautioning that he may not wield it arbitrarily.[285] The CFA's test was laid out as follows:

277 Danny Gittings, Introduction to the Hong Kong Basic Law 276–77 (2nd ed. 2016). In an early Bill of Rights decision, R v. Sin Yau Ming [1992] 1 H.K.C.L.R. 127, 145 (H.K.C.A.), Silke V-P unequivocally declared on behalf of the Court of Appeal: "The interests of the individual must be balanced against the interests of society generally but, in the light of the contents of the Covenant and its aim and objectives, with a bias towards the interests of the individual."

278 Bokhary, *supra* note 182, at 32–36.

279 Aharon Barak, Proportionality: Constitutional Rights and Their Limitations 375 (2012).

280 A.C.L. Davie & J.R. Williams, *Proportionality in English Law, in* The Judge and the Proportionate Use of Discretion: A Comparative Study 73, 81 (Sofia Ranchordás & Boudewijn de Waard eds.).

281 Leung Kwok Hung v. H.K.S.A.R. (2005) 8 H.K.C.F.A.R. 229 (H.K.C.F.A.).

282 Queensway is a busy highway near Central, the central business district.

283 Leung was popularly elected to the Legislative Council in 2004 and served until he was disqualified by the High Court under a Standing Committee Interpretation in 2017.

284 Public Order Ordinance, Cap. 245 (Hong Kong).

285 Leung Kwok Hung v. H.K.S.A.R. (2005) 8 H.K.C.F.A.R. 229, 268 (H.K.C.F.A.) (Li, C.J., Chan, P.J., Ribeiro, P.J., & Sir Anthony Mason, N.P.J.).

> (1) the restriction must be rationally connected with one or more of the legitimate purposes; and (2) the means used to impair the right of peaceful assembly must be no more than is necessary to accomplish the legitimate purpose in question.[286]

The majority decided that the Commissioner's discretion to impose limits on the right of peaceful assembly for the purpose of "public order (*ordre public*)" in Sections 14(1), 14(5), and 15(2) of the Ordinance was invalid as it was too vague to satisfy the constitutional requirement of "prescribed by law."[287] The Court, however, preserved the Commissioner's statutory discretion to restrict the right of peaceful assembly for the purpose of public order (in the law and order sense),[288] if the restrictions he imposed were proportionate.[289] In a different, anti-discrimination context, the Court fine-tuned this standard to a three-part "justification test," by which it ruled unconstitutional statutory provisions criminalizing homosexual but not heterosexual buggery for breaching the Basic Law's guarantee of legal equality:

> (1) "differential treatment" cannot be justified unless some "genuine need for such difference" exists, which must also (2) "be rationally connected to the legitimate aim," and (3) "be no more than is necessary to accomplish the legitimate aim."[290]

In *Hysan Development Co Ltd v Town Planning Board*[291] two property development companies challenged planning restrictions imposed on them by the Town Planning Board as contrary to Articles 6 and 105 of the Basic Law which guarantee private property rights.[292] The CFA accepted the companies'

[286] Leung Kwok Hung v. H.K.S.A.R. (2005) 8 H.K.C.F.A.R. 229, 253 (H.K.C.F.A.) (Li, C.J., Chan, P.J., Ribeiro, P.J., & Sir Anthony Mason, N.P.J.).

[287] Leung Kwok Hung v. H.K.S.A.R. (2005) 8 H.K.C.F.A.R. 229, 264 (H.K.C.F.A.) (Li, C.J., Chan, P.J., Ribeiro, P.J., & Sir Anthony Mason, N.P.J.).

[288] Leung Kwok Hung v. H.K.S.A.R. (2005) 8 H.K.C.F.A.R. 229, 265–66 (H.K.C.F.A.) (Li, C.J., Chan, P.J., Ribeiro, P.J., & Sir Anthony Mason, N.P.J.).

[289] Leung Kwok Hung v. H.K.S.A.R. (2005) 8 H.K.C.F.A.R. 229, 268 (H.K.C.F.A.) (Li, C.J., Chan, P.J., Ribeiro, P.J., & Sir Anthony Mason, N.P.J.).

[290] Secretary for Justice v. Yau Yuk Lung (2007) 10 H.K.C.F.A.R. 335, 349 (H.K.C.F.A.).

[291] Hysan Development Co. Ltd. v. Town Planning Bd. (2016) 19 H.K.C.F.A.R. 372 (H.K.C.F.A.).

[292] Basic Law, art. 6: "The Hong Kong Special Administrative Region shall protect the right of private ownership of property in accordance with law." Basic Law, art. 105: "The Hong Kong Special Administrative Region shall, in accordance with law, protect the right of individuals and legal persons to the acquisition, use, disposal and inheritance of property and their right to compensation for lawful deprivation of their property. Such compensation shall correspond to the real value of the property concerned at the time and shall be freely convertible and paid without undue

constitutional objections, and indeed seized the opportunity to modify the structured proportionality doctrine by adding a redoubtable fourth step:

> A fourth step should be added. In line with a substantial body of authority, where an encroaching measure has passed the three-step test, the analysis should incorporate a fourth step asking whether a reasonable balance has been struck between the societal benefits of the encroachment and the inroads made into the constitutionally protected rights of the individual, asking in particular whether pursuit of the societal interest results in an unacceptably harsh burden on the individual.[293]

This fourth step significantly obligates the legislature or public authorities to establish a non-disproportionality between the benefits of actualizing the impugned statute's purpose, and the damage to the claimant's constitutional rights; which is not satisfied unless the social utility of actualization exceeds that of avoiding the encroachment on constitutional rights.[294]

In *Kong Yunming v Director of Social Welfare*,[295] the applicant challenged the constitutionality of a policy issued by the Chief Executive in Council that excluded all non-permanent residents from receiving benefits under the Comprehensive Social Security Assistance scheme. It was in this decision that the CFA broke new ground in substantive review, when Ribeiro PJ ruled that "any restriction subsequently placed on [social welfare rights guaranteed by the Basic Law art.36] is subject to constitutional review by the Courts on the basis of a proportionality analysis."[296] Ostensibly, the CFA followed the standard proportionality analysis in proceeding through three stages, as involved in such an inquiry – Step One: inquire whether the restriction pursues "a legitimate societal aim";[297] if affirmative, Step Two: proceed to inquire whether the restriction may be said to be "rationally connected with the achievement of that end";[298] if again affirmative, Step Three: do not

delay. The ownership of enterprises and the investments from outside the Region shall be protected by law."

293 Hysan Development Co. Ltd. v. Town Planning Bd. (2016) 19 H.K.C.F.A.R. 372, 424 (H.K.C.F.A.) (Ribeiro, P.J.).

294 Barak, *supra* note 181, at 331.

295 Kong Yunming v. Dir. of Soc. Welfare (2013) 16 H.K.C.F.A.R. 950, 969 (H.K.C.F.A.).

296 Kong Yunming v. Dir. of Soc. Welfare (2013) 16 H.K.C.F.A.R. 950, 968 (H.K.C.F.A.). Basic Law, art. 36: "Hong Kong residents shall have the right to social welfare in accordance with law. The welfare benefits and retirement security of the labour force shall be protected by law."

297 Kong Yunming v. Dir. of Soc. Welfare (2013) 16 H.K.C.F.A.R. 950, 969 (H.K.C.F.A.) (Ribeiro, P.J.).

298 Kong Yunming v. Dir. of Soc. Welfare (2013) 16 H.K.C.F.A.R. 950, 969 (H.K.C.F.A.) (Ribeiro, P.J.).

inquire whether the restriction is "no further than necessary"[299] to achieve the legitimate aim, as would be applicable in the structured proportionality doctrine sensu stricto, but rather, whether it is "manifestly without reasonable foundation."[300] This substitution of a manifest unreasonableness standard for a minimal impairment one distinguishes the *Kong Yunming* doctrine from ordinary proportionality. Unlike minimum impairment, manifest unreasonableness implies that the governmental act in question should be invalidated only in the most extreme and unlikely circumstances, not merely because it is disproportionate.[301] The Court arguably misapplied Step Two of the proportionality test in *Kong Yunming* to invalidate the administrative denial of benefits;[302] nonetheless, the very high manifest unreasonableness threshold will predictably lead courts to uphold the vast majority of limitations on socio-economic rights.[303]

In this manner, the CFA has distinguished between "fundamental rights" and "socio-economic policies." The former encompasses rights such as freedom of expression and presumption of innocence, any encroachment on which should be condemned as "disproportionate" unless justifiable as no more than "minimal impairment," meaning "it goes no further than necessary to achieve the legitimate objective in question."[304] By contrast, it risks neither violation of "fundamental rights" nor "discrimination on inherently suspect grounds" to allocate to social welfare a limited share of the budget, a public good that is finite in quantity (exhaustion of which would impair the private economy) yet infinite in fungibility (anybody might legitimately lay claim to it). The CFA astonished many when it announced that "[the] right to social welfare is not a fundamental right but a right which intrinsically involves the Government setting rules determining eligibility and benefit levels."[305] Under the doctrine of the "margin of appreciation," drawn from European supranational jurisprudence, judges ought to intervene only if the impugned act is

299 Kong Yunming v. Dir. of Soc. Welfare (2013) 16 H.K.C.F.A.R. 950, 969 (H.K.C.F.A.) (Ribeiro, P.J.).

300 Kong Yunming v. Dir. of Soc. Welfare (2013) 16 H.K.C.F.A.R. 950, 970 (H.K.C.F.A.) (Ribeiro, P.J.).

301 Paul Daly, A Theory of Deference in Administrative Law: Basis, Application and Scope 181 (2012).

302 Po Jen Yap & Thomas Wong, *Public Welfare and the Judicial Over-Enforcement of Socio-Economic Rights in Hong Kong*, 44(1) Hong Kong L.J. 41, 48 (2014).

303 Eric C. Ip, Kong Yunming *Manifest Unreasonableness: The Doctrinal Future of Constitutional Review of Welfare Policy in Hong Kong'*, 44(1) Hong Kong L.J. 55, 66 (2014).

304 Kong Yunming v. Dir. of Soc. Welfare (2013) 16 H.K.C.F.A.R. 950, 969 (H.K.C.F.A.) (Ribeiro, P.J.).

305 Kong Yunming v. Dir. of Soc. Welfare (2013) 16 H.K.C.F.A.R. 950, 971 (H.K.C.F.A.) (Ribeiro, P.J.).

"manifestly without reasonable justification."[306] Thus, the Hong Kong courts ought to appreciate the informational advantages of the Government and Legislative Council, just as international courts do those of national governments, even if judges cannot be said to be unfamiliar with local conditions.[307] Earlier, in *Fok Chun Wa v. Hospital Authority*,[308] the CFA upheld an administrative policy denying non-resident spouses of permanent residents eligibility for subsidized services at public hospitals on the ground that "where limited public funds are involved, the courts have recognized that lines have had to be drawn by the executive or the legislature," which should not be disturbed unless "shown to be manifestly without reasonable foundation."[309]

In line with Macau's civil law tradition, its Código do Procedimento Administrativo (Code of Administrative Procedure)[310] provides a statutory proportionality principle that mandates that an administrative act that infringes the rights or legally protected interests of private persons may do so if and only if its purpose is proper and the means used proportionate.[311] The same Code provides an equality principle that obligates public authorities to avoid discriminating against or conferring undue privilege upon persons on the basis of their "descent, sex, race, language, place of origin, religion, political belief, ideological belief, education, financial conditions or social status."[312] Other principles relevant to judicial review of administrative acts that are codified therein include legality;[313] the public interest;[314] use of official languages;[315] justice and impartiality;[316] good faith;[317] cooperation;[318] participation;[319] the obligation to act;[320] efficiency;[321]

306 Kong Yunming v. Dir. of Soc. Welfare (2013) 16 H.K.C.F.A.R. 950, 970 (H.K.C.F.A.) (Ribeiro, P.J.).

307 Johannes M.M. Chan & C.L. Lim, *Interpreting Constitutional Rights and Permissible Restrictions, in* LAW OF THE HONG KONG CONSTITUTION 565, 602 (Johannes M.M. Chan & C.L. Lim eds., 2d ed. 2015).

308 Fok Chun Wa v. Hospital Auth. (2012) 15 H.K.C.F.A.R. 409 (H.K.C.F.A.).

309 Fok Chun Wa v. Hospital Auth. (2012) 15 H.K.C.F.A.R. 409, 438 (H.K.C.F.A.) (Ma, C.J.).

310 Código do Procedimento Administrativo (approved by Decree Law 57/99/M; amended by Decree Law 110/99/M) [hereinafter "Code of Administrative Procedure"].

311 Code of Administrative Procedure, s. 5.

312 Code of Administrative Procedure, s. 5.

313 Code of Administrative Procedure, s. 3.

314 Code of Administrative Procedure, s. 4.

315 Code of Administrative Procedure, s. 6.

316 Code of Administrative Procedure, s. 7.

317 Code of Administrative Procedure, s. 8.

318 Code of Administrative Procedure, s. 9.

319 Code of Administrative Procedure, s. 10.

320 Code of Administrative Procedure, s. 11.

321 Code of Administrative Procedure, s. 12.

non-compensation;[322] and oversight by the judiciary.[323] This compendious enumeration notwithstanding, as a practical matter the courts of Macau evaluate only the legality of administrative acts.[324] Unlike its Hong Kong counterpart, the principle of proportionality in Macau has been confined by the TUI (as expected) to the review of administrative acts, and never been deployed to invalidate legislation. Even in reviewing administrative acts, the TUI has been content in practice simply to check whether the impugned act has "manifestly violated" proportionality,[325] without analyzing step by step the true extent or legitimacy of this.[326] The Macau version of proportionality has been reaffirmed in the context both of immigration policy: "if in the exercise of free discretionary powers there exists obvious errors or circumstances of manifestly unreasonable exercises of free discretionary powers, then [the immigration authority] has to be subjected to judicial review";[327] and police powers: "[the police force enjoys] free discretionary powers, which constitute illegality and are judicially reviewable only if in the course of exercising these powers there are obvious errors and manifestly unreasonable circumstances."[328]

In a recent decision, Case 83/2016, the TUI rejected a Hong Kong permanent resident's suit to reverse the Secretary for Security's decision against issuing him a residential permit for reunion with his spouse, who is a Macau permanent resident, on the ground that the claimant committed a minor offence in Hong Kong a decade ago, which resulted in a fine of HK$1,000 (US$127.37) but was expunged from the record pursuant to Section 2(1) of Hong Kong's Rehabilitation of Offences Ordinance.[329] The claimant argued the Secretary's decision constituted a disproportionate restriction on his and his wife's right to family guaranteed by Article 38 of the Lei Básica. The TUI reiterated its test as follows: "it is only when in the exercise of jurisdictional rights there are obvious errors and manifest or total unreasonableness [manifesto ou a total desrazoabilidade] that the law will be breached, and judicial review becomes relevant."[330]

In Case 5/2010, the TUI was asked to decide an inconsistency between two laws dealing with the calculation of service hours of teachers assigned to the

322 Code of Administrative Procedure, s. 13.
323 Code of Administrative Procedure, s. 14.
324 Mai & Ho, *supra* note 99, at 82.
325 Case 6/2000, 14 (T.U.I.M.) (Chu, J.).
326 Chen et al., *supra* note 220, at 205–06.
327 Case 21/2014, 37 (T.U.I.M.) (Lima, J.).
328 Case 33/2014, 16 (T.U.I.M.) (Song, J.).
329 Rehabilitation of Offences Ordinance, Cap. 297 (Hong Kong).
330 Case 83/2016, 17 (T.U.I.M.) (Song, J.).

Direcção dos Serviços de Educação e Juventude (Education and Youth Affairs Bureau) in public universities and in public primary and secondary schools. Invoking the principle of equality enshrined in Article 25 of the Lei Básica,[331] the Tribunal stated the principle in these words: "to treat like cases alike, and to treat unlike cases unlike";[332] and "the principle is violated on the ground of the prohibition of arbitrariness if like cases are treated unequally."[333] The TUI compared the rules of the University of Macau, of the Macau Polytechnic Institute, and of secondary schools dependent on the Bureau, and found the norm to be in breach of the principle and so inapplicable.[334] The norm itself was not invalidated, just the administrative act based on it was quashed. The Tribunal seized the opportunity to caution that "'reasonableness', 'justice', and 'desirableness' ('razoável', 'justa' ou 'ideal')" are not grounds for judicial superintendence of the legality of legal norms, and that the principle of equality is an "essentially negative criterion (critério essencialmente negativo)" invalidating only what is "flagrantly and intolerably unequal (flagrante e intolerável desigualdade)," which practically does not happen unless the differential treatment by the legislator is "without justification, without objectivity, without rationality (não fundamentadas, não objectivas, não razoáveis)."[335] In Case 9/2012 a nurse in the Bureau of Health (Serviços de Saúde) challenged the Chief Executive's decision to refuse to adjust her salary. The claimant nurse alleged inter alia that the impugned act contravened the three principles of legal equality, legitimate expectation, and non-discrimination enshrined in the Lei Básica. The TUI dismissed her appeal from her lost case in the TSI, taking its caution in Case 5/2010 to its logical conclusion: "in the case in question, notwithstanding the fact that the legislature could have established identical [salary] arrangements for all nurses, the differential treatment between various categories of public servants in relation to the present question of transitional salaries does not constitute flagrant and intolerable inequality, for this belongs to the free discretion of the legislature."[336]

The TUI has statutory jurisdiction in cases of criminal acts alleged to have been committed by senior political officials. In that capacity, the Tribunal

331 Lei Básica, art. 25: "All Macao residents shall be equal before the law, and shall be free from discrimination, irrespective of their nationality descent, race, sex, language, religion, political persuasion or ideological belief, educational level, economic status or social conditions."

332 Case 5/2010, 31 (T.U.I.M.) (Lima, J.).

333 Case 5/2010, 32 (T.U.I.M.) (Lima, J).

334 Godinho & Cardinal, *supra* note 22, at 625.

335 Case 5/2010, 34–35 (T.U.I.M.) (Lima, J).

336 Case 5/2010, 37–38 (T.U.I.M.) (Lima, J).

rather idiosyncratically functions as the "first, single and last instance" court.[337] On July 13, 2017, in just such a case, the TUI sentenced Ho Chio Meng, the Macau SAR's inaugural Procurator-General (holding office from 1999 to 2014) and one-time Chief Executive hopeful, to 21 years in prison, and fined him MOP87 million (US$10.8 million) in total, for the offences of founding a criminal organization, money laundering, and aggravated fraud.[338] In Case 60/2015, delivered on August 15, 2017, Judge Song Man Lei, writing on behalf of the TUI, rejected Ho's contention that Sections 44(2)(7) and (8) of the Fundamental Law on Judicial Organization, prohibiting him from appealing his conviction at least once, was in breach of Article 14(5) of the ICCPR[339] – as incorporated in the Lei Básica's Article 40 – which states: "Everyone convicted of a crime shall have the right to his conviction and sentence being reviewed by a higher tribunal according to law." Without any substantive analysis of the impugned statute's compatibility with the ICCPR, Judge Song concluded prima facie that Ho's case must fail:

> The Legislature, in establishing the [TUI] as the first instance court for the judgment of specific persons, should have foreseen the non-availability of an even higher court to hear appeals from a case decided by the highest judicial organ, but have nonetheless decided to confer first instance jurisdiction on the [TUI] in relation to the specific persons, and refrained from providing any regulation on any possible appeal lodged against judgments by that Tribunal. From this, we can infer that, regardless of the absence of an expressed provision by the Legislature that forbids appeals against first instance decisions of the [TUI], it cannot be eliminated that the legislative intent was precisely so.[340]

337 Godinho & Cardinal, *supra* note 22, at 628.

338 Raquel Carvalho, *Macau's Former Chief Prosecutor Ho Chio-meng Jailed 21 years for Crimes including Fraud and Money Laundering*, South China Morning Post, Jul. 14, 2017, www.scmp.com/news/hong-kong/law-crime/article/2102603/macaus-former-chief-prosecutor-ho-chio-meng-jailed-21-years

339 International Covenant on Civil and Political Rights, 999 U.N.T.S. 171, Dec. 19, 1966.

340 Case 60/2015, 3 (Song, J.) ("O legislador ao determinar o referido Tribunal como aquele que tem competência para julgar em primeira instância determinados indivíduos, deveria ter previsto a questão de que, situando-se o Tribunal de Última Instância no topo dos órgãos judiciários, não haveria tribunal de nível mais alto para conhecer do recurso interposto das decisões proferidas por aquele Tribunal, mas mesmo assim, atribuiu ao Tribunal de Última Instância a competência de julgar em 1ª instância aqueles indivíduos, e não procedeu a qualquer regulação sobre a possibilidade da interposição do recurso dos acórdãos proferidas por aquele Tribunal. Daí podemos extrair a conclusão de que, apesar de o legislador não ter previsto explicitamente que não se pode interpor recurso do acórdão do Tribunal de Última Instância proferido em primeira instância, não se pode excluir que, esta tenha sido precisamente a sua intenção legislativa.")

In fact, Case 60/2015 merely restated what the TUI had decided in the similar Case 36/2007 concerning the former Secretary for Transport and Public Works, Ao Man Long, who had been sentenced by the Tribunal on January 30, 2008 to twenty-seven years in prison on corruption charges and fined him 800 million Macau patacas (US$99.4 million).[341] Ao's arrest and conviction had shattered public confidence in the Government,[342] as not a few residents came to suspect that this was not an isolated incident, but only the tip of an iceberg.[343] In this sensitive case, the Tribunal went as far as saying that legal consequences to its rejection of Ao's right to appeal, contrary to the ICCPR, are international, not domestic.[344] The most daunting problem in these two cases is that the ICCPR has direct legal effect in Macau's legal system, and that Macau has formulated no reservation to Article 14(5) in order to exempt its peculiar appellate arrangements from it, as have Belgium, Italy, Holland, and Switzerland.[345] Moreover, the Human Rights Committee of the United Nations has already spoken on this matter when it held Spain in breach of Article 14(5):

> Where the highest court of a country acts as first and only instance, the absence of any right to review by a higher tribunal is not offset by the fact of being tried by the supreme tribunal of the State party concerned; rather, such a system is incompatible with the Covenant, unless the State party concerned has made a reservation to this effect.[346]

It can be straightforwardly deduced from these principles that, unless and until such a reservation is made, Ho, Ao, and others like them should be allowed appeals against the TUI decisions of the first instance. It is for the Macau SAR to figure out how and to whom such appeals should proceed, as by enlarging the TUI to include an appellate chamber, or moving its first instance jurisdiction to lower courts.[347] Notwithstanding the weighty international law implications, the TUI in neither case conducted any kind of structured

[341] Jorge Godinho, *The Ao Man Long Corruption and Money Laundering Case*, 4 FREEDOM FROM FEAR MAGAZINE 26, 27 (2009).

[342] Ieong Meng U, *Macao and Hong Kong, Convergence or Divergence? The 2014 Retirement Package Bill Protest and Macao's Governance Crisis*, 57 (3) ASIAN SURV. 504, 507 (2017).

[343] VICTOR ZHENG & PO-SAN WAN, GAMBLING DYNAMISM: THE MACAO MIRACLE 137 (2014).

[344] Case 36/2007, 8 (T.U.I.M.) (Sam, P., Lima, J. & Lai., J.).

[345] Godinho & Cardinal, *supra* note 22, at 629.

[346] Human Rights Committee, *General Comment No. 32. Article 14: Right to equality before courts and tribunals and to a fair trial, doc.*, C.C.P.R./C./G.C./32 (2007).

[347] Godinho & Cardinal, *supra* note 22, at 630.

proportionality review of the impugned statute's compatibility with the Lei Básica or the ICCPR.

This stands in stark contrast to the CFA's largely consistent application of the structured proportionality standard, subject to the margin of appreciation. There is a grim irony here, as structured proportionality originated not in the courts of England and Wales, but in the Prussian Supreme Administrative Court in the late nineteenth century – within the Romano-Germanic civil law tradition.[348] The doctrine has grown in prominence throughout the twentieth century under the influence of the European Court of Justice and European Court of Human Rights,[349] and has become singular as the most widely discussed and resorted-to constitutional doctrine in the world, crossing legal traditions and transcending national boundaries in a way unmatched, for example, by the debate on originalism in the United States.[350] The CFA's proportionality standard directs constitutional scrutiny in three dimensions: (1) whether the statute limits a constitutional right; (2) whether the limitation satisfies the various conditions of proportionality analysis; and (3) whether any, and if so, what constitutional remedy should be granted.[351] It is the most intrusive form of substantive review,[352] obliging the state to respond to clear-cut judicial questions with reasoned justifications for the way it brought its powers to bear.[353] It differs markedly from the TUI's "flagrant inequality" and "manifest unreasonableness" standards, both one-dimensional inquiries able to recognize as invalid none but the most intolerable acts. But by Hong Kong's proportionality standard, a "tolerably irrational" act may be invalidated if it fails to clear just one of the three or four steps.

Judicial Petition

The Basic Law and the Lei Básica obligate all courts of Hong Kong and Macau, when in the course of final appellate adjudication they are bound to

348 David Dyzenhaus, *Proportionality and Deference in a Culture of Justification, in* PROPORTIONALITY AND THE RULE OF LAW: RIGHTS, JUSTIFICATION, REASONING 234, 236 (Grant Huscroft et al. eds., 2014).

349 Sofia Ranchordás & Boudewijn de Waard, *Proportionality Crossing Borders: Why It Is Still Difficult to Recognise Sparrows and Cannons, in* THE JUDGE AND THE PROPORTIONATE USE OF DISCRETION: A COMPARATIVE STUDY 1, 4 (Sofia Ranchordás & Boudewijn de Waard eds., 2016).

350 Vicki C. Jackson & Mark Tushnet, *Introduction, in* PROPORTIONALITY: NEW FRONTIERS, NEW CHALLENGES 1, 1 (Vicki C. Jackson & Mark Tushnet eds., 2017).

351 Barak, *supra* note 181, at 325.

352 STEPHEN GARDBAUM, THE NEW COMMONWEALTH MODEL OF CONSTITUTIONALISM: THEORY AND PRACTICE 225 (2013).

353 YAP, *supra* note 275, at 181.

resolve matters outside the limits of the Regions' autonomy, to "seek an interpretation of the relevant provisions from the Standing Committee of the National People's Congress," addressed via the CFA and the TUI, respectively.[354] Interestingly, the two basic laws do not define what provisions lie outside the SARs' autonomy, nor is the Standing Committee forbidden to circumscribe at will the scope of validity of Hong Kong's and Macau's legal doctrines embodied in their judicial precedents.[355] In theory, this mandatory referral procedure gives Beijing *carte blanche* to ensure the complete subordination of the SAR to China.[356] In Hong Kong it has been called "a nightmare to the Court of Final Appeal that it cannot get rid of."[357] If used with any frequency, it could seal the fate of the SARs as free-standing jurisdictions.[358] Thus far, the TUI has encountered no occasion to petition to the Standing Committee, nor has the Standing Committee found any instance for overturning a constitutional doctrine of the Tribunal. In neighboring Hong Kong, however, the issue of judicial petition has been very important and very controversial.

The CFA has reacted with constitutional jurisprudence that mediates the effect of the referral procedure through the so-called "predominant provision test" originally formulated in the *Ng Ka Ling* case. It divides Basic Law provisions into two types: "non-excluded provisions" (belonging to the Hong Kong SAR's autonomous powers), and "excluded provisions" (for which the Chinese Central People's Government has responsibility, or touching relations between the Centre and the SAR). In the case of an "excluded provision" the courts are to make a referral to the Standing Committee *only* if it is a "predominant provision" in that case, meaning that it bids fair to "affect the judgment on the case."[359] Even then, a referral may be avoided if the competent court demonstrates that the provision is not "essential" to the outcome of its decision. In practice, the CFA itself avoids referring matters to the Standing Committee with impunity.

The first-ever referral from Hong Kong was not made until 2011 – fourteen years after the resumption of Chinese sovereignty – in *Democratic Republic of*

354 Basic Law, art. 158.

355 Zhenmin Wang, *From the Judicial Committee of the British Privy Council to the Standing Committee of the Chinese National People's Congress – An Evaluation of the Legal Interpretive System after the Handover*, 37 HONG KONG L.J. 605, 611 (2007).

356 Ghai, *supra* note 227, at 345.

357 Benny Y.T. Tai, *The Constitutional Game of Article 158 (3) of the Basic Law*, 41 HONG KONG L.J. 377, 381 (2001).

358 *See* Cora Chan, *Reconceptualising the Relationship between the Mainland Chinese Legal System and the Hong Kong Legal System*, 6 ASIAN J. COMP. L. Iss. 1, art. 1 (2011).

359 Ng Ka Ling v. Dir. of Immigration (1999) 2 H.K.C.F.A.R. 4, 31 (H.K.C.F.A.) (Li, C.J.).

the Congo v. FG Hemisphere Associates LLC (No. 1),[360] which raised the issue of whether China's policy of granting foreign states absolute immunity[361] in its courts extended to Hong Kong, where the common law doctrine of restrictive immunity[362] has traditionally prevailed.[363] China's responsibility for "foreign affairs" is exclusive, whence the courts of Hong Kong in matters not falling under the SAR's wide-ranging "external affairs" competence,[364] are bound to defer to Beijing "on matters of foreign affairs relating to the People's Republic of China as a sovereign State."[365] China, through a letter addressed to the CFA through its foreign affairs commissioner in Hong Kong, had earlier threatened that,

> If the Hong Kong Special Administrative Region were to adopt a regime of state immunity which is inconsistent with the position of the state, it will undoubtedly prejudice the sovereignty of China and have a long-term impact and serious prejudice to the overall interests of China [...] it would be contradictory to the above-mentioned foreign policy of China and tarnish the international image of China [...] thus threatening the interests and security of the property of China abroad, as well as hampering the normal intercourse and co-operation in such areas as economy and trade between China and the states concerned.[366]

360 Democratic Republic of the Congo v. FG Hemisphere Associates LLC (No 1) (2011) 14 H.K.C.F.A.R. 95 (H.K.C.F.A.).

361 Xiaodang Yang, State Immunity in International Law 7 (2012) ("'absolute immunity' means that States enjoyed immunity before foreign courts with regard to any subject matter").

362 Hazel Fox & Philippa Webb, The Law of State Immunity 48 (3d ed. 2013) ("the restrictive doctrine [makes] a distinction between the State's exercise of public powers as opposed to engagement in private relations restricts immunity to the former allowing proceedings relating to commercial matters against a foreign State in national courts by private individuals").

363 Democratic Republic of the Congo v. FG Hemisphere Associates LLC (No 1) (2011) 14 H.K.C.F.A.R. 95, 165 (H.K.C.F.A.) (Chan, P.J., Ribeiro, P.J., & Sir Anthony Mason, N.P.J.).

364 Basic Law, art. 151: "The Hong Kong Special Administrative Region may on its own, using the name "Hong Kong, China," maintain and develop relations and conclude and implement agreements with foreign states and regions and relevant international organizations in the appropriate fields, including the economic, trade, financial and monetary, shipping, communications, tourism, cultural and sports fields." *See* Eric C. Ip, *Comparative Subnational Foreign Relations Law in the Chinese Special Administrative Regions*, 65(4) Int'l & Comp. L. Q. 953 (2016).

365 Democratic Republic of the Congo v. FG Hemisphere Associates LLC (No 1) (2011) 14 H.K.C.F.A.R. 95, 165 (H.K.C.F.A.) (Chan, P.J., Ribeiro, P.J., & Sir Anthony Mason, N.P.J.).

366 Democratic Republic of the Congo v. FG Hemisphere Associates LLC (No 1) (2011) 14 H.K.C.F.A.R. 95, 250, 252 (H.K.C.F.A.) (Chan, P.J., Ribeiro, P.J., & Sir Anthony Mason, N.P.J.).

Undoubtedly, the absolute immunity doctrine and other Chinese foreign policy positions, like all matters relating to national sovereignty, were intrinsic to a core set of preferences that Beijing would be willing to defend at all costs, indeed, all political transaction costs vis-à-vis the CFA. China would not tolerate any judgment by the Court that might complicate its plans for economic and political influence in Africa. For the CFA to act defiantly and uphold the restrictive immunity doctrine would amount to a colossal crisis that would inflict losses more devastating for the Court than for the Standing Committee of the National People's Congress.

The CFA, therefore, crafted a precedent in referring the matter to the Standing Committee, framing questions to all of which the Court in its own opinion provided ready answers consistent with China's preferences. The Standing Committee returned an Interpretation directly quoting each of the questions and provided acute and affirmative answers.[367] The Court then issued its own final judgment applying the Interpretation to the case in favour of the Congo.[368] By delivering a detailed and principled judgment that evaluated all relevant legal and policy issues, and rendering its own provisional ruling before the Standing Committee got at any Interpretation, the CFA wove a subtextual narrative that could claim that it remained de facto the real final adjudicative authority in Hong Kong. It had narrowly drafted each of the four questions in the referral so as to elicit only a binary ("yes" or "no") answer. This strategy has been commended as "a laudable attempt that reduces the arbitrariness of the referencing process."[369]

The "predominant provision" test stood the "test" of the first and only referral so far. Since then the CFA has stoutly resisted making further referrals to the Standing Committee even when the Hong Kong Government itself has specifically requested it. In *Vallejos v. Commissioner of Registration*[370] the constitutionality of a controversial statute was impugned which prohibited foreign domestic helpers to acquire permanent residency, no matter how long resident in Hong Kong, allegedly contrary to the Basic Law's permission for expatriates to acquire permanent residency "who have ordinarily resided in Hong Kong for a continuous period of not less than seven years."[371] Even in

367 Interpretation of Paragraph 1, Article 13 and Article 19 of the Basic Law of the Hong Kong Special Administrative Region of the People's Republic of China by the Standing Committee of the National People's Congress (Adopted by the Standing Committee of the Eleventh National People's Congress at its Twenty-Second Session on August 26, 2011).

368 Democratic Republic of the Congo v. FG Hemisphere Associates LLC (No. 2) (2011), 14 H.K.C.F.A.R. 395 (H.K.C.F.A.).

369 Chan, *supra* note 17, at 191.

370 Vallejos v. Comm'r of Registration (2013) 16 H.K.C.F.A.R. 45 (H.K.C.F.A.).

371 Basic Law, art. 24(2)(2).

affirming the Commissioner of Registration's position, the Court denied his request for a referral to the Standing Committee for a final interpretation of the meaning of certain parts of its 1999 Interpretation as a matter of obligation (in the teeth of the *Chong Fung Yuen* principles. The Court reaffirmed that the referral mechanism is mandatory only upon the two well-established conditions of the avoidance doctrine, *viz.* "classification" and "necessity." Both must be satisfied before one may proceed to a referral;[372] the Court jealously guarding its prerogative "to decide and for it alone to decide"[373] whether to make a referral, and dismissing the Commissioner's request as "unnecessary."[374] The provision in question may be an "excluded" one, but it has no legal application to foreign domestic helpers, who are "qualitatively so far-removed from what would traditionally be recognized as 'ordinary residence'."[375] Importantly, the Court formalized a third hurdle in the referral doctrine by ruling that any request must satisfy a third, "arguability" condition designed to eliminate "a risk of potential abuse" by avoiding a slippery slope down which "all sorts of fanciful arguments could then be made just to seek a reference to the Standing Committee."[376] Thus the Court has created for itself even greater latitude in avoiding engagement with the Standing Committee of the National People's Congress.

DISCUSSION AND CONCLUSION

If the Hong Kong Basic Law and the Lei Básica de Macau had established any systems of constitutional review, they were at best "weak-form review[s]."[377] Both the CFA and the TUI could easily have disclaimed any powers of constitutional adjudication by holding that they are vested in the Standing Committee of the National People's Congress exclusively, and that any local SAR act of state not vetoed by the latter must be presumed constitutional and enforced by the courts.[378] By asserting a constitutional jurisdiction for the Hong Kong Judiciary, the CFA has staked out a real primacy over constitutional meaning and enforcement, and legitimized judicial checks and balances on the political authorities, in a way only implicit in the constitutional text. The "living constitution" and purposive approaches to interpreting the

372 Vallejos v. Comm'r of Registration (2013) 16 H.K.C.F.A.R. 45, 83 (H.K.C.F.A.).
373 Vallejos v. Comm'r of Registration (2013) 16 H.K.C.F.A.R. 45, 86 (H.K.C.F.A.).
374 Vallejos v. Comm'r of Registration (2013) 16 H.K.C.F.A.R. 45, 86 (H.K.C.F.A.).
375 Vallejos v. Comm'r of Registration (2013) 16 H.K.C.F.A.R. 45, 76–77 (H.K.C.F.A.).
376 Vallejos v. Comm'r of Registration (2013) 16 H.K.C.F.A.R. 45, 85 (H.K.C.F.A.).
377 Tushnet & Dixon, *supra* note 149, at 105.
378 Chen, *supra* note 150, at 24.

Basic Law have freed the Hong Kong courts from the chains of original intent, actual or supposititious, so that they can confidently construe constitutional provisions in line with the common law tradition and in light of societal and technological metamorphoses. Structured proportionality standard of review has not only put explicit limits to arbitrary administrative decision-making, but even indicated effectual guidelines of constitutionally permissible legislation. The margin of appreciation has afforded the CFA the discretion to keep hands off the thorny issue of resource allocation without having to withdraw from the arena of social and economic rights altogether. And the referral avoidance doctrine has interdicted undue influence by the National People's Congress, Standing Committee in the Basic Law's interpretation, at least in an adjudicatory context.

The constitutional jurisprudence of the TUI exhibits astonishing contrasts with its Hong Kong counterpart by adhering to a literalist reading of the Lei Básica. Early on, the Tribunal has decided to preempt the recognition of any specific constitutional litigation procedure. It has declined to assert competence to find legislative provisions incompatible with the Lei Básica and so null to that extent.[379] It has chosen to affirm that no court in Macau has such competence, and has rarely, if ever, declined to apply Lei Básica-incompatible provisions on substantive constitutional rights grounds. The TUI's interpretive approach is premised on strongly emphasizing the literal meaning of law codes; deep respect for mainland Chinese juridical concepts; deference to political authorities, and, consequently, a virtual absence of high-energy constitutional review. It has been suggested that the TUI's practice is redolent rather of the courts in some former socialist jurisdictions of Eastern Europe than of the West European tradition whence the TUI sprang.[380] It has never yet seized any opportunity rendered it by the direct applicability of international human rights treaties in the Macau legal system to craft a more sophisticated structure of judicial doctrines on constitutional questions. It has never yet availed itself of the world-renowned, time-tested structured proportionality doctrine to gauge the compatibility of legislation with the Lei Básica, and even in its often-brief review of the constitutionality of administrative acts, it has been content to invoke only "manifest unreasonableness," which annuls only egregious acts. The TUI has evolved no judicial doctrine regulating its relationship to the Standing Committee of the National People's Congress, which in turn has never yet issued an Interpretation that reversed or preempted

379 Ignazio Castellucci, *Legal Hybridity in Hong Kong and Macau*, 57 McGill L. J. 665, 698 (2012).

380 *Id.* at 697.

a Macau court case. The Chapter 5 will study a variety of independent variables which may explain the fundamental divergence between the constitutional jurisprudence of the CFA and the TUI, notwithstanding their highly similar constitutional frameworks and the nearly identical time frames.

Appendix to Chapter 4

TABLE 4.1 *List of Judges of the Hong Kong Court of Final Appeal (1997–2017)*

Name	Position(s) in the Court	Judgeship held before appointment to the Court	Occupation(s) before becoming judge
Andrew Li	Chief Justice (1997–2010)	Deputy High Court judge, High Court, British Hong Kong	Barrister (Queen's Counsel) in private practice
Kemal Bokhary	Permanent Judge (1997–2012) Local Non-Permanent Judge (2012-)	Justice of Appeal, Court of Appeal, British Hong Kong	Barrister (Queen's Counsel) in private practice
Charles Ching	Permanent Judge (1997–2000) Local Non-Permanent Judge (2000)	Justice of Appeal, Court of Appeal, British Hong Kong	Barrister (Queen's Counsel) in private practice
Henry Litton	Permanent Judge (1997–2000) Local Non-Permanent Judge (2000–15)	Vice-President, Court of Appeal, British Hong Kong	Barrister (Queen's Counsel) in private practice
Patrick Chan	Permanent Judge (2000–13) Local Non-Permanent Judge (2013-)	Chief Judge of the High Court, Court of Appeal, Hong Kong SAR	Barrister in private practice
Robert Ribeiro	Permanent Judge (2000-)	Justice of Appeal, Court of Appeal, Hong Kong SAR	Barrister (Queen's Counsel) in private practice; legal academic

TABLE 4.1 (*continued*)

Name	Position(s) in the Court	Judgeship held before appointment to the Court	Occupation(s) before becoming judge
Geoffrey Ma	Chief Justice (2010-)	Chief Judge of the High Court, Court of Appeal, Hong Kong SAR	Barrister (Queen's Counsel) in private practice
Robert Tang	Local Non-Permanent Judge (2010–12) Permanent Judge (2012)	Vice-President, Court of Appeal, Hong Kong SAR	Barrister (Queen's Counsel) in private practice
Joseph Fok	Permanent Judge (2013)	Justice of Appeal, Court of Appeal, Hong Kong SAR	Barrister (Senior Counsel) in private practice
Philip Clough	Local Non-Permanent Judge (1997–2006)	Justice of Appeal, Court of Appeal, British Hong Kong	Federal Counsel, Malaya; Legal Affairs Advisor, Brunei
Sir Derek Cons	Local Non-Permanent Judge (1997–2006)	Vice President, Court of Appeal, British Hong Kong	Barrister in private practice
Kutlu Fuad	Local Non-Permanent Judge (1997–2009)	Vice President, Court of Appeal, British Hong Kong; President, Court of Appeal, Brunei	Director, Legal Division, Commonwealth Secretariat
Sir Alan Huggins	Local Non-Permanent Judge (1997–2003)	Vice President, Court of Appeal, British Hong Kong	Barrister in private practice
Neil MacDougall	Local Non-Permanent Judge (1997–2003)	Vice President, Court of Appeal, British Hong Kong	Principal Crown Counsel
Art McMullin	Local Non-Permanent Judge (1997–2003)	Justice of Appeal, Court of Appeal, British Hong Kong	Crown Counsel
John Mortimer	Local Non-Permanent Judge (1997–2015)	Vice President, Court of Appeal, Hong Kong SAR	Barrister (Queen's Counsel), in private practice
Gerald Nazareth	Local Non-Permanent Judge (1997–2012)	Vice President, Court of Appeal, Hong Kong SAR	Barrister (Queen's Counsel) in private practice

TABLE 4.1 (*continued*)

Name	Position(s) in the Court	Judgeship held before appointment to the Court	Occupation(s) before becoming judge
Sir Noel Power	Local Non-Permanent Judge (1997–2009)	Acting Chief Justice of Hong Kong, British Hong Kong	Barrister in private practice
Sir Denys Roberts	Local Non-Permanent Judge (1997–2003)	Chief Justice of Hong Kong, British Hong Kong	Chief Secretary, British Hong Kong; Attorney General, British Hong Kong; Solicitor-General, British Hong Kong
William Silke	Local Non-Permanent Judge (1997–2009)	Vice President, Court of Appeal, British Hong Kong	Barrister in private practice
Michael Hartmann	Local Non-Permanent Judge (2010–16)	Justice of Appeal, Court of Appeal, Hong Kong SAR	Deputy Principal Crown Counsel
Frank Stock	Local Non-Permanent Judge (2010)	Vice President, Court of Appeal, Hong Kong SAR	Solicitor-General, British Hong Kong
Lord Cooke	Overseas Non-Permanent Judge (1997)	Lord of Appeal in Ordinary, Appellate Committee, House of Lords, United Kingdom	Barrister (Queen's Counsel) in private practice
Sir Daryl Dawson	Overseas Non-Permanent Judge (1997–2003)	Justice, High Court of Australia	Barrister (Queen's Counsel) in private practice; Solicitor-General of Victoria
Sir Anthony Mason	Overseas Non-Permanent Judge (1997–2015)	Chief Justice of Australia	Barrister (Queen's Counsel) in private practice; legal academic; Solicitor-General of Australia
Lord Nicholls	Overseas Non-Permanent Judge (1997–2004)	Lord of Appeal in the Ordinary, Appellate	Barrister (Queen's Counsel) in private practice

TABLE 4.1 *(continued)*

Name	Position(s) in the Court	Judgeship held before appointment to the Court	Occupation(s) before becoming judge
		Committee, House of Lords, United Kingdom	
Sir Edward Somers	Overseas Non-Permanent Judge (1997–2002)	Judge, Court of Appeal New Zealand	Barrister and Solicitor (Queen's Counsel) in private practice
Lord Hoffmann	Overseas Non-Permanent Judge (1998)	Lord of Appeal in the Ordinary, Appellate Committee, House of Lords, United Kingdom	Barrister (Queen's Counsel) in private practice
Sir Gerard Brennan	Overseas Non-Permanent Judge (2000–12)	Chief Justice of Australia	Barrister (Queen's Counsel) in private practice
Sir Thomas Eichelbaum	Overseas Non-Permanent Judge (2000–09)	Chief Justice of New Zealand	Barrister (Queen's Counsel) in private practice
Lord Millett	Overseas Non-Permanent Judge (2000)	Lord of Appeal in the Ordinary, Appellate Committee, House of Lords, United Kingdom	Barrister (Queen's Counsel) in private practice
Sir Ivor Richardson	Overseas Non-Permanent Judge (2003–09)	President, Court of Appeal, New Zealand	Crown counsel; law firm partner; legal academic
Lord Scott	Overseas Non-Permanent Judge (2003–12)	Lord of Appeal in the Ordinary, Appellate Committee, House of Lords, United Kingdom	Barrister in private practice; Attorney General, Duchy of Lancaster
Lord Woolf	Overseas Non-Permanent Judge (2003–12)	Lord Chief Justice of England and Wales	Barrister in private practice
Sir Thomas Gault	Overseas Non-Permanent Judge (2006–15)	Judge, Supreme Court of New Zealand	Barrister and Solicitor (Queen's Counsel) in private practice

TABLE 4.1 *(continued)*

Name	Position(s) in the Court	Judgeship held before appointment to the Court	Occupation(s) before becoming judge
Michael McHugh	Overseas Non-Permanent Judge (2006–12)	Justice, High Court of Australia	Barrister (Queen's Counsel) in private practice
Murray Gleeson	Overseas Non-Permanent Judge (2009)	Chief Justice of Australia	Barrister (Queen's Counsel) in private practice
Lord Collins	Overseas Non-Permanent Judge (2009)	Justice, Supreme Court of the United Kingdom	Solicitor-advocate (Queen's Counsel) in private practice
Lord Neuberger	Overseas Non-Permanent Judge (2009)	President, Supreme Court of the United Kingdom	Barrister (Queen's Counsel) in private practice
Lord Walker	Overseas Non-Permanent Judge (2009)	Justice, Supreme Court of the United Kingdom	Barrister (Queen's Counsel) in private practice
Lord Clarke	Overseas Non-Permanent Judge (2011)	Justice, Supreme Court of the United Kingdom	Barrister (Queen's Counsel) in private practice
Lord Phillips	Overseas Non-Permanent Judge (2012)	President, Supreme Court of the United Kingdom	Barrister (Queen's Counsel) in private practice
James Spigelman	Overseas Non-Permanent Judge (2013)	Chief Justice of New South Wales	Barrister (Queen's Counsel) in private practice; Solicitor-General of New South Wales
William Gummow	Overseas Non-Permanent Judge (2013)	Justice, High Court of Australia	Barrister (Queen's Counsel) in private practice; legal academic
Robert French	Overseas Non-Permanent Judge (2017)	Chief Justice of Australia	Barrister and solicitor in private practice
Lord Reed	Overseas Non-Permanent Judge (2017)	Justice, Supreme Court of the United Kingdom	Barrister (Queen's Counsel) in civil service; Advocate Depute, Scotland

TABLE 4.2 *List of Judges of the Tribunal de Última Instância de Macau (1999–2017)*

Name	Position(s) in the Tribunal	Judgeship held before appointment to the Tribunal	Occupation(s) before becoming judge
Sam Hou Fai	President (1999)	Judge, Tribunal de Competência Genérica, Portuguese Macau	Judicial Advisor to the Courts and the Procuracy, Portuguese Macau
Chu Kin	Judge (1999–2011)	Judge, Tribunal de Competência Genérica, Portuguese Macau	Judicial Advisor to the Courts and the Procuracy, Portuguese Macau
Viriato Lima	Judge (1999)	Judge, Tribunal de Competência Genérica, Portuguese Macau	N/A
Song Man Lei	Judge (2011)	N/A	First Assistant Procurator General, Macau SAR

TABLE 4.3 *List of Hong Kong Court of Final Appeal decisions in which the constitutionality of primary legislation (ordinances) was reviewed* (1997–2017)

The following table contains a list of all Hong Kong Court of Final Appeal decisions in which the constitutionality of one or more provisions from primary legislation, known as "Ordinances" in Hong Kong, were reviewed for consistency with the Basic Law between July 1997 and December 2017. This list does not exhaust all constitutional review decisions, including politically significant ones, that do not involve the constitutionality of primary legislation, such as those that concern exclusively the constitutionality of administrative acts. There are thirty-four cases in the dataset. The list was compiled by searches of Court of Final Appeal decisions on Westlaw Asia and the Hong Kong Legal Information Institute (www.hklii.hk). According to this original dataset, during its first twenty decades of existence, the CFA had upheld the constitutionality of legislation in less than half of all cases (sixteen out of thirty-four, or 47 percent) in which the constitutionality of legislation was in question. Regarding constitutional remedies, out of the eighteen decisions in which statutory provisions were deemed unconstitutional, the Court issued declarations of unconstitutionality in eleven decisions, remedial interpretations in five decisions, and other forms of remedies in two other decisions.

Year	Case Name	Citation	Basic Law provision(s) engaged	Primary legislation reviewed	Impugned provisions constitutional?	Constitutional Remedy
1999	Ng Ka Ling v. Dir. of Immigration	(1999) 2 H.K.C.F.A. R. 4	24(2); 24(3); 25; 39	Immigration (Amendment) (No. 2) Ordinance, No. 122 of 1997; Immigration (Amendment) (No. 3) Ordinance, No. 124 of 1997	Unconstitutional	Invalidation
1999	Chan Kam Nga v. Dir. of Immigration	(1999) 2 H.K.C.F.A. R. 82	24(2)(3)	Immigration (No. 2) Ordinance, No. 122 of 1997	Unconstitutional	Invalidation
1999	Re Yung Kwan Lee	(1999) 2 H.K.C.F.A. R. 245	28; 153	Transfer of Sentenced Persons Ordinance, Cap. 513	Constitutional	N/A

1999	HKSAR v. Ng Kung Siu	(1999) 2 H.K.C.F.A. R. 442	27; 39	National Flag and National Emblem Ordinance, No. 116 of 1997; Regional Flag and Regional Emblem Ordinance, No. 117 of 1997	Constitutional	N/A
2001	Comm'r of Rating & Valuation v. Agrila Ltd.	(2001) 4 H.K.C.F.A. R. 83	121	Rating Ordinance, Cap. 116	Constitutional	N/A
2001	Fateh Muhammad v. Comm'r of Registration	(2001) 4 H.K.C.F.A. R. 278	25; 39	Immigration Ordinance, Cap. 115	Constitutional	N/A
2001	Dir. of Immigration v. Chong Fung Yuen	(2001) 4 H.K.C.F.A. R. 211	24(2)(1)	Immigration Ordinance, Cap. 115	Unconstitutional	Invalidation
2002	Lau Cheong v. HKSAR	(2002) 5 H.K.C.F.A. R. 415	28; 39	Offences against the Person Ordinance, Cap. 212; Criminal Procedure Ordinance, Cap. 221	Constitutional	N/A
2002	Gurung Kesh Bahadur v. Dir. of Immigration	(2002) 5 H.K.C.F.A. R. 480	31; 39	Immigration Ordinance, Cap. 115	Unconstitutional	Limited Reading
2003	Dir. of Lands v. Yin Shuen Enterprises Ltd.	(2003) 6 H.K.C.F.A. R. 1	105	Lands Resumption Ordinance, Cap. 124	Constitutional	N/A
2003	Prem Singh v. Dir. of Immigration	(2003) 6 H.K.C.F.A. R. 26	24(2)(4)	Immigration Ordinance, Cap. 115	Unconstitutional	Invalidation

TABLE 4.3 (*continued*)

Year	Case Name	Citation	Basic Law provision(s) engaged	Primary legislation reviewed	Impugned provisions constitutional?	Constitutional Remedy
2003	A Solicitor v. Law Soc'y of Hong Kong	(2003) 6 H.K.C.F.A. R. 570	82	Legal Practitioners Ordinance, Cap. 159	Unconstitutional	Invalidation
2003	Tse Mui Chun v. HKSAR	(2003) H.K.C.F.A. R. 601	87; 39	Copyright Ordinance, Cap. 121	Constitutional	N/A
2005	Leung Kwok Hung v. HKSAR	(2005) 8 H.K.C.F.A. R. 229	27; 39	Public Order Ordinance, Cap. 245	Unconstitutional	Severance
2005	Sec'y for Justice v. Lau Kwok Fai Bernard	(2005) 8 H.K.C.F.A. R. 304	100	Public Officers Pay Adjustment Ordinance, Cap. 574; Public Officers Adjustments (2004/2005) Ordinance, Cap. 580	Constitutional	N/A
2006	Solicitor (23/05) v. Law Soc'y of Hong Kong	(2006) 9 H.K.C.F.A. R. 175	35	Legal Practitioners Ordinance, Cap. 159	Constitutional	N/A
2006	So Wai Lun v. HKSAR	(2006) 9 H.K.C.F.A. R. 530	25; 28; 39	Crimes Ordinance, Cap. 200	Constitutional	N/A

2006	Koo Sze Yiu v. Chief Exec.	(2014) 17 H.K.C.F.A. R. 811	30	Telecommunications Ordinance, Cap. 106	Unconstitutional	Temporary Suspension of Invalidation for 6 months
2006	The Official Receiver & Tr. in Bankrupt of Chan Wing Hing, a bankrupt v. Chan Wing Hing	(2006) 9 H.K.C.F.A. R. 545	31; 39	Bankruptcy Ordinance, Cap. 6	Unconstitutional	Invalidation
2006	HKSAR v. Lam Kwong Wai	(2006) 9 H.K.C.F.A. R. 574	39; 87(2)	Firearms & Ammunition Ordinance, Cap. 238	Unconstitutional	Remedial Interpretation
2006	HKSAR v. Hung Chan Wa	(2006) 9 H.K.C.F.A. R. 614	39; 87(2)	Dangerous Drugs Ordinance, Cap. 134	Unconstitutional	Remedial Interpretation
2007	Sec'y for Justice v. Yau Yuk Lung Zigo	(2007) 10 H.K.C.F.A. R. 335	25; 39	Crimes Ordinance, Cap. 200	Unconstitutional	Invalidation
2008	HKSAR v. Ng Po On	(2008) 11 H.K.C.F.A. R. 91	39; 87(2)	Prevention of Bribery Ordinance, Cap. 201	Unconstitutional	Remedial Interpretation
2008	Koon Wing Yee v. Insider	(2008) 11 H.K.C.F.A. R. 170	39	Securities (Insider Dealing) Ordinance, Cap. 395	Unconstitutional	Invalidation

TABLE 4.3 *(continued)*

Year	Case Name	Citation	Basic Law provision(s) engaged	Primary legislation reviewed	Impugned provisions constitutional?	Constitutional Remedy
	Dealing Tribunal					
2008	Yeung Chung Ming v. Comm'r of Police	(2008) 11 H.K.C.F.A. R. 513	39; 87(2)	Police Force Ordinance, Cap. 232	Constitutional	N/A
2010	Mok Charles Peter v. Tam Wai Ho	(2010 13 H.K.C.F.A. R. 762	82	Legislative Council Ordinance, Cap. 542	Unconstitutional	Invalidation
2011	Catholic Diocese of Hong Kong v. Sec'y for Justice	(2011) 14 H.K.C.F.A. R. 754	136(1); 141(3)	Education Ordinance, Cap. 279	Constitutional	N/A
2012	Lee To Nei v. HKSAR	(2012) 15 H.K.C.F.A. R. 162	39; 87(2)	Trade Descriptions Ordinance, Cap. 362	Unconstitutional	Remedial Interpretation
2012	Fu Kor Kuen Patrick v. HKSAR	(2012) 15 H.K.C.F.A. R. 524	39; 87(2)	Securities and Futures Ordinance, Cap. 571	Constitutional	N/A
2013	W v. The Registrar of Marriages	(2013) 16 H.K.C.F.A. R. 112	37; 39	Matrimonial Causes Ordinance, Cap. 179; Marriage Ordinance, Cap. 181	Unconstitutional	Remedial Interpretation

2013	Leung Chun Ying v. Ho Chun Yan Albert	(2013) 16 H.K.C.F.A. R. 735	35	Chief Executive Election Ordinance, Cap. 569	Constitutional	N/A
2015	Official Receiver v. Zhi Charles	(2015) 18 H.K.C.F.A. R. 467	31	Bankruptcy Ordinance, Cap. 6	Unconstitutional	Invalidation
2017	Sam Woo Marine Works Ltd. v. I.O. of Po Hang Bldg.	(2017) 20 H.K.C.F.A. R. 240	82	District Court Ordinance, Cap. 336	Constitutional	N/A
2017	Kwok Cheuk Kin v. Sec'y for Constitutional & Mainland Aff.	[2017] 5 H.K.C. 242	26; 39	Legislative Council Ordinance, Cap. 542	Constitutional	N/A

5

Transaction Cost Politics in Hong Kong and Macau

INTRODUCTION

Instituting constitutional review is a political investment. Hybrid regimes are no less vulnerable to the risk and uncertainty associated with empowering constitutional courts because, by their own nature, they must be enmeshed in the antagonism of keeping up the appearance of liberal democracy while serving the authoritarian substance. The mere unity of executive and legislative powers in the hands of one ruling coalition by no means ensures that a hybrid regime will be able to act easily and decisively to avenge judicial insubordination. The transaction cost theory of hybrid constitutionalism set out in Chapter 2 implies greater explanatory and predictive power in analyzing political transaction costs borne by hybrid regimes than in focusing on formal constitutional design. Transaction costs can be estimated and compared only through gauging such frictions as regime ideological and organizational incoherence and the resistance, both within and without, to court-curbing proposals, not by formal indicators such as the number of parliamentary seats held by the ruling coalition.

Chapter 3 has shown that the Special Administrative Regions (SARs) were preprogrammed by the People's Republic of China to be hybrids that combine Western European legal systems with political command and control the origins of which trace back to the central Leninist Party-state in Beijing. From a formalist perspective, the Hong Kong Basic Law[1] and the Lei Básica de Macau[2] establish nearly identical jurisdictions featuring apex courts vested

[1] Basic Law of the Hong Kong Special Administrative Region of the People's Republic of China (adopted at the Third Session of the Seventh National People's Congress on Apr. 4, 1990, effective on Jul. 1, 1997).

[2] Lei Básica da Região Administrativa Especial de Macau da República Popular da China (Basic Law of the Macao Special Administrative Region of the People's Republic of China) (adopted by the First Session of the Eighth National People's Congress on Mar. 31, 1993, effective Dec. 20, 1999).

with the same constitutional interpretative competences subject to override by the abstract authority of the Standing Committee of the National People's Congress. Indeed, the Macau model "seems almost blindly copied from" Hong Kong.[3] Legally speaking, then, the constitutional jurisprudence of the two SARs in principle should not differ from each other. And yet, it was revealed in Chapter 4 that the case law on interpreting and enforcing the two SAR constitutions enormously diverges. After two decades of experiment, the Hong Kong Court of Final Appeal (CFA), with no enforcement or budgetary powers of its own,[4] has fashioned a fully fledged constitutional common law consisting of a sizeable repertory of substantive, procedural and remedial judicial doctrines that were inspired, but not strictly required, by the Basic Law.[5] The common law's gloss on the Basic Law is now instinct: "[t]here is an essential unity between the Basic Law and the common law that is denied if they are treated as if each occupies a separate watertight compartment,"[6] in the extrajudicial words of former Chief Justice of Australia Sir Anthony Mason, one of the Court's most influential judges. The Tribunal de Última Instância's (TUI's) Lei Básica decisions present a diametric opposite: they have eschewed laying claim to any power to invalidate legislation, as the CFA has repeatedly and unambiguously done, but have unswervingly adhered to a formal and minimalistic approach to constitutional issues in preference to the purposively activist one characteristic of CFA jurisprudence.[7] In short, the TUI has shunned "a more Western style" modus operandi in the exercise of its constitutional jurisdiction.[8] The continual absence of high-energy constitutional review that might have checked the SAR authorities had led Zhang Xiaoming, Director of the Hong Kong and Macau Affairs Office of the State Council in Beijing since September 2017, earlier to effuse that the "judicial organs [of the Macau SAR] have, in accordance with the provisions of the [Lei

[3] Paulo Cardinal, *Macau: Transformation of an Historic Autonomy*, *in* PRACTISING SELF-GOVERNMENT: A COMPARATIVE STUDY OF AUTONOMOUS REGIONS 383, 408 (Yash Ghai & Sophia Woodman eds., 2013).

[4] JON ELSTER, EXPLAINING SOCIAL BEHAVIOR: MORE NUTS AND BOLTS FOR THE SOCIAL SCIENCES 444 (2d ed. 2015).

[5] PO JEN YAP, CONSTITUTIONAL DIALOGUE IN COMMON LAW ASIA 80–85 (2015); Henry P. Monaghan, *Constitutional Common Law*, 89 HARV. L. REV. 1, 2 (1975).

[6] Anthony Mason, *The Common Law*, *in* HONG KONG'S COURT OF FINAL APPEAL: THE DEVELOPMENT OF THE LAW IN CHINA'S HONG KONG 327, 335 (Simon N.M. Young & Yash Ghai eds., 2014).

[7] Paolo Cardinal, *Revisiting the Macanese Amparo of Fundamental Rights: A Quest under the Searchlight of the Principle of Continuity with a Stopover in Comparative Law*, 83 PHIL. L.J. 833, 846 (2009).

[8] Ignazio Castellucci, *Legal Hybridity in Hong Kong and Macau*, 57 MCGILL L.J. 665, 698 (2012).

Básica], fulfilled their duties, assumed their responsibilities, brought about executive-led government with the chief executive at its core, maintained the efficiency of decision making and implementation."[9]

The purpose of this chapter is to explain this consequential antithesis of high- and low-energy constitutional review in Hong Kong and Macau, respectively, using the transaction cost theory of hybrid constitutionalism proposed herein, which has refined the standard strategic model. It yields the prediction that a regime's ability credibly to threaten consequences for judicial opportunism (and thus raise its cost) is the weaker, the higher its own political transaction costs; regardless of unified powers or systematic electoral irregularities favoring incumbents. Deploying this theory to constitutionalism in the Chinese SARs, one should expect that the CFA's entrenched high-energy constitutional review correlates to Hong Kong being a high transaction cost polity, and the TUI's entrenched low-energy constitutional review to Macau being a low transaction cost polity, the resemblance of their constitutions and the hybrid authoritarianism of their governing institutions notwithstanding. As the next section of this chapter will show, these expectations square with the available evidence, and confirm the explanatory power of the transaction cost analysis. The state of affairs in Hong Kong results from the high costs to the regime of overcoming staunch external resistance and its ongoing internal factionalism to rein in the CFA and suppress the demand for constitutional review. In contrast, the decisive unity and relative popularity of the Macau SAR regime, which imply much lower transaction costs in pursuing their policy preferences, undergird its will and ability to forestall any move of the TUI toward self-empowerment. The lack of popular opposition to the regime has shut the TUI out of any real opportunity to review the policy choices of decision-makers.

It is nevertheless insufficient to substantiate the validity of the transaction cost theory of hybrid constitutionalism with evidence from the Hong Kong and Macau SARs alone. The careful small-*n*, most-similar-cases analysis undertaken by this study strives to utilize controlled comparisons to explain dynamics and make inferences about cause and effect.[10] Such an approach is particularly apt for a study of constitutional review in Chinese SARs, which allows us to hold constant numerous political and socioeconomic variables.

9 Zhang Xiaoming, *Why Macao Is Not Implementing the Separation of Powers Political System*, 45 CHINESE L. & GOV'T 15, 24 (2012).

10 RAN HIRSCHL, COMPARATIVE MATTERS: THE RENAISSANCE OF COMPARATIVE CONSTITUTIONAL LAW 193 (2014).

In the researcher's ideal situation, the cases compared are in all measures the same except for the output of interest plus the proposed explanatory variable; in real-world circumstances, cases are often comparable only very generally: similar in measures that are theoretically relevant, but dissimilar in the dependent and explanatory variables.[11] This brings to mind the risk of omitted variable bias, which could occur if an alternative explanation for the divergence between the CFA and the TUI were available that had been omitted, entailing an overestimation of the significance of political transaction cost fluctuations.[12] The best research strategy, therefore, to affirm the persuasiveness and explanatory power of the present thesis is to review competing accounts purporting to explain the behavior of the Chinese SARs and to consider whether they are to be rejected. The potential competing explanatory variable that stands out the most is surely legal origins: that the common law tradition of Hong Kong is more receptive to an activist judiciary than the civil law tradition of Macau, which assigns courts the responsibility to apply all-foreseeing codes with little discretion. The third section of this chapter evaluates the explanatory power of legal origins in the present context. After comprehensively reviewing the best evidence in favor of it, the author shows why it must be rejected, and the transaction cost thesis reaffirmed, that the fate of constitutional review in the SAR hybrid regimes is determined more by political transactions than by formal legal rules. The fourth and final section concludes with a summary of the major findings of this chapter.

HIGH AND LOW TRANSACTION COST POLITICS IN THE CHINESE SPECIAL ADMINISTRATIVE REGIONS

Neither the Hong Kong nor the Macau constitutional order has fundamentally altered in the past two centuries: an unelected chief executive, first the colonial Governor, now an officially non-partisan Chief Executive appointed by Beijing, is advised by an appointed Executive Council, whose advice he can ignore.[13] Checking the Chief Executive is a weak, at best only partially elected, corporatist Legislative Council or the Legislative Assembly dominated by his own supporters (see Tables 5.1, 5.2, 5.3, and 5.4), to the bills passed by whom he can withhold

11 Julio Ríos-Figueroa, Constitutional Courts as Mediators: Armed Conflict, Civil-Military Relations, and the Rule of Law in Latin America 172 (2016).

12 Tom Ginsburg & Mila Versteeg, *Why Do Countries Adopt Constitutional Review?*, 30(3) J. Law. Econ. & Organ. 587, 616 (2014).

13 Sonny Shiu-Hing Lo, *Central Control and Local Welfare Autonomy in Guangzhou, Hong Kong and Macau*, 42(3) J. Current Chinese Aff. 3, 4 (2013).

TABLE 5.1 *Hong Kong Chief Executive elections (1996–2017)*

Year	Candidate	Affiliation	Nominations	Votes
1996	**C.H. Tung**	**Establishment**	**206**	**320**
	T.L. Yang	Establishment	82	42
	Peter Woo	Establishment	54	36
2002	**C.H. Tung**	**Establishment**	**712**	**Uncontested**
2005	**Donald Tsang**	**Establishment**	**674**	**Uncontested**
2007	**Donald Tsang**	**Establishment**	**641**	**649**
	Alan Leong	Pan-Democratic	132	123
2012	**C.Y. Leung**	**Establishment**	**305**	**689**
	Henry Tang	Establishment	390	285
	Albert Ho	Pan-Democratic	188	76
2017	**Carrie Lam**	**Establishment**	**580**	**777**
	John Tsang	Establishment	165	365
	Kwok-hing Woo	Independent	180	21

TABLE 5.2 *Macau Chief Executive elections (1999–2014)*

Year	Candidate	Affiliation	Nominations	Votes
1999	**Edmund Ho**	**Establishment**	**125**	**163**
	Stanley Au	Establishment	65	34
2004	**Edmund Ho**	**Establishment**	**297**	**296**
2009	**Fernando Chui**	**Establishment**	**286**	**282**
2014	**Fernando Chui**	**Establishment**	**331**	**380**

TABLE 5.3 *Partisan composition of the Legislative Council of Hong Kong*

	Hong Kong	
General election year	Number of establishment members of the Legislative Council	Number of non-establishment members of the Legislative Council
1998	40 (66.7%)	20 (33.3%)
2000	39 (65%)	21 (35%)
2004	35 (58.3%)	25 (41.7%)
2008	37 (61.7%)	23 (38.3%)
2012	43 (61.4%)	27 (38.6%)
2016	40 (57.1%)	30 (42.9%)

TABLE 5.4 *Partisan composition of the Legislative Assembly of Macau*

	Macau	
General election year	Number of establishment members of the Legislative Assembly	Number of non-establishment members of the Legislative Assembly
2001	25 (93%)	2 (7%)
2005	26 (89.7%)	3 (10.3%)
2009	25 (86.2%)	4 (13.8%)
2013	29 (88%)	4 (12%)
2017	29 (88%)	4 (12%)

necessary assent.[14] The formal constitutions of both SARs mandate "unified government" – the control of the executive and legislative by the same political grouping, the Establishment Coalition. What is more, the Basic Law and the Lei Básica impose identical formal constraints on the constitutional jurisdictions of their respective apex courts. The SARs' de facto common sovereign, the Communist Party-controlled Standing Committee of the National People's Congress, can, *sua sponte*, reinterpret the Basic Law or the Lei Básica to reverse any apex court interpretation of it; both SAR legislatures backed by their Chief Executives could, in theory, impeach overly independent judges, or curtail their jurisdiction by statute, or require extraordinary judicial majorities for decisions on constitutionality, or starve the judiciary budget, or pack them with supernumerary and subservient judges (see Figure 5.1).[15]

Recall that conventional strategic models theorize that undivided control of the political branches undermines judicial independence, while divided control facilitates it, as the legislature will check the chief executive and vice versa.[16] Applying this to the hybrid regimes of the SARs yields the prediction that both apex courts will similarly succumb to political pressures from their undivided regimes and act deferentially. This prediction, however, is belied by observation. As will be shown below, the incorporation of transaction cost calculus into this conventional strategic model yields an explanation far more

[14] Steve Tsang, A Modern History of Hong Kong 18 (2007); Bill K.P. Chou, *Legitimacy-Building and Public Sector Reform in Macao: Administrative Measures to Address Political Problems*, 10(3) China: An Int'l J. 133, 144 (2012).

[15] *See* Todd Schneider, *David v Goliath?: The Hong Kong Courts and China's National People's Congress Standing Committee*, 20 Berkeley J. Int'l L. 597 (2002).

[16] Rebecca Bill Chavez et al., *A Theory of the Politically Independent Judiciary: A Comparative Study of the United States and Argentina*, *in* Courts in Latin America 219, 220 (Gretchen Helmke & Julio Ríos-Figueroa eds., 2011).

	Ex ante	Ex post
Constitutional	New Basic Law/Lei Básica to: Define or redefine the CFA's/TUI's constitutional jurisdiction (accomplished in 1990 and 1993, respectively) New Interpretation of the Basic Law/Lei Básica by the Standing Committee of the National People's Congress to preempt an unwanted judgment by the CFA/TUI	Amendment to or Interpretation of the Basic Law/Lei Básica by the National People's Congress and its Standing Committee, respectively, to: overturn the CFA's/TUI's judgment; curtail the CFA's/TUI's jurisdiction; circumscribe provisions guaranteeing judges' security of tenure and salary, or suspend the CFA/TUI
Subconstitutional	Statutory amendment or binding legislative resolution to: control judicial appointments manipulate judicial procedures limit access to courts	Statutory amendment or binding legislative resolution to: undermine the effect of judgments; slash judicial budget; impeach independent judges

FIGURE 5.1 A typology of countermeasures against CFA/TUI

consistent with the facts. The superficial similarities between the formal aspects of the two SARs mask enormous differences in judicial and political dynamics. Put simply, the Macau SAR features a cohesive unified government; oppositional forces so weak that they are rarely accused of being proxies of Western governments; and very warm relations with Beijing in particular and mainland China in general – all of which are the reverse in the Hong Kong SAR.[17] The contrast is best viewed in a transaction cost perspective: Hong Kong features high political transaction costs, whereas Macau has low costs.

The underlying logic of political transaction costs is that politics is fundamentally about collective decision-making.[18] The difficulties of making and policing political agreements, whether by formal statutes or otherwise, cannot be ignored by any serious researcher.[19] Even the most autocratic polity cannot

[17] Lo, *supra* note 13, at 4.

[18] Jean-Jacques Laffont, Incentives and Political Economy 182 (2000).

[19] David Epstein & Sharyn O'Halloran, Delegating Powers: A Transaction Cost Politics Approach to Policy Making under Separate Powers 43 (1999); Murray

collect sufficient information on everything and all must sometimes encounter prohibitive internal disagreements, if only because of external pressures.[20] Courts conducting constitutional review anticipate regime response strategically to avoid retaliation. Regimes respond to defiant courts depending heavily on their differential political transaction costs: the less internal fragmentation or external resistance regimes face, the likelier they are to restrict opportunities for the courts to assert review competences; conversely, high internal transaction costs burden the regime with indecision about whether and how to respond to controversial judicial decisions. The opposition may capitalize on hybrid regimes' liberal façade to afflict the incumbents with the friction of mass mobilization and electoral victories, compelling them to choose moderation over repression.[21] The following two subsections describe the political transaction cost structures of the SARs with reference to the cohesiveness of unified government and the strength of popular support for the opposition.

High Transaction Cost Politics in the Hong Kong SAR

The Hong Kong Establishment Coalition is plagued by incohesion and rife with indecision, the hallmarks of high political transaction costs.[22] The Establishment is a loose coalition without an official unifying manifesto, clear lines of command, or even a standardized member enrollment procedure. This was Beijing's preference in part, to forestall the emergence of a strong ruling party, even a pro-Beijing one, which could end up on par with Singapore's People's Action Party, with a firm social base and mass support.[23] Deprived of the backing of a unified state machine, all the first three Chief Executives failed miserably to check, balance, and mediate

J. Horn, The Political Economy of Public Administration: Institutional Choice in the Public Sector 14–15 (1995).

20 Mushtaq H. Khan, *Markets, States and Democracy: Patron-Client Networks and the Case for Democracy in Developing Countries*, *in* Twenty Years of Studying Democratization: Vol 2: Democratization, Democracy and Authoritarian Continuity 33, 37–38 (Aurel Croissant & Jeffrey Haynes eds., 2016).

21 Steven Levitsky & Lucan A. Way, Competitive Authoritarianism: Hybrid Regimes after the Cold War 69 (2010).

22 Ngok Ma, *From Executive Dominance to Fragmented Authority: An Institutional and Political Analysis*, *in* Hong Kong 20 Years after the Handover: Emerging Social and Institutional Fractures after 1997 21, 22 (Brian C.H. Fong & Tai-lok Lui eds., 2018).

23 Brian C.H. Fong, *Executive-Legislative Disconnection in the HKSAR: Uneasy Partnership between Chief Executives and Pro-Government Parties, 1997–2016*, *in* Hong Kong 20 Years after the Handover: Emerging Social and Institutional Fractures after 1997 45, 58 (Brian C.H. Fong & Tai-lok Lui eds., 2018).

competing special interests with anything like the credibility and moral authority of the former colonial Governors.[24] A "perpetual governing crisis" has dogged the Hong Kong SAR regardless of who has become Chief Executive.[25] Unlike the position in Macau, so far, no Hong Kong Chief Executive has managed to complete two terms of ten years in office.

Establishment insider Lau Siu-kai, the founding Vice Chairman of the semi-governmental Chinese Association of Hong Kong and Macao Studies that reports to the State Council, and currently a National Delegate to the Chinese People's Political Consultative Conference,[26] recently admitted that the SAR "has been saddled with ineffective governance" because of "incapable leadership, lack of solidarity in the governing coalition, discord between the executive and the legislature, obstruction of the judiciary, weak public support, frequent collective protests, and difficulties in implementing new policies."[27] Head of the Central Policy Unit, the government's in-house think tank between 2002 and 2012, and thus well positioned to know, Lau rebuked the Establishment for its want of "cohesion and a unified leadership"[28] and blamed its factionalism on the skirmish between elites of the former colonial regime and traditional pro-Beijing forces, who "fought fiercely, with resulting hostility not only between the two camps, but also among individuals."[29]

While not wholly false, this is an oversimplification of Establishment infighting. Political scientists have identified three main factions in the Coalition, within which are manifold sub-factions: the powerful so-called "Administrative Officers (AO) Party"[30] or British-groomed senior civil service elite;[31] pro-business politicians and other agents of commercial corporations;

24 Peter W. Preston, The Politics of China-Hong Kong Relations: Living with Distant Masters 71 (2016).

25 Matthew Y.H. Wong, Comparative Hong Kong Politics: A Guidebook for Students and Researchers 39 (2017).

26 The Chinese People's Political Consultative Conference is sometimes viewed as the "upper house" of China's national political system. It is typically chaired by a member of the Communist Party's ultra-elite Politburo Standing Committee. Wei Shan & Lijun Yang, Governing Society In Contemporary China 153–54 (2017).

27 Siu-kai Lau, The Practice of "One Country Two Systems" Policy in Hong Kong 85 (2017).

28 *Id.* at 152.

29 *Id.* at 151.

30 Mathew Y.H. Wong, *Discussing without Deciding, Deciding without Acting: Veto Players in Hong Kong, and Beijing's Response*, 2(3) Asian J. Comp. Pol. 347, 351 (2017).

31 Eric C. Ip, *The Economic Structure of Hong Kong Administrative Law: Efficiency and Legality of Government Decision-Making since China's Resumption*, 12 Wash. U. Global Stud. L. Rev. 227, 234–36 (2013).

and classical pro-Communist splinter groups.[32] Originally, an implicit partnership between Beijing's handpicked Chief Executive and the AO Party subsisted.[33] C.H. Tung's first term was bedeviled by confrontations with his Chief Secretary, Anson Chan, widely seen as the spokeswoman of the AO Party, who had held that office since 1993 under Queen Elizabeth II and Governor Chris Patten.[34] The AO Party kept firm control of daily policy formulation and implementation, thanks to severe information asymmetry between itself and Tung, whom they pushed to the margin, an outsider in his own Government.[35] Nonetheless he prevailed: the power struggle culminated in Chan's forced retirement in 2001,[36] and Tung's removal of all AOs from ministerial positions in a de facto coup dubbed the Political Officials Accountability System (POAS), which empowered the Chief Executive, in the name of better political accountability, to pick his ministers independently of the civil service bureaucracy.[37]

Predictably, POAS created more problems than it fixed. The new appointees were a diverse mix, with some chosen from various factions of the Establishment, and others coopted directly from the business and professional world with little or no experience in politics or public administration. Assembled by Tung ad hoc, these political ministers had little in common with each other, even ideology, except a shared personal allegiance to the Chief Executive and Beijing.[38] Mutual distrust and tension reigned between the Chief Executive and his appointees on one side, and the AOs on the other, aggravating agency costs until they were handicapping the governing capacity of the government.[39] Information asymmetry obliged the new ministers to rely

32 *See* Steve Tsang, Governing Hong Kong: Administrative Officers from the Nineteenth Century to the Handover to China, 1862–1997 (2007).

33 Ma, *supra* note 22, at 33.

34 Brian C.H. Fong, *Ten Years of Political Appointments in Hong Kong – The Challenges and Prospects of Developing a Political Appointment System under a Semi-Democratic Regime, 2002–12*, *in* New Trends of Political Participation in Hong Kong 67, 72–73 (Joseph Y.S. Cheng ed., 2014).

35 *See* Ian Scott, *Legitimacy, Governance and Public Policy in Post-Handover Hong Kong*, 29 Asia Pac. J. Pub. Admin. 37 (2007).

36 Chan later switched her political allegiance to the Pan-Democratic Opposition and briefly served as a Member of the Legislative Council after winning a by-election in 2007. *See* Francis L.F. Lee & Joseph M. Chan, Media, Social Mobilisation and Mass Protests in Post-colonial Hong Kong: The Power of a Critical Event 128 (2010).

37 Anthony Cheung, *In Search of Trust and Legitimacy: The Political Trajectory of Hong Kong as Part of China*, *in* Trust and Governance Institutions: Asian Experiences 41, 58 (Clay Wescott et al. eds., 2012).

38 Ma, *supra* note 22, at 29.

39 Ip, *supra* note 31, at 239.

on (and thus compromise with) senior civil servants to implement policy.[40] Tung himself resigned in 2005, midway through his second term, after successive policy blunders during the Severe Acute Respiratory Syndrome (SARS) epidemic, and massive public resistance to his attempt two years earlier to introduce a national security bill that was deemed overtly draconian. The strained relationship between the political executive and the AO Party was temporarily relieved when Beijing decided to promote a former AO, Chief Secretary Sir Donald Tsang, as Tung's successor. It was an indication of just how high the transaction costs of governing Hong Kong had become that Harvard-educated and British-knighted Tsang, a practicing Roman Catholic and outsider in pro-Beijing circles, could receive China's anointment as Chief Executive.

Apart from the Chief Executive–AO clash, another quasi-faction within the government, according to Lau Siu-kai, comprised those handling legal policy: "a portion of government officials themselves, particularly officials in charge of legal affairs, have views about 'one country, two systems' and the Basic Law that are similar to those of the opposition activists."[41] Undoubtedly, the Department of Justice was well known for its sympathy with and deference to the CFA's views and constitutional review decisions throughout the tenures of Tung and Tsang.[42] In fact, Wong Yan Lung SC, Hong Kong's Secretary for Justice from 2005 to 2012, served his pupillage under Andrew Li QC, the founding Chief Justice of the CFA, and is a former deputy High Court judge. In 2008, Wong publicly noted that "[a]lthough defeats in judicial reviews can be hard to swallow immediately," there is a widespread "conviction" within the government, that "the commitment to the high standards of legality, reasonableness and fairness, and the metamorphosis brought about by judicial discipline at times, will improve public administration, and will make Hong Kong a better society."[43] Even his predecessor, Elsie Leung, a solicitor by training who had no formal ties with the courts, and no proponent of Westernized liberalization,[44] held constitutional review in high regard during

40 *See* Anthony Cheung, *Policy Capacity in Post-1997 Hong Kong: Constrained Institutions Facing a Crowding and Differentiated Polity*, 29 ASIA PAC. J. PUB. ADMIN. 51 (2007).

41 LAU, *supra* note 27, at 86.

42 P.Y. Lo, *An Internationalist, Consequentialist and Non-Progressive Court: Constitutional Adjudication in Hong Kong (1997–2009)*, 2 CITY U. HONG KONG L. REV. 234 (2010).

43 Yan Lung Wong, *Secretary for Justice's Speech at Conference on Effective Judicial Review: A Cornerstone of Good Governance*, PRESS RELEASES, Dec. 11, 2008, www.info.gov.hk/gia/general/200812/11/P200812110116.htm

44 Alex Ho, *Call to Disband Functional Constituencies is Wishful Thinking*, SOUTH CHINA MORNING POST, Feb. 3, 2015, www.scmp.com/comment/insight-opinion/article/1699883/call-disband-functional-constituencies-wishful-thinking

a public speech delivered on April 12, 2003 in honor of the thirteenth anniversary of the Basic Law's promulgation: "[Hong Kong residents] have learned how to defend their rights and interests by way of constitutional litigation. The Basic Law thus flourished, developed, and adequately demonstrated its life and power under the common law system through caselaw emerging from these litigations."[45]

With little guidance from the Basic Law, the Chief Executive had little leverage to secure a stable coalition in the Legislative Council.[46] Establishment Members of the Legislative Council (MLCs) were divided mainly into the business and Leftist factions, causing a scattering of preferences across the fiscal and social policy spectrum within the legislative Establishment, such that individual parliamentarians routinely cross the floor and oppose the Government of the day on a variety of specific issues.[47] For instance, the neoliberal Liberal Party was more pro-business than the flagship Establishment party, the centrist Democratic Alliance for the Betterment and Progress of Hong Kong (DAB), while the Hong Kong Federation of Trade Unions (FTU), another Establishment stalwart, historically espoused Maoist revolutionary and anti-imperialist ideologies.[48] Infighting between Establishment partisans unintendedly escalated with the introduction of proportional representation in 1998, a move aimed originally at fragmentizing the Pan-Democratic Opposition into smaller fringe groups.[49] Periodical pressures faced by Establishment MLCs for reelection, a problem not uncommon in hybrid regimes, systemically undermined their loyalty to the Chief Executive.[50] After all, unlike in the British era when Members of the Legislative Council were handpicked by the Governor, SAR parliamentarians no longer perceive themselves as advisors to the Head of Region but, rather, as agents of their own political parties and constituencies, whose interests are often at odds with the Chief Executive's.[51]

45 Elsie Leung, Footsteps in Time: Twenty Years of Basic Law in Hong Kong 169 (2017).

46 Eliza W.Y. Lee & Rikkie L.K. Yeung, *The "Principal Officials Accountability System": Its Underdevelopment as a System of Ministerial Government*, 39(2) Asia Pac. J. Pub. Admin. 120, 123 (2017).

47 Baohui Zhang, *Political Paralysis of the Basic Law Regime and the Politics of Institutional Reform in Hong Kong*, 49(2) Asian Surv. 312, 322–23 (2009).

48 Wong, *supra* note 25, at 152.

49 John M. Carey, *Electoral Formula and Fragmentation in Hong Kong*, 17 J. E. Asian Stud. 215, 220 (2017).

50 Ma, *supra* note 22, at 35.

51 Eric C. Ip; *Mapping Parliamentary Law and Practice in Hong Kong*, 3(1) Chinese J. Comp. L. 97, 117 (2015).

The assimilation of business elites into the Establishment Coalition did not proceed smoothly.[52] Compared with the Communist-groomed Leftists, the business right are uncoordinated and fragmented;[53] no nonpartisan mechanism for arbitrating intra-business political conflicts has ever existed.[54] Business parties such as the Liberal Party and Economic Synergy are but imperfect proxies for corporate interests; the major business associations bypassed them and lobbied the government directly over Hong Kong's first-ever antitrust bill in the early 2010s.[55] Freelance business agents, major business associations, unaffiliated pro-business parliamentarians and lone companies get involved in the policy process to varying degrees.[56] The SAR regime's cooptation tactics have fomented an "eclectic corporatist structure" in which business and professional elites, distributed unevenly across the many statutory authorities, advisory bodies, and policy commissions, bend public policy to their own interest, resist government initiatives, and seek rents.[57]

It was an open secret that the third Chief Executive, C.Y. Leung, was not on best terms with key business magnates, major land developers, and pro-business Establishment MLCs, who had supported textile tycoon and former Chief Secretary Henry Tang in his failed bid for Chief Executive in 2012.[58] Indeed, the unanticipated and unprecedented falling-out of the Establishment Coalition into partisan camps during the 2012 election fractured the Establishment itself. Mudslinging and smear campaigns between the two camps, previously unheard of, finally forced Beijing to assume direct control of the Election Committee selection process, and abandon Tang, its initially preferred candidate, for Leung, who had relatively more public support.[59] Leung reportedly engineered the takeover of important Government positions by his supporters, largely to the exclusion of the Tang camp.[60] In the next five years, Leung became a polarizing figure, unable to

52 Brian C.H. Fong, Hong Kong's Governance under Chinese Sovereignty: The Failure of the State-Business Alliance after 1997 121 (2015).

53 Wong, *supra* note 25, at 206.

54 Fong, *supra* note 52, at 155.

55 *Id.* at 147.

56 *Id.*

57 Ngok Ma, *Eclectic Corporatism and State Interventions in Post-Colonial Hong Kong, in* Repositioning the Hong Kong Government: Social Foundations and Political Challenges 63, 74–80 (Stephen Wing-kai Chiu et al. eds., 2012).

58 Ma, *supra* note 22, at 32.

59 Chiew Ping Yew, *The 2012 Chief Executive Election and after. Hong Kong under Chinese Rule, in* Hong Kong under Chinese Rule Economic Integration and Political Gridlock 237, 237 (Yongnian Zheng & Chiew Ping Yew eds., 2013).

60 Sonny Shiu-Hing Lo, *Factionalism and Chinese-style Democracy: The 2017 Hong Kong Chief Executive Election*, 39(2) Asia Pac. J. Pub. Admin. 100, 102–103 (2017).

forge consensus in the Legislative Council,[61] and his decision not to seek a second term in late 2016, possibly due to Beijing's need for a conciliatory Chief Executive, still left Hong Kong "stunned" and "in shock."[62]

To Beijing's unpleasant surprise,[63] again the Establishment split in two, in the leadup to the 2017 Chief Executive election, when former Chief Secretary Carrie Lam and former Financial Secretary John Tsang announced their candidacies. Both were leading figures in the AO Party, whose "moderate and technocratic style of governance" sharply contrasted with Leung's "combative style."[64] With Beijing's tacit approval, on March 26, 2017 Lam won the Election Committee's nomination for appointment by the State Council as Chief Executive with 777 electoral votes. Whether Lam will bring any substantial change to the status quo is questionable, her promises to heal divisions with a more inclusive style of administration notwithstanding, given her strong backing by incumbent Leung throughout the campaign. And she has held over a large part of his cabinet.[65]

The Hong Kong Chief Executive does not face the uncertainty of real, universal suffrage elections. But he still relies on good policy performance as a source of legitimacy, meaning that he cannot utterly ignore society's demands.[66] External resistance then all the more heaps political transaction costs onto such a regime. As Lau Siu-kai has criticized, a "fear of bringing about public dissatisfaction, of attacks from the opposition activists as well as external forces" vitiates the government.[67] The overarching clash between the Establishment and the Pan-Democratic Opposition is an ideological contest between advocates of transforming the SAR's hybrid institutions into genuine liberal democratic ones, and custodians of a regime characteristically capable of converging with mainland China.[68] In the course of more than 150 years of political dissociation from the mainland, Hong Kong residents have acquired

[61] Jermain T.M. Lam, *Political Decay in Hong Kong after the Occupy Central Movement*, 42(2) Asian Aff.: An Am. Rev. 99, 112 (2015).

[62] Gary Cheung & Joyce Ng, *Hong Kong in Shock as Chief Executive CY Leung Decides Not to Seek Re-election*, South China Morning Post, Dec. 10, 2016, www.scmp.com/news/hong-kong/politics/article/2053402/embattled-hong-kong-leader-cy-leung-wont-seek-re-election

[63] Gary Leung, *Carrie Lam may be Beijing's Choice, but Hong Kong still Needs a Fair Leadership Race*, South China Morning Post, Jan. 13, 2017, 13 January 2017, www.scmp.com/comment/insight-opinion/article/2064579/carrie-lam-may-be-beijings-choice-hong-kong-still-needs-fair

[64] Ma, *supra* note 22, at 33.

[65] Lo, *supra* note 60, at 102–103.

[66] Eliza W.Y. Lee et al., Public Policymaking in Hong Kong: Civic Engagement and State-society Relations in a Semi-Democracy 2 (2013).

[67] Lau, *supra* note 27, at 86.

[68] Lo, *supra* note 60, at 103.

a unique civic identity, with political values that differ radically from the mainland's.[69] Many in the local community adhere passionately to the rule of law bequeathed to them by the English common law as their core civic identity, in contradistinction to an authoritarianism guided only by "Leninist morality," as attested by the custom that persists long after Britain's withdrawal, of Hong Kong residents annually gathering in their tens of thousands in Victoria Park to commemorate Tiananmen Square; or by Falun Gong followers' freedom to practice and proselytize their religion in the teeth of the mainland's ban.[70] The supreme irony is that the Basic Law itself is what has facilitated the coordination of opposition to the regime it founded.[71] Its own civil liberties and its promise of eventual universal suffrage have inspired a popular ideal of democratic constitutional order supported by the victims of authoritarianism, from the political parties affiliated with the Pan-Democratic Opposition to the Catholic Church, academics, human rights nongovernmental organizations, public intellectuals on radio, social activists, and aggrieved citizens.[72] The upshot is that no government policy can now be carried through unless it can survive the exacting scrutiny of Opposition MLCs, the mass media, and opinion leaders.

Even a permanent parliamentary majority for the Establishment cannot guarantee the frictionless passage of government proposals.[73] Apart from delivering the critical vote when it was necessary, Establishment MLCs have managed to get no concerted strategy together to assist the Chief Executive.[74] None of the four Chief Executives has been afforded a dominant position in the legislative process in consequence.[75] This was reflected in the Hong Kong SAR governments' poor legislative success rates: their probability of passing their annual legislative program through the Legislative Council into actual legislation. The overall rate from 1998 to 2016 stood at an unremarkable 56.29 percent, given Hong Kong's hybrid authoritarian structure and the

69 CAROL A. G. JONES, LOST IN CHINA? LAW, CULTURE AND IDENTITY IN POST-1997 HONG KONG 251 (2015).

70 Albert H.Y. Chen, *The Theory, Constitution and Practice of Autonomy: The Case of Hong Kong*, *in* ONE COUNTRY, TWO SYSTEMS, THREE LEGAL ORDERS – PERSPECTIVES OF EVOLUTION 751, 758 (Jorge Costa Oliveira & Paulo Cardinal et al. eds., 2009).

71 Wai-Man Lam, *Changing Political Activism: Before and after the Umbrella Movement*, *in* HONG KONG 20 YEARS AFTER THE HANDOVER: EMERGING SOCIAL AND INSTITUTIONAL FRACTURES AFTER 1997 73, 99 (Brian C.H. Fong & Tai-lok Lui eds., 2018).

72 Elaine Chan & Joseph Chan, *Hong Kong 2007–2017: A Backlash in Civil Society*, 39(2) ASIA PAC. J. PUB. ADMIN. 135, 137 (2017).

73 WONG, *supra* note 25, at 224 n. 11.

74 Ma, *supra* note 22, at 39.

75 WONG, *supra* note 25, at 149.

Establishment's majority.[76] Withdrawal of bills by the Government of the day is not uncommon[77] – as witness the shelving or postponement of 39.84 percent of legislative initiatives that were originally planned in the Government's program.[78] From time to time the Pan-Democratic minority manages to leverage its residual institutional influence to exert negative control of public policy, mainly through filibustering through iterated questioning, lengthy speeches, and head-count requests to adjourn if a quorum is not seated.[79] In 2011 and 2012 the Legislative Council voted down a HK$60 billion provisional appropriations bill that bailed out the government; rejected a government proposal to bid for the 2023 Asian Games; invoked its statutory special powers to investigate allegations of a conflict of interest on the part of a Chief Executive-elect; and obliged a new Government to abandon a controversial Reorganization Programme.[80] On July 15, 2016, physician-politician Leung Ka-lau, MLC for the Medical Sector, widely seen as a nonpartisan politician leaning toward the Establishment, single-handedly filibustered the Government's Medical Registration (Amendment) Bill 2016 to death by making frequent quorum calls.[81] The Bill, to which other Establishment MLCs offered no active support, was interpreted by many inside the medical profession and out as a maneuver by Chief Executive C.Y. Leung to get control of statutory agencies through appointment and dismissal, not a genuine attempt to enhance physicians' professional accountability.[82] It was widely believed that Leung relied on appointments to reduce friction in the policy process.[83] Leung's Government was also compelled to withdraw the Copyright (Amendment) Bill in March 2016, which had stirred controversy for potentially infringing the freedom of expression.[84]

76 Fong, *supra* note 23, at 54–55
77 *Id.* at 46.
78 *Id.* at 55.
79 Ma, *supra* note 22, at 37.
80 Sonny Shiu-Hing Lo & Dennis K.K. Leung, *The Dynamics of Executive-Legislative Discord in Hong Kong: Conflict, Confrontation and Adaptation*, 15(2) PUB. ADMIN. & POL'Y 6, 18 (2012).
81 Owen Fung & Ng Kang chung, *"A Colossal Waste of Time and Money": Legco Quorum Calls Cost Hongkongers HK$45.6 Million*, SOUTH CHINA MORNING POST, Jul. 15, 2016, www.scmp.com/news/hong-kong/politics/article/1990207/colossal-waste-time-and-money-legco-quorum-calls-cost
82 Albert Cheng, *Hong Kong Doctors' Advice: Reject Medical Reform Bill, and then Get Rid of CY Leung*, SOUTH CHINA MORNING POST, Jul. 14, 2016, www.scmp.com/comment/insight-opinion/article/1989806/hong-kong-doctors-advice-reject-medical-reform-bill-and-then
83 YU GU, HONG KONG'S LEGISLATURE UNDER CHINA'S SOVEREIGNTY 1998–2013 227–28 (2015).
84 Stuart Lau, *Hong Kong Government's Shelving of Controversial Copyright Bill: What went Wrong?*, SOUTH CHINA MORNING POST, Feb. 25, 2016, www.scmp.com/news/hong-kong/politics/article/1917070/hong-kong-governments-shelving-controversial-copyright-bill

The SAR's authoritarianism has left many aggrieved citizens, who took the Basic Law's autonomy and democratization guarantees at face value,[85] with little choice but street politics to wrest a response to their complaints out of the regime.[86] Pan-Democratic political entrepreneurs, disaffected by the latest in a long line of patchy reform proposals by Chief Executive Tsang in 2009, began to explore less conventional means of mobilization. This eventuated in the Quasi-Referendum of 2010, in which the League of Social Democrats and the Civic Party, both relatively new Pan-Democratic groups, joined forces to pressure China to keep its promise to allow universal suffrage in 2012 according to the Basic Law. Five MLCs from these two parties, all popularly elected and representing all five electoral districts of Hong Kong, resigned in January 2010, then campaigned to regain their seats in a by-election on a platform of universal suffrage by 2012. Quasi-Referendum organizers announced that each vote for the five would be viewed as a proxy vote for universal suffrage. All five were re-elected, with nearly 90 percent of the votes being cast by half a million citizens, who turned out despite the SAR government's boycott.[87] This conjuncture seems to have impressed China enough unprecedentedly to enter into secret negotiations with the Democratic Party, whose plan for political reform, more conciliatory and moderate than the Quasi-Referendum's organizers', had always been stifled by the Establishment before.[88] Beijing eventually acceded to the Democratic Party's plan in exchange for its support of Tsang's 'reforms'. Following this internal split of the Pan-Democratic Opposition, which hamstrung its veto in the Legislative Council, in June 2010 the Standing Committee of the National People's Congress in enacted a decision that facilitated the broadening of the Chief Executive Election Committee from 800 to 1,200 members (but leaving intact the Committee's corporatist representatives), and of the Legislative Council from sixty MLCs to seventy (without altering the 50:50 ratio of functional to geographical constituencies); and permitted the five new seats allotted to functional constituencies (7 percent of the total) to be nominated by District Councilors, most of whom are popularly elected (by 3.3 million voters not concurrently electors of any other functional constituency). "Popular constitutionalism" expressing itself by way of a Quasi-Referendum led unexpectedly

85 Bill Chou, *Local Autonomy in Action: Beijing's Hong Kong and Macau Policies*, 42(3) J. CURRENT CHINESE AFF. 29, 39 (2013).

86 Anthony Cheung & Max Wong, *Judicial Review and Policy Making in Hong Kong: Changing Interface between the Legal and the Political*, 28 ASIA P. J. PUB. ADMIN. 117, 118 (2006).

87 Ho-fung Hung & Iam-chong Ip, *Hong Kong's Democratic Movement and the Making of China's Offshore Civil Society*, 52(3) ASIAN SURV. 504, 513 (2012).

88 *Id.* at 514.

to a minor yet very appreciated breakthrough that increased the proportion of the Legislative Council that is de facto popularly elected from 50 percent to 57 percent in the person of Members nominally belonging to functional constituencies.[89]

With no formal consultation but presuming public opinion to be on its side, the regime retaliated on the Quasi-Referendum with Legislative Council (Amendment) Bill 2011, which sought to abolish Legislative Council by-elections, substituting a system that fills legislative vacancies with the candidate from the previous election who ranked highest on the precedence list of that constituency.[90] This constitutionally questionable step backfired almost immediately, galvanizing the Pan-Democratic Opposition to reunite, and 60,000 demonstrators to take to the streets in July 2011 to demand rejection of the Bill, which was perceived as undermining their constitutional right to partake in public affairs without unreasonable restrictions. The public pressure forced the Government to postpone the second reading of the Bill for two months, so that the public might be formally consulted: a maneuver that did not, however, convince the Bar Association, the Law Society, or the academic community, more than 100 of whom petitioned to kill the Bill altogether. The Pan-Democratic Opposition proceeded to filibuster it.[91] Finally the Government conceded to offer a compromise – Legislative Council (Amendment) Ordinance 2012 – that left parliamentary by-elections intact, merely prohibiting parliamentarians who resigned before their term to run for the same office again for six months.

Public anxiety at the erosion of the Basic Law's "One China, Two Systems" and "high degree of autonomy" principles erupted in September 2012, when student activist groups staged a high-profile hunger strike and tens of thousands of protestors occupied Government Square to denounce the "moral and national education" curriculum slated to be injected into the primary school curriculum on a compulsory basis to the detriment of the freedom of conscience of school children; government spending on such courses mushroomed from HK$5 million (US$636,950) to HK$96 million (US$12,229,440) between 2006 and 2010.[92] The press and civil society joined in condemning it as "brainwashing" for maligning the multi-party elections so cherished by Hong Kong; glorifying the Chinese Communist Party as

[89] Eric C. Ip, *The High Court of the People: Popular Constitutionalism in Hong Kong under Chinese Sovereignty*, 36(3) LAW & POL'Y 314, 330 (2014).

[90] Peter S.C. Chau & Simon N.M. Young, *Abolishing By-elections to Fill Vacancies in the Legislative Council* 41(3) HONG KONG L. J. 601, 603–05 (2012).

[91] *Id.* at 608.

[92] JONES, *supra* note 69, at 234.

"progressive, selfless and cohesive"; and belittling Hong Kong's special identity in favor of Chinese nationalism. After all, freedom of conscience is guaranteed by Article 32(1) of the Basic Law. As a result, Chief Executive Leung had to back down and suspend the curriculum indefinitely. The vehement public reaction is not surprising; in Hong Kong "Chinese" is a cultural and ethnic identity, which has never entailed political support for or national allegiance to the People's Republic of China.[93] The most prominent leader of these protests, Joshua Wong, aged twelve in 2012, went on to become the global poster boy for Hong Kong's democratic movement, taking a leading role in the Umbrella Revolution in 2014.[94]

Repeatedly frustrated by Beijing's demurral to commit itself to abolishing screening mechanisms filtering the Hong Kong people's electoral will, their dissatisfaction with the entire Basic Law framework had metastasized. The "Occupy Central with Love and Peace" movement, a concept authored by Benny Tai, law professor at the University of Hong Kong, reckoned that 10,000 protestors committing civil disobedience in the very busy Central business district would paralyze traffic and pressure the SAR regime and China into abandon their existing plans to use an Establishment-controlled nomination committee to rig the ostensibly direct election of the Chief Executive in 2017.[95] On June 10, 2014, presumably in response to Occupy Central,[96] the State Council in Beijing released a controversial White Paper titled THE PRACTICE OF THE 'ONE COUNTRY, TWO SYSTEMS' POLICY IN THE HONG KONG SPECIAL ADMINISTRATIVE REGION, which asserted inter alia that China's "sovereignty, security and development interests"[97] were to be paramount in Hong Kong, and that officials, legislators and judges of the putatively autonomous SAR were required to be "loyal to the country [China]," and were "subject to oversight by the central government."[98] The overall tone of the White Paper signaled an escalation in Beijing's determination to rein in

93 TSANG, *supra* note 14, at 195.

94 Man Yee Karen Lee, *Lawyers and Hong Kong's Democracy Movement: From Electoral Politics to Civil Disobedience*, 25(1) ASIAN J. POL. SCI. 89, 98 (2017).

95 *See* Benny Yiu-ting Tai, *Civil Disobedience and the Rule of Law*, *in* CIVIL UNREST AND GOVERNANCE IN HONG KONG: LAW AND ORDER FROM HISTORICAL AND CULTURAL PERSPECTIVES 141 (Michael Ng & John Wong eds., 2017).

96 Stephen Ortmann, *The Umbrella Movement and Hong Kong's Protracted Democratization Process*, 46 ASIAN AFF. 32, 33 (2015).

97 INFORMATION OFFICE OF THE STATE COUNCIL OF THE PEOPLE'S REPUBLIC OF CHINA, THE PRACTICE OF 'ONE COUNTRY, TWO SYSTEMS' POLICY IN THE HONG KONG SPECIAL ADMINISTRATIVE REGION [Foreword] (2014).

98 *Id.* at [3].

Hong Kong.[99] Undeterred by its uncompromising tone, Occupy Central held an informal plebiscite in conjunction with the Public Opinion Program at the University of Hong Kong ten days later. Roughly 90 percent of the 800,000 participants voted for electoral reforms that featured citizen nomination of candidates for Chief Executive and a stipulation that the Legislative Council must reject any reform that falls short of "international standards" of free elections.[100] The turnout, comprising one-ninth of Hong Kong's entire population, has been interpreted as a massive public repudiation of the White Paper.[101]

On August 31, 2014 the Standing Committee of the National People's Congress formalized Beijing's imperative that all prospective candidates for Chief Executive in the 2017 election – if suffrage is universal – must be vetted by a 1,200-member Nomination Committee that would, for all practical purposes, be tightly controlled by the party-state, to qualify for candidacy (August 31 Decision).[102] The Standing Committee further determined that the Nomination Committee might nominate no more than three candidates having secured the consent of more than half the Committee's members; justifying such restrictions on the grounds of China's "sovereignty, security and development interests," and abiding by the White Paper line that a Chief Executive must "love the country [China] and love Hong Kong."[103] After all was said and done, the August 31 Decision effectively certified the Party Politburo Standing Committee's right to disqualify politically unacceptable Hong Kong residents from running as candidates for election to the office of Chief Executive. On September 28, 2014, Hong Kong made international headlines when riot police rained eighty-seven rounds of tear gas down on protesters outside Government Headquarters in Admiralty. Many protestors used umbrellas to resist the assault, upon which the movement was dubbed

99 Jones, *supra* note 69, at 6–7.

100 Alvin Y.H. Cheung, *Road to Nowhere: Hong Kong's Democratization and China's Obligations under Public International Law*, 40 Brook. J. Int'l L. 465, 495 (2015).

101 Tony Cheung et al., *Alliance for True Democracy Proposal Wins Occupy Central Poll as Nearly 800,000 Hongkongers Vote*, South China Morning Post, Jun. 29, 2014, www.scmp.com/news/hong-kong/article/1543231/alliance-true-democracy-proposal-wins-occupy-central-poll-nearly

102 Decision of the Standing Committee of the National People's Congress on Issues Relating to the Selection of the Chief Executive of the Hong Kong Special Administrative Region by Universal Suffrage and on the Method for Forming the Legislative Council of the Hong Kong Special Administrative Region in the Year 2016 (adopted by the Tenth Session of the Standing Committee of the Twelfth National People's Congress on Aug. 31, 2016).

103 Cheung, *supra* note 100, at 502.

the "Umbrella Revolution."[104] Ban Ki-moon, Secretary General of the United Nations, responded with an urgent statement asking "all stakeholders to resolve any differences in a manner that is peaceful and safeguards democratic principles."[105] The actions of the first protestors inspired tens of thousands more residents to join in, by blocking major roads not only in Admiralty, but also in Causeway Bay, Mongkok, and Tsimshatsui. It was estimated that as many as 1.2 million people out of the Region's total population of 7.2 million participated in the Umbrella Revolution at various times and in various ways.[106] As events unfolded, it transpired that it was students, not the originators of Occupy Central, who were at the forefront of Hong Kong's largest and longest popular protest movement.[107]

The Umbrella Revolution was a cause actuated by constitutional controversy.[108] Participants opposed any form of screening of the Chief Executive, as most flagrantly set forth in the August 31 Decision.[109] The movement merits special attention as it differs from previous efforts in ways too important to be ignored.[110] First of all, its many organizers and participants willfully disobeyed public order laws for a prolonged period of time, a radical break with the famed law-abidingness of participants in every other major public rally and demonstration in Hong Kong history. Noticeably, Revolution participants in Mongkok came to evolve a "militant protest identity" that markedly contrasted with the ordinary collective action ethos of "peaceful, rational, non-violent and non-profane."[111] Second, participants

104 Justin K.H. Tse, *Under the Umbrella: Grounded Christian Theologies and Democratic Working Alliances in Hong Kong*, 2(1) REV. RELIGION & CHINESE SOC'Y 109, 110–11 (2015).

105 Staff Reporters, *OCCUPY CENTRAL – NIGHT THREE: Full Coverage of All the Night's Events*, SOUTH CHINA MORNING POST, Sep. 30, 2014, www.scmp.com/news/hong-kong/article/1604648/live-thunder-rain-fail-dampen-spirits-hong-kong-democracy-protesters

106 Victoria Tin-bor Hui, *Hong Kong's Umbrella Movement: The Protests and Beyond*, 26(2) J. DEMOCRACY 111, 111 (2015).

107 *See* Samson Yuen, *Hong Kong after the Umbrella Movement: An Uncertain Future for the "One Country Two Systems*, 2015/1 CHINA PERSP. 49 (2015).

108 Marco Wan, *The Artwork of Hong Kong's Occupy Central Movement*, *in* CIVIL UNREST AND GOVERNANCE IN HONG KONG: LAW AND ORDER FROM HISTORICAL AND CULTURAL PERSPECTIVES 179, 193 (Michael Ng & John Wong eds., 2017).

109 Albert H.Y. Chen, *Social Movements and the Law: The Case of Hong Kong*, *in* CIVIL UNREST AND GOVERNANCE IN HONG KONG: LAW AND ORDER FROM HISTORICAL AND CULTURAL PERSPECTIVES 117, 131 (Michael Ng & John Wong eds., 2017); Paul S. N. Lee et al., *The Struggle for Hegemony: The Emergence of a Counter-public Sphere in Post-1997 Hong Kong*, 10(4) CHINESE J. COMM. 338, 339 (2017).

110 ERIC C. IP, LAW AND JUSTICE IN HONG KONG 134–35 (2d ed. 2016).

111 Samson Yuen, *Contesting Middle-class Civility: Place-based Collective Identity in Hong Kong's Occupy Mongkok*, SOC. MOVEMENT STUD. 1, 7 (2018), www.tandfonline.com/doi/abs/10.1080/14742837.2018.1434501

were demanding to override a nomination mechanism explicitly provided in the Basic Law and, indeed, no less than the Standing Committee's previously unquestioned supremacy over constitutional interpretation. Both demands evince a rising tendency in Hong Kong to resist any attempt by Beijing to overrule popular democratic demands under color of a narrow and literal reading of the Basic Law, or of security issues.[112] Chief Executive Leung condemned the Umbrella Revolution as unlawful, and claimed that it put the Standing Committee under duress to withdraw a lawful decision.[113] On the mainland, President Xi Jinping spoke against separatist forces behind the protest,[114] and the mainland Chinese Deputy Director of the Committee for the Basic Law under the Standing Committee even accused the Umbrella Revolution of being a Ukrainian-style, foreign-instigated "Color Revolution" hatched to subvert China's national sovereignty, and admonished the people of Hong Kong that they must be "re-enlightened" to embrace the Chinese national identity more fully.[115]

The government repeatedly urged the protestors to disband or resort to "lawful" means to express their views; whereas, the protestors wanted to continue the occupation until Beijing yielded. After sharp international and local criticism of their initial tactics, the regime conceded to fall back on a wait-it-out approach for the duration.[116] Self-supporting, orderly, peaceable occupier communities soon sprang up in Admiralty, Causeway Bay, and Mongkok, featuring camps, art exhibitions, study areas, and supply stations.[117] People from all walks of life participated in their own ways: doctors and nurses organized first-aid teams; workmen reinforced barricades; school teachers and university academics delivered lectures; college students helped high-schoolers with their homework; and artists created resistance-themed artworks from umbrellas damaged by tear gas.[118] The Umbrella Revolution, however, was unable to avoid polarizing society at large, so that animadversion spread between families, friends, colleagues, and neighbors; and disaffection with the consequent transportation gridlock and income losses, even among sympathizers, steadily

[112] Eric C. Ip, *Constitutional Conflict in Hong Kong under Chinese Sovereignty*, 8(1) Hague J. on Rule of Law 75, 76 (2016).

[113] Yuen, *supra* note 107, at 50.

[114] Lam, *supra* note 61, at 117.

[115] Eric C. Ip, *Prototype Constitutional Supervision in China: The Lessons of the Hong Kong Basic Law Committee*, 10(2) Asian J. Comp. L. 323, 339 (2016).

[116] Simon N.M. Young, *Hong Kong: End of Occupy Central, Government's Proposal for Universal Suffrage Reform*, 2015 Pub. L. 502, 502–03 (2015).

[117] Yuen, *supra* note 107, at 50.

[118] Hui, *supra* note 106, at 112.

grew.[119] The standoff was broken only after minibus unions and an investment company filed civil lawsuits claiming relief from the public nuisance that they alleged the protests constituted.[120] Outspoken criticism of the ensuing judgments did not prevent the clearances that were carried out according to the High Court's orders on December 11 and 15 in Admiralty and Causeway Bay. It was a peaceful end, for the most part, although it did result in more than 200 arrests. The willingness of so many protestors who, though exhausted and factionalized,[121] had carried on so far, to back down, owed more to the authority of the High Court than to respect for the Chief Executive.[122] In the end, the High Court did not truly address the plaintiffs' substantive claims brought under the tort of public nuisance.[123] The Court resolved the public order conflict between the SAR regime and protestors, but could do nothing about the constitutional conflict between Beijing and the democratic forces of Hong Kong.[124] The Pan-Democratic Opposition undertook a most proactive campaign to infiltrate the Election Committee in December 2016, and did achieve unprecedented success: as many as 352 out of 1,194 Electorships fell into the hands of the Opposition, with two Occupy originators, jurist Benny Tai and sociologist Chan Kin-man, becoming Chief Executive Electors for the Higher Education Subsector.[125]

The transaction cost theory of hybrid constitutionalism predicts that political transaction costs on such a scale will sap the Hong Kong SAR regime's power to suppress high-energy constitutional review by the CFA. Indeed, the role of resistance external to the regime in shielding the CFA from its aggressions seems to have been acknowledged by Kemal Bokhary, one of the CFA's founding and most outspoken judges: "Our people's assertiveness [is] the mainstay" of their own legal order. "However high a constitutional objective," he continued, "its attainment is possible if the judiciary is true to its duty and is supported in that duty by an alert population, a free media, a learned academy

[119] Jonathan Poon, *Umbrellas in Hong Kong: Youth and Reform in a Polarized City*, Winter Asia Pac. Aff. Counc J. 14, 14–15 (2015).

[120] Chiu Luen Public Light Bus Co. Ltd., Unrep., H.C.M.P. 3028/2014 (Hong Kong); Chiu Luen Public Light Bus Co. Ltd. [2014] 6 H.K.C. 298 (Hong Kong).

[121] Chris Buckley, *Three Months of Protests End Quietly in Hong Kong*, The New York Times, Dec. 14, 2014, www.nytimes.com/2014/12/15/world/asia/three-months-of-protests-end-quietly-in-hong-kong.html

[122] Young, *supra* note 116, at 502.

[123] Po Jen Yap, *Freedom of Assembly and Association*, *in* Law of the Hong Kong Constitution 821, 835 (Johannes M.M. Chan & C.L. Lim eds., 2d ed. 2015).

[124] Hui, *supra* note 106, at 120.

[125] Lee, *supra* note 94, at 102.

and a dedicated profession."[126] Inability on the parts of the authorities to pervert the Basic Law by amendment or to enact constitutionally suspect statutes reinforces the point that it is powerless to rein in ex ante and ex post the CFA with the kind of constitutional and subconstitutional countermeasures cataloged in Figure 5.1. The most spectacular, if not "paradigmatic," failure of the Establishment Coalition at the subconstitutional level was its aborted attempt to pass a Beijing-inspired national security bill into law in 2003.[127] Article 23 of the Basic Law obligates the SAR to enact "on its own" legislation to "prohibit any act of treason, secession, sedition, subversion against the Central People's Government, or theft of state secrets, to prohibit foreign political organisations or bodies from conducting political activities in the Region, and to prohibit political organisations or bodies of the Region from establishing ties with foreign political organisations or bodies." When the government moved to do just this, an estimated 500,000 people poured into the streets on July 1, 2003, the sixth anniversary of the establishment of the Hong Kong SAR, to express their anger against that bill in particular, and the Government of the day in general.[128] Establishment MLC James Tien, Leader of the Liberal Party, defected from Chief Executive Tung's Government by resigning from the Executive Council to oppose the bill, directly resulting in its defeat.

Between 2005 and 2015, the Legislative Council voted down two out of three government proposals to amend the Basic Law, despite the Establishment holding the majority of seats.[129] Riding his initial popularity, Chief Executive Tsang ventured a reform package that would have enlarged the Legislative Council, while saving the 50:50 ratio of Functional to Geographical Constituencies; although it would also have empowered District Council Members, 80 percent of whom are popularly elected, to take a stronger part in selecting the Chief Executive and the Functional Constituency MLCs. The package failed to win the hearts and minds of the Pan-Democratic Opposition, who, on December 4, 2005, mobilized 250,000 demonstrators against it.[130] Tsang's package, lacking either a roadmap to universal suffrage or an alternative to the Chief Executive appointing the 102 District Councilors,

126 Kemal Bokhary, *The Rule of Law in Hong Kong: Fifteen Years after the Handover*, 51 COLUM. J. TRANSNAT'L L. 287, 299 (2013).

127 Chen, *supra* note 109, at 131.

128 Scott, *supra* note 35, at 85.

129 Young, *supra* note 116, at 502–03.

130 Ming Sing, *Hong Kong at the Crossroads: Public Pressure for Democratic Reform*, *in* POLITICS AND GOVERNMENT IN HONG KONG: CRISIS UNDER CHINESE SOVEREIGNTY 112, 127 (Ming Sing ed., 2009).

was considered temporizing, if not indeed a conspiracy actually to adjourn liberalization under the color of reform. In the end, the Establishment was unable to shield its changeling from the veto of the 24 Pan-Democratic parliamentarians who voted against it. More recently, on June 18, 2015, the Legislative Council, in which the Pan-Democratic MLCs held nearly 40 percent of the seats, vetoed Chief Executive Leung's Government's electoral reform bill for the 2017 Chief Executive election, framed in accordance with the unpopular, abovementioned August 31 Decision and in contempt for the demands of Umbrella Revolution. Yet the Standing Committee has insisted that its Decision shall be the normative framework for any reform bill that should be preferred in future. The SAR regime is thus left with a severe legitimacy deficit that undermines its ability to advance needed electoral reforms, while all the other interested parties, including Beijing and the Pan-Democratic Opposition, never cease suffering political polarization and paralysis.[131]

Low Transaction Cost Politics in the Macau SAR

The Macau Establishment Coalition, like its counterpart in Hong Kong, controls both the executive and legislative branches of the Macau SAR. It has long comprised three main factions, or the so-called "Big Three"[132]: the Associação Comercial de Macau (ACM), the Macau Federation of Trade Unions (FTU), and the General Union of Neighbors Association of Macau (GUNA). These factions have never descended into the factionalism and infighting that have plagued Hong Kong's Establishment Coalition. A much clearer division of the spoils exists in Macau. The ACM, which represents the interests of businessmen of Chinese descent, has for many years wielded a tacit primacy. The ACM alone controlled fourteen out of thirty-three seats on the Legislative Assembly during the 2013–17 term.[133] As at 2015, ACM members occupied nearly half, and more than half of all Macau seats on the National People's Congress and the National Committee of the Chinese People's Political Consultative Conference, respectively.[134] Both the FTU and the GUNA looked after the interests, respectively, of labor and neighborhood interest groups, incorporated into the SAR ruling elite as instruments of social

131 Joseph Y.S. Cheng, *New Trends of Political Participation in Hong Kong*, *in* New Trends of Political Participation in Hong Kong 3, 34 (2014).

132 Bill K.P. Chou, *Politics and Social Organisations in Macao: A Historical Institutionalist Analysis*, 13(1) China: An Int'l J. 22, 28–29 (2015).

133 *Id.* at 30.

134 *Id.* at 28–29.

control.[135] These factions and their predecessors monopolized the representation of the local Chinese community to the colonial regime and during the Sino–Portuguese negotiations and the drafting of the Lei Básica. Ever since pro-Communist partisans in Macau capitalized on the outbreak of violent Maoist protests in the late 1960s to drive Kuomintang loyalists out of the Portuguese dependency with the assistance of Beijing, the latter's intervention has overmastered a weakened Macau government.[136] China has since maintained the strong political presence in Portuguese Macau that it failed to achieve in British Hong Kong.[137]

Inaugural Macau Chief Executive Edmund Ho was an experienced politician by the time he assumed power in 1999, having served as Deputy Speaker of the Legislative Assembly of Portuguese Macau for more than a decade between 1988 and 1999.[138] In contrast, inaugural Hong Kong Chief Executive and shipping magnate C.H. Tung was a layman in politics before taking office in 1997, apart from having served as an Unofficial Member of the Executive Council under Governor Chris Patten. Ho was also the son of an influential politician, businessman, and philanthropist, Ho Yin, President of the ACM from 1950 until his death in 1983 and a veteran middleman in quasi-diplomatic exchanges between rightist Estado Novo Portugal and leftist Communist China.[139] But over and above his prestigious political inheritance, Chief Executive Ho was an energetic and charismatic strongman in his own right,[140] whose leadership of Macau had proved stabilizing if not, in brief, "very powerful."[141] As a result, he commanded a large following with the public.[142] Ho's successor, Fernando Chui, Secretary for Social Affairs and Culture for Ho's two terms of office, also hailed from a political dynasty that counted among its members four current or former Assemblymen. With this background, the Macau Chief Executive has known how to radiate his

135 Ying-ho Kwong, *Ruling Coalition Restructuring under Macao's Hybrid Regime*, 17(3) CHINA REV. 111, 116–17 (2017).

136 Kevin K.S. Tso, *Fundamental Political and Constitutional Norms: Hong Kong and Macau Compared*, 13(1) AUSTRALIAN J. ASIAN L. 1, 12 (2012).

137 Yash Ghai, *The Basic Law of the Special Administrative Region of Macau: Some Reflections*, 49(1) INT'L & COMP. L. Q. 183, 197 (2000).

138 Bill K.P. Chou, *Public Sector Reform in Macao after the Handover*, 52/2004 CHINA PERSP. 1, 4 (2004).

139 *Id.* at 4.

140 SONNY SHIU-HING LO, POLITICAL CHANGE IN MACAO 33 (2008).

141 Herbert S. Yee, *The Theory and Practice of "One-Country-Two-Systems" in Macao*, *in* CHINA'S MACAO TRANSFORMED: CHALLENGE AND DEVELOPMENT IN THE 21ST CENTURY 3, 13 (Eilo W.Y. Yu and Ming K. Chan eds., 2014).

142 Chou, *supra* note 138, at 4.

penetrating political influence.[143] Unlike his Hong Kong counterpart, who lacks all such discretion, Macau's Chief Executive has conserved the Portuguese colonial practice of appointing lawmakers to the Legislative Assembly, and of issuing Decree Laws.[144] There is no equivalent of Hong Kong's powerful AO Party in the government. Due to the delay of bureaucratic localization by Portugal, the principal officials in Chief Executive Ho's Government were mostly in their thirties when appointed, and their merits chiefly rested with their proficiency in the Portuguese language, or ties to the Establishment.[145] As of 2001, a mere 16 percent of civil servants at the director rank (99 out of 633) had reached age forty-five or above.[146] Macau's strong political executive was immune from the friction of strong bureaucratic resistance. The bureaucracy has too little administrative savvy to challenge the leadership of Macau's succession of strong Chief Executives.[147] In sum, the Macau Chief Executive can, and often does, govern by himself.[148]

Following longstanding colonial tradition,[149] the Chief Executives have thus far relied heavily on political cooptation and consensus-building tactics, resulting in a near-absence of confrontation between Chief Executive and Legislative Assembly.[150] Indeed, the majority of Assemblymen cherish a convention of resolving differences and finding solutions informally before even proceeding to formal sessions.[151] There would appear to be a deep-seated belief that openly criticizing the Government in power might exude an unbecoming reek of social disharmony and conflict.[152] All Establishment Assemblymen, be they from the traditional factions or the newer casino-

143 Yufan Hao et al., Political Economy of Macao since 1999: The Dilemma of Success 169 (2017).

144 Chaoyuan Ji, *A Study of the Political Structure of the Macao Special Administrative Region from the Perspective of Constitutionalism*, 1 Academic J. "One Country, Two Systems" 68, 69–72 (2011).

145 Hao et al., *supra* note 143, at 155.

146 Chou, *supra* note 138, at 4.

147 Brian Brewer, *Civil Service Reform: Building Basic Administrative Capacity*, *in* Gaming, Governance and Public Policy in Macao 89, 89 (Newman M.K. Lam & Ian Scott, eds., 2011).

148 Eilo Wing-Yat Yu, *Executive-Legislative Relationships and the Development of Public Policy*, *in* Gaming, Governance and Public Policy in Macao 57, 57 (Newman M.K. Lam & Ian Scott eds., 2011).

149 Yee, *supra* note 141, at 29–33.

150 Sonny Shiu-Hing Lo, *Consultative Governance and Legitimacy in Macao: The Mix of Electoral and Public Sector Reforms*, 15(1) Pub. Admin & Pol'y 19, 23 (2012).

151 Sonny Shiu-Hing Lo, *Constitutional Conventions and Political Development in Macau*, *in* Macau on the Threshold of the Third Millennium 93, 97–98 (2001).

152 Kwong, *supra* note 135, at 123.

friendly ones, have kept to a tacit convention or "unwritten rule" that "vetoing government bills may create a perception of 'social disharmony' and 'disunity of pro-government force'."[153] Nothing has made an inroad in the entrenched cohesion of the Establishment Coalition, as witness the casual yet very sophisticated coordination mechanisms, reinforced by nepotism and authoritarianism,[154] that constantly steer the various Establishment factions away from discord and intra-competition in the course of fielding candidates for General Elections, who have had undeniable success.[155]

No viable opposition has arisen in Macau that might veto the regime's decisions on any issue. The Pro-Democracy Opposition in the Legislative Assembly is minuscule: in 2018 it could count only four out of thirty-three Assemblymen. Against a historical background in which a genuine political party system with popular support is lacking,[156] the Assembly's unwillingness to investigate former senior government official Ao Man Long, who, as mentioned in Chapter 4, allegedly received bribes from construction companies, has been construed as a failure of constitutional responsibility to hold the government accountable.[157] The Legislative Assembly has no specialized subcommittees, like the Finance Committee of the Hong Kong Legislative Council, that could scrutinize expenditure bills, especially public works projects and the creation of senior positions;[158] explicable by the fact that the Establishment majority never shows any enthusiasm for holding the government accountable for anything that it does,[159] not even to stamp out imprudent public spending practices.[160] Notably, two Opposition legislators, who held less than 10 percent of the parliamentary seats, raised 60 percent of all written questions before the government between 1999 and 2009.[161] Macau has been rebuked for not

153 *Id.* at 130.

154 Li Sheng, *The Transformation of Island City Politics: The Case of Macau*, 11(2) Island Stud. J. 521, 534 (2016).

155 Eilo Wing-Yat Yu, *Formal and Informal Politics in Macao Special Administrative Region Elections 2004–2005*, 16(52) J. Contemp. China 417, 427 (2007).

156 Eric C. Ip, *The Evolution of Constitutional Adjudication in the Chinese Special Administrative Regions: Theory and Evidence*, 61(4) Am. J. Comp. L. 799, 823 (2013).

157 Arnaldo Gonçalves, *Macau's Autonomy: Looking for a Fresh Awakening?*, *in* One Country, Two Systems, Three Legal Orders – Perspectives of Evolution: Essays on Macau's Autonomy after the Resumption of Sovereignty by China 733, 739 (Jorge Oliveira & Paulo Cardinal, eds., 2009).

158 Yee, *supra* note 141, at 12.

159 Bill K.P. Chou, *Interest Group Politics in Macau after Handover*, 14(43) J. Contemp. China 191, 200 (2005).

160 Sheng, *supra* note 154, at 529.

161 Yu, *supra* note 148, at 64–5.

having been "properly supervised by the local legislature, media or populace."[162]

The exceptionally high legislative success rate of Macau's government reflects the lowness of that SAR's political transaction costs. Astonishingly, the legislative success rate from 1998 to 2005 was nothing less than 100 percent: each and every one of the seventy-eight bills proposed by the Ho Government were approved by the Legislative Assembly[163] – and the cumulative rate between 1999 and 2013 stood at 98.4 percent.[164] Assemblymen from the Establishment maintained their conspicuous solidarity with the Chief Executive even in the passage of controversial laws such as the Labor Relations Law 2008, Antitobacco Law 2011, and Land Law 2014.[165] The bargaining power of the Pro-Democracy Opposition was so weak that the enacting procedures for bills proposed by individual MLCs, which are found in Hong Kong, and are so burdensome compared with government-sponsored bills, are completely unknown in the Legislative Assembly, because the sheer rarity of such bills renders them unnecessary.[166] The relationship between the Chief Executive and the Legislative Assembly can be described as a lopsided asymmetry of power.

A number of public processions celebrating various political rites are held each year on commemorative dates, such as National Day of the People's Republic of China on October 1, and Establishment Day of the Macau SAR on December 20.[167] Annual clashes between the police and street demonstrators inspired by labor activists almost invariably occur on International Labor Day on May 1.[168] Public protests have become an increasingly popular channel to express socioeconomic grievances – in the aftermath of gambling liberalization, for example, or after the odd business-government collusive scandal breaks,[169] but they have never really put the regime under any real pressure to democratize Macau. Protests focus single-mindedly on socioeconomic issues like labor rights, the rising cost of living, official venality, and even the scarcity of parking spaces.[170] Interest groups consist mostly of trade

162 Yee, *supra* note 141, at 18.

163 Kwong, *supra* note 135, at 132.

164 *Id.* at 131.

165 *Id.*

166 Sonny Shiu-Hing Lo, Political Development in Macau 204 (1995).

167 Victor Zheng & Po-san Wan, Gambling Dynamism: The Macao Miracle 135 (2014).

168 Lo, *supra* 150, at 23.

169 Zheng & Wan, *supra* note 166, at 135.

170 Newman M.K. Lam, *The Impact of Gaming Liberalisation on Public Opinion and Political Culture*, *in* Gaming, Governance and Public Policy in Macao 37, 38 (Newman M.K. Lam & Ian Scott eds., 2011).

unions and neighborhood associations, and they usually depend on Establishment Coalition support, and the media is not critical of the government. When a flagship Pro-Democracy group, New Macau Association, rallied public support in 2012 for a proposal on electoral reform, Establishment bodies Jiangmen Communal Society and United Citizens Association counteracted with 17,000 signatures and 6,800 reports in support of the government's position.[171] Compared with Hong Kong's Pan-Democratic Opposition, the minuscule Pro-Democracy Opposition in Macau wields too little manpower or financial resources to mobilize the citizenry en masse effectively to resist regime transgressions of rights and liberties.[172] A sufficient explanation of its weakness lies in the government's preeminence in the economy, other than the gambling industry: it is the largest employer in professions known to foment potential dissidents, such as civil servants, physicians, university professors, and media reporters; the gambling and finance industries, even though not directly under government control, have prudently opted for friendly relations with it.[173]

Opinion polls consistently indicate that the general ethos of the people of Macau is to show little or no interest in public affairs;[174] in the prevalent belief that "politics is for the elites." Most Macau residents eschew political mobilization to concentrate on making a living.[175] Pro-Democracy groups almost universally demur to advocate rapid democratization in the light of the aversion of large segments of the electorate to social instability and drastic political changes.[176] The contrasting political attitudes of citizens of Macau and Hong Kong is likely down to two factors. First, Macau's economic and tourism performance, particularly after the deregulation of the gambling industry, was far better than Hong Kong's.[177] And the rare public resentments that may arise from causes such as the unexpected arrest of Ao Man-long in 2006 and the subsequent disclosure of his corruption record, are allayed by the government deploying such remedies as ad hoc social welfare benefits, public subsidies, even "cash handouts" to each Macau resident under the "Wealth Partaking Scheme."[178] Secondly, Macau's cohesive society of community leaders and

[171] Kwong, *supra* note 135, at 127.

[172] Lo, *supra* note 150, at 96.

[173] Ieong Meng U, *Macao and Hong Kong, Convergence or Divergence? The 2014 Retirement Package Bill Protest and Macao's Governance Crisis*, 57 (3) Asian Surv. 504, 525 (2017).

[174] Zheng & Wan, *supra* note 166, at 137.

[175] *Id.* at 146.

[176] Herbert S. Yee, Macau in Transition: From Colony to Autonomous Region 164 (2001).

[177] Zheng & Wan, *supra* note 166, at 158.

[178] *Id.* at 187.

neighborhood associations is very receptive to cooptation by the SAR regime and Beijing.[179] Historically, Macau residents have held a more positive view of Communist China than their Hong Kong neighbors. After the Sino–Portuguese Joint Declaration, and even after the Tiananmen Square crackdown, there was no Hong Kong-style mass exodus or fear over the imminent transfer of sovereignty.[180] Opinion polls have suggested that the people of Macau identify as "Chinese" notably more than Hong Kong residents or Taiwanese.[181] Equally dissimilarly, the Macau populace rarely if ever second-guesses the SAR regime's deference to Beijing, even in policy domains that fall squarely within the scope of its "high degree of autonomy."[182] Consider the following incident. The government neglected to limit the height of three proposed office and residential towers that were liable to blot out, from the harbor and from the city, the view of Guia Lighthouse, built by the Portuguese in the nineteenth century and in 2005 listed as a United Nations Educational, Scientific and Cultural Organization (UNESCO) World Heritage Site. In 2007, UNESCO expressed its dissatisfaction and warned Macau that it might delist the site. Acutely attuned to the necessity of conserving and building up China's global soft power on the eve of the 2008 Beijing Olympics, the authorities in Beijing stepped in to "lean" on the Macau officials to reset the height limits for the buildings in question.[183] This dénouement sparked no discontent on either side.

The transaction cost theory of hybrid constitutionalism predicts that such low political transaction costs will buttress regime capacity to squelch constitutional review by way of constitutional and subconstitutional measures that stultify consequential, high-energy constitutional review. Constitutional amendments and constitutionally controversial statutes have proved largely frictionless to pursue in Macau. Contrast the enactment of the Macau Lei relativa à defesa da segurança do Estado (National Security Law) with its Hong Kong counterpart, which triggered more than half a million people to protest against it in the streets in 2003. A far tougher national security law sailed through the Macau Legislative Assembly in January 2009 with little opposition from civil society groups, based on the verbatim transposition in the Lei Básica

179 Richard C. Bush, Hong Kong in the Shadow of China: Living with the Leviathan 224 (2016).

180 Tso, *supra* note 136, at 20.

181 *See* Wai-man Lam, *Promoting Hybridity: The Politics of the New Macau Identity*, 203 China Q. 656 (2010).

182 Sheng, *supra* note 154, at 525.

183 Ming K. Chan, *Beyond the Luso Twilight: Into the Sino Glow: A Historical Sketch of Macao's Transformation, in* China's Macao Transformed: Challenge and Development in the 21st Century lxiii, lxxxviii (Eilo W.Y. Yu and Ming K. Chan eds., 2014).

of article 23 of the Basic Law, as noted above. Macau's National Security Law now criminalizes vague "preparatory acts" to treason, secession, and subversion, treating convicts to a minimum of three years and a maximum of twenty-five years in prison.[184] Note that the National Security Bill had been introduced less than three months earlier in October 2008.[185] Disputes between Beijing and Macau on the matter, if any, went unnoticed.[186] Chief Executive Fernando Chui's 2011 proposal to reform the political system was widely regarded as an initiative of Beijing and not the Macau community, which has collectively petitioned for no electoral progress. On December 31, 2011 the National People's Congress, Standing Committee decided that the first and last word on amendments to the political system rested with the Committee itself, although the SAR was allowed to participate in the interstices.[187] In January 2012 the government conducted a one-month consultation on electoral reform, providing the public with restricted options allowing for only a small increase in the number of elected Assemblymen and Chief Executive Electors.[188] In the end, backed by the Standing Committee, and met by nearly no public resistance,[189] Macau added a mere two directly elected and two indirectly elected legislators, and just 100 members to the Election Committee, leaving the power distribution in statu quo.[190] As of March 2018, it is noteworthy that the Standing Committee has interpreted no provision of the Lei Básica in anticipation of or response to a judgment of the TUI, in marked contrast with its dealings with Hong Kong. Ex ante constraints on the Tribunal are doubtlessly more than adequate from the perspective of the regime.

Implications

The above offered the reader thick, contextualized descriptions of the contrasting cases of Hong Kong and Macau as, respectively, high and low political transaction cost jurisdictions. This empirical background is essential to the type of judicial behavior research attempted in this book, given that it is next to

184 Sonny Shiu-Hing Lo, *Hong Kong*, *in* POLITICS IN CHINA: AN INTRODUCTION 451, 455 (William A. Joseph ed., 2d ed. 2014).
185 Chou, *supra* note 85, at 42.
186 *Id.* at 42.
187 *Id.* at 36.
188 Sonny Shiu-Hing Lo, *Consultative Governance and Legitimacy in Macao: The Mix of Electoral and Public Sector Reforms*, 15(1) PUB. ADMIN. & POL'Y 19, 31 (2012).
189 Chou, *supra* note 132, at 33.
190 Zhidong Hao, *Social Stratification and Ethnic and Class Politics in Macao before and after the Handover in 1999*, 13(1) CHINA: AN INT'L J. 66, 85 (2015).

impossible to obtain reliable empirical psychological evidence about how judges in hybrid regimes, appointed by non-partisan procedures, anticipate regime responses, especially when the regime has never visibly retaliated, as in Macau.[191] Judges are hung on the horns of a central dilemma: self-restraint avoids being purged but precludes expression of their heartfelt preferences; assertiveness enables assertion of their actual preferences, but exposes them to the risk of backlash.[192] When judicial appointment procedures are non-transparent, and the ideological position of each judge cannot be ascertained by external circumstantial evidence such as party affiliation, the absence on record of judicial invalidations of regime acts or retaliations against the constitutional court is, without further information, very ambiguous. It could imply that the court restrained itself; or that the regime incorporated its expectations of the court's preferences into the laws that it enacted; or that the regime was incompetent to retaliate.[193,194] The independent evidence that Hong Kong is a high political transaction cost polity, where enacting controversial statutes and amendments is "constitutionally" (in an informal, conventional sense) fraught with difficulty, buttresses the inference that the regime was incapable of acting coherently to overcome resistance in pursuing court-curbing measures. The fragility of the Hong Kong Establishment Coalition, particularly on matters that are not crucial to Beijing, has opened up significant policy space for the CFA to invalidate legislation and administrative acts on constitutional grounds.[195] The cohesion of the Macau Establishment Coalition, reinforced by the near absence of state-society conflict and any local identity opposed to mainland China, has rendered the threat of backlash against TUI defiance so imminently credible that no TUI has dared risk it.[196] On the basis of the theory, it is very probable that the TUI's persistent low-energy constitutional review was anchored in the anticipation that judicial aggression will quickly trigger a court-curbing response.

191 Juan Carlos Rodriguez-Raga, *Strategic Deference in the Colombian Constitutional Court 1992–2006*, *in* COURTS IN LATIN AMERICA 81, 84 (Gretchen Helmke & Julio Ríos-Figueroa eds., 2011).

192 Gretchen Helmke & Jeffrey K. Staton, *The Puzzling Judicial Politics of Latin America: A Theory of Litigation, Judicial Decisions and Interbranch Conflict*, *in* COURTS IN LATIN AMERICA 306, 326 (Gretchen Helmke & Julio Ríos-Figueroa eds., 2011).

193 John Ferejohn et al., *Comparative Judicial Politics*, *in* THE OXFORD HANDBOOK OF COMPARATIVE POLITICS 727, 747 (Carles Boix & Susan C. Stokes eds., 2007).

194 Rodriguez-Raga, *supra* note 190, at 85.

195 PO JEN YAP, COURTS AND DEMOCRACIES IN ASIA 203 (2017).

196 Ieong, *supra* note 172, at 527.

LEGAL ORIGINS AS AN ALTERNATIVE EXPLANATION

It is not disputed that the CFA and the TUI spring from very different legal traditions. Hong Kong's common law is closely modeled on England's, and CFA decisions are issued solely in English. CFA judgments have been cited with approval by courts of last resort across the common law world, from England and Wales, Scotland, Australia, Canada, New Zealand to Malaysia, Singapore, the Eastern Caribbean territories, the Cayman Islands, Trinidad and Tobago, Fiji, and Tonga.[197] Macau's civil law legacy, on the other hand, stems from the Continent (ultimately from Roman law) and is heavily influenced by contemporary Portugal and the European Union.[198] It is not unusual for Hong Kong courts to cite foreign precedents from the common law world in constitutional cases,[199] and for Macau courts to quote Portuguese academic works and legal opinions even in public law adjudication;[200] indeed, Portuguese references are used more abundantly than Chinese ones.[201] Not surprisingly, then, the divergence between Hong Kong's and Macau's jurisprudence has been attributed to the differences between the common law and civil law, respectively.[202] This is the well-known legal origins hypothesis all over again,[203] as applied to the study of the Chinese SARs, which generally holds that common law and civil law, the world's two dominant secular legal traditions, predictably yield significant political-economic differences in terms of investor protection, government regulation, and judicial discretion;[204] accordingly, Hong Kong's judges tend to enjoy more freedom to make their own rules and more independence from the administrative state than their counterparts in

[197] P.Y. Lo, *Impact of Jurisprudence beyond Hong Kong," in* HONG KONG'S COURT OF FINAL APPEAL: THE DEVELOPMENT OF THE LAW IN CHINA'S HONG KONG 579, 580 (Simon N.M. Young & Yash Ghai eds., 2014).

[198] Guangjian Tu, *The Conflict of Laws System in Macau*, 40 HONG KONG L.J. 85, 90 (2010).

[199] IP, *supra* note 110, at 13–15.

[200] Jorge Godinho & Paulo Cardinal, *Macau's Court of Final Appeal, in* HONG KONG'S COURT OF FINAL APPEAL: THE DEVELOPMENT OF THE LAW IN CHINA'S HONG KONG 608, 625 (Simon N.M. Young & Yash Ghai eds., 2014).

[201] Denis de Castro Halis, *"Post-Colonial" Legal Interpretation in Macau, China: Between European and Chinese Influences, in* EAST ASIA'S RENEWED RESPECT FOR THE RULE OF LAW IN THE 21ST CENTURY: THE FUTURE OF LEGAL AND JURIDICAL LANDSCAPES IN EAST ASIA 68, 80 (Setsuo Miyazawa et al., 2015).

[202] CHAOYANG JIANG, A STUDY ON THE BASIC LAW OF MACAU AND THE RULE OF LAW OF THE MACAU SPECIAL ADMINISTRATIVE REGION 131 (2016); Castellucci, *supra* note 8, at 699.

[203] Edward L. Glaeser & Andrei Shleifer, *Legal Origins*, 117(4) Q J. ECON. 1193, 1200 (2002).

[204] *See* Rafael La Porta et al., *Law and Finance*, 106(6) J. POL. ECON. 1113 (1998).

Macau, because they make like common law judges everywhere, while Macau judges follow the rest of the civil law world.[205]

Without passing judgment on the efficacy of the legal origins hypothesis in other domains of research such as law and finance,[206] this book has evidenced that it cannot convincingly explain the data of Hong Kong and Macau. If the hypothesis is to preempt the transaction cost theory of hybrid constitutionalism, we should expect the following: constitutional review at a global level should be systemically stronger in the common law than in the civil law tradition; high-energy constitutional review should be more entrenched in the United Kingdom than in Portugal; a stronger tradition of review should exist in British Hong Kong than in Portuguese Macau; and the patterns of judicial assertiveness and deference in the CFA and TUI, respectively, should be reversed. Every one of these predictions was negated by the evidence. The refutation of the legal origins hypothesis in this one case does not necessarily imply that history and institutions do not factor into judicial calculi,[207] or that legal culture is negligible in the comparative study of constitutional law.[208] And even if constitutional politics is not predetermined by historical factors, historical contexts remain important to it.[209] The argument here is a narrow one: when it comes to constitutional review, particularly of legislation, variables related to political transaction costs tend to be most decisive compared with other variables like legal origins and culture.

Common Law versus Civil Law

The common law in its several versions governs one third of the world's population.[210] Major jurisdictions include Australia, Canada, England, India, New Zealand, and the United States. In terms of global influence, it is rivaled only by the Romano-Germanic civil law family, which has significantly shaped the legal systems of all contemporary jurisdictions in East Asia

[205] Peter H. Solomon, Jr., *Courts and Judges in Authoritarian Regimes*, 60 World Pol. 122, 139 (2007).

[206] *See* Stefan Voigt, *Are International Merchants Stupid? A Natural Experiment Refutes the Legal Origin Theory*, 5(1) J. Empirical Legal Stud. 1 (2008); Thorsten Beck et al., *Law and Finance: Why Does Legal Origin Matter?*, 31(4) J. Comp. Econ. 653 (2003).

[207] Rachel E. Brown, The Achilles Heel of Democracy: Judicial Autonomy and the Rule of Law in Central America 19 (2017).

[208] Diana Kapiszewski et al., *Introduction*, *in* Consequential Courts: Judicial Roles in Global Perspective 1, 5 (Diana Kapiszewski et al. eds., 2013).

[209] Nuno Garoupa and Tom Ginsburg, Judicial Reputation: A Comparative Theory 74 (2015).

[210] Penny Darbyshire, Darbyshire on the English Legal System 13 (10th ed. 2011).

except Hong Kong.[211] Former colonies generally received their legal systems from their colonial rulers; no British colony has ever adopted a civil law system nor any continental European colony a common law one.[212] The ancient Roman tradition of civil law (ius civile, in Latin) was recovered with the revival of Latin in the High Middle Ages in the work of scholars of the new-founded universities of Paris, Bologna and the like, who endeavored to develop a law that would be autonomous from canon law, yet superior in rational plasticity to the patchwork of local custom. For the basis of their endeavor they took up the rediscovered CORPUS JURIS CIVILIS (BODY OF CIVIL LAW) commissioned in the sixth century by the Eastern Roman Emperor Justinian. In the course of expounding this law, European jurists conceived of law as an abstract, sophisticated body of precepts related to theology and philosophy.[213] Their refinement of Roman law culminated in the magisterial Napoleonic Code of 1804,[214] which was carried across Continental Europe to Belgium, Italy, Luxembourg, the Low Countries, and Rhenish provinces, and Poland by Napoleon's invasions; and felt in Portugal, Spain, and some cantons of Switzerland as well.[215]

There are undeniable systemic differences between common and civil law. One is that a common law statute, unlike a civil law code, is normally premised on the expectation that courts will work out the details in case law. Frequently, this is because the statute was drafted to modify rather than abandon the prior state of the common law; seldom, if ever, is it intended to shape or reshape fundamental common law norms. In the system of civil law, courts are expected to apply legal codes meant to be compendious, literally and cautiously by default.[216] In sum, the "philosopher-kingship" is vested in the Lawgiver in the civil law tradition, but in the appellate judges under the common law.[217] No less diversity exists between legal systems conventionally labeled as "common law" and "civil law," however, contrary to common

211 IP, *supra* 110, at 11.

212 Daniel M. Klerman et al., *Legal Origin or Colonial History?*, 3 J. LEGAL ANALYSIS 379, 385 (2011) (several former British colonies such as South Africa and Sri Lanka have evolved "mixed" legal systems that feature elements of both civil with common law.)

213 Reinhard Zimmermann, *Roman Law in the Modern World*, *in* THE CAMBRIDGE COMPANION TO ROMAN LAW 452, 458–59 (David Johnston ed., 2015).

214 CRAIG ANDERSON, ROMAN LAW 115 (2009).

215 Rafael La Porta et al., *The Economic Consequences of Legal Origins*, 46(2) J. ECON. LITERATURE 285, 289–291 (2008).

216 Gani Aldashev, *Legal Institutions, Political Economy, and Development*, 25(2) OXFORD REV. ECON. POL'Y 257, 265 (2009).

217 GAROUPA & GINSBURG, *supra* note 208, at 44.

stereotypes.[218] In the common law world, judges in the United States seem readier to ignore precedent than those of England and Wales.[219] Not all civil law judges necessarily ignore previous decisions, or resist acknowledging that they can have policy-making influence.[220] Striking similarities between the French civil and English common law approaches to statutory interpretation have been discovered, in the sense that they apply nearly identical criteria to the construction of statutory texts in light of their "purpose," within a "context" that includes the legal system at large and extralegal values.[221]

The single most significant argument against the legal origins hypothesis as applied to the Chinese SARs is that, as a rule, constitutional review is no less energetic or entrenched in the civil law than in the common law world. During the twentieth century, numerous civil law constitutional democracies, such as Austria, France, Germany, Italy, Portugal, and Spain, have departed from the classical model by establishing specialized constitutional courts that regularly conduct aggressive and sometimes even preemptive constitutional review of legislation.[222] These constitutional courts have adopted expansive modes of interpretation that do not conform to the image of a judiciary bound by legislative dictates.[223] The power of constitutional interpretation has brought civil law judges, traditionally presumed politically neutral, to the forefront of policy making by experts,[224] endowing them with such great prerogatives that they have become "negative legislator[s]."[225] It is only to be expected that contemporary comparative constitutional law scholars today are deliberately steering their investigation away from legal families to particular legal institutions, such as constitutional review.[226] A survey of the empirical

218 Nuno Garoupa & Andrew P. Morriss, *The Fable of the Codes: The Efficiency of the Common Law, Legal Origins, and Codification Movements*, 2012 Univ. Ill. L. Rev. 1443, 1451 (2012).

219 Nuno Garoupa & Carlos Gómez Ligüerre, *The Evolution of the Common Law and Efficiency*, 40(2) Ga. J. Int'l & Comp. L. 307, 325 (2012).

220 Roderick A. Macdonald & Hoi Kong, *Judicial Independence as a Constitutional Virtue*, *in* The Oxford Handbook of Comparative Constitutional Law 831, 852 (Michael Rosenfeld and Andras Sajo eds., 2012).

221 Gerard Carney, *Comparative Approaches to Statutory Interpretation in Civil Law and Common Law Jurisdictions*, 36(1) Statute L. Rev. 46, 58 (2015).

222 Georg Vanberg, *Constitutional Courts in Comparative Perspective: A Theoretical Assessment*, 18 Annu. Rev. Polit. Sci. 167, 176 (2015).

223 Macdonald & Kong, *supra* note 220, at 852.

224 Walter F. Murphy, *Civil Law, Common Law, and Constitutional Democracy*, 52 La. L. Rev. 98, 98 (1991).

225 Gustavo Femandes de Andrad, *Comparative Constitutional Law: Judicial Review*, 3(3) J. Const. L. 977, 983 (2001).

226 Macdonald & Kong, *supra* note 220, at 850.

literature suggests that any correlation of degrees of judicial independence with either the common law or civil law tradition is nowadays anything but self-evident.[227]

Proponents of the legal origins hypothesis may try to argue that the non-permanent judges from overseas common law jurisdictions have prodded the CFA toward a more assertive stance than was traditional for Hong Kong's bench. The data does not support this line of argument. The presence of one overseas non-permanent judge on the CFA is not a sufficient explanatory factor of the CFA–TUI divergence. A conclusive riposte to the Establishment politicians who belittle them as "parachute judges"[228] is that they are actually too likely to defer to local views, as would any polite guest in unfamiliar surroundings.[229] Adequate representation of local experts on the Court all but guarantees that any liberties that overseas judges might take with Hong Kong laws, conventions, and culture will be kept in check.[230] Indeed, the overseas non-permanent judge was in the majority in the CFA's unprecedented decision to petition the Standing Committee of the National People's Congress for an Interpretation, regarded by not a few as unnecessary or damaging to judicial independence,[231] in *Democratic Republic of the Congo v. FG Hemisphere*.[232] In every single reported case in which the CFA has upheld the constitutionality of primary legislation between July 1997 and July 2017, not one overseas non-permanent judge dissented. Indeed, dissent, generally, is very rare on both the TUI,[233] and to a slightly lesser extent the

[227] *Id.* at 852.

[228] Cliff Buddle, *Why Criticising Hong Kong's Foreign Judges for Not Understanding the City Is Ridiculous*, SOUTH CHINA MORNING POST, Jan. 13, 2018, www.scmp.com/week-asia/opinion/article/2128060/why-criticising-hong-kongs-foreign-judges-not-understanding-city

[229] Mark Daly, *A Human Rights Lawyer's Perspective*, *in* HONG KONG'S COURT OF FINAL APPEAL: THE DEVELOPMENT OF THE LAW IN CHINA'S HONG KONG 207, 220 (Simon N.M. Young & Yash Ghai eds., 2014).

[230] Simon N.M. Young & Antonio Da Roza, *The Judges*, *in* HONG KONG'S COURT OF FINAL APPEAL: THE DEVELOPMENT OF THE LAW IN CHINA'S HONG KONG 253, 263 (Simon N.M. Young & Yash Ghai eds., 2014).

[231] Kin-ming Kwong & Chiew Ping Yew, *Fifteen Years after Hong Kong's Handover: Is This City Dying?*, *in* EAST ASIA: DEVELOPMENTS AND CHALLENGES 165, 178 (Yongnian Zheng & Fook Lye Liang eds., 2013).

[232] Democratic Republic of the Congo v. F.G. Hemisphere (2011) 14 H.K.C.F.A.R. 95 (H.K.C.F.A.).

[233] The first TUI decision in which a dissent was recorded was Case No. 14/2010 (T.U.I.M.): Jorge Godinho & Paulo Cardinal, *Macau's Court of Final Appeal*, *in* HONG KONG'S COURT OF FINAL APPEAL: THE DEVELOPMENT OF THE LAW IN CHINA'S HONG KONG 608, 617 (Simon N.M. Young & Yash Gahi eds., 2014).

CFA.[234] It is therefore difficult to argue that overseas judges have been the vanguard defending Hong Kong's rule of law or high degree of autonomy.[235]

Constitutional Review in the United Kingdom and Portugal

If the legal origins hypothesis had any predictive power over actual cases in Hong Kong and Macau, we would expect to find entrenched high-energy constitutional review as much in the United Kingdom as in Hong Kong, but no established system of constitutional review in Portugal any more than in Macau. The opposite, in fact, is true. Historically, a "strong intellectual tradition" in the United Kingdom rejects empowering the courts under the pretext of protecting human rights.[236] The most characteristic statement of this position was offered by Oxford constitutional theorist Albert Venn Dicey (1835–1922), the nineteenth-century successor to Blackstone as Vinerian Professor of English Law:

> [T]hat Parliament has, under the English constitution, the right to make or unmake any law whatever; and, further, that no person or body is recognised by the law of England as having a right to override or set aside the legislation of Parliament.[237]

This is the doctrine of parliamentary sovereignty, under which the role of judges is to interpret and apply, rather than review, an Act passed by Parliament.[238] Unconstrained by any canonical constitutional instrument and constitutional review, Parliament was able swiftly to pass statutes that

234 One empirical study of CFA judgments (1997–2010) indicated that the vast majority of judgments were unanimously decided without dissent or concurrence (95.7 percent): Jill Cottrell & Yash Ghai, *Concurring and Dissenting in the Hong Kong Court of Final Appeal*, *in* Hong Kong's Court of Final Appeal: The Development of the Law in China's Hong Kong 283, 298 (Simon N.M. Young & Yash Ghai eds., 2014).

235 Danny Gittings, Introduction to the Hong Kong Basic Law 195 (2d ed. 2016); N. Balakrishnan, *Hong Kong's Rule of Law Depends on People's Values, Not Foreign Judges*, South China Morning Post, Mar. 22, 2017, www.scmp.com/comment/insight-opinion/article/2080831/hong-kongs-rule-law-depends-peoples-values-not-foreign ("Hong Kong people queue up and support freedom of speech because they have been schooled in it for many years and not because of some foreign judges sitting in the Court of Final Appeal. Hong Kong's rule of law and its freedoms will rise or fall depending on the attitudes of society at large, and foreign judges are only bit players in that drama.")

236 Aileen Kavanagh, Constitutional Review under the UK Human Rights Act 3 (2009).

237 Albert Venn Dicey, Introduction to the Study of the Law of the Constitution 37–38 (8th ed. 1982 [1915]).

238 Fiona Cownie et al., English Legal System in Context 101 (6th ed. 2013).

have stirred controversy from the standpoint of individual rights, such as the Public Order Act 1936 or the Criminal Justice and Public Order Act 1994, as well as successive Prevention of Terrorism Acts from 1974 onwards.[239] The English courts not only lack power to review Acts of Parliament; even judicial review of administrative action prior to the 1960s has been described as "superficial."[240] Only since then have the courts asserted themselves more in this connection.[241] But even this development of public law was not motivated by the protection of rights, but was chiefly concerned with holding public officials to account on behalf of Parliament.[242] The courts were nonetheless powerless to check the rather poor state of civil rights affairs during the 1980s.[243] Constitutional review of any kind did not exist in the United Kingdom until the passage of the Human Rights Act 1998, after the Chinese had resumed sovereignty over Hong Kong. In sum, throughout the entire history of British Hong Kong, the United Kingdom never had any cognizable tradition of constitutional review. Few, if any, precedents were available to the Hong Kong courts from the Appellate Committee of the House of Lords that could have guided the constitutional review of legislative and administrative acts in the light of a canonical constitution.[244] Even the form of review that was permitted by the Human Rights Act is weaker than in the aforementioned civil law countries, in that courts may not strike down primary legislation, but only alert Parliament in a "declaration of incompatibility" issued against impugned provisions for contradicting the European Convention on Human Rights.[245] Parliament conserves all power to legislate in spite of the Convention under the Human Rights Act provided only that it is explicit about doing so.[246] Section 4(6)(a) and (b) of the Act affirms that any

239 Martin Loughlin, The British Constitution: A Very Short Introduction 93 (2013).

240 Adam Tomkins, Public Law 171 (2003).

241 Eric C. Ip, *Taking a "Hard Look" at "Irrationality": Substantive Review of Administrative Discretion in the US and UK Supreme Courts*, 34(3) Oxford J. Legal Stud. 481, 491 (2014); *see* Eric C. Ip, *Doctrinal Antithesis in Anglo-American Administrative Law*, 22(1) Sup. Ct Econ. Rev. 147 (2015).

242 Tom Hickman, Public Law after the Human Rights Act 13 (2010).

243 Keith D. Ewing & Conor A. Gearty, Freedom under Thatcher: Civil Liberties in Modern Britain 77–78 (1990).

244 Michael C. Davis, Constitutional Confrontation in Hong Kong: Issues and Implications of the Basic Law 61 (1990).

245 Ginsburg & Versteeg, *supra* note 12, at 600.

246 Cownie et al., *supra* note 237, at 116; see Eric C. Ip, *The Judicial Review of Legislation in the United Kingdom*, 37(2) Eur. J. L. & Econ. 221 (2014); Eric C. Ip, *The Institutional Foundations of Supreme Court Power in Britain's Representative Democracy*, 49(3) Representation: J. Representative Democracy 281 (2013).

incompatibility denounced by courts shall "not affect the validity, continuing operation or enforcement of the provision in respect of which it is given; and is not binding on the parties to the proceedings in which it is made." At present, more than two decades after the departure of Hong Kong from the British Crown, ultimate constitutional authority lies utterly in the hands of Parliament.[247]

By contrast, modern Portugal has a vibrant history of constitutional review.[248] In 1911, it became the first European country to establish judicial review of legislation on the basis of a written constitutional instrument.[249] At the dawn of the Macau Handover, Portugal already possessed perhaps the most comprehensive and sophisticated system of constitutional review that could ever exist in any jurisdiction,[250] combining centralized review by a specialized court, the Tribunal Constitucional, an arrangement clearly inspired by the best practices in leading Continental European legal systems such as France and Germany,[251] with decentralized review at all levels of the ordinary courts; akin to the robust kind of constitutional review which exists in common law states like the United States and Australia.[252] Portugal has a long history of canonical constitutions dating back to 1822. The current Constitution of Portugal, first ratified in 1976, was heavily influenced by the Universal Declaration of Human Rights and by the European Convention on Human Rights.[253] At 296 articles it is doubtlessly "very long and detailed."[254] Article 277(1) unequivocally asseverates the principle of constitutional supremacy: "Rules that contravene any of the provisions of this Constitution or the principles enshrined therein shall be unconstitutional."

[247] Colm O'Cinneide, *Human Rights and the UK Constitution*, *in* The Changing Constitution 67, 68 (Jeffrey Jowell et al. eds., 8th ed. 2015).

[248] Judith R. Krebs, *One Country, Three Systems? Judicial Review in Macau after* Ng Ka Ling, 10 (1) Pac. Rim L. & Pol'y J. 111, 138 (2000).

[249] Antonio Cortes & Teresa Violante, *Concrete Control of Constitutionality in Portugal: A Means towards Effective Protection of Fundamental Rights*, 29(4) Pa. St. Int'l L. Rev. 759, 761 (2011).

[250] *Id.* at 760.

[251] António Goucha Soares, *Portugal: An Incomplete Europeanization*, *in* Portugal in the Twenty-First Century 121, 132 (Sebastián Royo ed., 2012).

[252] Sofia Amaral-Garcia et al., *Judicial Independence and Party Politics in the Kelsenian Constitutional Court: The Case of Portugal*, 6(2) J. Empirical Legal Stud. 381, 385 (2009).

[253] Vitalino Canas, *The General Regime of Fundamental Rights in the Basic Law and in the International Instruments*, *in* One Country, Two Systems, Three Legal Orders – Perspectives of Evolution: Essays on Macau's Autonomy after the Resumption of Sovereignty by China 672 (Jorge Oliveira & Paulo Cardinal eds., 2009).

[254] Amaral-Garcia et al., *supra* note 252, at 384.

Consider the thirteen-member Tribunal Constitucional, which has prominent status under the Constitution. Established by Article 221 as "the court with specific responsibility for administering justice in matters of a legal and constitutional nature," it is capable of invalidating unconstitutional norms retrospectively, but also revalidating constitutionally compatible norms abrogated by unconstitutional ones.[255] None of the Tribunal decisions can be appealed further, not even to the parliament: the Assembleia da República.[256] The Tribunal was endowed not only with the standard concrete, abstract, and preemptive review powers typically found in European constitutional courts, but even the competence to strike down legislation or official acts for "unconstitutionality by omission";[257] to resolve electoral disputes and interbranch conflicts, cases concerning referenda, and the regulation of political parties.[258] Portugal's Tribunal Constitucional in fine enjoys powers possessed by no court in England or Wales, not even the Supreme Court of the United Kingdom: first and foremost, the power to excise unconstitutional legislation from the legal system once for all with *erga omnes* effect.[259] What is more, the Tribunal's judgments have proved to be consequential.[260] Amendments are routinely made to national laws in the aftermath of Tribunal Constitucional decisions;[261] even powerful parties tend to respect and comply with them.[262] While Macau was still a Portuguese dependency, the Tribunal was already reviewing important legislation enacted by sizeable parliamentary majorities, sometimes at the behest of the President; including anti-corruption laws and the Official Secrets Act 1993.[263] More recently, the Tribunal Constitucional scrutinized the constitutionality of Portugal's austerity policy infrastructure as demanded by the "troika" of leading bailout creditors, namely the European Union, the European Central Bank, and the International Monetary Fund, and invalidated austerity measures that would have enabled government layoffs, for breaching guarantees for public-

255 Jorge Bacelar Gouveia, Constitutional Law in Portugal 130 (2d ed., 2015).

256 Cortes & Violante, *supra* note 249, at 761.

257 Gouveia, *supra* note 255, at 130.

258 *Id.*

259 Joaquim de Sousa Ribeiro & Esperança Mealha, *Portugal: Constitutional Courts as Positive Legislators*, *in* Constitutional Courts as Positive Legislators: A Comparative Law Study 721, 724 (Allan R. Brewer-Carías ed., 2011).

260 *Id.* at 730.

261 *Id.* at 733.

262 Amaral-Garcia et al., *supra* note 252, at 387.

263 Octavio Amorim Neto & Marina Costa Lobo, *Portugal's Semi-Presidentialism (Re) Considered: An Assessment of the President's Role in the Policy Process, 1976–2006*, *in* Portugal in the Twenty-First Century 49, 61 (Sebastián Royo ed., 2012).

sector employment.[264] Portuguese legal scholar Jorge Bacelar Gouveia has remarked:

> Nowadays more than ever, to study and examine the rulings of the Constitutional Court, as well as those of the other courts (albeit less relevant), for many reasons, the least of which is not that they have been entrusted with the task of filling in, through their intervention within the margin left to subconstitutional power, many spaces the Constitution has not occupied.[265]

Notably, the Tribunal Constitucional does not exhaust constitutional review in Portugal. Article 204 of the Constitution provides, "in matters brought before them for decision, the courts shall not apply any rules that contravene the provisions of this Constitution or the principles contained there."[266] Closely resembling American-style decentralized judicial review, every Portuguese court may be regarded in the light of a constitutional court competent to disapply legislation on grounds of unconstitutionality.[267], [268] And the Supreme Court of Justice and Supreme Administrative Court's constitutional decisions enjoy considerable persuasive weight in the eyes of the lower courts. Importantly, these courts routinely override the legislature,[269] which consigns to the dustbin of legal history the stigmatization of civil law courts by the legal origins hypothesis as mere uncreative civil service automatons.

Constitutional Review in British Hong Kong and Portuguese Macau

Contrary, once again, to the predictions of the legal origins hypothesis, judicial review of legislation and administrative acts on human rights grounds did not exist for 150 out of 156 years (96.2 percent) of British rule in Hong Kong.[270] In stark contrast with Portuguese Macau, the formal constitutional protection of human rights was non-existent for most of British Hong Kong's existence. No principles of fundamental rights or liberties were

264 Evan J. Criddle, Human Rights in Emergencies 257 (2016)

265 Gouveia, *supra* note 255, at 49.

266 Ribeiro & Mealha, *supra* note 259, at 721.

267 Cortes & Teresa Violante, *supra* note 249, at 759–61.

268 Ribeiro & Mealha, *supra* note 259, at 721.

269 Krebs, *supra* note 249, at 128.

270 Albert H.Y. Chen et al., *Constitutional Order under "One Country, Two Systems": A Comparative Study of Constitutional Judicial Review and the Application of the Proportionality Principle in the Courts of the Hong Kong and Macau Special Administrative Regions*, *in* Studies of the Political System of the Hong Kong SAR 185, 194 (Guobin Zhu ed., 2017).

enshrined in the Letters Patent. Constitutional review had nominally existed at least since 1913, when the Full Court said, in *R. v. Ibrahim*,[271] that if the Legislative Council purported to enact any law beyond the scope of the Letters Patent, the courts "would have no hesitation in pronouncing it bad."[272] The Judicial Committee of the Privy Council nonetheless decided in *Reil v. The Queen*[273] that the only constraints on the colonial government was language like "peace, order and good government," which warranted "the utmost discretion of enactment."[274] Recently, the CFA admitted that "until the advent of the Hong Kong Bill of Rights on June 8, 1991 there was little real scope for the exercise in Hong Kong of the judicial power of constitutional review by which legislation incompatible with the constitution is struck down."[275]

Successive Governors fended off calls for a statutory bill of rights until the last decade of British rule.[276] As mentioned above, only in 1991 did Whitehall pressure the Government under Governor David Wilson to pass one in response to the urgent, unprecedented calls from local and international stakeholders for rights protection in the face of the 1989 Tiananmen Square crackdown. Recollect that the doctrine of parliamentary sovereignty, loyally upheld by the British Hong Kong courts, forbade England's own courts to strike down an Act of Parliament. Even after enactment of the Hong Kong Bill of Rights Ordinance,[277] most British Hong Kong judges, including several future CFA judges, apparently felt uneasy about exercising powers that their more prestigious counterparts in the United Kingdom had never enjoyed.[278] Most competent at commercial adjudication, like the courts of Singapore, the British Hong Kong judiciary played but a marginal role in constitutional governance.[279] The few constitutional decisions rendered by them at the dawn of the Handover made

[271] R v. Ibrahim (1913) 8 H.K.L.R. 1 (H.K.F.C.).

[272] R v. Ibrahim (1913) 8 H.K.L.R. 1, at 18 (H.K.F.C.).

[273] Reil v. The Queen (1885) 10 App. Cas. 675, at 678 (U.K.P.C.).

[274] A v. Commissioner of Independent Commission (2012) 15 H.K.C.F.A.R. 362, at 381 (H.K.C.F.A.).

[275] A v. Commissioner of Independent Commission (2012) 15 H.K.C.F.A.R. 362, at 381 (H.K.C.F.A.).

[276] *See* Nihal Jayawickrama, *Human Rights in the Draft Basic Law – A Critique*, 18 HONG KONG L. J. 370 (1988).

[277] Hong Kong Bill of Rights Ordinance (1990) Cap. 383 (Hong Kong).

[278] *See* Andrew Byrnes, *And Some Have Bills of Rights Thrust upon Them: The Experience of Hong Kong's Bill of Rights*, *in* PROMOTING HUMAN RIGHTS THROUGH BILLS OF RIGHTS 318 (Philip Alston ed., 2000).

[279] *See* Yash Ghai, *The Past and the Future of Hong Kong's Constitution*, 128 CHINA Q. 794 (1991).

"very little impact."[280] Overall, in a century and a half, the colonial judiciary was consistently deferential to the Governor and his Government.[281]

The colonial constitution of Portuguese Macau provided for civil rights, at least since the Carnation Revolution of 1974, far better than the Letters Patent, and the judges of British Hong Kong were never more activist than those of Macau. Article 2 of the Estatuto Orgânico de Macau 1976 (Organic Statute of Macau) expressly referred to the rights and privileges of the Portuguese Constitution as obligatory limits on legislation enacted by the Legislative Assembly of Macau.[282] Article 41 of the Estatuto provided that the courts of Macau ought to disapply any norms inconsistent with the Portuguese Constitution, the Estatuto itself, or principles established by them.[283] Under Portugal's dual track system of constitutional review, marrying a "Kelsenian" constitutional court with American-style decentralized review, which offers litigants multiple avenues for challenging the constitutionality of laws,[284] Macau's courts were entitled to review the constitutionality of both legislation and executive decrees, and their decisions could be appealed to the Tribunal Constitucional in Lisbon.[285] In 1995, just four years before the Handover, the Tribunal Constitucional, in an internationally consequential judgment that showcased Portugal's commitment to constitutional review and human rights,[286] overruled a controversial decision of Macau's Tribunal Superior de Justiça to extradite two ethnic Chinese prisoners to the People's Republic of China for crimes punishable by death,[287] holding it to be a violation of the prohibition on extradition to face the death penalty in Article 33 of the Portuguese Constitution.[288]

Portugal's juridical legacy continues to embolden the lower levels of the Macau SAR judiciary. As the intermediate appellate court since the Handover, the Tribunal de Segunda Instância (TSI) has been far more receptive than the TUI to rights adjudication and constitutional review, and has in fact defied the government, repeatedly. In *Case 166/2003*,[289] for

280 *See* Kevin Zervos, *Constitutional Remedies under the Basic Law*, 40 HONG KONG L. J. 687 (2010).
281 LAU, *supra* note 27, at 114.
282 Krebs, *supra* note 248, at 134.
283 Chen et al., *supra* note 270, at 204.
284 *See* Chris Hanretty, *Dissent in Iberia: The Ideal Points of Justices on the Spanish and Portuguese Constitutional Tribunals*, 51 EUR. J. POL. RESEARCH 671 (2012).
285 U.S. Department of State, *Macau*, 19 ANN. HUM. RTS. REP. SUBMITTED TO CONG. 922, 924–26 (1994).
286 Krebs, *supra* note 248, at 135–136.
287 U.S. Department of State, *supra* note 282, at 923.
288 Krebs, *supra* note 248, at 135.
289 Case 166/2003 (T.S.I.M.).

example, it used a more activist version of proportionality review to determine the permissible limits to fundamental rights and liberties.[290] And in *Case 280/2005*[291] it struck down Decree Law 17/2004,[292] which had criminalized illegal employment, for inconsistency with primary legislation, the Illegal Immigrant Law and the Civil Code. Premising itself on the principles of democracy, the rule of law, and the separation of powers, it ruled that its "refusal to apply illegal laws is an unquestionable obligation in the exercise of judicial power";[293] that "the Legislative Assembly of the Macao Special Administrative Region, as the sole legislative organ of the Macao Special Administrative Region, enjoys an exclusivist power over local legislative affairs";[294] and that "the Chief Executive does not possess lawmaking powers"[295] independent of the Assembly; and that a Decree "only evidences the government's administrative management powers, rather than the scope of its lawmaking competence; administrative regulations must not contradict the Basic Law as well as primary legislation made by the Legislative Assembly."[296] The significance of this case lies in its unequivocal declaration that post-Handover Decree Laws issued by the Chief Executive no longer command the status of those of the colonial Governors that were equal to laws enacted by the Legislative Assembly.[297] The majority also rejected the dissenting view that the Lei Básica ought to be interpreted according to mainland legal principles.[298]

Predictably, on July 18, 2007 in *Case 28/2006*,[299] the TUI reversed the TSI's ruling in *Case 280/2005*,[300] and reinstated the Decree Law, holding that prior authorization by the Legislative Assembly is not necessary before the Chief

290 Paulo Cardinal, *A Panoramic View on Fundamental Rights in Macau: From Territory under Portuguese Administration to Special Administrative Region of the P.R. China*, *in* Studies on Macau Civil, Commercial, Constitutional and Criminal Law 1, 26 (Jorge A.F. Godinho ed., 2010).

291 Case 280/2005 (T.S.I.M.).

292 Decree Law 17/2004 (Macau).

293 Case 280/2005, at 4 (T.S.I.M.).

294 Case 280/2005, at 9 (T.S.I.M.).

295 Case 280/2005, at 9 (T.S.I.M.).

296 Case 280/2005, at 9 (T.S.I.M.).

297 Paulo Cardinal, *Macau: Transformation of an Historic Autonomy*, *in* Practising Self-Government: A Comparative Study of Autonomous Regions 383, 403 (Yash Ghai & Sophia Woodman eds., 2013).

298 Denis de Castro Halis, *"Post-Colonial" Legal Interpretation in Macau, China: Between European and Chinese Influences*, *in* East Asia's Renewed Respect for the Rule of Law in the 21st Century: The Future of Legal and Juridical Landscapes in East Asia 68, 81 (Setsuo Miyazawa et al. eds., 2015).

299 Case 28/2006 (T.U.I.M.).

300 Case 280/2005 (T.S.I.M.).

Executive can make Decree Laws.[301] Notably, Judge Lima, for the TUI, emphasized that "in deciding this case, we must take into consideration the norms, theories, and experiences of the interaction between administrative regulations and laws in the Constitution of China."[302] This led the Tribunal to conclude that "it is impossible to derive from any provision of the Lei Básica a rule that forbids administrative regulations from imposing obligations and restrictions on individuals"; that "insofar as the relevant matter has not been reserved for the laws of the Legislative Assembly, nothing can prevent administrative regulations from imposing obligations and restrictions on individuals."[303] This line of reasoning was harshly criticized by the TSI in *Case 223/2005(II)*,[304] handed down on December 13, 2007. Judge Chan Kuong Seng for the TSI opined that the TUI judgment, in practically constitutionalizing Decree Laws as a separate source of law, had "substantially altered the distribution of powers and checks and balances between the Legislative Assembly and the Chief Executive provided by the Lei Básica."[305] The TSI also cautioned against the TUI's uninhibited use of mainland Chinese analogues in interpreting the Lei Básica: "given that the Legislation Law that is currently implemented in mainland China has no effect in Macau, it appears to be groundless to invoke the provisions of that Law to justify the view that the Chief Executive of the Macau Special Administrative Region has the power to make administrative regulations independently [from the Legislative Assembly]."[306] The TSI posed the following rhetorical question that evidenced its commitment to the rule of law: given that "anything not expressly permitted by law is forbidden to public authorities . . . [who also] are prohibited from acting on the logic of 'anything not expressly forbidden by law is permitted'; [and yet] anything not expressly forbidden by law is indeed permitted to the community-at-large [given this asymmetric] logic of public power emanating from the principle of the rule of law, how is it possible [for the TUI] to derive the conclusion that the Chief Executive may independently issue administrative regulations from the observation that the Lei Básica has not expressly forbidden administrative regulations that impose obligations or restrictions on individuals?"[307]

301 Yu, *supra* note 148, at 62.
302 Case 28/2006, at 103 (T.U.I.M.) (Lima, J.).
303 Case 28/2006, at 108 (T.U.I.M.) (Lima, J.).
304 Case 223/2005(II) (T.S.I.M.) (Chan, J.).
305 Case 223/2005(II), at 64 (T.S.I.M.) (Chan, J.).
306 Case 223/2005(II), at 66 (T.S.I.M.) (Chan, J.).
307 Case 223/2005(II), at 67 (T.S.I.M.) (Chan, J.).

Such assertiveness in the second-highest court of the Macau SAR dispels any idea that low-energy constitutional review necessarily prevails across the judiciary of the former Portuguese dependency. It is likely that the TUI's revealed preference for strategic restraint does not stem from its unhindered attitudinal preferences, which might be as rights-receptive and assertive as the TSI, but rather that, to survive under a credible threat of retaliation, the TUI felt constrained to a minimalist approach; especially because an apex court is more exposed than lower courts to political retaliation. Ironically, history suggests that the TUI has gone too far in defending the Chief Executive's prerogatives. On July 27, 2009 the Legislative Assembly enacted the Regime Jurídico de Enquadramento das Fontes Normativas Internas (Juridical Framework for the Formulation of Internal Norms)[308] in order to determine the exact relationship between primary legislation and administrative regulations. Chiming more with the TSI's stand, the Juridical Framework affirms that the Legislative Assembly's statutes prevail over inconsistent administrative regulations of the Chief Executive;[309] and reserves a long list of important policy domains[310] that may be regulated only by primary legislation, not Decree Laws.[311]

CONCLUSION

This book has used the "most similar cases" research design in conducting its inference-oriented and controlled constitutional review comparison between

308 Juridical Framework for the Formulation of Internal Norms, Law 13/2009 (Macau) [hereinafter Juridical Framework].

309 Juridical Framework, s. 3(2).

310 Juridical Framework, s. 6 ("(1) fundamental rights and liberties and the legal system guaranteed by the Lei Básica and other legal provisions; (2) qualifications of Macao Residents; (3) residency system of Macao; (4) voter registration and electoral system; (5) provision of criminal offence, light offence, criminal punishment, security penalty, and related premises; (6) provision of general system for administrative illegal behavior, related procedure, and penalty, but without prejudice to provisions in s. 7(1)(6); (7) rules of procedure of Members of the Legislative Assembly; (8) auxiliary organizations of the Legislative Assembly, and the legal system on their operation and personnel; (9) Civil Code and Commercial Code; (10) Administrative Procedure Code; (11) systems for civil litigation, criminal litigation, administrative litigation and arbitration systems; (12) Registration Code and Notary Code; (13) normative documents and other documentary forms that ought to be promulgated; (14) fundamental systems for public administration personnel; (17) legal system on currency, finance, and external trade activities; (18) property right system, and systems for public confiscation and eminent domain; (19) other items authorized to the legislative jurisdiction of the Legislative Assembly by the Lei Básica.")

311 Wang Tao, *Rule of Law in SAR Macao since its Return to China*, 5 CHINA LEGAL DEV. Y. B. 119, 125 (2011).

the apex courts of the Hong Kong and Macau Special Administrative Regions. The logic of this research design compares and contrasts cases that share overall similarities on all variables that are not critical to the research question, but exhibits variance in the values of the crucial independent and dependent variables. As an approach to controlling variables that are peripheral to the investigation, most similar cases research "isolates" the significance of variance on the key independent variable in determining the variance on the dependent variable, so finessing the impossibility or undesirability of statistical or experimental control.[312] This chapter adduced empirical evidence to substantiate the explanations offered by the transaction cost theory of hybrid constitutionalism that the Hong Kong apex court's constant high-energy constitutional review diverged from the Macau apex court's constant low-energy constitutional review not so much because of the dividedness of government, but because of the differing political transaction cost structures confronting the Hong Kong and Macau hybrid regimes. In Hong Kong the Chief Executive's legitimacy has always been "extremely vulnerable," and the Government and the Establishment parties inside the Legislative Council distrust each other.[313] By contrast, the powerful Chief Executive of Macau and the unassertive Legislative Assembly have nearly always had an enormously harmonious relationship. What is more, contrary to Beijing's preferences, the Hong Kong Establishment Coalition has openly split twice in the Chief Executive selection in 2012 and 2017. Nothing close has never happened to Macau's Establishment.

It is argued that the state of affairs in Hong Kong stems from the high transaction costs to the regime of overcoming staunch external resistance, and of coping with its own ongoing internal factionalism and incohesion, in order to rein in the CFA and to suppress demand for judicial review. It is therefore the CFA's common law constitutionalism, underpinning, and transcending all cases of constitutional litigation in Hong Kong, which has been shaping the meaning and meaningfulness of the Basic Law in the minds of millions of residents of the SAR, making of it a morally, not just legally, binding document.[314] It is the far lower transaction cost structure within which the Macau Establishment pursues its controversial constitutional and statutory options, witnessed by its relative popularity and decisiveness, that furnishes its

[312] Ran Hirschl, *On the Blurred Methodological Matrix of Comparative Constitutional Law*, *in* THE MIGRATION OF CONSTITUTIONAL IDEAS 39, 48 (Sujit Choudhry ed. 2006).

[313] Jermain T.M. Lam, *After Ten Years of Transfer of Sovereignty: Political Stability and Reforms in Hong Kong*, 10(2) NEW ZEALAND J. ASIAN STUD. 21, 23 (2008).

[314] Eric C. Ip, *The Politics of Constitutional Common Law in Hong Kong under Chinese Sovereignty*, 25(3) WASHINGTON INT'L L. J. 565, 594 (2016).

political will to forestall any tendency of the TUI toward self-aggrandizement. The lack of external friction or popular resistance to the regime has shut the Tribunal out of any real opportunity to question the policy choices of decision-makers. Finally, so as to reduce the risks of confirmation bias in the present research, this chapter has scrutinized the legal origins hypothesis as an alternative explanation of the divergence between the CFA and TUI. It demonstrated that, contrary to intuition, the common/civil law difference between Hong Kong and Macau is not a theoretically decisive variable; nor does it have any special bearing on the behavior of constitutional courts around the world.

6

Epilogue

The Transaction Cost Politics of Hybrid Constitutionalism

INTRODUCTION

Since the end of the Cold War, the number of authoritarian regimes caparisoned in the splendor of institutions that characterize liberal democracy, such as popular elections and multiparty legislatures, has been continually on the rise.[1] Courts vested with some semblance of constitutional review authority have been set up by these hybrid regimes to stake a credible claim to the mantle of democracy;[2] to restrain majoritarian institutions, both national and subnational; and to protect property rights the better to foster economic development;[3] and in other ways too meaningful to be dismissed as "facile caricatures of telephone justice."[4] The concept of "hybrid constitutionalism" as used herein seeks to capture the unenviable task of a constitutional court, which, broadly, is to mediate the essential tensions between the liberal democratic ideals and the authoritarian realities underlying any hybrid regime. This book selected as its core case studies the development of hybrid constitutionalism in the Chinese Special Administrative Regions (SARs) of Hong Kong and Macau, former West European colonies, now cosmopolitan and

[1] Grigorii V. Golosov, *Why and How Electoral Systems Matter in Autocracies*, 51(3) Australian J. Pol. Sci. 367, 367 (2016); Dawn Brancati, *Democratic Authoritarianism: Origins and Effects*, 17 Annu. Rev. Polit. Sci. 313, 314 (2014); Jeremy Wallace, *Cities, Redistribution, and Authoritarian Regime Survival*, 75(3) J. Pol. 632, 639 (2013); Joseph Wright & Abel Escribà-Folch, *Authoritarian Institutions and Regime Survival: Transitions to Democracy and Subsequent Autocracy*, 42(2) British J. Pol. Sci. 283, 284 (2012).

[2] Rachel E. Brown, The Achilles Heel of Democracy: Judicial Autonomy and the Rule of Law in Central America 222–25 (2017).

[3] Tom Ginsburg, *Judicial Independence in East Asia: Lessons for China*, *in* Judicial Independence in China: Lessons for Global Rule of Law Promotion 247, 249 (Randall Peerenboom ed., 2010).

[4] Tamir Moustafa, *Law and Courts in Authoritarian Regimes*, 10 Annu. Rev. Law Soc. Sci. 281, 294 (2014).

economically prosperous, whose Basic Laws, ratified by the National People's Congress of the People's Republic of China shortly before and shortly after the dissolution of the Soviet Union, set up "de facto self-regulated"[5] subnational liberal authoritarian regimes enjoying "a high degree of autonomy,"[6] which were supposed to govern until the middle of the twenty-first century, if not beyond. In so doing, this book has contributed substantially to several academic literatures: to those on comparative constitutional law, especially subnational constitutional law; comparative Asian law; and Chinese law and politics.

The Hong Kong and Macau SARs provide ideal natural laboratories to examine the political dynamics of constitutional review under hybrid regimes. They are "most similar" cases, nearly identical in nearly all independent variables that are not central to the inquiry. Being only sixty kilometers apart from each other by sea,[7] and overseen by the same authoritarian party-state globally known for its antipathy to liberal constitutionalism,[8] the two Chinese SARs have a great deal in common in terms of history, ethnicity, language, culture, and demographics.[9] As was thoroughly explained in Chapter 3, the political systems set up by the Hong Kong Basic Law and the Lei Básica de Macau are undoubtedly hybrid by design, as evidenced by elaborate guarantees of individual freedoms, judicial independence, and official accountability, yet combined with corporatism and the want of universal suffrage in the selection of the Chief Executives and the majority of seats in the Legislative

5 Weiqing Song, *A Special Regional Actor in the World: Conceptualising Macao's Diplomatic Behaviour*, 13(3) CHINA: AN INT'L J. 154, 154 (2015).

6 Basic Law of the Hong Kong Special Administrative Region of the People's Republic of China (adopted at the Third Session of the Seventh National People's Congress on Apr. 4, 1990, effective on Jul. 1, 1997) [hereinafter "Basic Law"], art. 2; Lei Básica da Região Administrativa Especial de Macau da República Popular da China (Basic Law of the Macao Special Administrative Region of the People's Republic of China) (Adopted by the First Session of the Eighth National People's Congress on Mar. 31, 1993, effective Dec. 20, 1999) [hereinafter "Lei Básica"], art. 2.

7 In November 2017, a bridge connecting Hong Kong and Macau, known as the Hongkong-Zhuhai-Macau Bridge, was completed. This was to be accompanied by mainland China's proactive attempts to economically integrate the two Special Administrative Regions and their neighboring Guangdong Province into a "Pearl Delta Great Bay Area." *See* Chi-yuk Choi et al., Top Beijing Leader Will Take Charge of China's Ambitious Bay Area Integration Plan, SOUTH CHINA MORNING POST, Mar. 28, 2018, www.scmp.com/news/hong-kong/politics/article/2139185/top-beijing-leader-will-take-charge-chinas-ambitious-bay

8 Martin S. Flaherty, *Hong Kong Fifteen Years after the Handover: One Country, Which Direction?*, 51 COLUM. J. TRANSNAT'L L. 275, 276 (2013).

9 *See* Ivan W.H. Funga et al., *A Review on Historic Building Conservation: A Comparison between Hong Kong and Macau Systems*, 71 RENEWABLE & SUSTAINABLE ENERGY REV. 927 (2017).

Council or the Legislative Assembly. The two most westernized societies in East Asia were thereby artificially prevented from participating in the dramatic democratic transition that occurred in Eastern Europe, Latin Africa, and many parts of the British Commonwealth.[10]

Intriguingly, the Lei Básica de Macau "largely copies the Hong Kong Basic Law and ignores Macau's political tradition";[11] both apex courts, the Hong Kong Court of Final Appeal (CFA) and the Tribunal de Última Instância de Macau (TUI), were empowered with identical final adjudicatory powers to the detriment of the Chinese Supreme People's Court,[12] and constitutional interpretive authority second only to the Standing Committee of the National People's Congress in Beijing. And yet each Court's constitutional jurisprudence in the two decades since resumption of Chinese sovereignty could not be more different, as is laid out in Chapter 4. Owing to the CFA's activism, anyone who consults constitutional law in Hong Kong, be they politicians, judges, lawyers, journalists, or activists, must consult not just the Basic Law itself, but the voluminous case law of the CFA, too – like it or not.[13] The ascent of this body of constitutional common law of "exceptionally high quality"[14] is dazzling in light of the Basic Law's undisputed socialist civil law pedigree.[15] The contrast with the TUI is stark: it has minimized its role in judging the compatibility of legislation and administrative acts with the Lei Básica, and avoided invalidating a single statutory provision for any

10 Waikeung Tam, *Do Female Legislators Have Different Policy Priorities Than Their Male Colleagues in an Undemocratic/Semi-democratic Legislature? The Case of Hong Kong*, 23(1) J. LEGIS. STUD. 44, 45 (2017).

11 HERBERT S. YEE, MACAU IN TRANSITION: FROM COLONY TO AUTONOMOUS REGION 30 (2001). Differences between the two constitutions exist nonetheless. The most important is undoubtedly the Basic Law's expressed promises of Chief Executive and Legislative Council elections by universal suffrage at an indefinite date. The absence of such promises in the Lei Básica de Macau has significantly lowered public expectations that the SAR regime is under any positive obligation to phase out appointed members of the Legislative Assembly, let alone introduce substantial political reforms. *See* Francisco Gonçalves Pereira, *Accommodating Diversity: Macau under China's Constitution*, *in* MACAU ON THE THRESHOLD OF THE THIRD MILLENNIUM 101, 116 (Macau Ricci Institute ed., 2001).

12 Eric C. Ip, *The Supreme People's Court and the Political Economy of Judicial Empowerment in Contemporary China*, 24 COLUM. J. ASIAN L. 367, 432–33 (2011).

13 The CFA's high-energy constitutional review has attracted much criticism from mainland Chinese legal circles. For an excellent review of this literature, *see* P.Y. LO, THE JUDICIAL CONSTRUCTION OF HONG KONG'S BASIC LAW: COURTS, POLITICS AND SOCIETY AFTER 1997 185–203 (2014).

14 Yash Ghai, *Themes and Arguments*, *in* HONG KONG'S COURT OF FINAL APPEAL: THE DEVELOPMENT OF THE LAW IN CHINA'S HONG KONG 1, 13 (Simon N.M. Young & Yash Ghai eds., 2014).

15 P.Y. Lo, *Hong Kong: Common Law Courts in China*, *in* ASIAN COURTS IN CONTEXT 183, 223 (Jiunn-Rong Yeh & Wen-Chen Chang eds., 2015).

incompatibility with the constitution. Yet the TUI's entrenched low-energy constitutional review was never an outcome predetermined by the civil law tradition that Macau hailed from; indeed, had it but adopted the modus operandi of the Portuguese Tribunal Constitucional,[16] it would have been reviewing the constitutionality of official acts more expansively, if anything, than its Hong Kong counterpart.[17]

How did such radical variance in the dependent variable – that is, the constitutional jurisprudence of the SAR apex court – come to pass? The CFA's vibrant independence, activism, and defense of the rule of law against unified government and hybrid authoritarianism are particularly puzzling.[18] In comparative constitutional law scholarship, especially the strand that investigates strategic judicial behavior, a great truism is that prolonged control of both executive and legislature by one political group is not conducive to constitutional review.[19] Such an executive, if it moves to curb the courts by legislation, constitutional amendment, or court packing, will encounter no resistance from a legislature controlled by the same group. The mere prospect of such retaliation is often sufficient to deter the court from engaging in activism. On this view, the costs to rulers of reining-in a defiant court tend to be lower in hybrid regimes than in liberal democracies, especially if in hybrids judicial independence and freedom of the press are less institutionalized.[20] Both the Hong Kong Legislative Council and the Macau Legislative Assembly are competent to enact court-curbing subconstitutional measures, such as legislation that regulates the organization and decisional procedures of the courts. More importantly, the Standing Committee of the National People's Congress has power to decree Interpretations or move amendments of the Basic Law and Lei Básica to quash either the

16 *See* Daniele Gallo & Cisotta Roberto, *The Portuguese Constitutional Court Case Law on Austerity Measures: A Reappraisal*, *in* Social Rights in Times of Crisis in the Eurozone: The Role of Fundamental Rights' Challenges 133 (Stefano Civitarese Matteucci & Simon Halliday eds., 2014).

17 Ignazio Castellucci, *Legal Hybridity in Hong Kong and Macau*, 57 McGill L. J. 665, 698 (2012).

18 Agnes Shuk Mei Ku, *From Civil Disobedience to Institutional Politics: Conflict over the Public Order Ordinance in 2000*, *in* Civil Unrest and Governance in Hong Kong: Law and Order from Historical and Cultural Perspectives 163, 164 (Michel H.K. Ng & John D. Wong eds., 2017).

19 *See* Michael A. Bailey & Forrest Maltzman, The Constrained Court: Law, Politics, and the Decisions Justices Make 155 (2011); Lee Epstein & Jack Knight, The Choices Justices Make (1998); Walter Murphy, Elements of Judicial Strategy (1964).

20 Maria Popova, Politicized Justice in Emerging Democracies: A Study of Courts in Russia and Ukraine 169 (2012).

constitutional jurisdiction or jurisprudence staked out by the CFA or the TUI,[21] rendering either Court "as powerless as the citizen who has started the judicial review proceeding."[22] It is a striking fact that the Standing Committee has never denied the constitutional review authority of either Court.[23]

To solve this puzzle, this book proposed a transaction cost theory of hybrid constitutionalism, a remediation of the standard strategic account that educes political transaction costs as pivotal to shaping how a constitutional court will interact with its hybrid regime. "Political transaction cost" means the cost of defining, establishing, maintaining, transferring, and enforcing political agreements, usually in terms of legislation, that emerges from informational uncertainty.[24] The core insight of the transaction cost analysis of politics is that political decision-making, regardless of regime type, is not frictionless and costless, and these costs can significantly affect the substance of policy.[25] Recognizing the weightiness of political transaction costs can, in principle, assist political actors in better choosing, comprehending, and refining the kind of agreements they intend to make with each other.[26] It follows that, regardless of whether a given regime has a unified government or noncompetitive elections, higher political transaction costs, observable in factional infighting and external pressures, translate to lower defiance costs for courts, allowing them to conduct constitutional review more aggressively; and also vice versa. The amount of political transaction costs is inversely proportional to the capacity of the regime to rein in controversial judicial acts. A politically fragmented regime will be burdened by high transaction costs, and is bound to be indecisive about whether and how to react to aggressive judicial review: agreements on constitutional or subconstitutional, ex ante or ex post countermeasures to judicial activism will become exceedingly difficult to achieve. Chapter 2 has corroborated the external validity of this theory by testing its explanatory power in the "most different" cases of Singapore and Turkey, two

[21] Michael C. Davis, *Interpreting Constitutionalism and Democratization in Hong Kong*, *in* INTERPRETING HONG KONG'S BASIC LAW: THE STRUGGLE FOR COHERENCE 90 (Hualing Fu et al. eds., 2007).

[22] *See*, Benny Y.T. Tai, *The Judiciary*, in CONTEMPORARY HONG KONG POLITICS: GOVERNANCE IN THE POST-1997 ERA 72 (Wai-man Lam et al. eds., 2007).

[23] Tahirih V. Lee, *"Apres Moi Le Deluge?" Judicial Review in Hong Kong since Britain Relinquished Sovereignty*, 11 IND. INT'L & COMP. L. REV. 323 (2001).

[24] Anthea Coggan et al., *Influences of Transaction Costs in Environmental Policy*, 69(9) ECOLOGICAL ECON. 1777, 1778 (2010).

[25] Kerry Krutilla & Alexander Alexeev, *The Political Transaction Costs and Uncertainties of Establishing Environmental Rights*, 107 ECOLOGICAL ECON. 299, 307 (2014).

[26] Coggan et al., *supra* note 24, at 1782.

national-level hybrid regimes featuring low and high transaction cost structures, respectively. Accounting for shifts in the regimes' transaction cost calculus enabled reliable prediction of corresponding changes to apex constitutional jurisprudence.

Applying the transaction cost theory of hybrid constitutionalism to the Chinese SARs unveiled that, beneath their constitutions' similarity and the durability of authoritarianism, factional infighting inside Hong Kong's Establishment Coalition and formidable popular resistance to its initiatives have "costed it out" of credibly threatening the CFA, while reinforcing popular demand for its constitutional review of unpopular policies; whereas Macau's Establishment Coalition enjoys exceptional executive–legislative harmony, minimal popular unrest, and very weak pressure to democratize. In Hong Kong, the impasse over democratization[27] perpetuates a political system that is trapped in "continuing friction and conflict."[28] Beijing's hostility to Opposition parties translates to an adversarial relationship between the Chief Executive and the Pan-Democratic Opposition in the Legislative Council.[29] Inurement to a pervasive lack of comity has turned the latter adversarial, with open confrontation superseding the old colonial consensual politics.[30] This should surprise no one, as legislatures with policy objectives distinct from those of the executive may find it in their interest to establish competing centers of legislative power and oversight.[31] Rampant intra-elite conflicts have plunged Hong Kong "into a political quagmire of pervasive public discontent and distrust"[32] and galvanized external resistance to any controversial Government action. "Very damaging divisions" further fragmented the ruling elite in the aftermath of the 2012 Chief Executive election, in which two Establishment candidates bitterly divided the Coalition itself.[33]

27 *See* Kit Poon, *The Impasse over Constitutional Reform: Negotiating Democracy in Hong Kong*, *in* THE IMPASSE OVER CONSTITUTIONAL REFORM: NEGOTIATING DEMOCRACY IN HONG KONG 3 (Brian C.H. Fong & Tai-lok Lui eds., 2017).

28 Toru Kurata, *Support for and Opposition to Democratization in Hong Kong*, 22(1) ASIA-PACIFIC REV. 16, 32 (2015).

29 ELIZA W.Y. LEE ET AL., PUBLIC POLICYMAKING IN HONG KONG: CIVIC ENGAGEMENT AND STATE-SOCIETY RELATIONS IN A SEMI-DEMOCRACY 9 (2013).

30 Jeremiah T.M. Lam, *The Hong Kong Legislative Council: A Friend or an Enemy of Donald Tsang?*, *in* THE SECOND CHIEF EXECUTIVE OF HONG KONG: EVALUATING THE TSANG YEARS 2005–2012 59, 60–64 (Joseph Y.S. Cheng ed., 2013).

31 DAVID EPSTEIN & SHARYN O'HALLORAN, DELEGATING POWERS: A TRANSACTION COST POLITICS APPROACH TO POLICY MAKING UNDER SEPARATE POWERS 243–44 (1999).

32 BRIAN C.H. FONG, HONG KONG'S GOVERNANCE UNDER CHINESE SOVEREIGNTY: THE FAILURE OF THE STATE-BUSINESS ALLIANCE AFTER 1997 233 (2015).

33 Joseph Y.S. Cheng, *The 2012 Chief Executive Election in Hong Kong and the Challenges for the Chinese Authorities*, 5(4) E. ASIAN POL'Y 91, 100 (2013).

The state of affairs may be summarized as follows: "the [Hong Kong] elite cannot provide leadership; the masses cannot effectively engage in political life; and the population as a whole can only defend the status quo."[34] Macau presents a strikingly different political scene. The Chief Executive is backed by a fully complicit Legislative Assembly of Establishment factions.[35] He exercises massive political power, opposed by no viable check or balance, and, according to survey results, most Macau residents are not interested in public affairs in general, let alone in democratization.[36] The sophistication of social media notwithstanding, there is little prospect that a critical number of middle-class residents will mobilize for political change.[37]

Legislative success rates are good, objective indicators of political transaction cost, which is otherwise difficult to quantify. As was discussed in Chapter 5, Macau's Government has so far secured an almost 100 percent success rate, while its Hong Kong counterpart cannot persuade the legislature it dominates (by seats) to enact more than 60 percent of its proposals into law. The capacity of each SAR regime credibly to threaten judges with sanctioning their misadventures can be partially proxied by their ability to get through the legislature a national security law obligated by common Article 23 of the Basic Law and of the Lei Básica. Hong Kong's proposed national security legislation was introduced in the Legislative Council in February 2003; popular discontent with it, and with the SAR regime in general, snowballed into a half-a-million-strong multipartisan demonstration on July 1, 2003. The bill was shelved indefinitely when a member party of the Establishment defected shortly thereafter. As of March 2018, fifteen years later, the Government has yet to suggest another deadline for reintroducing its national security law proposal. Macau was able smoothly and irresistibly to enact the same within four months of the bill first being proposed. This explanation coheres with the general picture of contemporary politics in the Chinese SAR. Beijing has gradually come to see Macau as the role-model of "One China, Two Systems" for Hong Kong and Taiwan,[38] while the Hong Kong community, as evidenced by the outbreak of the Umbrella Revolution of 2014, exhibits a dramatic resentment of what may be politely called China's underdeveloped

[34] Peter W. Preston, The Politics of China-Hong Kong Relations: Living with Distant Masters 106 (2016).

[35] Bill K.P. Chou, *Politics and Social Organisations in Macao: A Historical Institutionalist Analysis*, 13(1) China: An Int'l J. 22, 30 (2015).

[36] Zhidong Hao, Macau: History and Society 48–50 (2011).

[37] Chou, *supra* note 35, at 42.

[38] Meng U. Ieong, *Macao and Hong Kong, Convergence or Divergence? The 2014 Retirement Package Bill Protest and Macao's Governance Crisis*, 57(3) Asian Surv. 504, 519 (2017).

rights regime and bluntly called its Leninist dictatorship. The radical differences in Hong Kong's and Macau's political dynamics have largely been reflected in the constitutional doctrines of the CFA and the TUI. What caused the levels of political transaction costs in Hong Kong and Macau to diverge only after China resumed sovereignty is beyond the scope of this book. Let us avoid the infinite regression (or regression back to the Big Bang, for that matter), that inevitably ensues if no causal explanation can be acceptable absent prior causal explanation, for we would then be obliged to reject all causal explanations, lest we reach an infinity of explanations for each of the earlier phenomena, which needless to say is practically impossible.[39] We should therefore be content to leave the study of the causes of variant transaction cost structures to economists, political scientists, international relations scholars, historians, sociologists, and so on. One potentially fruitful research direction is to inquire if the relative sizes of Hong Kong's and Macau's populations impact the transaction cost structure of either polity.[40] In accordance with strategic analysis in general, this book has taken the preferences of CFA and TUI judges, and Hong Kong and Macau SAR politicians, too, as given, leaving to future empirical research the investigation of whence these actors' preferences came and how they evolved.

It was demonstrated that the legal origins hypothesis, the only serious contender with the transaction cost theory of hybrid constitutionalism, is unable to account for the CFA–TUI constitutional review divergence. The constitutional jurisprudential divide between Hong Kong and Macau is not convincingly explained by differences between the common and civil law traditions from which the CFA and the TUI sprang. First, the variation in the common law and civil law approaches to constitutional interpretation has been exaggerated. In Europe, the purposive or teleological method and structured proportionality doctrine can be found in both common law and civil law jurisdictions. Secondly, constitutional review is no more widespread in the common law than in the civil law world; Commonwealth countries typically conserve some version of parliamentary sovereignty at the expense of judicial supremacy. Thirdly, Portugal, as a result of the Carnation Revolution of 1974, has adopted literally the most powerful system of constitutional review in the world, combining centralized review by a Tribunal Constitucional with decentralized review by ordinary courts; whereas, the United Kingdom did not

[39] Joseph Wayne Smith, Reductionism and Cultural Being: A Philosophical Critique of Sociobiological Reductionism and Physicalist Scientific Unificationism 36 (1984).

[40] Ying-ho Kwong & Mathew Y.H. Wong, *State Size and Democratization in Hybrid Regimes: The Chinese Island Cities of Macau and Hong Kong*, 12(2) Island Stud. J. 113, 117–118 (2017).

adopt even its current weak form of judicial review under the Human Rights Act 1998 until a year after it withdrew from Hong Kong. Fourthly, Macau's intermediate appellate court, the Tribunal de Segunda Instância (TSI), exhibits an activism and jealousy in defense of the SAR's legal autonomy not far removed from that of the CFA, which hints that low-energy constitutional review is not necessarily entrenched in the legal culture of Macau. If the legal origins hypothesis had held true, we should have expected to see the TUI be the activist, and the CFA the deferrer. The opposite proved to be the case, entailing that the legal origins hypothesis must fall before the transaction cost theory of hybrid constitutionalism. Indeed, the constitutional jurisprudence of Macau's TUI and Singapore's Court of Appeal have much more in common with each other than they do with that of Hong Kong's CFA, notwithstanding the supposed consequences of legal origins. It follows that the trajectories of constitutional review in Hong Kong and Macau will converge only if fundamental changes to one or the other polity occur: either there emerges in Hong Kong a strongman Chief Executive, who can suppress factionalism within the Establishment and dismantle public resistance, or else Macau's ruling elite fragments, so that a viable Opposition becomes consolidated. This brings us to the following section, which explores whether, in Xi Jinping's China, creeping authoritarianism in Hong Kong or occasional sparks of civil activism in Macau may invert the prevailing constitutional doctrines of the CFA and the TUI.

HYBRID CONSTITUTIONALISM UNDER XI JINPING

Xi Jinping is widely regarded as China's most powerful leader since Deng Xiaoping.[41] Compared with Hu Jintao, his predecessor as State President, General Secretary of the Party, and Chairman of the Central Military Commission, Xi has been more decisive in stifling dissent and exploiting nationalist propaganda to shore up his party's legitimacy.[42] In fact, the number of arrests and indictments for state security crimes tripled in Xi's first year in office compared with Hu's first year a decade ago.[43] Xi's aggressive anti-corruption campaign, spearheaded by waves of arrests of senior Party and military officials, also showcased his capacity to overcome resistance from

41 Lowell Dittmer, *Xi Jinping's "New Normal": Quo Vadis?*, 22(3) J. CHINESE POL. SCI. 429, 429 (2017).

42 Robert S. Ross & Jo Inge Bekkevold, *New Leaders, Stronger China, Harder Choices*, *in* CHINA IN THE ERA OF XI JINPING 265, 277 (Robert S. Ross & Jo Inge Bekkevold eds., 2016).

43 BRUCE J. DICKSON, THE DICTATOR'S DILEMMA: THE CHINESE COMMUNIST PARTY'S STRATEGY FOR SURVIVAL 39 (2016).

entrenched Party factions and powerful state-owned enterprises.[44] The impact of this campaign on the flow of mainland Chinese cash abroad has been keenly felt by the gaming business in Macau.[45] Xi has clearly moved Chinese governance away from "apparent softness" toward "more undisguised hardness."[46] His tough authoritarian style of government has now reset the broader context of Chinese politics.[47] In March 2018, the National People's Congress ratified an amendment to the Constitution of 1982 to remove term limits on the State Presidency, prompting speculation that Xi would remain paramount leader indefinitely, contrary to the convention that predecessors Jiang Zemin and Hu Jintao abided by.[48] Under these auspices, the State Council released a White Paper asserting that "China's central government has comprehensive jurisdiction over all local administrative regions, including the [Hong Kong SAR],"[49] and that "judges of the courts at different levels, and other judicial personnel, have on their shoulders the responsibility of correctly understanding and implementing the Basic Law, of safeguarding the country's sovereignty, security and development interests, and of ensuring the long-term prosperity and stability of Hong Kong."[50] In his closing speech to the National People's Congress on March 20, 2018, Xi unambiguously asserted authority over the two SARs: "[We will] support Hong Kong and Macau in integrating into the State's development strategies, strengthen the national identity and patriotism of compatriots [in the two SARs], and maintain the long-term prosperity and stability of Hong Kong and Macau."[51] The two SARs would most heavily be affected by Xi's so-called One Belt-One Road Initiative (the Silk Road Economic Belt and Maritime Silk Road Initiative of the

44 Yongnian Zheng & Cuifen Weng, *The Development of China's Formal Political Structures*, *in* China in the Era of Xi Jinping 32, 56 (Robert S. Ross & Jo Inge Bekkevold eds., 2016).

45 Stein Ringen, The Perfect Dictatorship: China in the 21st Century 88 (2016).

46 *Id.* at 174.

47 Peter T.Y. Cheung, *In Beijing's Tightening Grip*, *in* Hong Kong 20 Years after the Handover: Emerging Social and Institutional Fractures after 1997 255, 279 (Brian C.H. Fong & Tai-lok Lui eds., 2018).

48 Chun Han Wong, *Xi Jinping Clear to Rule Indefinitely as China Scraps Presidential Term Limits*, Wall Street Journal, Mar. 11, 2018, www.wsj.com/articles/xi-jinping-clear-to-rule-indefinitely-as-china-scraps-presidential-term-limits-1520757321

49 Information Office of the State Council of the People's Republic of China, The Practice of "One Country, Two Systems" Policy in the Hong Kong Special Administrative Region [1] (2014).

50 *Id.* at [3].

51 Tony Cheung & Kimmy Chung, *Xi Jinping Vows to Strengthen National Identity and Patriotism in Hong Kong and Macau*, South China Morning Post, Mar. 20, 2018, www.scmp.com/news/hong-kong/politics/article/2137990/xi-jinping-vows-strengthen-national-identity-and-patriotism

Twenty-first Century), a grand strategy that seeks to integrate China with Asia, Europe, and Africa.[52]

The Hong Kong SAR

Unprecedented attempts by the Hong Kong SAR to reduce political transaction costs have coincided with Xi's rise to power. Xi had been outspoken in condemning the separation of powers in the SARs even as Vice President under Hu Jintao. On July 8, 2008, he publicly stated that "solidarity and sincere cooperation with the governing team" and "mutual understanding and support amongst the executive, the legislature, and the judiciary" should prevail in the SARs.[53] This line-to-take has since then been rote-repeated by Establishment and mainland Chinese political figures. Most notably, Chief Executive C.Y. Leung and Director of the Liaison Office of the Central People's Government Zhang Xiaoming both asserted in September 2015 that the Chief Executive has a "special," "superior," and "transcendent" legal position above the Government, the Legislative Council, and the judiciary,[54] only to be indirectly rebuked by Chief Justice Geoffrey Ma in a rare public statement making the point that judicial independence and equal justice under the law remain inviolable constitutional principles in the Region.[55] Besides that, Leung reportedly exercised relatively more hostile rhetoric toward judicial intervention.[56]

At all events, throughout Chief Executive Leung's term in office (2012–17), the SAR authorities took unambiguous, concrete steps to re-coordinate and reorganize the splintered Establishment forces.[57] Emerging as the winner of a divisive contest that had vitiated the Establishment,[58] Leung began by

52 Julan Du & Yifei Zhang, *Does One Belt One Road Initiative Promote Chinese Overseas Direct Investment?*, 47 China Econ. Rev. 189, 193 (2018); Kelvin Hiu Fai Kwok, *Antitrust Enforcement and State Restraints at the Mainland China-Hong Kong Interface: The Importance of Bilateral Antitrust Co-operation*, 12(2) Asian J. Comp. L. 335, 338 (2017).

53 Cheung, *supra* note 47, at 262.

54 *Id.* at 263.

55 Tony Cheung et al., *No One Is above the Law, Says Hong Kong's Top Judge in Surprise Rebuke to Leader CY Leung's Defence of His Transcendent Position*, South China Morning Post, Sep. 16, 2015, www.scmp.com/news/hong-kong/politics/article/1858653/hong-kong-leader-cy-leung-makes-fresh-defence-beijing

56 *See* Ying-kit Lai & Christy Leung, *Hong Kong Leader CY Leung Blames Legal Challenges for Transport Infrastructure Project Delays*, South China Morning Post, Oct. 27, 2015, www.scmp.com/news/hong-kong/economy/article/1872668/hong-kong-leader-cy-leung-blames-legal-challenges-transport

57 Cheung, *supra* note 47, at 278.

58 Fong, *supra* note 32, at 261.

passing over traditional professional political and business elites for his personal supporters in appointments to the Executive Council and top state apparatus.[59] Reversing the bottom-up convention of personnel selection for administrative agencies, advisory committees, and statutory authorities, Leung adopted an abrasively top-down, hands-on approach[60] to control governmental organs through promotions and dismissals and reduce friction in the policy process.[61] He reportedly placed his own allies in agencies ranging from the Independent Police Complaints Council and the Airport Authority to the Trade Development Council and the Hong Kong Science and Technology Parks Corporation.[62] He established new agencies to implement an agenda favoring greater integration with mainland China, such as the Consultative Committee on Economic and Trade Co-operation between Hong Kong and the Mainland, the Financial Services Development Council, and the Economic Development Commission.[63] The Liaison Office of the Central People's Government made its presence felt through its activism in shaping election results and criticizing or commenting on Hong Kong affairs.[64] In his purely ceremonial capacity as Chancellor, the Chief Executive made divisive appointments to various university councils, which were interpreted as retaliatory steps against academics and students who were involved in the Umbrella Revolution.[65]

There was an undeniable trend nudging Hong Kong politics away from liberal toward electoral authoritarianism, which relatively neglects individual liberties to concentrate on defeating opposition politicians through elections rigged with a variety of tactics,[66] such as intimidating dissidents, disqualifying candidates and elected parliamentarians, and selectively prosecuting activists, especially those of the Umbrella Revolution.[67] In the 2016 General Election,

59 Gu Yu, Hong Kong's Legislature under China's Sovereignty 1998–2013 227–29 (2015).

60 Eliza W.Y. Lee & Rikkie L.K. Yeung, *The "Principal Officials Accountability System": Its Underdevelopment as a System of Ministerial Government*, 39(2) Asia Pac. J. Pub. Admin. 120, 123 (2017).

61 Yu, *supra* note 59, at 227.

62 *Id.* at 228.

63 *Id.*

64 Kin Ming Kwong & Chiew Ping Yew, *Hong Kong Politics: Weak Leadership, Frustrated Society and Prospect*, 5(1) E. Asian Pol'y 55, 56 (2013).

65 Cheung, *supra* note 47, at 276.

66 Brian C.H. Fong, *In-between Liberal Authoritarianism and Electoral Authoritarianism: Hong Kong's Democratization under Chinese Sovereignty, 1997–2016*, 24(4) Democratization 724, 728 (2017).

67 Antony Dapiran, City of Protest: A Recent History of Dissent in Hong Kong 106 (2017).

Returning Officers of the Electoral Affairs Commission, who are supposed to be politically neutral, took the previously unheard-of step of rejecting the candidacies of six applicants on the ground of being sympathetic to pro-independence causes.[68] In spite of the ban, several radical separatists or self-determination activists did contest the General Election and won five seats in the Legislative Council.[69]

On November 7, 2016 the Standing Committee delivered its fifth Interpretation of the Basic Law.[70] It was handed down in the midst of a High Court judicial review proceeding, paradoxically and unprecedentedly initiated by Chief Executive C. Y. Leung and Secretary for Justice Rimsky Yuen SC against Legislative Council President and senior Establishment politician Andrew Leung. The Interpretation directly responded to alleged derogatory acts by Regine Yau and Baggio Leung, two separatists and popularly elected Members of the Legislative Council at their oath-taking ceremonies a month earlier, and addressed the growing trend of irregular oath-taking by Pan-Democratic Opposition Members in general. Based on Article 104 of the Basic Law, the Interpretation mandated the legal novelty of empowering the unidentified "person administering the oath" to disqualify officials, parliamentarians, or judges from office simply if the oath-giver deems, in his sole discretion, that they took their oaths to "bear allegiance to the Hong Kong Special Administrative Region of the People's Republic of China" in some way ambiguously designated "not sincere or not solemn," or if one hears them "intentionally reading out words which do not accord with the wording of the oath prescribed by law."[71] The Interpretation also directs that oath-takers "shall bear legal responsibility" should they "engage in conduct in breach of the oath,"[72] an obligation with considerable political ramifications. Riding high on the tide of the Interpretation, the Chief Executive and the Secretary for Justice applied for judicial review of four more Opposition Members who had taken their oaths irregularly. Before the fifth Interpretation, the convention in the Legislative Council was to view oath-taking as a mere formality.

68 Joyce Ng, *Lawyers Question Power of Returning Officers to Disqualify Hong Kong Poll Candidates*, South China Morning Post, Aug. 3, 2016, www.scmp.com/news/hong-kong/politics/article/1998842/lawyers-question-power-returning-officers-disqualify-hong

69 Ian Scott, *"One Country, Two Systems": The End of a Legitimating Ideology?*, 39(2) Asia Pac. J. Pub. Admin. 83, 87 (2017).

70 Interpretation of Article 104 of the Basic Law of the Hong Kong Special Administrative Region of the People's Republic of China by the Standing Committee of the National People's Congress, 7 November 2016 (adopted by the Twenty-fourth Session of the Standing Committee of the Twelfth National People's Congress on Nov. 7, 2016).

71 *Id.* s.2(4).

72 *Id.* s.3.

Constrained by the Interpretation, the High Court in the end disqualified, with retroactive effect, six Opposition Members altogether, five popularly elected by hundreds of thousands of voters, and one a functional constituency representative.[73] This exposed them to legal claims by the Legislative Council for the remission of salaries and allowances, not to mention harsh litigation fees.[74] The Establishment Coalition instantly seized the historic opportunity catalyzed by this drastic weakening of the Pan-Democratic Opposition to pass amendments to the Legislative Council's Rules of Procedure, which would increase the difficulty of filibustering and of commissioning committees to investigate government malfeasance.[75]

Beijing's anxiety lest Hong Kong's westernized and localist ideas infiltrate into the mainland was reflected in the SAR's decline of press freedom indicators.[76] Hong Kong ranked 18 out of 134 countries in the first World Press Freedom Index launched by Reporters without Borders in 2002; by 2016, it had dropped to 69 out of 179 countries.[77] Earlier, on February 26, 2014, renowned pro-democracy journalist and former editor-in-chief of respected local newspaper MING PAO, Kevin Lau, was critically wounded by an assailant who stabbed him multiple times in Sai Wan Ho, Hong Kong Island.[78] The buyout, in December, 2015, of the SOUTH CHINA MORNING POST, a 113-year-old flagship English-language newspaper by Alibaba Group, the mainland Chinese e-commerce giant, reportedly stirred fears of infiltration of local journalism from higher up.[79] In January 2016, Michael Gui, co-owner of a bookshop in Causeway Bay, Hong Kong Island specializing in banned books on Chinese politics, suspiciously appeared on Party mouthpiece China Central Television (CCTV) confessing that he had killed someone

[73] *See* The Chief Executive of the HKSAR v. Yau Wai Ching [2017] 1 H.K.L.R.D. 460 (H.K.C.A.); Secretary for Justice v. Nathan Law [2017] 4 H.K.L.R.D. 115 (H.K.C.F.I.).

[74] Ying-ho Kwong, *Political Repression in a Sub-national Hybrid Regime: The PRC's Governing Strategies in Hong Kong*, CONTEMP. POL. 1, 13 (2018), www.tandfonline.com/doi/citedby/10.1080/13569775.2017.1423530?scroll=top&needAccess=true

[75] Kimmy Chung, *Legco Approves Rule Book Changes after Dramatic Debate with 11 Pan-dems Booted out of Chamber*, SOUTH CHINA MORNING POST, Dec. 15, 2017, www.scmp.com/news/hong-kong/politics/article/2124467/two-pan-dems-kicked-out-legco-meeting-after-disrupting

[76] Paul S. N. Lee et al., *The Struggle for Hegemony: The Emergence of a Counter-public Sphere in Post-1997 Hong Kong*, 10(4) CHINESE J. COMM. 338, 340 (2017).

[77] Hualing Fu, *Political Protest in High-Income Societies: The Case of the Occupy Central Movement in Hong Kong*, *in* LAW AND POLITICS OF THE TAIWAN SUNFLOWER AND HONG KONG UMBRELLA MOVEMENTS 83, 89 (Brian Christopher Jones ed., 2017).

[78] Stuart Lau, *"My Pelvic Bone Blocked the Knife": Kevin Lau Says His Attacker Showed No Mercy*, SOUTH CHINA MORNING POST, Mar. 10, 2014, www.scmp.com/news/hong-kong/article/1445322/my-waist-bones-blocked-knife-kevin-lau-says-his-attacker-showed-no

[79] Cheung, *supra* note 47, at 266.

in a drunk driving accident over a decade previously; it was also later revealed that the bookshop's other shareholders and staff members had mysteriously disappeared to the mainland.[80]

Relations between the central state and Hong Kong have gradually descended into a "vicious cycle"[81]: the erosion of its commitment to Hong Kong's internationally guaranteed autonomy ignites protest from the community, which in turn leads to still more political interference from the center.[82] The failure of the Umbrella Revolution hinted that Beijing would offer no more concessions to electoral competition in Hong Kong, even in face of unprecedented popular mobilization.[83] Yet, at the same time, the Revolution has given new momentum to youth political activism,[84] as well as the so-called "localism" movement, whose adherents range from the advocates of outright independence from China to those who accept Chinese sovereignty but lobby rather for self-determination.[85] The so-called "Fishball Revolution,"[86] a riot instigated by localist forces in Mongkok on the lunar New Year in 2016, proved that an event as minor as a government crackdown on unlicensed street food sellers, construed by some as the regime's deliberate suppression of a distinct cultural artefact of the Hong Kong identity, could easily explode into a full-blown violent conflict.[87] Localist challenges to the benevolence of China

80 *Id.* at 267.

81 Michael C. Davis, *The Basic Law, Universal Suffrage and the Rule of Law in Hong Kong*, 38(2) Hastings Int'l & Comp. L. Rev. 275, 295 (2015).

82 Ming Sing & Karena Tang, *Mobilization and Conflicts over Hong Kong's Democratic Reform*, *in* Contemporary Hong Kong Government and Politics 137, 147 (Wai-man Lam et al. eds., 2012). *See* Eric C. Ip, *Constitutional Conflict in Hong Kong under Chinese Sovereignty*, 8(1) Hague J. on Rule of Law 75 (2016).

83 Tai Wei Lim & Xiaojuan Ping, Contextualizing Occupy Central in Contemporary Hong Kong 147 (2015).

84 Man Yee Karen Lee, *Lawyers and Hong Kong's Democracy Movement: From Electoral Politics to Civil Disobedience*, 251(1) Asian J. Pol. Sci. 89, 102 (2017).

85 Elaine Chan & Joseph Chan, *Hong Kong 2007–2017: A Backlash in Civil Society*, 39(2) Asia Pac. J. Pub. Admin. 135, 142 (2017).

86 Tai Wei Lim, *"Fishball Revolution" and Hong Kong's Identity, in* Politics, Culture and Identities in East Asia: Integration and Division 35, 35–36 (Lam Peng Er & Lim Tai Wei eds., 2017).

87 Ray Yep, *A Historical Perspective on Hong Kong Autonomy: Traditions of British Imperialism, Maritime Enclave and Contending Views of British Interest, in* Hong Kong 20 Years after the Handover: Emerging Social and Institutional Fractures after 1997 231, 233 (Brian C.H. Fong & Tai-lok Lui eds., 2018); Siu-Yau Lee, *Profit Seeking and Intergroup Conflict in Hong Kong: A Case Study of the Private Health Care Sector*, 56(2) Asian Surv. 348, 350 (2016) ("A typical urban intergroup conflict is usually ignited by a salient appeal to localism, in which existing urban dwellers identify themselves as a community with distinctive cultural and economic characteristics, whereas out-group members are depicted as parasitic, invasive, or both.")

highlight the fact that food and water supplies from the mainland do not come free of charge.[88]

What might Hong Kong's future hold for hybrid constitutionalism in general, and the CFA's constitutional jurisprudence in particular, under Xi Jinping's rulership? The premeditated reduction of external political transaction costs has weakened the liberal aspect of the SAR's liberal authoritarian polity and increasingly succeeded in fracturing the Opposition and societal resistance, but it has yet to mitigate the high internal political transaction costs intrinsic to factional infighting in the Establishment. The Chief Executive remains heavily dependent on Legislative Council support to pass bills, and loyalist Establishment forces have yet to canvass comprehensively the majority support of the electorate or speak with one voice.[89] Leung's successor as Chief Executive, British-groomed veteran Administrative Officer Carrie Lam, has, since taking office in July 2017, distanced herself from the many unconventional and polarizing practices of her immediate predecessor,[90] including aggressive strategies of political transaction cost reduction. The diametrically opposed views of Beijing and the Pan-Democratic Opposition and radical localist groups on democratic reform almost certainly guarantee the protraction of constitutional conflict.[91] As well, the former British dependency remains an open and internationalized jurisdiction that is closely watched by foreign investors and the global community.[92] But it is equally true that to dismantle popular resistance to regime aggression is to expose the Court to greater peril should it intend to go against the wishes of the Government of the day. Electoral reform is one domain that the CFA ideally avoids. Any substantive interpretation of the Basic Law's electoral reform provisions must deeply provoke either the rulers or the ruled, an outcome fraught with the peril of weakening the political foundations of constitutional common law to devastating effect.[93] In the aftermath of the deeply polarizing Umbrella

88 Siu-Keung Cheung, *Reunification through Water and Food: The Other Battle for Lives and Bodies in China's Hong Kong Policy*, 220 China Q. 1012, 1030 (2014).

89 Po Jen Yap, Constitutional Dialogue in Common Law Asia 37 (2015).

90 Kimmy Chung & Jeffie Lam, *New Hong Kong Leader Denies Trying to Shed "CY 2.0" Label by Undoing Leung Policies*, South China Morning Post, Jul. 4, 2017, www.scmp.com/news/hong-kong/politics/article/2101196/hong-kong-leader-carrie-lam-denies-attempts-shed-cy-20-label

91 Michael C. Davis, *Hong Kong's Umbrella Movement: Beijing's Broken Promises*, 26(2) J. Democracy 101, 109 (2015).

92 Tai Wei Lim, *The Future of Hong Kong Governance: The Pro-independence Legislators' Election Fallout and Beijing's Political Voice in Hong Kong*, 4(2) Asia & Pac. Pol'y Stud. 343, 352 (2017).

93 Eric C. Ip, *The Constitution of Economic Liberty in Hong Kong*, 26(3) Const. Pol. Econ. 307, 351 (2015).

Revolution, however, it is uncertain how long the Court can stay aloof from democratization controversies.

The Macau SAR

Just as Hong Kong was undergoing a nascent wave of authoritarianism, Macau was, ironically, witnessing new signs of civic activism and the rise of new factions within the Establishment Coalition. Since 2006, two annual demonstrations have stood out: the Labor Day protest, coordinated by non-Establishment trade unions and youth groups, and the Democratic Rally, organized on the anniversary of the Handover by the New Macau Association, the main faction of the Pro-Democracy Opposition, the latter of which adopted as its rallying cry "Oppose Corruption, Battle for Democracy, Safeguard Livelihood."[94] None of them has ever broken the record-high turnout at the May 1989 protests in favor of the student movement on the eve of the Tiananmen Square crackdown in Beijing, which numbered 170,000 to 200,000 participants.[95] And their political significance was dwarfed by what happened in the year 2014, the same year in which the Umbrella Revolution erupted in Hong Kong, and which proved to be a turbulent one for the former Portuguese dependency as well. In a rare turn of events, two consecutive demonstrations related to constitutional matters broke out during the summer: the "Anti-Welfare Package" demonstrations in May and the Civil Referendum from July to August.

On May 25, 2014, roughly 20,000 residents championed the cause of Opposition group Macau Conscience, and marched from Tap Seac Square to Nam Van Lake in what turned out to be the largest mass mobilization since the resumption of Chinese sovereignty over Macau,[96] to protest the Welfare Package for Designated, Incumbent and Former Chief Executives and Principal Officials Bill offered by the Government of Chief Executive Fernando Chui.[97] Protestors carried with them signs composed in Chinese and Portuguese, with messages such as "No Shame at All," and "Ali Baba and the 40 Thieves."[98] Among the provisions that stirred the public the most was

94 Hio Hei Albert Wong, *The Summer 2014 Protests in Macau: Their Contexts and Continuities*, 6 (1) ASIAN EDUC. & DEV. STUD. 57, 59 (2017).

95 *Id.* at 58.

96 Ieong, *supra* note 38, at 505.

97 Zhidong Hao, *Social Stratification and Ethnic and Class Politics in Macao before and after the Handover in 1999*, 13(1) CHINA: AN INT'L J. 66, 86 (2015).

98 Ying Ho Kwong, *Protests against the Welfare Package for Chief Executives and Principal Officials*, 2014/4 CHINA PERSP. 61, 62 (2014), 2014, http://journals.openedition.org/chinaperspectives/6588

Section 4, which created immunity from criminal prosecutions for acts of the Chief Executive while in office,[99] and Section 5, which guaranteed a monthly allowance equivalent to 70 percent of the Chief Executive's monthly salary for retirees from that office.[100] Many residents came to suspect that the bill constituted an outrageous abuse of public power, legitimating corruption in the legal system.[101] Opposition to the bill percolated through the middle class and grass roots, students and civil servants alike.[102] Perhaps taken by surprise, the next day Chui asked the Legislative Assembly to postpone reading the bill.[103] The motion of Pro-Democracy Assemblyman António Ng to rescind the bill permanently was rejected by the Establishment, which, however, immediately triggered 7,000 angry protestors to encircle the Legislative Assembly building. Finally, on May 29, the Chief Executive convened a press conference to announce that the Government would withdraw the bill.[104] This signal success, however, did not signify a sea-change in the overall political apathy of Macau residents. Subsequent public scandals attracted very little public attention, let alone consequential action.[105] Sulu Sou, a Pro-Democracy Assemblyman and one of the organizers of the May 25 Protest, disappointedly joked that the protest "was merely a pee at midnight," and that the Macau people "decided to go back to sleep right afterwards."[106] In other words, the low level of external political transaction costs in Macau was not fundamentally altered by this one-time event. Rather, the Legislative Assembly voted to suspend Sou's office in December 2017, after he was prosecuted for "aggravated disobedience" while folding up protest letters into paper airplanes and tossing them over the fence of the Chief Executive's residence during a peaceful demonstration in May 2016.[107]

Earlier, in July, 2014, one month before the upcoming Chief Executive Election, several Opposition groups co-organized a Civil Referendum to gauge whether the citizenry wanted "one-person, one-vote" universal suffrage

99 Ieong, *supra* note 38, at 506.

100 *Id.* at 507.

101 *Id.*

102 HON-FAI CHEN, CATHOLICS AND EVERYDAY LIFE IN MACAU: CHANGING MEANINGS OF RELIGIOSITY, MORALITY AND CIVILITY 2 (2017).

103 Jeffie Lam, *Macau Protests Force Chief Executive Fernando Chui to Scrap Controversial Perks Bill*, SOUTH CHINA MORNING POST, May 29, 2014,www.scmp.com/news/hong-kong/article/1520998/macau-scraps-retirement-perk-bill-after-mass-rallies

104 Hao, *supra* note 97, at 86–88.

105 CHEN, *supra* note 102, at 6.

106 Jeffie Lam, *Macau Protest Leader Sulu Sou Remains Defiant after Protests over Contentious Bill*, SOUTH CHINA MORNING POST, Aug. 10, 2015, www.scmp.com/news/hong-kong/politics/article/1848052/macau-protest-leader-sulu-sou-remains-defiant-after-protests

107 Sarah Cook, *China's Stealthy Holiday Crackdowns*, 124 CHINA MEDIA BULL. 2, 7 (2017).

at the next Chief Executive election, and whether they had confidence in Chief Executive Chui.[108] This time, the SAR authorities responded with a hard line. The physical Referendum polling stations were seized.[109] Referendum organizer Jason Chao and his assistants were arrested for privacy violations related to their collection of personal information for the informal plebiscite. He and two others were also charged with the offence of "misuse of signage" related to the unauthorized appearance of the Judicial Police emblem in a satirical work.[110] As was briefly alluded to in Chapter 4, the TUI has refrained from being involved in the constitutional dispute between the Referendum organizers and the Government. In the same month when the Referendum took place, political scientists Éric Sautede and Bill Chou, both outspoken critics of the Establishment, lost their professorships under dubious circumstances.[111] What is more, successive polls reveal that, unlike the Hong Kong identity, the Macau identity and the Chinese are both well integrated and non-exclusive in the hearts and minds of the Macau community, which is much less polarized than its Hong Kong neighbors.[112] Hence no credible localist movement has ever arisen in Macau.

The rise of new Establishment factions such as the United Citizens Association[113] should not be mistaken for a proliferation of internal political transaction costs in any way analogous to that in the Hong Kong Establishment. Newly elected Assemblymen connected to the casino and construction industries may question the Government more actively than their allies from the traditional Establishment.[114] The advent of a "casino faction" was inevitable: tax contributions from gaming in the ten years between 2004 and 2014 rose 913 percent, from MOP15 billion (US$1,856,700,000) to MOP 137 billion (US$16,957,860,000).[115] In spite of the differences between the casino faction and traditional Establishment constituents, however, they share the same overarching dogma that all

108 Stuart Lau, *Macau Unofficial Democracy Poll Halted as Police Detain Five Activists*, SOUTH CHINA MORNING POST, Aug. 24, 2014, www.scmp.com/news/china/article/1580359/casino-hub-macau-holds-informal-poll-democracy

109 Wong, *supra* note 94, at 60.

110 *Id.* at 66.

111 Raquel Carvalho, *Macau Scholars Warn of Rising Censorship*, SOUTH CHINA MORNING POST, Jul. 22, 2014, www.scmp.com/news/china/article/1557068/macau-scholars-warn-rising-censorship-loss-confidence-one-country-two

112 Ieong, *supra* note 38, at 522.

113 Sonny Shiu-Hing Lo & Eric King-Man Chong, *Casino Interests, Fujian* Tongxianghui *and Electoral Politics in Macao*, 46(2) J. CONTEMP. ASIA 286, 286 (2016).

114 Ying-ho Kwong, *Ruling Coalition Restructuring under Macao's Hybrid Regime*, 17(3) CHINA REV. 111, 123 (2017).

115 *Id.* at 118.

electoral reform questions must be settled by instructions from Beijing, and that society should concentrate on economic rather than political matters. They all keep to the same discipline of preserving comity with other Establishment parties and, above all, with the Chief Executive.[116] It has been suggested, more importantly, that the casino faction had Beijing's blessing: it was accepted that the dearth of internal competition within the Macau Establishment would jeopardize the legitimacy of the entire SAR regime in the long run. Not only would the casino faction's existence not weaken the Establishment, it would offer another nominal option to voters who wanted neither the traditional Establishment nor the Pro-Democracy Opposition.[117]

Constitutional review by the TUI during the Xi Jinping era is unlikely to depart from its deferential, low-energy, path, given that the levels of political transaction costs in enacting court-curbing measures remain notably low. The Establishment Coalition has retained its cohesion and subservience to a Chief Executive who, except for the 2014 protests, has been unfettered by a politically uninterested citizenry. Nonetheless, the Tribunal has perhaps been overtly cautious, systemically overestimating the probabilities of regime retaliation even when it is not imminent. The Legislative Assembly's enactment of the Regime Jurídico de Enquadramento das Fontes Normativas Internas (Juridical Framework for the Formulation of Internal Norms) in July 2009 implies that the TUI could well move on to take up the relatively assertive approach already adopted by the intermediate court below, without provoking a political backlash. There is still room for the TUI to emphasize over and over again the importance of the SAR's legal autonomy.

In early February 2018, the Secretary for Administration and Justice, Sonia Chan, signaled an amendment to the Lei de Bases da Organização Judiciária (Fundamental Law on Judicial Organization), mandating the exclusion of non-Chinese judges from national security cases. Jorge Neto Valente, the non-Chinese President of the Macau Lawyers' Association, reportedly criticized the proposal as a "bad solution" contrary to the Lei Básica.[118] Yet the Macau Government's gambit apparently resonated with views in certain hardline quarters in the Hong Kong Establishment, which have long been discontent with the presence of non-Chinese in the judiciary. When non-Chinese Principal Magistrate Bina Chainrai sentenced a retired police superintendent

116 *Id.* at 130.

117 *Id.*

118 Niall Fraser, *Macau Proposal to Ban Foreign Judges on Some Cases would 'Dent Confidence' in Hong Kong, Says Legal Expert*, South China Morning Post, Feb. 21, 2018, www.scmp.com/news/hong-kong/law-crime/article/2134009/macau-proposal-ban-foreign-judges-some-cases-would-dent

to three months' imprisonment in December 2017, for assaulting a pedestrian mistaken for an Umbrella Revolution protester, pro-Establishment mobs reacted with spiteful, racist name calling as well as exacting demands for an all-Chinese bench at all levels of the judiciary.[119] In a high-profile act that reflected the magnitude of disagreement in the Hong Kong Establishment, in March 2018 Chief Executive Carrie Lam decided to appoint to the CFA Lady Hale, the incumbent President of the Supreme Court of the United Kingdom, and Beverley McLachlin, a former Chief Justice of Canada, neither of whom was famous for judicial deference,[120] subject to the Legislative Council's confirmation.

CONCLUDING REMARKS

This book has studied the political dynamics for consequential constitutional review in subnational hybrid regimes in the cases of the Chinese Special Administrative Regions of Hong Kong and Macau. It has reconsidered fundamental theoretical assumptions long prevalent in contemporary comparative constitutional law scholarship. It argues that the increasingly prevalent regime types that are neither liberal democracies nor closed autocracies, nor yet midway houses between liberal democracy and closed autocracy, merit closer scholarly attention. The instability inherent in the strange marriage of liberal democratic institutions with authoritarianism hardwired into the constitution of a hybrid regime is bound to defy conventional understandings. Despite persistent authoritarianism, a form of genuine constitutionalism pushes ahead in the universe of hybrid regimes: high-energy constitutional review has emerged in some places but not others.[121] Hybrid constitutionalism needs to be explained. This book has endeavored to make sense of how the diametrically opposite constitutional jurisprudence of the Hong Kong Court of Final Appeal and the Tribunal de Última Instância de Macau could have diverged so enduringly despite so many similarities in the history, ethnicity, language, culture, demographics and, above all, the constitutional frameworks of the two SARs.

119 Karen Cheung, *Retired Cop Frankly Chu Found Guilty of Assault after Hitting Pedestrian with a Baton During Occupy*, South China Morning Post, December 18, 2017, www.hongkongfp.com/2017/12/18/retired-cop-frankly-chu-found-guilty-assault-hitting-pedestrian-baton-occupy/

120 Alvin Lum, *Two Foreign Female Judges make History with Appointments to Hong Kong's Top Court*, South China Morning Post, Mar. 21, 2018, www.scmp.com/news/hong-kong/law-crime/article/2138271/two-female-foreign-judges-appointed-hong-kongs-top-court

121 Julio Ríos-Figueroa & Paloma Aguilar, *Justice Institutions in Autocracies: A Framework for Analysis*, 25(1) Democratization 1, 1 (2018).

The diachronic comparison[122] of Hong Kong with Macau reminds us how vastly different in judicial outcomes hybrid regimes endowed with the same set of political institutions can be.

The solution revealed herein lies not in superficial differences between common law and civil law systems, for if legal origins were a reliable predictor of judicial acts, the TUI instead of the CFA should have been the activist court. A transaction cost theory of hybrid constitutionalism has been presented, the central insight of which is that observable changes in regime political transaction cost structures reliably predict correlative changes to the constitutional jurisprudence of the apex court. The higher a regime's political transaction costs mount, the lower its ability credibly to threaten to sanction judicial opportunism, whence a lower cost of opportunism. *Ceteris paribus*, the CFA asserted and continually exercised a competence to strike down legislation *erga omnes*, while the TUI constantly avoided gauging the compatibility of legislation with constitutional rights even case by case, let alone *erga omnes*. According to this theory, Hong Kong and Macau should be analyzed as a high political transaction cost polity and a low transaction cost polity, respectively. Empirical evidence has rigorously confirmed this prediction: factional infighting and vibrant popular resistance in Hong Kong have obsoleted "nuclear options" against constitutional review, while high regime cohesion and low levels of oppositional activism in Macau have exposed independent constitutional review to the perils of court curbing. The theory has two major implications for the future of constitutional review in both SARs. The first is that the rise of strongman politics in mainland China, the incremental growth of authoritarianism in Hong Kong, and the occasional occurrence of civic activism in Macau will not likely produce any fundamental change in the constitutional jurisprudence of the CFA or the TUI insofar as the transaction cost structures of both polities stay intact; and no fundamental change in political transaction costs is in sight. To change the status quo is either too costly or too harmful to the powerful. The second implication is that, given a constant political transaction cost structure in Hong Kong and Macau, the current constitutional review trajectories of the CFA and the TUI are unlikely to change in any meaningful way in the unlikely, but not entirely impossible, event of rapid democratization. And there is no reason to suppose that elections would reduce Hong Kong's snowballing political transaction costs or drastically remake Macau's cohesive Government and unpolarized society.

122 Rebecca Bill Chavez, The Rule of Law in Nascent Democracies: Judicial Politics in Argentina 164 (2004).

Finally, this book has three lessons for contemporary comparative constitutional law scholars. First, hybrid regimes, although authoritarian, do not always act decisively or with ease. Therefore, weighing up their decisional and informational costs in quashing constitutional judgments or curbing court powers should yield more insights than obsessing over the formal provisions of constitutional documents, the nominal separation of powers, or the presence or number of veto gates. Secondly, while culturally embedded legal and moral principles provide judges with powerful justifications for judicial intervention in politics on constitutional grounds, legal origins do not predetermine the precise doctrinal development of constitutional jurisprudence in either system. The third lesson is that the durability of high-energy constitutional review does not have to be a one-sided story of regime acquiescence under high political transaction costs. Aggressive review doctrines that maximize judicial power yet return substantial benefits to diverse actors inside and outside the regime, in ways that raise the opportunity and transaction costs of court-curbing measures, are more likely than not to survive against all odds,[123] and are not necessarily normatively undesirable.[124]

[123] Eric C. Ip, *The Politics of Constitutional Common Law in Hong Kong under Chinese Sovereignty*, 25(3) WASHINGTON INT'L L. J. 565, 591–92 (2016) ("Credible judicial remedies, upheld by the separation of powers principle have convinced aggrieved citizens that they will lessen their costs by seeking legal remedies under the [Hong Kong] Basic Law rather than by acting extra-constitutionally, even if power-holders do oftentimes get affirmed. The living constitution doctrine enables the courts to adapt the Basic Law enacted more than a quarter of a century ago to present conditions, at low cost to the polity, in light of shifting social attitudes, the demands of rapid technological change, and other modern challenges. It has spared public officials not only the cost of formally amending the Basic Law for the foregoing considerations, but also the burden of interpreting it themselves simply to remove the uncertainty proceeding from the ambiguity of incompleteness inherent in all constitutions and owing to the inevitable informational and organizational limitations of its drafters. Standards of constitutionally appropriate behavior, like proportionality and legality, benefit the whole political system by confirming the legitimacy of policies and statutes that the courts maintain or forbear to nullify through constitutional review. Proportionality in particular tests arbitrariness by obliging officials and lawmakers to duly weigh the pros and cons of their acts, consistent with the percepts of cost-benefit analysis. Improved legislative and administrative rationality in turn promotes market rationality, eases pressures on elites to reform the political system, and offers aggrieved citizens a sense of vindication. The opportunity costs to the SAR authorities of voiding the Court's constitutional jurisprudence would be high.").

[124] Eric C. Ip, *The Democratic Foundations of Judicial Review under Authoritarianism: Theory and Evidence from Hong Kong*, 12(2) INT'L J. CONST. L. 330, 353 (2014) ("Judicial review has often been described as 'countermajoritarian' and anti-democratic in form and substance. Few studies, however, have inquired into the role of judicial review in non-democratic settings. Might it be that the countermajoritarian nature of authoritarian regimes renders autonomous judicial review relatively more democratic than the political branches?").

References

Note: This list contains only published academic sources, such as journal articles, books, and book sections. References to other archival sources, such as laws, judgments, and newspaper reports, appear in the footnotes of the individual chapters of this book.

Sherzod Abdukadirov, *The Problem of Political Calculation in Autocracies*, 21 (4) CONST. POL. ECON. 360 (2010)

DARON ACEMOGLU & JAMES A. ROBINSON, ECONOMIC ORIGINS OF DICTATORSHIP AND DEMOCRACY (Cambridge Univ. Press 2007)

İsmet Akça & Evren Balta-Paker, *Beyond Military Tutelage? Turkish Military Politics and the AKP Government*, *in* DEBATING SECURITY IN TURKEY: CHALLENGES AND CHANGES IN THE TWENTY-FIRST CENTURY 77 (Ebru Canan-Sokullu ed., Lexington Books 2013)

Michael Albertus & Victor Menaldo, *The Political Economy of Autocratic Constitutions*, *in* CONSTITUTIONS IN AUTHORITARIAN REGIMES 53 (Tom Ginsburg & Alberto Simpser eds., Cambridge Univ. Press 2014)

Gani Aldashev, *Legal Institutions, Political Economy, and Development*, 25 (2) OXFORD REV. ECON. POL'Y 257 (2009)

Sofia Amaral-Garcia et al., *Judicial Independence and Party Politics in the Kelsenian Constitutional Court: The Case of Portugal*, 6 (2) J. EMPIRICAL LEGAL STUD. 381 (2009)

CRAIG ANDERSON, ROMAN LAW (Dundee Univ. Press 2009)

Aylin Aydin, *Judicial Independence across Democratic Regimes: Understanding the Varying Impact of Political Competition*, 47 (1) LAW & SOC'Y REV. 105 (2013)

MICHAEL A. BAILEY & FORREST MALTZMAN, THE CONSTRAINED COURT: LAW, POLITICS, AND THE DECISIONS JUSTICES MAKE (Princeton Univ. Press 2011)

Miklos Bankuti et al., *Hungary's Illiberal Turn: Disabling the Constitution*, *in* THE HUNGARIAN PATIENT: SOCIAL OPPOSITION TO AN ILLIBERAL DEMOCRACY 37 (Peter Krasztev et al. eds., Central European Univ. Press 2015)

Aharon Barak, *A Research Agenda for the Future*, *in* PROPORTIONALITY: NEW FRONTIERS, NEW CHALLENGES 322 (Vicki C. Jackson & Mark Tushnet eds., Cambridge Univ. Press 2017)

AHARON BARAK, PROPORTIONALITY: CONSTITUTIONAL RIGHTS AND THEIR LIMITATIONS (Cambridge Univ. Press 2012)

Gabrielle Bardall, *Coding Competitive Authoritarianism*, 10 Z. VGL. POLIT. WISS. (SUPPL.) 19 (2016)

Emily Johnston Barton, *Pricing Judicial Independence: An Empirical Study of Post-1997 Court of Final Appeal Decisions in Hong Kong*, 43 (2) HARV. INT'L L.J. 361 (2002)

Robert H. Bates et al., *The Analytical Narrative Project*, 94 AM. POL. SCI. REV. 696 (2000)

Thorsten Beck et al., *Law and Finance: Why Does Legal Origin Matter?*, 31 (4) J. COMP. ECON. 653 (2003)

Jacqueline Behrend & Laurence Whitehead,, *Setting the Comparative Agenda: Territorially Uneven Democratization Processes in Large Federations*, *in* ILLIBERAL PRACTICES: TERRITORIAL VARIANCE WITHIN LARGE FEDERAL DEMOCRACIES 1 (Jacqueline Behrend & Laurence Whitehead eds., Johns Hopkins Univ. Press 2016)

DANIEL A. BELL,. THE CHINA MODEL: POLITICAL MERITOCRACY AND THE LIMITS OF DEMOCRACY (Princeton Univ. Press 2016)

Ceren Belge, *Friends of the Court: The Republican Alliance and Selective Activism of the Constitutional Court of Turkey*, 40 (3) LAW & SOC'Y REV. 653 (2006)

Mario Bergara et al., *Modeling Supreme Court Strategic Decision-making: the Congressional Constraint*, 28 LEGIS. STUD. Q. 247 (2003)

Niclas Berggreni & Nils Karlson, *Constitutionalism, Division of Power and Transaction Costs*, 117 PUB. CHOICE 99 (2003)

Kemal Bokhary, *The Rule of Law in Hong Kong: Fifteen Years after the Handover*, 51 COLUM. J. TRANSNAT'L L. 287 (2013)

KEMAL BOKHARY, HUMAN RIGHTS: SOURCE, CONTENT AND ENFORCEMENT (Sweet & Maxwell 2015)

André Borges, *Subnational Hybrid Regimes and Democratization in Brazil: Why Party Nationalization Matters*, *in* ILLIBERAL PRACTICES: TERRITORIAL VARIANCE WITHIN LARGE FEDERAL DEMOCRACIES 162 (Jacqueline Behrend & Laurence Whitehead eds., Johns Hopkins Univ. Press 2016)

Clara Boulianne Lagacé & Jennifer Gandhi, *Authoritarian Institutions*, *in* ROUTLEDGE HANDBOOK OF COMPARATIVE POLITICAL INSTITUTIONS 278 (Jennifer Gandhi & Rubén Ruiz-Rufino eds., Routledge 2015)

C.R. BOXER, THE AFFAIR OF THE MADRE DE DEUS: A CHAPTER IN THE HISTORY OF THE PORTUGUESE IN JAPAN (Routledge 2010)

Dawn Brancati, *Democratic Authoritarianism: Origins and Effects*, 17 ANNU. REV. POLIT. SCI. 313 (2014)

DENIS BRAY, HONG KONG METAMORPHOSIS (Hong Kong Univ. Press 2001)

Geoffrey Brennan & Alan Hamlin, *Constitutions as Expressive Documents*, *in* THE OXFORD HANDBOOK OF POLITICAL ECONOMY 329 (Barry R. Weingast & Donald A. Wittman eds., Oxford Univ. Press 2006)

Brian Brewer, *Civil Service Reform: Building Basic Administrative Capacity*, *in* GAMING, GOVERNANCE AND PUBLIC POLICY IN MACAO 89 (Newman M.K. Lam & Ian Scott eds., Hong Kong Univ. Press 2011)

ALLAN R. BREWER-CARÍAS, CONSTITUTIONAL PROTECTION OF HUMAN RIGHTS IN LATIN AMERICA: A COMPARATIVE STUDY OF AMPARO PROCEEDINGS (Cambridge Univ. Press 2009)

PAUL BROOKER, NON-DEMOCRATIC REGIMES (Palgrave Macmillan, 3d ed. 2014)

RACHEL E. BROWN, THE ACHILLES HEEL OF DEMOCRACY: JUDICIAL AUTONOMY AND THE RULE OF LAW IN CENTRAL AMERICA (Cambridge Univ. Press 2017)

Jason Brownlee, *Portents of Pluralism: How Hybrid Regimes Affect Democratic Transitions*, 53 (3) AM. J. POL. SCI. 515 (2009)

JASON BROWNLEE, AUTHORITARIANISM IN AN AGE OF DEMOCRATIZATION (Cambridge Univ. Press 2007)

James M. Buchanan, *Same Players, Different Game: How Better Rules Make Better Politics*, 19 CONST. POL. ECON. 171 (2008)

John Burns et al., *Changing Governance Structures and the Evolution of Public Services Bargains in Hong Kong*, 79 (1)INT'L REV. ADMIN. SCI. 135 (2012)

John P. Burns, *Editorial Introduction: Special Issue on the Second Decade of the Hong Kong Special Administrative Region of China: Themes and Overview*, 39 (2) ASIA PAC. J. PUB. ADMIN. 79 (2017)

John P. Burns, *Administrative Reform in Hong Kong: An Institutional Analysis of Food Safety*, 17 RESEARCH IN PUB. POL'Y ANALYSIS & MANAGEMENT 21 (2008)

RICHARD C. BUSH, HONG KONG IN THE SHADOW OF CHINA: LIVING WITH THE LEVIATHAN (Brookings Institution Press 2016)

Andrew Byrnes, *And Some Have Bills of Rights Thrust upon Them: The Experience of Hong Kong's Bill of Rights*, *in* PROMOTING HUMAN RIGHTS THROUGH BILLS OF RIGHTS 318 (Philip Alston ed., Univ. of New South Wales Press 2000)

Gonzalo Caballero & David Soto Oñate, *Why Transaction Costs Are so Relevant in Political Governance? A New Institutional Survey*, 36 (2) BRAZILIAN J. POL. ECON. 330 (2016)

Dingjian Cai, *The Mechanism for Resolving the Conflict of Laws in China: Ratifying, Recording and Interpreting Law*, *in* HONG KONG'S CONSTITUTIONAL DEBATE 45 (Johannes M.M. Chan & Lison Harris eds., Hong Kong Law Journal Ltd 2005)

Vitalino Canas, *The General Regime of Fundamental Rights in the Basic Law and in the International Instruments*, *in* ONE COUNTRY, TWO SYSTEMS, THREE LEGAL ORDERS – PERSPECTIVES OF EVOLUTION: ESSAYS ON MACAU'S AUTONOMY AFTER THE RESUMPTION OF SOVEREIGNTY BY CHINA 672 (Jorge Oliveira & Paulo Cardinal eds., Springer 2009)

Paulo Cardinal, *Autonomy as a Tool for Peace: Some Topics Using as a Reference Point the Chinese SARs Seasoned with a Kantian Perpetual Peace Fragrance*, 89 BOL. FAC. DIREITO U. COIMBRA 925 (2013)

Paulo Cardinal, *Macau: Transformation of an Historic Autonomy*, *in* PRACTISING SELF-GOVERNMENT: A COMPARATIVE STUDY OF AUTONOMOUS REGIONS 383 (Yash Ghai & Sophia Woodman eds., Cambridge Univ. Press 2013)

Paulo Cardinal, *The Writ of Amparo: A New Lighthouse for the Rule of Law in the Philippines*, 87 PHIL. L.J. 229 (2012)

Paulo Cardinal, *A Panoramic View on Fundamental Rights in Macau: From Territory under Portuguese Administration to Special Administrative Region of the P.R. China*, *in* STUDIES ON MACAU Civil, COMMERCIAL, CONSTITUTIONAL AND CRIMINAL LAW 1 (Jorge A.F. Godinho ed., LexisNexis 2010)

Paulo Cardinal, *The Judicial Guarantees of Fundamental Rights in the Macau Legal System: A* Parcours *Under the Focus of Continuity and of Autonomy*, *in* ONE

COUNTRY, TWO SYSTEMS, THREE LEGAL ORDERS – PERSPECTIVES OF EVOLUTION 221 (Jorge Costa Oliveira & Paulo Cardinal et al. Springer 2009)

Paolo Cardinal, *Revisiting the Macanese Amparo of Fundamental Rights: A Quest under the Searchlight of the Principle of Continuity with a Stopover in Comparative Law*, 83 PHIL. L.J. 833 (2009)

Paulo Cardinal, *Macau: The Internationalization of an Historical Autonomy*, 122 BOLETIN: MEXICANO DE DERECHO COMPARADO 637 (2008)

Paulo Cardinal & Pereira Vidal, *An Outline of the Macau Legal System*, 23 HONG KONG L.J. 358 (1993)

Paulo Cardinal & Yihe Zhang, *Subnational Constitutionalism in the SARS of the People's Republic of China: An Exceptional Tailored Suit Model?*, 4 (2) PERSP. ON FEDERALISM 101 (2012)

John M. Carey, *Electoral Formula and Fragmentation in Hong Kong*, 17 J. E. ASIAN STUD. 215 (2017)

Gerard Carney, *Comparative Approaches to Statutory Interpretation in Civil Law and*, 36 (1) STATUTE L. REV. 46 (2015)

Thomas Carothers, *The End of the Transition Paradigm*, 13 (1) J. DEMOCRACY 5 (2002)

JOHN M. CARROLL, CONCISE HISTORY OF HONG KONG (Rowman & Littlefield Publishers 2007)

IGNAZIO CASTELLUCCI, RULE OF LAW AND LEGAL COMPLEXITY IN THE PEOPLE'S REPUBLIC OF CHINA (Università degli Studi di Trento 2012)

Ignazio Castelucci, *Rule of Law with Chinese Characteristics*, 13 ANN. SURV. INT'L & COMP. L. 35 (2007)

Cora Chan; *A Preliminary Framework for Measuring Deference in Rights Reasoning*, 14 (4) INT'L J. CONST. L. 851 (2016)

Cora Chan, *Reconceptualising the Relationship between the Mainland Chinese Legal System and the Hong Kong Legal System*, 6 ASIAN J. COMP. L. Iss. 1, art. 1 (2011)

Elaine Chan & Joseph Chan, *Hong Kong 2007–2017: A Backlash in Civil Society*, 39 (2) ASIA PAC. J. PUB. ADMIN. 135 (2017)

Johannes Chan, *Basic Law and Constitutional Review*, 37 HONG KONG L.J. 407 (2007)

Johannes Chan, *Hong Kong's Constitutional Journey, 1997–2011, in* CONSTITUTIONALISM IN ASIA IN THE EARLY TWENTY-FIRST CENTURY 169 (Albert H.Y. Chen ed., Cambridge Univ. Press 2014)

Johannes M.M. Chan, *Clarified in Its Clarification: Jurisdiction and Amicus Intervention, in* HONG KONG'S CONSTITUTIONAL DEBATE: CONFLICT OVER INTERPRETATION 171 (Hong Kong Univ. Press 2000)

Johannes M.M. Chan, *Immigration Policies and Human Resources Planning, in* HONG KONG MOBILE: MAKING A GLOBAL POPULATION 149 (Helen F. Siu & Agnes S. Ku eds., Hong Kong Univ. Press 2008)

Johannes M.M. Chan, *Right to Judicial Remedies, in* LAW OF THE HONG KONG CONSTITUTION 1109 (Johannes M.M. Chan & C.L. Lim eds., Sweet & Maxwell, 2d ed. 2015)

JOHANNES M.M. CHAN & KEMAL BOKHARY, HALSBURY'S LAWS OF HONG KONG: CONSTITUTIONAL AND HUMAN RIGHTS LAW (LexisNexis Butterworths 2015)

Johannes M.M. Chan & C.L. Lim, *Interpreting Constitutional Rights and Permissible Restrictions*, *in* LAW OF THE HONG KONG CONSTITUTION 565 (Johannes M.M. Chan & C.L. Lim eds., Sweet & Maxwell, 2d ed. 2015)

Ming K. Chan, *Beyond the Luso Twilight: Into the Sino Glow: A Historical Sketch of Macao's Transformation*, *in* CHINA'S MACAO TRANSFORMED: CHALLENGE AND DEVELOPMENT IN THE 21ST CENTURY lxiii (Eilo W.Y. Yu and Ming K. Chan eds., City Univ. of Hong Kong Press 2014)

Ming K. Chan, *Democracy Derailed: Realpolitik in the Making of the Hong Kong Basic Law, 1985–90*, *in* THE HONG KONG BASIC LAW: BLUEPRINT FOR "STABILITY AND PROSPERITY" UNDER CHINESE SOVEREIGNTY? 6 (Ming K. Chan & David J. Clark eds., Hong Kong Univ. Press 1991)

Ming K. Chan, *Different Roads to Home: The Retrocession of Hong Kong and Macau to Chinese Sovereignty*, 12 (36) J. CONTEMP. CHINA 493 (2003)

MING K. CHAN & Shiu-Hing Lo, THE A TO Z OF THE HONG KONG SAR AND THE MACAO SAR (Scarecrow Press 2010)

MING K. CHAN & SHIU-HING LO, HONG KONG SAR AND THE MACAO SAR (Scarecrow Press 2006)

Jaw-ling Joanne Chang, *Settlement of the Macao Issue: Distinctive Features of Beijing's Negotiating Behavior*, 20 CASE W. RES. J. INT'L L. 253 (1988)

Peter S.C. Chau & Simon N.M. Young, *Abolishing By-elections to Fill Vacancies in the Legislative Council*, 41(3) HONG KONG L. J. 601 (2012)

REBECCA BILL CHAVEZ, THE RULE OF LAW IN NASCENT DEMOCRACIES: JUDICIAL POLITICS IN ARGENTINA (Stanford Univ. Press 2004)

Rebecca Bill Chavez et al., *A Theory of the Politically Independent Judiciary: A Comparative Study of the United States and Argentina*, *in* COURTS IN LATIN AMERICA 219 (Gretchen Helmke & Julio Ríos-Figueroa eds., Cambridge Univ. Press 2011)

Kathleen Cheek-Milby, *The Changing Political Role of the Hong Kong Civil Servant*, 62 (2) PAC. AFF. 219 (1989)

Albert H.Y. Chen, *The Achievement of Constitutionalism in Asia: Moving beyond "Constitutions without Constitutionalism,"* *in* CONSTITUTIONALISM IN ASIA IN THE EARLY TWENTY-FIRST CENTURY 1 (Albert H.Y. Chen ed., Cambridge Univ. Press 2014)

Albert H.Y. Chen, *Another Case of Conflict between the CFA and the NPC Standing Committee?*, 31 (1) HONG KONG L.J. 179 (2001)

Albert H.Y. Chen, *The Constitution and the Rule of Law*, *in* THE FIRST TUNG CHEE-HWA ADMINISTRATION: THE FIRST FIVE YEARS OF THE HONG KONG SPECIAL ADMINISTRATIVE REGION 69 (Siu-kai Lau ed., Chinese Univ. Press 2002)

Albert H.Y. Chen, *Constitutional Adjudication in Post-1997 Hong Kong*, 15 PAC. RIM L. & POL'Y J. 627 (2006)

Albert H.Y. Chen, *The Court of Final Appeal's Ruling in the "Illegal Migrant" Children Case: Congressional Supremacy and Judicial Review*, *in* HONG KONG'S CONSTITUTIONAL DEBATE: CONFLICT OVER INTERPRETATION 73 (Johannes M.M. Chan et al. eds., Hong Kong Univ. Press 2001)

ALBERT H.Y. CHEN, AN INTRODUCTION TO THE LEGAL SYSTEM OF THE PEOPLE'S REPUBLIC OF CHINA (LexisNexis Butterworths, 4th ed. 2011)

Albert H.Y. Chen, *The Relationship between the Central Government and the SAR*, *in* THE BASIC LAW AND HONG KONG'S FUTURE 107 (Peter Wesley-Smith & Albert H.Y. Chen eds., Butterworths 1988)

Albert H.Y. Chen, *Social Movements and the Law: The Case of Hong Kong*, *in* CIVIL UNREST AND GOVERNANCE IN HONG KONG: LAW AND ORDER FROM HISTORICAL AND CULTURAL PERSPECTIVES 117 (Michael Ng & John Wong eds., Routledge 2017)

Albert H.Y. Chen, *A Tale of Two Islands: Comparative Reflections on Constitutionalism in Hong Kong and Taiwan*, 37 (2) HONG KONG L. J. 647 (2007)

Albert H.Y. Chen, *The Theory, Constitution and Practice of Autonomy: The Case of Hong Kong*, *in* ONE COUNTRY, TWO SYSTEMS, THREE LEGAL ORDERS – PERSPECTIVES OF EVOLUTION 751 (Jorge Costa Oliveira & Paulo Cardinal et al. Springer 2009)

Albert H.Y. Chen et al., *The Constitutional Orders of "One Country, Two Systems": A Comparative Study of Constitutional Review and Proportionality Analysis in the Hong Kong and Macau Special Administrative Regions*, *in* THE STUDY OF POLITICAL STRUCTURE OF THE HONG KONG SPECIAL ADMINISTRATIVE REGION 185 (Guobin Zhu ed., City Univ. of Hong Kong Press 2017)

Albert H.Y. Chen & Anne S.Y. Cheung, *Debating Rule of Law in the Hong Kong Special Administrative Region, 1997–2002*, *in* ASIAN DISCOURSES OF RULE OF LAW 250 (Randall Peerenboom ed., Routledge 2004)

Albert H.Y. Chen & P.Y. Lo, *Hong Kong's Judiciary under "One Country, Two Systems,"* *in* ASIA-PACIFIC JUDICIARIES: INDEPENDENCE, IMPARTIALITY AND INTEGRITY 131 (H.P. Lee ed., Cambridge Univ. Press 2018)

Albert H.Y. Chen & Miguel Poiares Maduro, *The Judiciary and Constitutional Review*, *in* ROUTLEDGE HANDBOOK OF CONSTITUTIONAL LAW 97 (Mark Tushnet et al. eds., Routledge 2015)

HON-FAI CHEN, CATHOLICS AND EVERYDAY LIFE IN MACAU: CHANGING MEANINGS OF RELIGIOSITY, MORALITY AND CIVILITY (Routledge 2017)

Edmund W. Cheng, *Street Politics in a Hybrid Regime: The Diffusion of Political Activism in Post-colonial Hong Kong*, 226 CHINA Q. 383 (2016)

Joseph Y.S. Cheng, *New Trends of Political Participation in* Hong Kong, *in* NEW TRENDS OF POLITICAL PARTICIPATION IN HONG KONG 3 (City Univ. of Hong Kong Press 2014)

Joseph Y.S. Cheng, *The 2012 Chief Executive Election in Hong Kong and the Challenges for the Chinese Authorities*, 5 (4) E. ASIAN POL'Y 91 (2013)

Kevin Kwok-yin Cheng, *Prosecutorial Procedural Justice and Public Legitimacy in Hong Kong*, 57 (1) BRIT. J. CRIMINOL. 94 (2017)

Alvin Y.H. Cheung, *Road to Nowhere: Hong Kong's Democratization and China's Obligations under Public International Law*, 40 BROOK. J. INT'L L. 465 (2015)

Anthony Cheung, *In Search of Trust and Legitimacy: The Political Trajectory of Hong Kong as Part of China*, *in* TRUST AND GOVERNANCE INSTITUTIONS: ASIAN EXPERIENCES 41 (Clay Wescott et al. eds., Information Age Publishing 2012)

Anthony Cheung, *Policy Capacity in Post-1997 Hong Kong: Constrained Institutions Facing a Crowding and Differentiated Polity*, 29 ASIA PAC. J. PUB. ADMIN. 51 (2007)

Anthony Cheung & Max Wong, *Judicial Review and Policy Making in Hong Kong: Changing Interface between the Legal and the Political*, 28 ASIA P. J. PUB. ADMIN. 117 (2006)

Peter T.Y. Cheung, *In Beijing's Tightening Grip*, *in* HONG KONG 20 YEARS AFTER THE HANDOVER: EMERGING SOCIAL AND INSTITUTIONAL FRACTURES AFTER 1997 225 (Brian C.H. Fong & Tai-lok Lui eds., Palgrave Macmillan 2018)

Peter T.Y. Cheung, *Who's Influencing Whom? Exploring the Influence of Hong Kong on Politics and Governance in China*, 51 (4) ASIAN SURV. 718 (2011)

Siu-Keung Cheung, *Reunification through Water and Food: The Other Battle for Lives and Bodies in China's Hong Kong Policy*, 220 CHINA Q. 1012 (2014)

Bill Chou, *Local Autonomy in Action: Beijing's Hong Kong and Macau Policies*, 42 (3) J. CURRENT CHINESE AFF. 29 (2013)

Bill K.P. Chou, *Elections in Hong Kong: International Perspectives and Implications for China*, *in* CHINA AND EAST ASIA: AFTER THE WALL STREET CRISIS 75 (Peng Er Lam et al. eds., World Scientific 2013)

Bill K.P. Chou, *Interest Group Politics in Macau after Handover*, 14 (43) J. CONTEMP. CHINA 191 (2005)

Bill K.P. Chou, *Legitimacy-Building and Public Sector Reform in Macao: Administrative Measures to Address Political Problems*, 10(3) CHINA: AN INT'L J. 133 (2012)

Bill K.P. Chou, *Local Autonomy Matters: One-Country Two-System Policy in Macao and its Implications to China's Policies towards Borderlands*, *in* CHINA'S POLICIES ON ITS BORDERLANDS AND INTERNATIONAL RELATIONS 225 (Yufan Hao & Bill K P Chou eds., World Scientific 2010)

Bill K.P. Chou, *Politics and Social Organisations in Macao: A Historical Institutionalist Analysis*, 13(1) CHINA: AN INT'L J. 22 (2015)

Bill K.P. Chou, *Public Sector Reform in Macao after the Handover*, 52 CHINA PERSP. 1 (2004)

CINDY YIK-YI CHU, CHINESE COMMUNISTS AND HONG KONG CAPITALISTS: 1937–1997 (Palgrave Macmillan 2010)

Lynette J. Chua & Stacia L. Haynie, *Judicial Review of Executive Power in the Singaporean Context, 1965–2012*, 4(1) J. L. & CTS. 43 (2016)

Ümit Cizre, *The Justice and Development* Party *and* the Military: Recreating the Past after Reforming It?, *in* SECULAR AND ISLAMIC POLITICS IN TURKEY: THE MAKING OF THE JUSTICE AND DEVELOPMENT PARTY 132 (Ümit Cizre ed., Routledge 2007)

TOM S. CLARK, THE LIMITS OF JUDICIAL INDEPENDENCE (Cambridge Univ. Press 2011)

RONALD H. COASE, THE FIRM, THE MARKET, AND THE LAW (Univ. of Chicago Press 1988)

Ronald H. Coase, *The Relevance of Transaction Costs in the Economic Analysis of Law*, *in* THE ORIGINS OF LAW AND ECONOMICS: ESSAYS BY THE FOUNDING FATHERS 119 (Francesco Parisi & Charles K. Rowley eds., Edward Elgar 2005)

Anthea Coggan et al., *Influences of Transaction Costs in Environmental Policy*, 69 (9) ECOLOGICAL ECON. 1777 (2010)

DANIEL COMPAGNON, A PREDICTABLE TRAGEDY: ROBERT MUGABE AND THE COLLAPSE OF ZIMBABWE (Univ. of Pennsylvania Press 2011)

Roger D. Congleton & Birgitta Swedenborg, *Introduction: Rational Choice Politics and Institutions*, *in* DEMOCRATIC CONSTITUTIONAL DESIGN AND PUBLIC POLICY: ANALYSIS AND EVIDENCE 1 (Roger D. Congleton & Birgitta Swedenborg eds., M.I.T. Press 2006)

Sarah Cook, *China's Stealthy Holiday Crackdowns*, 124 CHINA MEDIA BULL. 2 (2017)

ROBERT D. COOTER, THE STRATEGIC CONSTITUTION (Princeton Univ. Press 2000)

Antonio Cortes & Teresa Violante, *Concrete Control of Constitutionality in Portugal: A Means towards Effective Protection of Fundamental Rights*, 29 (4) PA. ST. INT'L L. REV. 759 (2011)

Jill Cottrell & Yash Ghai, *Concurring and Dissenting in the Hong Kong Court of Final Appeal*, *in* HONG KONG'S COURT OF FINAL APPEAL: THE DEVELOPMENT OF THE LAW IN CHINA'S HONG KONG 283 (Simon N.M. Young & Yash Ghai eds., Cambridge Univ. Press 2014)

FIONA COWNIE ET AL., ENGLISH LEGAL SYSTEM IN CONTEXT (Oxford Univ. Press, 6th ed. 2013)

JAMES CRAWFORD, THE CREATION OF STATES IN INTERNATIONAL LAW (Oxford Univ. Press, 2d ed. 2006)

EVAN J. CRIDDLE, HUMAN RIGHTS IN EMERGENCIES (Cambridge Univ. Press 2016)

Mark Daly, *A Human Rights Lawyer's Perspective*, *in* HONG KONG'S COURT OF FINAL APPEAL: THE DEVELOPMENT OF THE LAW IN CHINA'S HONG KONG 207 (Simon N.M. Young & Yash Ghai eds., Cambridge Univ. Press 2014)

PAUL DALY, A THEORY OF DEFERENCE IN ADMINISTRATIVE LAW: BASIS, APPLICATION AND SCOPE (Cambridge Univ. Press 2012)

ANTONY DAPIRAN, CITY OF PROTEST: A RECENT HISTORY OF DISSENT IN HONG KONG (Penguin Books 2017)

PENNY DARBYSHIRE, DARBYSHIRE ON THE ENGLISH LEGAL SYSTEM (Sweet & Maxwell, 10th ed. 2011)

A.C.L. Davie & J.R. Williams, *Proportionality in English Law*, *in* THE JUDGE AND THE PROPORTIONATE USE OF DISCRETION: A COMPARATIVE STUDY 73 (Sofia Ranchordás & Boudewijn de Waard eds., Routledge 2016)

Michael C. Davis, *The Basic Law and Democratization in Hong Kong*, 3 LOY. U. CHI. INT'L L. REV. 165 (2006)

Michael C. Davis, *The Basic Law, Universal Suffrage and the Rule of Law in Hong Kong*, 38 (2) HASTINGS INT'L & COMP. L. REV. 275 (2015)

MICHAEL C. DAVIS, CONSTITUTIONAL CONFRONTATION IN HONG KONG: ISSUES AND IMPLICATIONS OF THE BASIC LAW (Palgrave Macmillan 1990)

Michael C. Davis, *Constitutionalism in Hong Kong: Politics versus Economics*, 18 (1) U. PA. INT'L ECON. L. 157 (1997)

Michael C. Davis, *Hong Kong's Umbrella Movement: Beijing's Broken Promises*, 26 (2) J. DEMOCRACY 101 (2015)

Michael C. Davis, *Interpreting Constitutionalism and Democratization in Hong Kong*, *in* INTERPRETING HONG KONG'S BASIC LAW: THE STRUGGLE FOR COHERENCE 90 (Hualing Fu et al. eds., Palgrave Macmillan 2007)

Larry J. Diamond, *Thinking about Hybrid Regimes*, 13 (2) J. DEMOCRACY 21 (2002)

ALBERT VENN DICEY, INTRODUCTION TO THE STUDY OF THE LAW OF THE CONSTITUTION (Liberty Classics, 8th ed. 1982 [1915])

Bruce J. Dickson, The Dictator's Dilemma: The Chinese Communist Party's Strategy for Survival (Oxford Univ. Press 2016)

Michael Dietrich, Transaction Cost Economics and Beyond: Toward a New Economics of the Firm (Routledge 1994)

Lowell Dittmer, *Xi Jinping's "New Normal": Quo Vadis?*, 22 (3) J. Chinese Pol. Sci. 429 (2017)

Avinash K. Dixit, The Making of Economic Policy: A Transaction-Cost Politics Perspective (M.I.T. Press 1996)

Rosalind Dixon & Tom Ginsburg, *The Forms and Limits of Constitutions as Political Insurance*, 15 (4) Int'l J. Const. L. 988 (2017)

Rosalind Dixon & Tom Ginsburg, *Introduction, in* Comparative Constitutional Law in Asia 1 (Rosalind Dixon & Tom Ginsburg ed., Edward Elgar 2014)

Michael E. Degolyer, *The Civil Service, in* The Other Hong Kong Report 73 (Joseph Y.S. Cheng ed., Chinese Univ. Press 1990)

Giacomo Delledonne, *Subnational Constitutionalism: A Matter of Review*, 4 (2) Persp. on Federalism 294 (2012)

Michael W. Dowdle, *Constitutionalism in the Shadow of the Common Law: The Dysfunctional Interpretive Politics of Article 8 of the Hong Kong Basic Law*, in Interpreting Hong Kong's Basic Law: The Struggle for Coherence 55 (Hualing Fu et al. eds., Palgrave Macmillan 2007)

Björn Dressel, *The Judicialization of Politics in Asia: Towards a Framework of Analysis, in* The Judicialization of Politics in Asia 1 (Björn Dressel ed., Routledge 2012)

Julan Du & Yifei Zhang, *Does One Belt One Road Initiative Promote Chinese Overseas Direct Investment?*, 47 China Econ. Rev. 189 (2018)

Dennis Duncanson, *Hong Kong as a Crown Colony, in* A Hong Kong: Chinese and International Concern 9 (Jürgen Domes & Yu-ming Shaw eds., Westview Press 1988)

Stephen Dunn, The "Uncertain" Foundations of Post Keynesian Economics: Essays in Exploration (Routledge 2010)

Arthur Dyevre, *Unifying the Field of Comparative Judicial Politics: Towards a General Theory of Judicial Behaviour*, 2 (2) Eur. Pol. Sc. Rev. 297 (2010)

David Dyzenhaus, *Proportionality and Deference in a Culture of Justification, in* Proportionality and the Rule of Law: Rights, Justification, Reasoning 234 (Grant Huscroft et al. eds., Cambridge Univ. Press 2014)

Richard Louis Edmonds & Herbert S. Yee, *Macau: From Portuguese Autonomous Territory to Chinese Special Administrative Region*, 160 China Q. 801 (1999)

Zachary Elkins et al., *The Content of Authoritarian Constitutions, in* Constitutions in Authoritarian Regimes 141 (Tom Ginsburg & Alberto Simpser eds., Cambridge Univ. Press 2014)

Zachary Elkins et al., The Endurance of National Constitutions (Cambridge Univ. Press 2009)

Jon Elster, Explaining Social Behavior: More Nuts and Bolts for the Social Sciences (Cambridge Univ. Press, 2d ed. 2015)

G.B. Endacott, A History of Hong Kong (Oxford Univ. Press 1964)

Brad Epperly, *Political Competition and de facto Judicial Independence in Non-Democracies*, 56 (2) Eur. J. Pol. Research 279 (2017)

David Epstein & Sharyn O'Halloran, Delegating Powers: A Transaction Cost Politics Approach to Policy Making under Separate Powers (Cambridge Univ. Press 1999)

Lee Epstein & Jack Knight, The Choices Justices Make (C.Q. Press 1998)

Hasan Ersel, *Political and Economic Developments in Turkey and the Transformation of Political Islam (1950–2010), in* Understanding the Political Economy of the Arab Uprisings 193 (Ishac Diwan ed., World Scientific Publishing Co. 2014)

Laarni Escresa & Nuno Garoupa, *Testing the Logic of Strategic Defection: The Case of the Philippine Supreme Court—An Empirical Analysis (1986–2010)*, 21 (2) Asian J. Pol. Sci. 189 (2013)

Berk Esen & Sebnem Gumuscu, *Rising Competitive Authoritarianism in Turkey*, 37 (9) Third World Q. 1581 (2016)

William N. Eskridge, *Overriding Supreme Court Statutory Interpretation Decisions*, 101 Yale L. J. 331 (1991).

Keith D. Ewing and Conor A. Gearty, Freedom under Thatcher: Civil Liberties in Modern Britain (Clarendon Press 1990)

Norbert C. Y. Fan, The Electoral System of the Hong Kong Special Administrative Region (Joint Publishing 2006)

John Ferejohn, *Independent Judges, Dependent Judiciary: Explaining Judicial Independence*, 72 S. Cal. L. Rev. 353 (1999)

John A. Ferejohn, *Judicial Power: Getting It and Keeping It, in* Consequential Courts: Judicial Roles in Global Perspective 349 (Diana Kapiszewski et al. eds., Cambridge Univ. Press 2013)

John Ferejohn, *Law, Legislation, and Positive Political Theory, in* Modern Political Economy 191 (Jeffrey S. Banks & Eric A. Hanushek eds., Cambridge Univ. Press 1995)

John Ferejohn et al., *Comparative Judicial Politics, in* The Oxford Handbook of Comparative Politics 727 (Carles Boix & Susan C. Stokes eds., Oxford Univ. Press 2007)

John A. Ferejohn & Barry R. Weingast, *A Positive Theory of Statutory Interpretation*, 12 Int'l Rev. L. & Econ. 263 (1992)

William D. Ferguson, Collective Action and Exchange: A Game-Theoretic Approach to Contemporary Political Economy (Stanford Univ. Press 2013)

Moisés Silva Fernandes, *The Normalisation of Portuguese-Chinese Relations and Macao's Handover to Mainland China, 1974–79*, 13 (1) China: An Int'l J. 3 (2015)

Gustavo Femandes de Andrad, *Comparative Constitutional Law: Judicial Review*, 3 (3) J. Const. L. 977 (2001)

Jodi Finkel, Judicial Reform as Political Insurance: Argentina, Peru, and Mexico in the 1990s (Univ. of Notre Dame Press 2008)

Michael A. Fitts, *The Foibles of Formalism: Applying a Political 'Transaction Cost Analysis' to Separation of Powers*, 47 (4) Case W.Res. L. Rev. 1643 (1997)

Martin S. Flaherty, *Hong Kong Fifteen Years after the Handover: One Country, Which Direction?*, 51 Colum. J. Transnat'l L. 275 (2013)

Kaicheong Fok, *The Existence of Macau: A Chinese Perspective*, in Macau on the Threshold of the Third Millennium 13 (Macau Ricci Institute ed., Instituto Ricci de Macau, 2001)

Brian C.H. Fong, *Executive-Legislative Disconnection in the HKSAR: Uneasy Partnership between Chief Executives and Pro-Government Parties, 1997–2016, in* HONG KONG 20 YEARS AFTER THE HANDOVER: EMERGING SOCIAL AND INSTITUTIONAL FRACTURES AFTER 1997 45 (Brian C.H. Fong & Tai-lok Lui eds., Palgrave Macmillan 2018)

Brian C.H. Fong, HONG KONG'S GOVERNANCE UNDER CHINESE SOVEREIGNTY: THE FAILURE OF THE STATE-BUSINESS ALLIANCE AFTER 1997 (Routledge 2015)

Brian C.H. Fong, *In-between Liberal Authoritarianism and Electoral Authoritarianism: Hong Kong's Democratization under Chinese Sovereignty, 1997–2016*, 24 (4) DEMOCRATIZATION 724 (2017)

Brian C.H. Fong, *State-Society Conflicts under Hong Kong's Hybrid Regime*, 53 (5) ASIAN SURV. 854 (2013)

Brian C.H. Fong, *Ten Years of Political Appointments in Hong Kong – The Challenges and Prospects of Developing a Political Appointment System under a Semi-Democratic Regime, 2002–12, in* NEW TRENDS OF POLITICAL PARTICIPATION IN HONG KONG 67 (Joseph Y.S. Cheng ed., City Univ. Press 2014)

HAZEL FOX & PHILIPPA WEBB, THE LAW OF STATE IMMUNITY (Oxford Univ. Press, 3d ed. 2013)

Markus Freitag & Adrian Vatter, *Patterns of Democracy: A Subnational Analysis of the German Lander*, 44 (4) ACTA POLITICA 410 (2009)

Barry Friedman, *The Will of the People and the Process of Constitutional Change*, 78 GEO. WASH. L. REV. 1232 (2010)

Hualing Fu, *Political Protest in High-Income Societies: The Case of the Occupy Central Movement in Hong Kong, in* LAW AND POLITICS OF THE TAIWAN SUNFLOWER AND HONG KONG UMBRELLA MOVEMENTS 83 (Brian Christopher Jones ed., Routledge 2017)

Francis Fukuyama, *Development and the Limits of Institutional Design', in* POLITICAL INSTITUTIONS AND DEVELOPMENT: FAILED EXPECTATIONS AND RENEWED HOPES 21 (Natalia Dinello & Vladimir Popov eds., Edward Elgar 2007)

Ivan W.H. Funga et al., *A Review on Historic Building Conservation: A Comparison between Hong Kong and Macau Systems*, 71 RENEWABLE & SUSTAINABLE ENERGY REV. 927 (2017)

ERIK G. FURUBOTN & RUDOLF RICHTER, INSTITUTIONS AND ECONOMIC THEORY: THE CONTRIBUTION OF THE NEW INSTITUTIONAL ECONOMICS (Univ. of Michigan Press 2000)

Mary-Ann Gallagher, *Macau (Macao), in* COLUMBIA CHRONOLOGIES OF ASIAN HISTORY AND CULTURE 244 (John Brown ed., Columbia Univ. Press 2000)

Daniele Gallo & Cisotta Roberto, *The Portuguese Constitutional Court Case Law on Austerity Measures: A Reappraisal, in* SOCIAL RIGHTS IN TIMES OF CRISIS IN THE EUROZONE: THE ROLE OF FUNDAMENTAL RIGHTS' CHALLENGES 133 (Stefano Civitarese Matteucci & Simon Halliday eds., Routledge 2014)

JENNIFER GANDHI, POLITICAL INSTITUTIONS UNDER DICTATORSHIP (Cambridge Univ. Press 2008)

Stephen Gardbaum, *Are Strong Constitutional Courts Always a Good Thing for New Democracies?*, 53 COLUM. J. TRANSNAT'L L. 285 (2015)

STEPHEN GARDBAUM, THE NEW COMMONWEALTH MODEL OF CONSTITUTIONALISM: THEORY AND PRACTICE (Cambridge Univ. Press 2013)

Nuno Garoupa, *Comparing Judicial Activism – Can We Say that the US Supreme Court Is More Activist Than the German Constitutional Court?*, 72 (4) REVISTA PORTUGUESA DE FILOSOFIA 1089 (2016)

NUNO GAROUPAET AL., LEGAL ORIGINS AND THE EFFICIENCY DILEMMA (Routledge 2016)

Nuno Garoupa & Tom Ginsburg, *The Comparative Law and Economics of Judicial Councils*, 27 BERKELEY J. INT'L LAW. 53 (2009)

NUNO GAROUPA & TOM GINSBURG, JUDICIAL REPUTATION: A COMPARATIVE Theory (Univ. of Chicago Press 2015)

Nuno Garoupa & Carlos Gómez Ligüerre, *The Evolution of the Common Law and Efficiency*, 40 (2) GA. J. INT'L & COMP. L. 307 (2012)

Nuno Garoupa & Maria Maldonado, *The Judiciary in Political Transitions: The Critical Role of U.S. Constitutionalism in Latin America*, 19 CARDOZO J. INT'L & COMP. L. 593 (2011)

Nuno Garoupa & Andrew P. Morriss, *The Fable of the Codes: The Efficiency of the Common Law, Legal Origins, and Codification Movements*, UNIV. ILL. L. REV. 1443 (2012)

SCOTT GEHLBACH, FORMAL MODELS OF DOMESTIC POLITICS (Cambridge Univ. Press 2013)

Carlos Gervasoni, *The Dimensions of Democratic and Hybrid Subnational Regimes: Evidence from an Expert Survey in Argentina*, *in* ILLIBERAL PRACTICES: TERRITORIAL VARIANCE WITHIN LARGE FEDERAL DEMOCRACIES 120 (Jacqueline Behrend & Laurence Whitehead eds., Johns Hopkins Univ. Press 2016)

Yash Ghai, *The Basic Law of the Special Administrative Region of Macau: Some Reflections*, 49 (1) INT'L & COMP. L.Q. 183 (2000)

Yash Ghai, *Hong Kong's Autonomy: Dialects of Powers and Institutions*, *in* PRACTISING SELF-GOVERNMENT: A COMPARATIVE STUDY OF AUTONOMOUS REGIONS 315 (Yash Ghai & Sophia Woodman eds., 2013)

Yash Ghai, *Hong Kong's Autonomy: Dialects of Powers and Institutions*, *in* PRACTISING SELF-GOVERNMENT: A COMPARATIVE STUDY IF AUTONOMOUS REGIONS 315 (Cambridge Univ. Press 2013)

YASH GHAI, HONG KONG'S NEW CONSTITUTIONAL ORDER: THE RESUMPTION OF CHINESE SOVEREIGNTY AND THE BASIC LAW (Hong Kong Univ. Press, 2d ed. 1999)

Yash Ghai, *The Past and the Future of Hong Kong's Constitution*, 128 CHINA Q. 794 (1991)

Yash Ghai, *The Rule of Law and Capitalism: Reflections on the Basic Law*, *in* HONG KONG, CHINA AND 1997: ESSAYS IN LEGAL THEORY 365 (Raymond Wacks ed., Hong Kong Univ. Press 1993)

Yash Ghai, *Themes and Arguments*, *in* HONG KONG'S COURT OF FINAL APPEAL: THE DEVELOPMENT OF THE LAW IN CHINA'S HONG KONG 1 (Simon N.M. Young & Yash Ghai eds., 2014)

EDWARD L. GIBSON, BOUNDARY CONTROL: SUBNATIONAL AUTHORITARIANISM IN FEDERAL DEMOCRACIES (Cambridge Univ. Press 2012)

James L. Gibson, *Judicial Institutions*, *in* The Oxford Handbook of Political Institutions 514, 522 (R.A.W. Rhodes et al. eds., Oxford Univ. Press 2006)
Leah Gilbert & Payam Mohseni, *Beyond Authoritarianism: The Conceptualization of Hybrid Regimes*, 46 St. Comp. Int'l Dev. 270 (2011)
Tom Ginsburg, *The Design of Constitutions*, *in* The Oxford Handbook of Law and Economics: Volume III: Public Law & Legal Institutions 28 (Francesco Parisi ed., Oxford Univ. Press 2017)
Tom Ginsburg, *East Asian Constitutionalism in Comparative Perspective*, in Constitutionalism in Asia in the Early Twenty-First Century 32 (Albert H.Y. Chen ed., Cambridge Univ. Press 2014)
Tom Ginsburg, *Judicial Independence in East Asia: Lessons for China*, *in* Judicial Independence in China: Lessons for Global Rule of Law Promotion 247 (Randall Peerenboom ed., Cambridge Univ. Press 2010)
Tom Ginsburg, Judicial Review in New Democracies: Constitutional Courts in Asian Cases (Cambridge Univ. Press 2003)
Tom Ginsburg, *The Politics of Courts in Democratization*, *in* Global Perspectives on the Rule of Law 175 (James J. Heckman et al. eds., Routledge 2010)
Tom Ginsburg, *Public Choice and Constitutional Design*, *in* Research Handbook on Public Choice and Public Law 261 (Daniel A. Farber & Anne Joseph O'Connell eds., Edward Elgar 2010)
Tom Ginsburg & Aziz Z. Huq, *Assessing Constitutional Performance*, in Assessing Constitutional Performance 3 (Tom Ginsburg & Aziz Z. Huq eds., Cambridge Univ. Press 2016)
Tom Ginsburg & Robert Kagan, *Introduction: Institutionalist Approaches to Courts as Political Actors*, *in* Institutions and Public Law: Comparative Approaches 1 (Tom Ginsburg & Robert Kagan eds., Peter Lang 2005)
Tom Ginsburg & Eric Posner, *Subconstitutionalism*, 62 Stan. L. Rev. 1583 (2010)
Tom Ginsburg & Alberto Simpser, *Introduction: Constitutions in Authoritarian Regimes*, *in* Constitutions in Authoritarian Regimes 1 (Tom Ginsburg & Alberto Simpser eds., Cambridge Univ. Press 2014)
Tom Ginsburg & Mila Versteeg, *Why Do Countries Adopt Constitutional Review?*, 30 (3) J. Law. Econ. & Organ. 587 (2014)
Agustina Giraudy, Democrats and Autocrats: Pathways of Subnational Undemocratic Regime Continuity within Democratic Countries 37 (Oxford Univ. Press 2015)
Danny Gittings, Introduction to the Hong Kong Basic Law (Hong Kong Univ. Press, 2d ed. 2016)
Edward l. Glaeser & Andrei Shleifer, *Legal Origins*, 117(4)Q J. Econ. 1193 (2002)
Jorge Godinho, *The Ao Man Long Corruption and Money Laundering Case*, 4 Freedom From Fear Magazine 26 (2009)
Jorge Godinho, *Electoral Reform and Political Representation in Macao*, *in* China's Macao Transformed: Challenge and Development in the 21st Century 43 (Eilo W.Y. Yu & Ming K. Chan eds., City Univ. of Hong Kong Press 2014)
Jorge A.F. Godinho, Macau Business Law & Legal System (LexisNexis 2007)
Jorge Godinho & Paulo Cardinal, *Macau's Court of Final Appeal*, *in* Hong Kong's Court of Final Appeal: The Development of the Law in China's

HONG KONG 608 (Simon N.M. Young & Yash Ghai eds., Cambridge Univ. Press 2014)

Grigorii V. Golosov, *Why and How Electoral Systems Matter in Autocracies*, 51 (3) AUSTRALIAN J. POL. Sci. 367 (2016)

Arnaldo Gonçalves, *Macau's Autonomy: Looking for a Fresh Awakening?*, in ONE COUNTRY, TWO SYSTEMS, THREE LEGAL ORDERS – PERSPECTIVES OF EVOLUTION: ESSAYS ON MACAU'S AUTONOMY AFTER THE RESUMPTION OF SOVEREIGNTY BY China 733 (Jorge Oliveira & Paulo Cardinal eds., Springer 2009)

Jian-guo Gong, *Interpretation of the Constitution and Statutes of the People's Republic of China*, 14 (2) CRIM. JUST. REV. 166 (1989)

RICHARD GORDON & JOHNNY MOK, JUDICIAL REVIEW IN HONG KONG (LexisNexis, 2d ed. 2014)

JORGE BACELAR GOUVEIA, CONSTITUTIONAL LAW IN PORTUGAL (Kluwer Law International 2d ed. 2015)

Mark A. Graber, *Constitutional Politics in the Active Voice*, *in* CONSEQUENTIAL COURTS: JUDICIAL ROLES IN GLOBAL PERSPECTIVE 363 (Diana Kapiszewski et al. eds., Cambridge Univ. Press 2013)

Mark A. Graber, *Judicial Supremacy and the Structure of Partisan Conflict*, 50 IND. L. REV. 141 (2016)

GRAHAM GREENLEAF, ASIAN DATA PRIVACY LAWS: TRADE & HUMAN RIGHTS PERSPECTIVES (Oxford Univ. Press 2014)

Carlo Guarnieri, *Judicial Independence in Authoritarian Regimes: Lessons from Continental Europe*, *in* JUDICIAL INDEPENDENCE IN CHINA: LESSONS FOR GLOBAL RULE OF LAW PROMOTION 234 (Randall Peerenboom ed., Cambridge Univ. Press 2010)

Ameze Guobadia, *Constitutional Adjudication in Nigeria: Formal Structures and Substantive Impact*, *in* CONSTITUTIONAL ADJUDICATION IN AFRICA 136 (Charles M. Fombad ed., Oxford Univ. Press 2017)

Stephen Haber, *Authoritarian Government*, *in* THE OXFORD HANDBOOK OF POLITICAL ECONOMY 693 (Barry R. Weingast & Donald A. Wittman eds., Oxford Univ. Press 2006)

STEPHAN HAGGARD & ROBERT R. KAUFMAN, THE POLITICAL ECONOMY OF DEMOCRATIC TRANSITIONS (Princeton Univ. Press 1995)

ROD HAGUE ET AL., COMPARATIVE GOVERNMENT AND POLITICS: AN INTRODUCTION (Palgrave Macmillan, 10th ed. 2016)

Henry E. Hale, *The Informal Politics of Formal Constitutions: Rethinking the Effects of "Presidentialism" and "Parliamentarism" in the Cases of Kyrgyzstan, Moldova, and Ukraine*, *in* CONSTITUTIONS IN AUTHORITARIAN REGIMES 218 (Tom Ginsburg & Alberto Simpser eds., Cambridge Univ. Press 2014)

HENRY E. HALE, PATRONAL POLITICS: EURASIAN REGIME DYNAMICS IN COMPARATIVE PERSPECTIVE (Cambridge Univ. Press 2015)

Denis de Castro Halis, *"Post-Colonial" Legal Interpretation in Macau, China: Between European and Chinese Influences*, *in* EAST ASIA'S RENEWED RESPECT FOR THE RULE OF LAW IN THE 21ST CENTURY: THE FUTURE OF LEGAL AND JURIDICAL LANDSCAPES IN EAST ASIA 68 (Setsuo Miyazawa et al. eds., Brill Nijhoff 2015)

Terence C. Halliday, *Why the Legal Complex Is Integral to Theories of Consequential Courts*, *in* CONSEQUENTIAL COURTS: JUDICIAL ROLES IN GLOBAL GOVERNANCE 337 (Diana Kapiszeswiki et al. eds., Cambridge Univ. Press 2013)

Linda Hancock & Zhidong Hao, *Gambling Regulatory Regimes and the Framing of "Responsible Gambling" by Transnational Casino Corporations: Asia-Pacific Regimes in Comparative Perspective*, 38 (3) ASIA PAC. J. PUB. ADMIN. 139 (2016)

Samuel Handlin, *Observing Incumbent Abuses: Improving Measures of Electoral and Competitive Authoritarianism with New Data*, 24 (1)DEMOCRATIZATION 41 (2017)

Chris Hanretty, *Dissent in Iberia: The Ideal Points of Justices on the Spanish and Portuguese Constitutional Tribunals*, 51 EUR. J. POL. RESEARCH 671 (2012)

YUFAN HAO ET AL., Political Economy of Macao since 1999: THE DILEMMA OF SUCCESS (Springer 2017)

ZHIDONG HAO, MACAU: HISTORY AND SOCIETY (Hong Kong Univ. Press 2011)

Zhidong Hao, *Social Stratification and Ethnic and Class Politics in Macao before and after the Handover in 1999*, 13 (1) CHINA: AN INT'L J. 66 (2015)

PATRICK H. HASE, THE SIX-DAY WAR OF 1899: HONG KONG IN THE AGE OF IMPERIALISM (Hong Kong Univ. Press 2008)

Yasuo Hasebe & Cesare Pinelli, *Constitutions, in Routledge Handbook of Constitutional Law* 9 (Mark Tushnet et al. eds., Routledge 2015)

CHARLES HAUSS & MELISSA HAUSSMAN, COMPARATIVE POLITICS: DOMESTIC RESPONSES TO GLOBAL CHALLENGES (Wadsworth, 8th ed. 2013)

Xin He, *Black Hole of Responsibility: The Adjudication Committee's Role in a Chinese Court*, 47 (4) LAW & SOC'Y REV. 681 (2009)

TIMOTHY R. HEATH, CHINA'S NEW GOVERNING PARTY PARADIGM: POLITICAL RENEWAL AND THE PURSUIT OF NATIONAL REJUVENATION (Routledge 2014)

Gretchen Helmke, *The Logic of Strategic Defection: Court-Executive Relations in Argentina under Dictatorship and Democracy*, 96 (2) AM. POL. SCI. REV. 291 (2002)

Gretchen Helmke & Julio Ríos-Figueroa, *Introduction: Courts in Latin America*, *in* COURTS IN LATIN AMERICA 1 (Gretchen Helmke & Julio Ríos-Figueroa eds., Cambridge Univ. Press 2011)

Gretchen Helmke & Frances Rosenbluth, *Regimes and the Rule of Law: Judicial Independence in Comparative Perspective*, 12 ANNU. REV. LAW POL. SCI. 345 (2009)

Gretchen Helmke & Jeffrey K. Staton, *The Puzzling Judicial Politics of Latin America: A Theory of Litigation, Judicial Decisions and Interbranch Conflict*, *in* COURTS IN LATIN AMERICA 306 (Gretchen Helmke & Julio Ríos-Figueroa eds., Cambridge Univ. Press 2011)

JANE HENDERSON, THE CONSTITUTION OF THE RUSSIAN FEDERATION: A CONTEXTUAL ANALYSIS (Hart Publishing 2011)

IAN HENDRY & SUSAN DICKSON, BRITISH OVERSEAS TERRITORY LAW (Hart Publishing 2011)

Witold J. Henisz & Bennet A. Zelner, *Explicating Political Hazards and Safeguards: A Transaction Cost Politics*, 13 (6) INDUSTRIAL & CORP. CHANGE 901 (2004)

Lilly W.Y. Heong, *One Country, Two Ideologies: The Rule of Law in the Hong Kong Special Administrative Region*, 16 TEMP. INT'L & COMP. L. J. 447 (2002)

Tom Hickman, Public Law after the Human Rights Act (Hart Publishing 2010)
Ran Hirschl, Comparative Matters: The Renaissance of Comparative Constitutional Law (Oxford Univ. Press 2014)
Ran Hirschl, Constitutional Theocracy (Harvard Univ. Press 2010)
Ran Hirschl, *On the Blurred Methodological Matrix of Comparative Constitutional Law, in* The Migration of Constitutional Ideas 39 (Sujit Choudhry ed., Cambridge Univ. Press 2006)
Ran Hirschl, *The Strategic Foundations of Constitutions, in* Social and Political Foundations of Constitutions 157 (Denis J. Galligan & Mila Versteeg eds., Cambridge Univ. Press 2013)
Ran Hirschl, Towards Juristocracy: The Origins and Consequences of the New Constitutionalism (Harvard Univ. Press 2004)
Randall G. Holcombe, Advanced Introduction to Public Choice (Edward Elgar Publishing 2016)
Theodore Holo, *Handling of Petitions by the Constitutional Court of Benin, in* Constitutional Adjudication in Africa 315 (Charles M. Fombad ed., Oxford Univ. Press 2017)
Murray J. Horn, The Political Economy of Public Administration: Institutional Choice in the Public Sector (Cambridge Univ. Press 1995)
Robert M. Howard & Amy Steigerwalt, Judging Law and Policy: Courts and Policymaking in the American Political System 177 (Routledge 2012)
Christopher R. Hughes, Chinese Nationalism in the Global Era (Routledge 2006)
Victoria Tin-bor Hui, *Hong Kong's Umbrella Movement: The Protests and Beyond*, 26 (2) J. Democracy 111 (2015)
Ho-fung Hung & Iam-chong Ip, *Hong Kong's Democratic Movement and the Making of China's Offshore Civil Society*, 52 (3) Asian Surv. 504 (2012)
Meng U. Ieong, *Macao and Hong Kong, Convergence or Divergence? The 2014 Retirement Package Bill Protest and Macao's Governance Crisis*, 57 (3) Asian Surv. 504 (2017)
Information Office of the State Council of the People's Republic of China, The Practice of "One Country, Two Systems" Policy in the Hong Kong Special Administrative Region (2014)
Matthew C. Ingram, Crafting Courts in New Democracies: The Politics of Subnational Judicial Reform in Brazil and Mexico (Cambridge Univ. Press 2016)
Eric C. Ip, *A Positive Theory of Constitutional Judicial Review: Evidence from Singapore and Taiwan*, 2 (4) Asian J. L. & Econ. art. 5 (2011)
Eric C. Ip, Kong Yunming *Manifest Unreasonableness: The Doctrinal Future of Constitutional Review of Welfare Policy in Hong Kong*, 44 (1) Hong Kong L.J. 55 (2014)
Eric C. Ip, *The Constitution of Economic Liberty in Hong Kong*, 26 (3) Const. Pol. Econ. 307 (2015)
Eric C. Ip, *Constitutional Competition between the Hong Kong Court of Final Appeal and the Chinese National People's Congress Standing Committee: A Game Theory Perspective*, 39 (4) Law & Soc. Inquiry 824 (2014)

Eric C. Ip, *Constitutional Conflict in Hong Kong under Chinese Sovereignty*, 8 (1) HAGUE J. ON RULE OF LAW 75 (2016)

Eric C. Ip, *The Democratic Foundations of Judicial Review under Authoritarianism: Theory and Evidence from Hong Kong*, 12 (2)INT'L J. CONST. L. 330 (2014)

Eric C. Ip, *Doctrinal Antithesis in Anglo-American Administrative Law*, 22 (1) SUP. CT. ECON. REV. 147 (2015)

Eric C. Ip, *The Economic Structure of Hong Kong Administrative Law: Efficiency and Legality of Government Decision-Making since China's Resumption*, 12 (2) WASH. U. GLOBAL STUD. L. REV. 227 (2013)

Eric C. Ip, *The Evolution of Constitutional Adjudication in the Chinese Special Administrative Regions: Theory and Evidence*, 61 (4) AM. J. COMP. L. 799 (2013)

Eric C. Ip, *The High Court of the People: Popular Constitutionalism in Hong Kong under Chinese Sovereignty*, 36 (3) LAW & POL'Y 314 (2014)

Eric C. Ip, *The Institutional Foundations of Supreme Court Power in Britain's Representative Democracy*, 49 (3) REPRESENTATION: J. REPRESENTATIVE DEMOCRACY 281 (2013)

Eric C. Ip, *Interpreting Interpretations: A Methodology for the Judicial Enforcement of Legislative Interpretations of the Hong Kong Basic Law*, PUB. L. 552 (2017)

Eric C. Ip, *Judicial Review in China: A Positive Political Economy Analysis*, 8 (2) REV. L. & ECON. 331 (2012)

Eric C. Ip, *The Judicial Review of Legislation in the United Kingdom*, 37 (2) EUR. J. L. & ECON. 221 (2014)

ERIC C. IP, LAW AND JUSTICE IN HONG KONG (Sweet & Maxwell, 2d ed. 2016)

Eric C. Ip; *Mapping Parliamentary Law and Practice in Hong Kong*, 3 (1) CHINESE J. COMP. L. 97, 117 (2015)

Eric C. Ip, *The Politics of Constitutional Common Law in Hong Kong under Chinese Sovereignty*, 25 (3) WASHINGTON INT'L L. J. 565 (2016)

Eric C. Ip, *Prototype Constitutional Supervision in China: The Lessons of the Hong Kong Basic Law Committee*, 10 (2) ASIAN J. COMP. L. 323 (2016)

Eric C. Ip, *The Supreme Court and the Making of Public Policy in Contemporary China*, 7 MICH. J. PUB. AFF. 1 (2010)

Eric C. Ip, *The Supreme People's Court and the Political Economy of Judicial Empowerment in Contemporary China*, 24 COLUM. J. ASIAN L. 367 (2011)

Eric C. Ip, *Taking a "Hard Look" at "Irrationality": Substantive Review of Administrative Discretion in the US and UK Supreme Courts*, 34 (3) OXFORD LEGAL STUD. 481 (2014)

Eric C. Ip & Kelvin H. F. Kwok, *Judicial Control of Local Protectionism in China: Antitrust Enforcement against Administrative Monopoly on the Supreme People's Court*, 13 (3) J. COMPETITION L. & ECON. 549 (2017)

Eric C. Ip, *Comparative Subnational Foreign Relations Law in the Chinese Special Administrative Regions*, 65 (4) INT'L & COMP. L. Q. 953 (2016)

SAMUEL ISSACHAROFF, FRAGILE DEMOCRACIES: CONTESTED POWER IN THE ERA OF CONSTITUTIONAL COURTS 6 (Cambridge Univ. Press 2015)

Vicki C. Jackson & Mark Tushnet, *Introduction*, *in Proportionality: New Frontiers, New Challenges* 1 (Vicki C. Jackson & Mark Tushnet eds., Cambridge Univ. Press 2017)

Tonja Jacobi, *The Impact of Positive Political Theory on Old Questions of Constitutional Law and the Separation of Powers*, 100 NW. U. L. REV. 259 (2006)

Nihal Jayawickrama, *Human Rights in the Draft Basic* Law – *A Critique*, 18 HONG KONG L. J. 370 (1988)

SWATI JHAVERI ET AL., ADMINISTRATIVE LAW IN HONG KONG (LexisNexis, 2d ed. 2013)

Swati Jhaveri & Anne Scully-Hill, *Executive and Legislative Reactions to Judicial Declarations of Constitutional Invalidity in Hong Kong: Engagement, Acceptance or Avoidance?*, 13 (2) INT'L J. CONST. L. 507 (2015)

Chaoyuan Ji, *A Study of the Political Structure of the Macao Special Administrative Region from the Perspective of Constitutionalism*, 1 Academic J. "One Country., Two Systems" 68 (2011)

CHAOYANG JIANG, A STUDY ON THE BASIC LAW OF MACAU AND THE RULE OF LAW OF THE MACAU SPECIAL ADMINISTRATIVE REGION (Social Sciences Academic Press China 2016)

Chaoyang Jiang & Feng Yang, *The Administrative Litigation System in Macao*, *in* ADMINISTRATIVE LITIGATION SYSTEMS IN GREATER CHINA AND EUROPE 73 (Yuewen Li ed., Routledge 2016)

Emily Johnston Barton, *Pricing Judicial Independence: An Empirical Study of Post-1997 Court of Final Appeal Decisions in Hong Kong*, 43 (2) HARV. INT'L L.J. 361 (2002)

CAROL A. G. JONES, LOST IN CHINA? LAW, CULTURE AND IDENTITY IN POST-1997 HONG KONG (Cambridge Univ. Press 2015)

David Martin Jones, *Asian Values and the Constitutional Order of Contemporary Singapore*, 8 (4) CONST. POL. ECON. 283 (1997)

Philip Jones & John Hudson, *The Role of Political Parties: An Analysis Based on Transaction Costs*, 94 (1/2) PUB. CHOICE 175 (1998)

Fok Kaicheong, *The Existence of Macau: A Chinese Perspective*, *in* MACAU ON THE THRESHOLD OF THE THIRD MILLENNIUM 13 (Macau Ricci Institute ed., Instituto Ricci de Macau, 2001)

Steffen Kailitz, *Classifying Political Regimes Revisited: Legitimation and Durability*, 20 (1) DEMOCRATIZATION 39 (2013)

Diana Kapiszeswiki et al., *Introduction*, *in* CONSEQUENTIAL COURTS: JUDICIAL ROLES IN GLOBAL GOVERNANCE 1 (Diana Kapiszeswiki et al. eds., Cambridge Univ. Press 2013)

Ira Katznelson, *Historical Approaches to the Study of Congress: Toward a Congressional Vantage on American Political Development*, *in* THE OXFORD HANDBOOK OF THE AMERICAN CONGRESS 115 (Eric Schickler & Frances E. Lee eds., Oxford Univ. Press 2011)

AILEEN KAVANAGH, CONSTITUTIONAL REVIEW UNDER THE UK HUMAN RIGHTS ACT (Cambridge Univ. Press 2009)

Mushtaq H. Khan, *Markets, States and Democracy: Patron-Client Networks and the Case for Democracy in Developing Countries*, *in* TWENTY YEARS OF STUDYING DEMOCRATIZATION: VOL 2: DEMOCRATIZATION, DEMOCRACY AND AUTHORITARIAN CONTINUITY 33 (Aurel Croissant & Jeffrey Haynes eds., Routledge 2016)

Mushtaq H. Khan, *Rent-seeking as Process, in Rents, in* RENT-SEEKING AND ECONOMIC DEVELOPMENT: THEORY AND EVIDENCE IN ASIA 70 (Mushtaq H. Khan & K.S. Jomo eds., Cambridge Univ. Press 2000)

Suna Kili, *Kemalism in Contemporary Turkey*, 1 (3) INT'L POL. SCI. REV. 381 (1980)

Ambrose Y.C. King, *The Hong Kong Talks and Hong Kong Politics, in* HONG KONG: A CHINESE AND INTERNATIONAL CONCERN 42 (Jürgen Domes & Yu-ming Shaw eds., Westview Press 1988)

Zentaro Kitagawa, *Development of Comparative Law in East Asia, in* THE OXFORD HANDBOOK OF COMPARATIVE LAW 237 (Mathias Reiman & Reinhard Zimmermann eds., Oxford Univ. Press 2006)

JAN KLABBERS, INTERNATIONAL LAW (Cambridge Univ. Press 2013)

Daniel M. Klerman et al., *Legal Origin or Colonial History?*, 3 J. LEGAL ANALYSIS 379 (2011)

Dicle Kogacioglu, *Progress, Unity, and Democracy: Dissolving Political Parties in Turkey*, 38 (3) LAW & SOC'Y REV. 433 (2004)

Judith R. Krebs, *One Country, Three Systems? Judicial Review in Macau after* Ng Ka Ling, 10 (1) PAC. RIM L. & POL'Y J. 111 (2000)

Kerry Krutilla & Alexander Alexeev, *The Political Transaction Costs and Uncertainties of Establishing Environmental Rights*, 107 ECOLOGICAL ECON. 299 (2014)

Agnes Shuk Mei Ku, *From Civil Disobedience to Institutional Politics: Conflict over the Public Order Ordinance in 2000, in* CIVIL UNREST AND GOVERNANCE IN HONG KONG: LAW AND ORDER FROM HISTORICAL AND CULTURAL PERSPECTIVES 163 (Michel H.K. Ng & John D. Wong eds., Routledge 2017)

Vikas Kumar, *Negotiating Constitutions for Political Unions*, 31 INT'L REV. L. & ECON. 58 (2011)

Toru Kurata, *Support for and Opposition to Democratization in Hong Kong*, 22 (1) Asia-Pacific Rev. 16 (2015)

Tamara O. Kuznetsova ET AL., RUSSIAN CONSTITUTIONAL LAW (Cambridge Scholars Publishing 2014)

Kelvin Hiu Fai Kwok, *Antitrust Enforcement and State Restraints at the Mainland China-Hong Kong Interface: The Importance of Bilateral Antitrust Co-operation*, 12 (2) ASIAN J. COMP. L. 335 (2017)

Bruce K.K. Kwong, *Patron-Clientelism and Elections in Macao: The 2009 Chief Executive Election, in* CHINA'S MACAO TRANSFORMED: CHALLENGE AND DEVELOPMENT IN THE 21st Century 55 (Eilo W.Y. Yu & Ming K. Chan eds., City Univ. of Hong Kong Press 2014)

Kin-ming Kwong & Chiew Ping Yew, *Fifteen Years after Hong Kong's Handover: Is This City Dying?, in* EAST ASIA: DEVELOPMENTS AND CHALLENGES 165 (Yongnian Zheng & Fook Lye Liang eds., World Scientific 2013)

Kin Ming Kwong & Chiew Ping Yew, *Hong Kong Politics: Weak Leadership, Frustrated Society and Prospect*, 5 (1) E. ASIAN POL'Y 55 (2013)

Kin Ming Kwong & Hong Yu, *Identity Politics, in* HONG KONG UNDER CHINESE RULE ECONOMIC INTEGRATION AND POLITICAL GRIDLOCK 125 (Yongnian Zheng & Chiew Ping Yew eds., World Scientific 2013)

Ying-ho Kwong, *Political Repression in a Sub-national Hybrid Regime: The PRC's Governing Strategies in Hong Kong*, Contemp. Pol. 1, 13 (2018), www.tandfonline.com/doi/citedby/10.1080/13569775.2017.1423530?scroll=top&needAccess=true

Ying Ho Kwong, *Protests against the Welfare Package for Chief Executives and Principal Officials*, 4 CHINA PERSP. 61, 62 (2014), http://journals.openedition.org/chinaperspectives/6588

Ying-ho Kwong, *Ruling Coalition Restructuring under Macao's Hybrid Regime*, 17 (3) CHINA REV. 111 (2017)

Ying-ho Kwong & Mathew Y.H. Wong, *State Size and Democratization in Hybrid Regimes: The Chinese Island Cities of Macau and Hong Kong*, 12 (2) ISLAND STUD. J. 113 (2017)

Rafael La Porta et al., *The Economic Consequences of Legal Origins*, 46 (2) J. ECON. LITERATURE 285 (2008)

Rafael La Porta et al., *Law and Finance*, 106 (6) J. POL. ECON. 1113 (1998)

JEAN-JACQUES LAFFONT, INCENTIVES AND POLITICAL ECONOMY (Oxford Univ. Press 2000)

David A. Lake, *Hobbesian Hierarchy: The Political Economy of Political Organization*, 12 ANNU. REV. POLIT. SCI. 263 (2009)

David Landau, *Abusive Constitutionalism*, 47 U.C. DAVIS L. REV. 189 (2013)

William Landes & Richard Posner, *The Independent Judiciary in an Interest-Group Perspective*, 18 J. L. & ECON. 875 (1975)

JAN-ERIK LANE, CONSTITUTIONS AND POLITICAL THEORY (Manchester Univ. Press, 2d ed. 2011)

LAURA LANGER, JUDICIAL REVIEW IN STATE SUPREME COURTS: A COMPARATIVE STUDY (State Univ. of New York Press 2002)

Jermain T.M. Lam, *After Ten Years of Transfer of Sovereignty: Political Stability and Reforms in Hong Kong*, 10 (2) New Zealand J. Asian Stud. 21 (2008)

Jermain T.M. Lam, *The Hong Kong Legislative Council: A Friend or an Enemy of Donald Tsang?*, *in* THE SECOND CHIEF EXECUTIVE OF HONG KONG: EVALUATING THE TSANG YEARS 2005–2012 59 (Joseph Y.S. Cheng ed., 2013)

Jermain T.M. Lam, *Political Decay in Hong Kong after the Occupy Central Movement*, 42 (2) ASIAN AFF.: AN AM. REV. 99 (2015)

Newman M.K. Lam, *The Impact of Gaming Liberalisation on Public Opinion and Political Culture*, *in* GAMING, GOVERNANCE AND PUBLIC POLICY IN MACAO 37 (Newman M.K. Lam & Ian Scott eds., 2011)

Wai Fung Lam & Kwan Nok Chan, *How Authoritarianism Intensifies Punctuated Equilibrium: The Dynamics of Policy Attention in Hong Kong*, 28 (4) GOVERNANCE: AN INT'L J. POL'Y ADMIN. & INSTITUTIONS 549 (2015)

Wai-Man Lam, *Changing Political Activism: Before and after the Umbrella Movement*, *in* HONG KONG 20 YEARS AFTER THE HANDOVER: EMERGING SOCIAL AND INSTITUTIONAL FRACTURES AFTER 1997 73 (Brian C.H. Fong & Tai-lok Lui eds., Palgrave Macmillan 2018)

Wai-man Lam, *Promoting Hybridity: The Politics of the New Macau Identity*, 203 CHINA Q. 656 (2010)

SIU-KAI LAU, THE PRACTICE OF "ONE COUNTRY TWO SYSTEMS" POLICY IN HONG KONG (The Commercial Press 2017)

SIU-KAI LAU & HSIN-CHI KUAN, THE ETHOS OF THE HONG KONG CHINESE (Chinese Univ. Press 1988)

David S. Law, *Judicial Comparativism and Judicial Diplomacy*, 163 U. PA. L. REV. 927 (2015)

David S. Law & Mila Versteeg, *Constitutional Variation among Strains of Authoritarianism*, *in* CONSTITUTIONS IN AUTHORITARIAN REGIMES 165 (Tom Ginsburg & Albert Simpser eds., 2014)

David S. Law & Mila Versteeg, *Sham Constitutions*, 101 CAL. L. REV. 863 (2013)

ELIZA W.Y. Lee ET AL., PUBLIC POLICYMAKING IN HONG KONG: CIVIC ENGAGEMENT AND STATE-SOCIETY RELATIONS IN A SEMI-DEMOCRACY (Routledge 2013)

Eliza W.Y. Lee & Rikkie L.K. Yeung, *The "Principal Officials Accountability System": Its Underdevelopment as a System of Ministerial Government*, 39 (2) ASIA PAC. J. PUB. ADMIN. 120 (2017)

FRANCIS L.F. LEE & JOSEPH M. CHAN, Media, SOCIAL MOBILISATION AND MASS PROTESTS IN POST-COLONIAL HONG KONG: THE POWER OF A CRITICAL EVENT (Routledge 2010)

Jack Tsen-Ta Lee, *According to the Spirit and Not to the Letter: Proportionality and the Singapore Constitution*, 8 VIENNA J. ON INT'L CONST. L. 276 (2014)

Jack Tsen-Ta Lee, *Constraint or Restraint? Singapore's Constitution at 50*, in SINGAPORE: NEGOTIATING STATE AND SOCIETY, 1965–2015 15 (Jason Lim & Terence Lee eds., Routledge 2016)

Man Yee Karen Lee, *Lawyers and Hong Kong's Democracy Movement: From Electoral Politics to Civil Disobedience*, 251 (1) ASIAN J. POL. SCI. 89 (2017)

Paul S. N. Lee et al., *The Struggle for Hegemony: The Emergence of a Counter-public Sphere in Post-1997 Hong Kong*, 10 (4) CHINESE J. COMM. 338 (2017)

Siu-Yau Lee, *Profit Seeking and Intergroup Conflict in Hong Kong: A Case Study of the Private Health Care Sector*, 56 (2) ASIAN SURV. 348 (2016)

Tahirih V. Lee, *"Apres Moi Le Deluge?" Judicial Review in Hong Kong since Britain Relinquished Sovereignty*, 11 IND. INT'L & COMP. L. REV. 323 (2001)

JIM LEITZEL, CONCEPTS IN LAW AND ECONOMICS: A GUIDE FOR THE CURIOUS (Oxford Univ. Press 2015)

ELSIE LEUNG, FOOTSTEPS IN TIME: TWENTY YEARS OF BASIC LAW IN HONG KONG (City Univ. of Hong Kong Press 2017)

Daryl J. Levinson, *Parchment and Politics: The Positive Puzzle of Constitutional Commitment*, 124 (3) HARV. L. REV. 657 (2011)

STEVEN LEVITSKY & LUCAN A. WAY, COMPETITIVE AUTHORITARIANISM: HYBRID REGIMES AFTER THE COLD WAR (Cambridge Univ. Press 2010)

Steven Levitsky & Lucan A. Way, *The Rise of Competitive Authoritarianism*, 13 J. DEMOCRACY 51 (2002)

ANDREW LI, REFLECTIONS ON THE RETROSPECTIVE AND PROSPECTIVE EFFECT OF CONSTITUTIONAL JUDGMENTS, THE COMMON LAW LECTURE SERIES 2010 (Jessica Young & Rebecca Lee eds., Faculty of Law, the University of Hong Kong 2011)

Yahong Li, *The Central-HKSAR Legislative Relationship: A Constitutional Assessment*, *in* THE NEW LEGAL ORDER IN HONG KONG 163 (Raymond Wacks ed., Hong Kong Univ. Press 1999)

Tai Wei Lim, *"Fishball Revolution" and Hong Kong's Identity*, *in* POLITICS, CULTURE AND IDENTITIES IN EAST ASIA: INTEGRATION AND DIVISION 35 (Lam Peng Er & Lim Tai Wei eds., World Scientific 2017)

Tai Wei Lim, *The Future of Hong Kong Governance: The Pro-independence Legislators' Election Fallout and Beijing's Political Voice in Hong Kong*, 4 (2) ASIA & PAC. POL'Y STUD. 343 (2017)

TAI WEI LIM & XIAOJUAN PING, CONTEXTUALIZING OCCUPY CENTRAL IN CONTEMPORARY HONG KONG (Imperial College Press 2015)

Jolene Lin, *The Judicialization of Governance: The Case of Singapore*, *in* ADMINISTRATIVE LAW AND GOVERNANCE IN ASIA: COMPARATIVE PERSPECTIVES 287 (Tom Ginsburg & Albert H.Y. Chen eds., Routledge 2009)

Laifan Lin & Mingkang Gu, *Can Courts in Hong Kong Examine the Constitutionality of the Legislative Conduct of the PRC?*, *in* HONG KONG IN TRANSITION: ONE COUNTRY, TWO SYSTEMS 175 (Robert Ash et al. eds., Routledge 2003)

Bing Ling, *Subject Matter Limitation on the NPCSC's Power to Interpret the Basic Law*, 37 HONG KONG L.J. 619 (2007)

Yiu-chu Liu, *Interpretation and Review of the Basic Law of the Hong Kong Special Administrative Region*, 2 J. CHINESE L. 49 (1988)

P.Y. LO, *An Internationalist, Consequentialist and Non-Progressive Court: Constitutional Adjudication in Hong Kong (1997–2009)*, 2 CITY U. HONG KONG L. REV. 234 (2010)

P.Y. LO, THE HONG KONG BASIC LAW (LexisNexis 2011)

P.Y. LO, *Hong Kong: Common Law Courts in China*, *in Asian Courts in Context* 183 (Jiunn-Rong Yeh and Wen-Chen Chang eds., 2015)

P.Y. LO, *Impact of Jurisprudence beyond Hong Kong*," *in* HONG KONG'S COURT OF FINAL APPEAL: THE DEVELOPMENT OF THE LAW IN CHINA'S HONG KONG 579 (Simon N.M. Young & Yash Ghai eds., Cambridge Univ. Press 2014)

P.Y. LO, THE JUDICIAL CONSTRUCTION OF HONG KONG'S BASIC LAW: COURTS, POLITICS AND SOCIETY AFTER 1997 (Hong Kong Univ. Press 2014)

Sonny Lo, *Hong Kong*, *in* Politics in China: An Introduction (William A. Joseph ed., 2010)

Sonny S.H. Lo & Herbert S. Yee, *Legitimacy-Building in the Macau Special Administrative Region: Colonial Legacies and Reform Strategies*, 13 (1) ASIAN J. POL. SCI. 51 (2005)

Sonny Shiu-Hing Lo, *Central Control and Local Welfare Autonomy in Guangzhou, Hong Kong and Macau*, 42 (3) J. CURRENT CHINESE AFF. 3 (2013)

SONNY SHIU-HING LO, CONSTITUTIONAL CONVENTIONS AND POLITICAL DEVELOPMENT IN MACAU, IN MACAU ON THE THRESHOLD OF THE THIRD MILLENNIUM 93 (Instituto Ricci de Macau 2001)

Sonny Shiu-Hing Lo, *Consultative Governance and Legitimacy in Macao: The Mix of Electoral and Public Sector Reforms*, 15 (1) PUB. ADMIN. & POL'Y 19 (2012)

Sonny Shiu-Hing Lo, *Factionalism and Chinese-style Democracy: The 2017 Hong Kong Chief Executive Election*, 39 (2) ASIA PAC. J. PUB. ADMIN. 100 (2017)

Sonny Shiu-Hing Lo, Hong Kong, in POLITICS IN CHINA: AN INTRODUCTION 451 (William A. Joseph ed., Oxford Univ. Press, 2d ed. 2014)

SONNY SHIU-HING LO, POLITICAL CHANGE IN MACAO (Routledge 2008)

SONNY SHIU-HING LO, POLITICAL DEVELOPMENT IN MACAU (Chinese Univ. Press 1995)

Sonny Shiu-Hing Lo & Eric King-Man Chong, *Casino Interests, Fujian Tongxianghui and Electoral Politics in Macao*, 46 (2) J. CONTEMP. ASIA 286 (2016)

Sonny Shiu-Hing Lo & Dennis K.K. Leung, *The Dynamics of Executive-Legislative Discord in Hong Kong: Conflict, Confrontation and Adaptation*, 15 (2) PUB. ADMIN. & POL'Y 6 (2012)

JOHN B. LONDREGAN, LEGISLATIVE INSTITUTIONS AND IDEOLOGY IN Chile (Cambridge Univ. Press 2007)

Ceren Lord, *Situating Change Under the AKP*, *in* CONTEMPORARY TURKEY AT A GLANCE II: TURKEY TRANSFORMED? POWER, HISTORY, CULTURE 7 (Meltem Ersoy & Ersa Ozyurek eds., Springer VS 2017)

MARTIN LOUGHLIN, THE BRITISH CONSTITUTION: A VERY SHORT INTRODUCTION (Oxford Univ. Press 2013)

Tai-lok Lui & Stephen S.W. Chiu, *Governance Crisis and Changing State-Business Relations: A Political Economy Perspective*, *in* REPOSITIONING THE HONG KONG GOVERNMENT: Social Foundations and Political Challenges 91 (Stephen W. K. Chiu & Siu Lune eds., Hong Kong Univ. Press 2012)

Ngok Ma, *Eclectic Corporatism and State Interventions in Post-Colonial Hong Kong*, in REPOSITIONING THE HONG KONG GOVERNMENT: SOCIAL FOUNDATIONS AND POLITICAL CHALLENGES 63 (Stephen Wing-kai Chiu et al. eds., Hong Kong Univ. Press 2012)

Ngok Ma, *From Executive Dominance to Fragmented Authority: An Institutional and Political Analysis'*, *in* HONG KONG 20 YEARS AFTER THE HANDOVER: EMERGING SOCIAL AND INSTITUTIONAL FRACTURES AFTER 1997 21 (Brian C.H. Fong & Tai-lok Lui eds., Palgrave Macmillan 2018)

Ngok Ma, *The Making of a Corporatist State in Hong Kong: The Road to Sectoral Intervention*, 46 (2) J. CONTEMP. ASIA 247 (2016)

NGOK MA, POLITICAL DEVELOPMENT IN HONG KONG: STATE, POLITICAL SOCIETY, AND CIVIL SOCIETY (Hong Kong Univ. Press 2007)

Roderick A. Macdonald & Hoi Kong, *Judicial Independence as a Constitutional Virtue*, *in* THE OXFORD HANDBOOK OF COMPARATIVE CONSTITUTIONAL LAW 831 (Michael Rosenfeld and Andras Sajo eds., Oxford Univ. Press 2012)

JONATHAN R. MACEY, *Transaction Costs and the Normative Elements of the Public Choice Model: An Application to Constitutional Theory*, 74 (2) VA. L. REV. 471 (1988)

BEATRIZ MAGALONI, *The Game of Electoral Fraud and the Ousting of Authoritarian Rule*, 54 (3) AM. J. POL. SCI. 751 (2010)

MAN LENG MAI & WAI NENG HO, ADMINISTRATIVE LITIGATION IN MACAO: SYSTEM, LEGISLATION AND CASES (Zhejiang Univ. Press 2011)

Joseph Marko, *Foreign Judges: A European Perspective*, *in* HONG KONG'S COURT OF FINAL APPEAL: THE DEVELOPMENT OF THE LAW IN CHINA'S HONG KONG 637 (Simon N.M. Young & Yash Ghai eds., Cambridge Univ. Press 2014)

Jerry Mashaw, *Public Law and Public Choice: Critique and Rapprochement*, *in* RESEARCH HANDBOOK ON PUBLIC CHOICE AND PUBLIC LAW 19 (Daniel A. Farber & Anne Joseph O'Connell eds., Edward Elgar 2010)

Anthony Mason, *The Common Law*, *in* HONG KONG'S COURT OF FINAL APPEAL: THE DEVELOPMENT OF THE LAW IN CHINA'S HONG KONG 327 (Simon N.M. Young & Yash Ghai eds., Cambridge Univ. Press 2014)

J.F. Matthews, *The Legal System of the Hong Kong Special Administrative Region*, 18 U. PA. J. INT'L L. 3 (1997)

Honorata Mazepusa et al., *A Comparative Study of Legitimation Strategies in Hybrid Regimes*, 37 (4) POL'Y STUD. 350 (2016)

Mathew D. McCubbins & Daniel B. Rodriguez, *The Judiciary and the Role of Law*, *in* THE OXFORD HANDBOOK OF POLITICAL ECONOMY 273 (Barry R. Weingas & Donald A. Wittman eds., Oxford Univ. Press, 2006)

CHARLES R. MCELWEE, ENVIRONMENTAL LAW IN CHINA: MITIGATING RISK AND ENSURING COMPLIANCE (Oxford Univ. Press 2011)

KELLY M. MCMANN, ECONOMIC AUTONOMY AND DEMOCRACY: HYBRID REGIMES IN RUSSIA AND KYRGYZSTAN 174 (Cambridge Univ. Press 2006)

Carmen Amado Mendes, *Macau in China's Relations with the Lusophone World*, 57 REV. BRAS. POLÍT. INT. 225 (2014)

CARMEN AMADO MENDES, PORTUGAL, CHINA AND THE MACAU NEGOTIATIONS 1986–1999 (Hong Kong Univ. Press 2013)

Fernando Mendez & Jonathan Wheatley, *Introduction*, *in* PATTERNS OF CONSTITUTIONAL DESIGN: THE ROLE OF CITIZENS AND ELITES IN CONSTITUTION-MAKING 1 (Jonathan Wheatley & Fernando Mendez eds., Ashgate 2013)

Claude Ménard, *Facing Crises: Economy, Democracy, and Political Transaction Costs*, *in* DEMOCRACY AND AN OPEN-ECONOMY WORLD ORDER 109 (George C. Bitros & Nicholas C. Kyriazis eds., Springer 2017)

Paul Milgrom & John Roberts, *Bargaining Costs, Influence Costs, and the Organization of Economic Activity*, *in* PERSPECTIVES ON POSITIVE POLITICAL ECONOMY 57 (James E. Alt & Kenneth A. Shepsle eds., 1990)

NORMAN J. MINERS, *Constitution and Administration*, *in* THE OTHER HONG KONG REPORT 1 (Joseph Y.S. Cheng ed., Chinese Univ. Press 1990)

Jihong Mo, *The Constitutional Law of the People's Republic of China and its Development*, 23 COLUM. J. ASIAN L. 137 (2009)

Henry P. Monaghan, *Constitutional Common Law*, 89 HARV. L. REV. 1 (1975)

Lee Morgenbesser, *The Autocratic Mandate: Elections, Legitimacy and Regime Stability in Singapore*, 30 (2) PAC. REV. 205 (2017)

Robert J. Morris, *The "Replacement" Chief Executive's Two-Year Term: A Pure and Unambiguous Common Law Analysis*, 35 HONG KONG L.J. 17 (2005)

Tamir Moustafa, *Law and Courts in Authoritarian Regimes*, 10 ANNU. REV. LAW SOC. SCI. 281 (2014)

TAMIR MOUSTAFA, THE STRUGGLE FOR CONSTITUTIONAL POWER: LAW, POLITICS, AND ECONOMIC DEVELOPMENT IN EGYPT (Cambridge Univ. Press 2007)

Tamir Moustafa & Tom Ginsburg, *Introduction: The Function of Courts in Authoritarian Politics*, *in* RULE BY LAW: THE POLITICS OF COURTS IN AUTHORITARIAN REGIMES 1 (Tom Ginsburg & Tamir Moustafa eds., Cambridge Univ. Press 2008)

Christopher Munn, *The Rule of Law and Criminal Justice in the Nineteenth Century*, *in* JUDICIAL INDEPENDENCE AND THE RULE OF LAW IN HONG KONG 19 (Steve Tsang ed., Hong Kong Univ. Press 2001)

Walter F. Murphy, *Civil Law, Common Law, and Constitutional Democracy*, 52 LA. L. REV. 98 (1991)

WALTER MURPHY, ELEMENTS OF JUDICIAL STRATEGY (Univ. of Chicago Press 1964)

Andrew J. Nathan, *China's Challenge, in* AUTHORITARIANISM GOES GLOBAL 23 (Larry Diamond et al. eds., Johns Hopkins Univ. Press 2016)

Jaclyn L. Neo, *Balancing Act: The Balancing Metaphor as Deference and Dialogue in Constitutional Adjudication, in* CONSTITUTIONAL INTERPRETATION IN SINGAPORE: THEORY AND PRACTICE 159 (Routledge 2017)

Octavio Amorim Neto & Marina Costa Lobo, *Portugal's Semi-Presidentialism (Re) Considered: An Assessment of the President's Role in the Policy* Process, 1976–2006, *in* PORTUGAL IN THE TWENTY-FIRST CENTURY 49 (Sebastián Royo ed., Lexington Books 2012)

DAVID W. NEUBAUER & STEPHEN S. MEINHOLD, JUDICIAL PROCESS; LAW, COURTS, AND POLITICS IN THE UNITED STATES (Wadsworth, 5th ed. 2010)

PAULA NEWBERG, JUDGING THE STATE: COURTS AND CONSTITUTIONAL POLITICS IN PAKISTAN (Cambridge Univ. Press 2002)

KWAI HANG NG, THE COMMON LAW IN TWO VOICES: LANGUAGE, LAW, AND THE POSTCOLONIAL PREDICAMENT IN HONG KONG (2009)

KWAI HANG NG & XIN HE, EMBEDDED COURTS: JUDICIAL DECISION-MAKING IN CHINA (Cambridge Univ. Press 2017)

Antonio Nicita & Ugo Pagano, *Law and Economics in Retrospect, in* NEW INSTITUTIONAL ECONOMICS: A GUIDEBOOK 409 (Éric Brousseau & Jean-Michel Glachant eds., Cambridge Univ. Press 2008)

Douglass C. North, *A Transaction Cost Theory of Politics*, 2 J. THEORETICAL POL. 355 (1990)

Douglass C. North, INSTITUTIONS, INSTITUTIONAL CHANGE AND ECONOMIC PERFORMANCE (Cambridge Univ. Press)

DOUGLASS C. NORTH, TRANSACTION COSTS, INSTITUTIONS, AND ECONOMIC PERFORMANCE (International Center for Economic Growth 1992)

Colm O'Cinneide, *Human Rights and the UK Constitution, in* THE CHANGING CONSTITUTION 67, 68 (Jeffrey Jowell et al. eds., Oxford Univ. Press 8th ed. 2015)

Stephen Ortmann, *The Umbrella Movement and Hong Kong's Protracted Democratization Process*, 46 ASIAN AFF. 32 (2015)

Esin Örücü, *The Constitutional Court of Turkey: The Anayasa Mahkemesi as the Protector of the System, in* CONSTITUTIONAL COURTS: A COMPARATIVE STUDY 196 (Andrew Harding and Peter Leyland eds., Wildy, Simmonds & Hill 2009)

C. L. OSTBERG & MATTHEW E. WETSTEIN, ATTITUDINAL DECISION MAKING IN THE SUPREME COURT OF CANADA (Univ. of British Columbia Press 2007)

MARINA OTTAWAY, DEMOCRACY CHALLENGED: THE RISE OF SEMI-AUTHORITARIANISM (Carnegie Endowment of International Peace 2003)

RICHARD L. PACELLE, JR. ET AL., DECISION MAKING BY THE MODERN SUPREME COURT (Cambridge Univ. Press 2011)

Francesco Parisi, *Political Coase Theorem*, 115 PUB. CHOICE 1 (2003)

FRANCESCO PARISI & VINCY FON, THE ECONOMICS OF LAWMAKING (Oxford Univ. Press 2009)

William Partlett & Eric C. Ip, *Is Socialist Law Really Dead?*, 48 N.Y.U. J. INT'L L. & POL. 463 (2016)

Haig Patapan, *Leadership, Law, and Legitimacy: Reflections on the Changing Nature of Judicial Politics in Asia*, *in* THE JUDICIALIZATION OF POLITICS IN ASIA 219 (Björn Dressel ed., Routledge 2012)

Randall Peerenboom, *Introduction*, *in* JUDICIAL INDEPENDENCE IN CHINA: LESSONS FOR GLOBAL RULE OF LAW PROMOTION 1 (Randall Peerenboom ed., Cambridge Univ. Press 2010)

Francisco Gonçalves Pereira, *Accommodating Diversity: Macau under China's Constitution*, *in* MACAU ON THE THRESHOLD OF THE THIRD MILLENNIUM 101 (Macau Ricci Institute ed., Instituto Ricci de Macau 2001)

Torsten Persson & Guido Tabellini, *Constitutions and Economic Policy*, 18 (1) JOURNAL OF ECONOMIC PERSPECTIVES 75 (2004)

DAVID L. PHILLIPS, AN UNCERTAIN ALLY: TURKEY UNDER ERDOGAN'S DICTATORSHIP (Routledge 2017)

Frederick J. Phillips-Patrick, *Political Risk and Organizational Form*, 34 (2) J. L. & ECON. 675 (1991)

PAUL PIERSON, POLITICS IN TIME: HISTORY, INSTITUTIONS, AND SOCIAL ANALYSIS (Princeton Univ. Press, 2011)

Antonio Costa Pinto, *Corporatism and "Organic Representation" in European Dictatorships*, *in* CORPORATISM AND FASCISM: THE CORPORATIST WAVE IN EUROPE 3 (Antonio Costa Pinto ed., Routledge 2017)

Jean-Philippe Platteau, *The Causes of Institutional Inefficiency: A Development Perspective*, *in* NEW INSTITUTIONAL ECONOMICS: A GUIDEBOOK 443 (Éric Brousseau & Jean-Michel Glachant eds., Cambridge Univ. Press 2008)

Jonathan Poon, *Umbrellas in Hong Kong: Youth and Reform in a Polarized City*, Winter ASIA PAC. AFF. COUNC J. 14 (2015)

Kit Poon, *The Impasse over Constitutional Reform: Negotiating Democracy in Hong Kong*, *in* THE IMPASSE OVER CONSTITUTIONAL REFORM: NEGOTIATING DEMOCRACY IN HONG KONG 3 (Brian C.H. Fong & Tai-lok Lui eds., Palgrave Macmillan 2017)

MARIA POPOVA, POLITICIZED JUSTICE IN EMERGING DEMOCRACIES: A STUDY OF COURTS IN RUSSIA AND UKRAINE (Cambridge Univ. Press, 2012)

Eric A. Posner, *Controlling Agencies with Cost-Benefit Analysis: A Positive Political Theory Perspective*, 68 U. CHI. L. REV. 1137 (2001)

Richard A. Posner, *The Constitution as an Economic Document*, 56 GEO. WASH. L. REV. 4 (1987)

RICHARD A. POSNER, ECONOMIC ANALYSIS OF LAW (Wolters Kluwer, 9th ed. 2014)

PETER W. PRESTON, THE POLITICS OF CHINA-HONG KONG RELATIONS: LIVING WITH DISTANT MASTERS (Edward Elgar 2016)

Alvin Rabushka, *A Free-Market Constitution for Hong Kong: A Blueprint for China*, 8 CATO J. 641 (1989)

J. Mark Ramseyer, *The Puzzling (In)Dependence of Courts: A Comparative Approach*, 23 J. LEGAL STUD. 721 (1994)

J. Mark Ramseyer & Eric B. Rasmusen, *Judicial Independence in a Civil Law Regime: The Evidence from Japan*. 13 (2) J. L. ECON. & ORG. 259 (1997)

Sofia Ranchordás & Boudewijn de Waard, *Proportionality Crossing Borders: Why It Is Still Difficult to Recognise Sparrows and Cannons*, *in* THE JUDGE AND THE PROPORTIONATE USE OF DISCRETION: A COMPARATIVE STUDY 1 (Sofia Ranchordás & Boudewijn de Waard eds., Routledge)

RETHINK INSTITUTE, 2015 TURKEY COUNTRY REPORT (Rethink Institute 2014)

THOMAS F. REMINGTON, POLITICS IN RUSSIA (Routledge 2015)

Joaquim de Sousa Ribeiro & Esperança Mealha, *Portugal: Constitutional Courts as Positive Legislators*, *in* CONSTITUTIONAL COURTS AS POSITIVE LEGISLATORS: A COMPARATIVE LAW STUDY 721 (Allan R. Brewer-Carías ed., Cambridge Univ. Press 2011)

STEIN RINGEN, THE PERFECT DICTATORSHIP: CHINA IN THE 21ST CENTURY (Hong Kong Univ. Press 2016)

JULIO RÍOS-FIGUEROA, CONSTITUTIONAL COURTS AS MEDIATORS: ARMED CONFLICT, CIVIL-MILITARY RELATIONS, AND THE RULE OF LAW IN LATIN AMERICA (Cambridge Univ. Press 2016)

Julio Ríos-Figueroa & Paloma Aguilar, *Justice Institutions in Autocracies: A Framework for Analysis*, 25 (1) DEMOCRATIZATION 1 (2018)

DAVID ROBERTSON, THE JUDGE AS POLITICAL THEORIST: CONTEMPORARY CONSTITUTIONAL REVIEW (Princeton Univ. Press 2010)

GRAEME B. ROBERTSON, THE POLITICS OF PROTEST IN HYBRID REGIMES: MANAGING DISSENT IN POST-COMMUNIST RUSSIA (Cambridge Univ. Press 2011)

Juan Carlos Rodriguez-Raga, *Strategic Deference in the Colombian Constitutional Court 1992–2006*, *in* COURTS IN LATIN AMERICA 81 (Gretchen Helmke & Julio Ríos-Figueroa eds., Cambridge Univ. Press 2011)

Robert S. Ross & Jo Inge Bekkevold, *New Leaders, Stronger China, Harder Choices*, *in China in the Era of Xi Jinping* 265 (Robert S. Ross & Jo Inge Bekkevold eds., Georgetown Univ. Press 2016)

YANIV ROZNAI, UNCONSTITUTIONAL CONSTITUTIONAL AMENDMENTS: THE LIMITS OF AMENDMENT POWERS (Oxford Univ. Press 2017)

Yaniv Roznai & Serkan Yolcu, *An Unconstitutional Constitutional Amendment – The Turkish Perspective: A Comment on the Turkish Constitutional Court's Headscarf Decision*, 10 (1) INT'L J. CONST. L. 175 (2012)

Yusuf Sarfati & Aviad Rubin, *Introduction: Israel and Turkey in Comparative Perspective*, *in* THE JARRING ROAD TO DEMOCRATIC INCLUSION: A COMPARATIVE ASSESSMENT OF STATE–SOCIETY ENGAGEMENTS IN ISRAEL AND TURKEY 1 (Aviad Rubin, Yusuf Sarfati eds., Lexington Books 2016)

Andreas Schedler, *The Logic of Electoral Authoritarianism*, *in* ELECTORAL AUTHORITARIANISM: THE DYNAMICS OF UNFREE COMPETITION 1 (Andreas Schedler ed., Lynne Rienner Publishers 2006)

Bernard Schlink, *Proportionality in Constitutional Law: Why Everywhere But Here?*, 22 DUKE J. COMP. & INT'L L. 291 (2012)

Todd Schneider, *David v Goliath? The Hong Kong Courts and China's National People's Congress Standing Committee*, 20 BERKELEY J. INT'L L. 575 (2002)

Andrew Scobell, *Hong Kong's Influence on China: The Tail That Wags the Dog?*, 28 (6) ASIAN SURV. 599 (1988)

Ian Scott, *Legitimacy, Governance and Public Policy in Post-Handover Hong Kong*, 29 ASIA PAC. J. PUB. ADMIN. 37 (2007)

Ian Scott, *"One Country, Two Systems": The End of a Legitimating Ideology?*, 39 (2) ASIA PAC. J. PUB. ADMIN. 83 (2017)

IAN SCOTT, PUBLIC ADMINISTRATION IN HONG KONG: REGIME CHANGE AND ITS IMPACT ON THE PUBLIC SECTOR (Marshall Cavendish International 2005)

IAN SCOTT, THE PUBLIC SECTOR IN HONG KONG (Hong Kong Univ. Press 2010)

Ian Scott, *Social Stability and Economic Growth*, *in* GAMING, GOVERNANCE AND PUBLIC POLICY IN MACAO 1 (Newman M.K. Lam & Ian Scott eds., Hong Kong Univ. Press 2011)

JEFFREY A. SEGAL & HAROLD J. SPAETH, THE SUPREME COURT AND THE ATTITUDINAL MODEL REVISITED (Cambridge Univ. Press 2002)

Hootan Shambayati, *Courts in Semi-Democratic/Authoritarian Regimes: The Judicialization of Turkish (and Iranian) Politics*, *in* RULE BY LAW: THE POLITICS OF COURTS IN AUTHORITARIAN REGIMES 283 (Tom Ginsburg & Tamir Moustafa eds., Cambridge Univ. Press 2008)

WEI SHAN & LIJUN YANG, GOVERNING SOCIETY IN CONTEMPORARY CHINA (World Scientific 2017)

Martin Shapiro, *The Mighty Problem Continues*, *in* CONSEQUENTIAL COURTS: JUDICIAL ROLES IN GLOBAL PERSPECTIVE 380 (Diana Kapiszewski et al. eds., Cambridge Univ. Press 2013)

Li Sheng, *The Transformation of Island City Politics: The Case of Macau*, 11 (2)ISLAND STUD. J. 521 (2016)

Mingjie Shenga & Chaolin Gub, *Economic Growth and Development in Macau (1999–2016): The Role of the Booming Gaming Industry*, 75 CITIES 72 (2018)

KENNETH A. SHEPSLE, ANALYZING POLITICS: RATIONALITY, BEHAVIOR, AND INSTITUTIONS (W.W. Norton, 2d ed. 2010)

MING SING, *Hong Kong at the Crossroads: Public Pressure for Democratic Reform*, *in* POLITICS AND GOVERNMENT IN HONG KONG: CRISIS UNDER CHINESE SOVEREIGNTY 112 (Ming Sing ed., Routledge 2009)

Ming Sing, *To What Extent Have Members of the Functional Constituencies Performed the "Balancing Role" in Hong Kong?*, *in* THE HONG KONG SPECIAL ADMINISTRATIVE REGION IN ITS FIRST DECADE 109, 110 (Joseph Y.S. Cheng ed., City Univ. of Hong Kong Press 2007)

Ming Sing & Karena Tang, *Mobilization and Conflicts over Hong Kong's Democratic Reform*, *in* CONTEMPORARY HONG KONG GOVERNMENT AND POLITICS 137 (Wai-man Lam et al. eds., Hong Kong Univ. Press 2012)

BILVEER SINGH, POLITICS AND GOVERNANCE IN SINGAPORE: AN INTRODUCTION (McGraw Hill Press, 2d ed. 2012)

Victor F.S. Sit ET AL., ENTREPRENEURS AND ENTERPRISES IN MACAU: A STUDY OF INDUSTRIAL DEVELOPMENT (Hong Kong Univ. Press 1991)

DAN SLATER, ORDERING POWER: CONTENTIOUS POLITICS AND AUTHORITARIAN LEVIATHANS IN SOUTHEAST ASIA (Cambridge Univ. Press 2010)

JOSEPH WAYNE SMITH, REDUCTIONISM AND CULTURAL BEING: A PHILOSOPHICAL CRITIQUE OF SOCIOBIOLOGICAL REDUCTIONISM AND PHYSICALIST SCIENTIFIC UNIFICATIONISM (Martinus Nijhoff Publishers 1984)

Jan M. Smits, *What Is Legal Doctrine? On The Aims and Methods of Legal-Dogmatic Research*, *in* RETHINKING LEGAL SCHOLARSHIP: A TRANSATLANTIC DIALOGUE 207 (Rob van Gestel et al. eds., Cambridge Univ. Press 2017)

Russell Smyth & Vinod Mishra, *The Transmission of Legal Precedent across the Australian State Supreme Courts*, 45 (1) L. & Soc'y Rev. 139 (2011)

Alvin Y. So, *Hong Kong's Problematic Democratic Transition: Power Dependency or Business Hegemony?*, 59 (2) J. Asian Stud. 359 (2000)

António Goucha Soares, *Portugal: An Incomplete Europeanization*, *in* Portugal in the Twenty-First Century 121 (Sebastián Royo ed., Lexington Books 2012)

Peter H. Solomon, Jr., Courts *and Judges in Authoritarian Regimes*, 60 World Pol. 122 (2007)

Peter H. Solomon, Jr., *Judicial Power in Authoritarian States: The Russian Experience*, *in* Rule by Law: The Politics of Courts in Authoritarian Regimes 261 (Tom Ginsburg & Tamir Moustafa eds., Cambridge Univ. Press 2008)

Weiqing Song, *A Special Regional Actor in the World: Conceptualising Macao's Diplomatic Behaviour*, 13 (3) China: An Int'l J. 154 (2015)

Nikolaos Stelgias, *Turkey's Hybrid Competitive Authoritarian Regime: A Genuine Product of Anatolia's Middle Class*, 4 Levantine Rev. 201 (2015)

Matthew C. Stephenson, *"When the Devil Turns ... ": The Political Foundations of Independent Judicial Review*, 32 J. Legal Stud. 59 (2003)

David A. Strauss, The Living Constitution (Oxford Univ. Press 2010)

Milan W. Svolik, The Politics of Authoritarian Rule (Cambridge Univ. Press 2012)

Benny Y.T. Tai, *The Constitutional Game of Article 158 (3) of the Basic Law*, 41 Hong Kong L.J. 377 (2001)

Benny Y.T. Tai, *The Judiciary*, *in* Contemporary Hong Kong Politics: Governance in the Post-1997 Era 72 (Wai-man Lam et al. eds., Hong Kong Univ. Press 2007)

Benny Yiu-ting Tai, *Civil Disobedience and the Rule of Law*, *in* Civil Unrest and Governance in Hong Kong: Law and Order from Historical and Cultural Perspectives 141 (Michael Ng & John Wong eds., Routledge 2017)

Waikeung Tam, *Do Female Legislators Have Different Policy Priorities Than Their Male Colleagues in an Undemocratic/Semi-democratic Legislature? The Case of Hong Kong*, 23 (1) J. Legis. Stud. 44 (2017)

Daniel Tan, *An Analysis of Substantive Review in Singaporean Administrative Law*, 25 Singapore Academy of Law J. 296 (2013)

Kenneth Paul Tan, Governing Global-City Singapore: Legacies and Futures after Lee Kuan Yew (Routledge 2017)

Kenneth Paul Tan, *The Singapore Parliament: Representation, Effectiveness, and Control*, *in* Parliaments in Asia: Institution Building and Political Development 27 (Zheng Yongnian et al. eds., Routledge 2014)

Kevin Y.L. Tan, *As Efficient as the Best Businesses: Singapore's Judicial System*, *in* Asian Courts in Context 228 (Jiunn-Rong Yeh & Wen-Chen Chang eds., Cambridge Univ. Press 2015)

Kevin Y.L. Tan, The Constitution of Singapore: A Contextual Analysis (Hart Publishing 2015)

Netina Tan, *Institutionalized Succession and Hegemonic Party Cohesion in Singapore*, *in* Party System Institutionalization in Asia: Democracies, Autocracies, and the Shadows of the Past 49 (Allen Hicken & Erik Martinez Kuhonta eds., Cambridge Univ. Press 2015)

Shu-hung Tang, *The Hong Kong Fiscal Policy: Continuity or Redirection?, in* POLITICAL ORDER AND POWER TRANSITION IN HONG KONG 189 (Pang-kwong Li ed., Chinese Univ. Press 1997)

Wang Tao, *Rule of Law in Sar Macao since its Return to China*, 5 CHINA LEGAL DEV. Y. B. 119 (2011)

C. Neal Tate, *Why the Expansion of Judicial Power?*, in THE GLOBAL EXPANSION OF JUDICIAL POWER 27 (C. Neal Tate & Torbjörn Vallinder eds., New York Univ. Press 1995)

Güneş Murat Tezcür, *Judicial Activism in Perilous Times: The Turkish Case*, 43 (2) LAW & SOC'Y REV. 305 (2009)

LI-ANN THIO, A TREATISE ON SINGAPORE CONSTITUTIONAL LAW (Academy Publishing 2012)

Li-ann Thio, *Lex Rex or Rex Lex? Competing Conceptions of the Rule of Law in Singapore*, 20 U.C.L.A. PAC. BASIN L. J. 1 (2002)

Li-ann Thio, *"We are Feeling Our Way Forward, Step by Step": The Continuing Singapore Experiment in the Construction of Communitarian Constitutionalism in the Twenty-First Century's First Decade, in* CONSTITUTIONALISM IN ASIA IN THE EARLY TWENTY-FIRST CENTURY 270 (Albert H.Y. Chen ed., Cambridge Univ. Press 2014)

CARLA L. THORSON, POLITICS, JUDICIAL REVIEW AND THE RUSSIAN CONSTITUTIONAL COURT (Palgrave Macmillan 2012)

Emerson H. Tiller, *The "Law" and Economics of Judicial Decision-Making: A Positive Political Theory Perspective, in* THE OXFORD HANDBOOK OF LAW AND ECONOMICS: *Volume 1: Methodology and Concepts* 222 (Francesco Parisi ed., Oxford Univ. Press 2017)

Emerson H. Tiller & Frank B. Cross, *What is Legal Doctrine?*, 100 (1) NW. U. L. REV. 517 (2006)

ADAM TOMKINS, PUBLIC LAW (Oxford Univ. Press 2003)

JOEL P. TRACHTMAN, THE ECONOMIC STRUCTURE OF INTERNATIONAL LAW (Harvard Univ. Press 2008)

Alexei Trochev, *Fragmentation? Defection? Legitimacy? Explaining Judicial Roles in Post-Communist "Colored Revolutions," in* CONSEQUENTIAL COURTS: JUDICIAL ROLES IN GLOBAL PERSPECTIVE 367 (Diana Kapiszewski et al. eds., Cambridge Univ. Press 2013)

ALEXEI TROCHEV, JUDGING RUSSIA: CONSTITUTIONAL COURT IN RUSSIAN POLITICS 1990–2006 (Cambridge Univ. Press 2008)

Alexei Trochev, *Less Democracy, More Courts: A Puzzle of Judicial Review in Russia*, 38 L. & SOC'Y REV. 513 (2004)

STEVE TSANG, A MODERN HISTORY OF HONG KONG (Hong Kong Univ. Press 2007)

Steve Tsang, *China and Political Reform in Hong Kong*, 2 (1) PAC. REV. 68 (1989)

STEVE TSANG, GOVERNING HONG KONG: ADMINISTRATIVE OFFICERS FROM THE NINETEENTH CENTURY TO THE HANDOVER TO CHINA, 1862–1997 (Hong Kong Univ. Press 2007)

Justin K.H. Tse, *Under the Umbrella: Grounded Christian Theologies and Democratic Working Alliances in Hong Kong*, 2 (1)REV. RELIGION & CHINESE SOC'Y 109 (2015)

Kevin K.S. Tso, *Fundamental Political and Constitutional Norms: Hong Kong and Macau Compared*, 13 (1) AUSTRALIAN J. ASIAN L. 1 (2012)

Guangjian Tu, *The Conflict of Laws System in Macau*, 40 HONG KONG L.J. 85 (2010)
MARK TUSHNET, ADVANCED INTRODUCTION TO COMPARATIVE CONSTITUTIONAL LAW (Edward Elgar 2014)
Mark Tushnet, *The Rise of Weak-Form Judicial Review*, *in* COMPARATIVE CONSTITUTIONAL LAW 321 (Tom Ginsburg & Rosalind Dixon eds., Edward Elgar 2011)
Mark Tushnet & Rosalind Dixon, *Weak-Form Review and Its Constitutional Relatives: An Asian Perspective*, *in* COMPARATIVE CONSTITUTIONAL LAW IN ASIA 102 (Rosalind Dixon & Tom Ginsburg eds., Edward Elgar 2014)
Mark Tushnet & Madhav Khosla, *Unstable Constitutionalism*, *in* UNSTABLE CONSTITUTIONALISM: LAW AND POLITICS IN SOUTH ASIA 3 (Mark Tushnet & Madhav Khosla eds., Cambridge Univ. Press 2015)
Mark V. Tushnet, *Authoritarian Constitutionalism*, 100 CORNELL L. REV. 391 (2015)
Charlotte Twight, *Political Transaction-Cost Manipulation: An Integrating Theory*, 6 J. THEORETICAL POL. 189 (1994)
CHARLOTTE A. TWIGHT, DEPENDENT ON D.C.: THE RISE OF FEDERAL CONTROL OVER THE LIVES OF ORDINARY AMERICANS (Palgrave 2002)
ALI RESUL USUL, DEMOCRACY IN TURKEY: THE IMPACT OF EU POLITICAL CONDITIONALITY (Routledge 2010)
Mehrdad Vahabi, *Appropriation, Violent Enforcement, and Transaction Costs: A Critical Survey*, 147 (1) PUB. CHOICE 227 (2011)
Georg Vanberg, *Constitutional Courts in Comparative Perspective: A Theoretical Assessment*, 18 ANNU. REV. POLIT. SCI. 167 (2015)
GEORG VANBERG, THE POLITICS OF CONSTITUTIONAL REVIEW IN GERMANY (Cambridge Univ. Press 2005)
JOHN M. VANDERLIPPE, POLITICS OF TURKISH DEMOCRACY, THE: ISMET INONU AND THE FORMATION OF THE MULTI-PARTY SYSTEM, 1938–1950 (State Univ. of New York Press 2012)
Stefan Voigt, *Are International Merchants Stupid? A Natural Experiment Refutes the Legal Origin Theory*, 5 (1) J. EMPIRICAL LEGAL STUD. 1 (2008)
Stefan Voigt, *Constitutional Political Economy: Analyzing Formal Institutions at the Most Elementary Level*, *in* NEW INSTITUTIONAL ECONOMICS: A GUIDEBOOK 363 (Éric Brousseau & Jean-Michel Glachant eds., Cambridge Univ. Press 2008)
Mary L. Volcansek, *Constitutional Courts as Veto Players: Divorce and Decrees in Italy*, 39 EUR. J. POL. RESEARCH 347 (2001)
Graham Walker, *The Idea of Nonliberal Constitutionalism*, *in* ETHNICITY AND GROUP RIGHTS 164 (Ian Shapiro & Will Kymlicka eds., New York Univ. Press 1997)
Jeremy Wallace, *Cities, Redistribution, and Authoritarian Regime Survival*,75(3) J. POL. 632 (2013)
Marco Wan, *The Artwork of Hong Kong's Occupy Central Movement*, *in* CIVIL UNREST AND GOVERNANCE IN HONG KONG: LAW AND ORDER FROM HISTORICAL AND CULTURAL PERSPECTIVES 179 (Michael Ng & John Wong eds., Routledge 2017)
Gungwu Wang & John Wong, *After Smooth Handover, Now the Hard Part*, *in* HONG KONG UNDER CHINESE RULE ECONOMIC INTEGRATION AND POLITICAL GRIDLOCK 3 (Yongnian Zheng & Chiew Ping Yew eds., World Scientific 2013)

Zhenmin Wang, *From the Judicial Committee of the British Privy Council to the Standing Committee of the Chinese National People's Congress – An Evaluation of the Legal Interpretive System after the Handover*, 37 HONG KONG L.J. 605 (2007)

Zhenmin Wang & Kai Tu, *Chinese Constitutional Dynamics: A Decennial Review*, *in* CONSTITUTIONALISM IN ASIA IN THE EARLY TWENTY-FIRST CENTURY 118 (2014)

Peter Wesley-Smith, *Comment: The SAR Constitution: Law or Politics*, 27 HONG KONG L. J. 125 (1997)

PETER WESLEY-SMITH, CONSTITUTIONAL AND ADMINISTRATIVE LAW IN HONG KONG (Longman 2d ed. 1994)

Peter Wesley-Smith, *The Present Constitution of Hong Kong*, *in* THE BASIC LAW AND HONG KONG'S FUTURE 5 (Peter Wesley-Smith & Albert Chen eds., Butterworths 1988)

Keith E. Whittington, *Legislative Sanctions and the Strategic Environment of Judicial Review*, 1 (3) INT'L J. CONST. L. 446 (2003)

KEITH E. WHITTINGON, POLITICAL FOUNDATIONS OF JUDICIAL SUPREMACY: THE PRESIDENCY, THE SUPREME COURT, AND CONSTITUTIONAL LEADERSHIP IN U.S. HISTORY (Princeton Univ. Press 2007)

Mikael Wigell, *Mapping "Hybrid Regimes": Regime Types and Concepts in Comparative Politics*, 15 (2) DEMOCRATIZATION 230 (2008)

ROBERT F. WILLIAMS, THE LAW OF AMERICAN STATE CONSTITUTIONS (Oxford Univ. Press 2009)

OLIVER E. WILLIAMSON, THE MECHANISMS OF GOVERNANCE (Oxford Univ. Press 1996)

DONALD WITTMAN, ECONOMIC FOUNDATIONS OF LAW AND ORGANIZATION (Cambridge Univ. Press 2006)

Hio Hei Albert Wong, *The Summer 2014 Protests in Macau: Their Contexts and Continuities*, 6 (1) ASIAN EDUC. & DEV. STUD. 57 (2017)

MATTHEW Y.H. WONG, COMPARATIVE HONG KONG POLITICS: A GUIDEBOOK FOR STUDENTS AND RESEARCHERS (Palgrave Macmillan 2017)

Matthew Y.H. Wong, *Discussing without Deciding, Deciding without Acting: Veto Players in Hong* Kong, *and* Beijing's Response, 2 (3) ASIAN J. COMP. POL. 347 (2017)

Matthew Y.H. Wong, *Party Models in a Hybrid Regime: Hong Kong 2007–2012*, 15 (1) CHINA REV. 67 (2015)

Stan Hok-Wui Wong, *Resource Disparity and Multi-Level Elections in Competitive Authoritarian Regimes: Regression Discontinuity Evidence from Hong Kong*, 33 ELECTORAL STUD. 200 (2014)

B. Dan Wood & John Bohte, *Political Transaction Costs and the Politics of Administrative Design*, 66 (1) J. POL. 176 (2004)

Sophia Woodman, *Legislative Interpretation by China's National People's Congress Standing Committee: A Power with Roots in the Stalinist Conception of Law*, *in* INTERPRETING HONG KONG'S BASIC LAW: THE STRUGGLE FOR COHERENCE 229 (Palgrave Macmillan 2007)

Joseph Wright & Abel Escribà-Folch, *Authoritarian Institutions and Regime Survival: Transitions to Democracy and Subsequent Autocracy*, 42 (2) BRITISH J. POL. SCI. 283 (2012)

Chien-Huei Wu, WTO AND THE GREATER CHINA: ECONOMIC INTEGRATION AND DISPUTE RESOLUTION (Martinus Nijhoff Publishers 2012)

Jianfan Wu, *Several Issues Concerning the Relationship between the Central Government of the People's Republic of China and the Hong Kong Special Administrative Region*, 2 J. CHINESE L. 65 (1988)

Weiyun Xiao et al., *Why the Court of Final Appeal Was Wrong: Comments of the Mainland Scholars on the Judgment of the Court of Final Appeal*, *in* HONG KONG'S CONSTITUTIONAL DEBATE: CONFLICTS OVER INTERPRETATION 53 (Johannes M.M. Chan et al. eds., Hong Kong Univ. Press 2000)

Julius Yam, *The Role of Courts in Hybrid* Regimes *and a Reconceptualization of Separation of Powers: The Case of Filibuster in Hong Kong*, 17 (1) AUSTRALIAN J. ASIAN L. art. 3 (2016)

XIAODANG YANG, STATE IMMUNITY IN INTERNATIONAL LAW (Cambridge Univ. Press 2012)

Xiaonan Yang, *Legislative Interpretations by the Standing Committee of the National People's Congress in China*, 38 (1) HONG KONG L. J. 255 (2008)

Xiaonan Yang, *Two Interpreters of the Basic Law*, *in* HONG KONG'S COURT OF FINAL APPEAL: THE DEVELOPMENT OF THE LAW IN CHINA'S HONG KONG 69 (Simon N.M. Young & Yash Ghai eds., Cambridge Univ. Press 2014)

PO JEN YAP, CONSTITUTIONAL DIALOGUE IN COMMON LAW ASIA (Oxford Univ. Press 2015)

PO JEN YAP, COURTS AND DEMOCRACIES IN ASIA (Cambridge Univ. Press 2017)

Po Jen Yap, *The "Dead" Constitution: Crime and Punishment in Singapore*, 40 (3) HONG KONG L. J. 577 (2010)

Po Jen Yap, *Freedom of Assembly and Association*, *in* LAW OF THE HONG KONG CONSTITUTION 821 (Johannes M.M. Chan & C.L. Lim eds., Sweet & Maxwell, 2d ed. 2015)

Po Jen Yap, *Interpreting the Basic Law and the Adjudication of Politically Sensitive Questions*, 6 CHINESE J. INT'L L. 543 (2007)

Po Jen Yap, *10 Years of the Basic Law: The Rise, Retreat and Resurgence of Judicial Power in Hong Kong*, 36 (2) COMMONWEALTH L. WORLD REV. 166 (2007)

Po Jen Yap & Thomas Wong, *Public Welfare and the Judicial Over-Enforcement of Socio-Economic Rights in Hong Kong*, 44 (1) HONG KONG L.J. 41 (2014)

M. HAKAN YAVUZ, ISLAMIC POLITICAL IDENTITY IN TURKEY (Oxford Univ. Press 2003)

HERBERT S. YEE, MACAU IN TRANSITION: FROM COLONY TO AUTONOMOUS REGION (Palgrave Macmillan, 2001)

Herbert S. Yee, *The Theory and Practice of "One-Country-Two-Systems" in Macao*, *in* CHINA'S MACAO TRANSFORMED: CHALLENGE AND DEVELOPMENT IN THE 21ST CENTURY 3 (Eilo W.Y. Yu and Ming K. Chan eds., City Univ. of Hong Kong Press 2014)

Herbert S. Yee, The 2001 *Legislative Assembly Elections and Political Development in Macau*, 14 (43) J. CONTEMP. CHINA 225 (2005)

Jiunn-Rong Yeh & Wen-Chen Chang, *Introduction: Asian Courts in Context: Tradition, Transition and Globalization*, *in* ASIAN COURTS IN CONTEXT 1 (Jiunn-Rong Yeh & Wen-Chen Chang eds., Cambridge Univ. Press 2015)

Ray Yep, *A Historical Perspective on Hong* Kong *Autonomy: Traditions of British Imperialism, Maritime Enclave and Contending Views of British Interest*', *in* HONG KONG 20 YEARS AFTER THE HANDOVER: EMERGING SOCIAL AND

INSTITUTIONAL FRACTURES AFTER 1997 231 (Brian C.H. Fong & Tai-lok Lui eds., Palgrave Macmillan 2018)

Chiew Ping Yew, *Political Reform and Dilemma, in* HONG KONG UNDER CHINESE RULE ECONOMIC INTEGRATION AND POLITICAL GRIDLOCK 209 (Yongnian Zheng & Chiew Ping Yew eds., World Scientific 2013)

Chiew Ping Yew, *The 2012 Chief Executive Election and After. Hong Kong under Chinese Rule, in* HONG KONG UNDER CHINESE RULE ECONOMIC INTEGRATION AND POLITICAL GRIDLOCK 237 (Yongnian Zheng & Chiew Ping Yew eds., World Scientific 2013)

Simon N.M. Young, *Constitutional Rights in Hong Kong's Court of Final Appeal*, 27 CHINESE (TAIWAN) Y. B. INT'L L. & AFF. 67 (2011)

Simon N.M. Young, *Fundamental Rights and the Basic Laws of the Hong Kong and Macau Special Administrative Regions, in* ONE COUNTRY, TWO SYSTEMS, THREE LEGAL ORDERS – PERSPECTIVES OF EVOLUTION: ESSAYS ON MACAU'S AUTONOMY AFTER THE RESUMPTION OF SOVEREIGNTY BY CHINA 683 (Jorge Oliveira & Paulo Cardinal eds., Springer 2009)

Simon N.M. Young, *Hong Kong: End of Occupy Central, Government's Proposal for Universal Suffrage Reform*, PUB. L. 502 (2015)

Simon N.M. Young, *Human Rights*, in HONG KONG'S COURT OF FINAL APPEAL: THE DEVELOPMENT OF THE LAW IN CHINA'S HONG KONG 391 (Simon N.M. Young & Yash Ghai eds., Cambridge Univ. Press 2014)

Simon N.M. Young et al., *Genesis of Hong Kong's Court of Final Appeal, in Hong Kong's Court of Final Appeal: The Development of the Law in China's Hong Kong* 121 (Simon N.M. Young & Yash Ghai eds., Cambridge Univ. Press 2014)

Simon N.M. Young et al., *Role of the Chief Justice, in* HONG KONG'S COURT OF FINAL APPEAL: THE DEVELOPMENT OF THE LAW IN CHINA'S HONG KONG 225 (Simon N.M. Young & Yash Ghai eds., Cambridge Univ. Press 2014)

SIMON YOUNG & RICHARD CULLEN, ELECTING HONG KONG'S CHIEF EXECUTIVE (Hong Kong Univ. Press 2010)

Simon N.M. Young & Antonio Da Roza, *The Judges, in* HONG KONG'S COURT OF FINAL APPEAL: THE DEVELOPMENT OF THE LAW IN CHINA'S HONG *Kong* 253 (Simon N.M. Young & Yash Ghai eds., Cambridge Univ. Press 2014)

Eilo Wing-Yat YU, *Executive-Legislative Relationships and the Development of Public Policy, in* GAMING, GOVERNANCE AND PUBLIC POLICY IN MACAO 57 (Newman M.K. Lam & Ian Scott eds., Hong Kong Univ. Press 2011)

Eilo Wing-Yat Yu, *Formal and Informal Politics in Macao Special Administrative Region Elections* 2004–2005, 16 (52) J. CONTEMP. CHINA 417 (2007)

Eilo Wing-yat YU, *Macao's "One Country, Two Systems": High Autonomy or Intervention?, in* NEGOTIATING AUTONOMY IN GREATER CHINA: HONG KONG AND ITS SOVEREIGN BEFORE AND AFTER 1997 207 (Ray Yep ed., Nordic Institute of Asian Studies2013)

Gu Yu, HONG KONG'S LEGISLATURE UNDER CHINA'S SOVEREIGNTY 1998–2013 (Brill Nijhoff 2015)

Samson Yuen, *Contesting Middle-class Civility: Place-based Collective Identity in Hong Kong's Occupy Mongkok*, SOC. MOVEMENT STUD. 1 (2018), www.tandfonline.com/doi/abs/10.1080/14742837.2018.1434501

Samson Yuen, *Hong Kong after the Umbrella Movement: An Uncertain Future for the "One Country Two Systems"*, 1 CHINA PERSP. 49 (2015)

Fareed Zakaria, *The Rise of Illiberal Democracy*, 76 (6) FOREIGN AFF. 22 (1997)

Kevin Zervos, *Constitutional Remedies under the Basic Law*, 40 HONG KONG L. J. 687 (2010)

Baohui Zhang, *Political Paralysis of the Basic Law Regime and the Politics of Institutional Reform in Hong Kong*, 49 (2) ASIAN SURV. 312 (2009)

QIANFAN ZHANG, THE CONSTITUTION OF CHINA: A CONTEXTUAL ANALYSIS (Hart Publishing 2012)

Xiaoming Zhang, *Why Macao Is Not Implementing the Separation of Powers Political System*, 45 CHINESE L. & GOV'T 15 (2012)

YUANYUAN ZHANG, ROLE ANALYSIS IN THE LEGALIZATION OF MACANESE GOVERNANCE (One Country, Two Systems Research Centre of the Macao Polytechnic Institute 2009)

LINLIN ZHAO, A NEW STUDY ON MACAU JUDICIAL SYSTEM (Social Sciences Academic Press (China) 2015)

VICTOR ZHENG & PO-SAN WAN, GAMBLING DYNAMISM: THE MACAO MIRACLE (Springer-Verlag 2014)

Yongnian Zheng & Cuifen Weng, *The Development of China's Formal Political Structures*, in CHINA IN THE ERA OF XI JINPING 32 (Robert S. Ross & Jo Inge Bekkevold eds., Georgetown Univ. Press)

Reinhard Zimmermann, *Roman Law in the Modern World, in* THE CAMBRIDGE COMPANION TO ROMAN LAW 452 (David Johnston ed., Cambridge Univ. Press 2015)

Franklin E. Zimring et al., *Executions, Deterrence, and Homicide: A Tale of Two Cities*, 7 (1) J. EMPIRICAL LEGAL STUD. 1 (2010)

Index